FOLK SONG STYLE and CULTURE

FOLK SONG STYLE
and
CULTURE

By

Alan Lomax

*With Contributions by the Cantometrics Staff
and With the Editorial Assistance of
Edwin E. Erickson*

Transaction Publishers
New Brunswick (U.S.A.) and London (U.K.)

Library of Congress Catalog Number: 77-80865
0-87855-640-0 (paper)
Printed in the United States of America
First paperback edition 1978 by Transaction Publishers, New Brunswick, New Jersey 08903.

Library of Congress Cataloging in Publication Data

Lomax, Alan, 1915-
    Folk song style and culture.

    Reprint of the 1968 ed. published by American Association for the Advancement of Science. II. Title. III. Series: American Association for the Advancement of Science. Publication; no. 88.
[ML3545.L63 1978]   784.4'9   77-80865
ISBN 0-87855-640-0 pbk.

A Staff Report on Cantometrics

Presented at the Washington Meeting of the
American Association for the Advancement
of Science, December, 1966.

Alan Lomax, Project Director
Conrad Arensberg, Co-Director
Edwin E. Erickson, Ethnologist
Victor Grauer, Musicologist
Norman Berkowitz, Programmer
Irmgard Bartenieff, Director of Dance Research
Forrestine Paulay, Dance Specialist
Joan Halifax, Research Assistant
Barbara Ayres, Ethnologist
Norman N. Markel, Consulting Linguist
Roswell Rudd, Music Analyst
Monika Vizedom, Ethnologist
Fred Peng, Linguist
Roger Wescott, Consulting Linguist
David Brown, Consulting Statistician

*The Cantometrics Project is administered by the Bureau of
Applied Social Research of Columbia University.*

Foreword

MANY of the chapters in this volume were first presented orally at the Annual Meeting of the American Association for the Advancement of Science in Washington on December 27, 1966, when the staff of the Cantometrics Project of Columbia University gave a day-long report to the Anthropology Section (H), entitled *Frontiers of Anthropology: Cantometrics and Culture.* The length of this symposium was, perhaps, warranted by the novelty of the method discussed, the applications and the tests to which it had been subjected during a four-year period, and the importance for social science of its principal finding—that song style symbolizes and reinforces certain important aspects of social structure in all cultures. For the first time, predictable and universal relationships have been established between the expressive and communication processes, on the one hand, and social structure and culture pattern, on the other. A science of social aesthetics which looks at all social process in terms of stylistic continuity and change may now be envisaged. We wish to thank both the Association and its officers for making this distinguished platform available for a report on a scientific enterprise in its early stages of development.

A word or two about the history of this research may be of interest. Such a broad, comparative study of singing qualities was not possible until the 1940's when large numbers of good recordings of folk songs from all over the world became available, and one could hear and compare the music of the world's peoples for the first time. In reviewing this material I saw that characteristics of sung performance, such as voice quality and mode of presentation, seemed to define large musical regions even without considering melody and rhythm. For example, the singing styles of the African Pygmies and Bushmen apparently belonged to the same musical family, in spite of the fact that the two peoples were racially different, had lived in contrasting environments, and had no known cultural connection for many centuries (p. 91). Islands of this African Hunter music are surrounded by a sea of Negro song that covers the whole of the continent south of the Sahara (p. 91). In the same sense one could perceive a high degree of continuity in the music of the Australian Aborigines from all quarters of that continent (p. 100), while the chants of the Indian tribes of North America, at least as far South as the Yaqui, have a family resemblance to one another in spite of local singularities (p. 85). Yet no empirical method existed for describing and assessing these grand stylistic continuities.

The first step toward this goal came in the course of two field trips in the

Mediterranean. In 1953, while making high-fidelity recordings of folk singing in every province of Spain, I observed that Spanish performance style varied in terms of the severity of prohibitions against feminine premarital intercourse. In southern Spain, where sexual sanctions were Oriental in their stringency, a piercing, high-pitched, squeezed, narrow vocal delivery was cultivated which made choral performance all but impossible. North of the Pyrenees, among the Basques, Gallegos, and Asturians, where sexual sanctions were mild and contact between the sexes was easy and relaxed, there was a strong preference for well-blended choirs singing in open and low-pitched voices.

In 1955 a more extensive field survey of Italian folk singing established a similar north-south correlation between sexual mores and vocal tension. Moving south from central Italy the severity of sexual mores and the intensity of masculine jealousy increases until a condition of virtual purdah is reached in the rural villages of Sicily and southern Calabria. The star singers of southern Italy use a tense, sometimes even strangulated, vocal attack much like that of North Africa, and group singing is both rare and diffusely organized. Crossing the Apennines into the Po Valley and mounting the foothills of the Alps, one finds an easy camaraderie between young people and, at the same time, mixed choirs of blending, bell-like, dewy voices.

In an article written for an Italian journal, *Nuovi Argomenti* (Lomax, 1955–1956), I argued that vocal stance varies with the strictness of sexual sanctions, not only in Mediterranean Europe, but in the rest of the world as well, citing as evidence recordings from every continent. This correlation has since been firmly established in the present study (p. 194). The substance of this idea, with a particular emphasis on Italian ethnography, was presented at the 1958 meeting of the American Anthropological Association under the aegis of Margaret Mead. Walter Goldschmidt, then editor of *The American Anthropologist,* asked for an article on song style for the journal. In this piece, there appears a preliminary regional classification of world singing styles, based on three criteria—degree of vocal tension, the dominance of solo or choral organization or performance, and the level of tonal unity in choral singing (Lomax, 1959). This layout of song styles has been largely confirmed by the present research (Chapter 4).

Work on the Cantometrics Project began in the summer of 1961 with the help of a pilot grant, sponsored by Jack Harrison of the Humanities Division of the Rockefeller Foundation. The proposal was to develop ways of describing recorded folk song performances in empirical terms so that songs could be compared and clustered from culture to culture. The first invention of that summer was *phonotactics,* by means of which the assonance pattern in sung verse can be diagrammed. When Edith Trager applied this system of analysis to a sample of songs from a cross-section of European cultures, it was found that each areal folk song style had a distinctive model of vowel color which held the frequencies of the vowels in its songs to a certain proportion. The most typical songs conformed closely to this model, a rudimentary form of which was exhibited in the popular lullabies of the region. These vowel diagrams, each with its distinctive patterns of vowel frequency, appeared to be an efficient means of classifying regional song styles. So far as Indo-European languages were concerned, a marked preference for high front (tense) vowels appeared in languages spoken in Mediterranean lands, where feminine premarital sexual intercourse was forbidden. On the other hand, low back vowels, together with oscillations toward back enunciation, characterized the song styles of areas with more permissive sexual standards, such as in northern Italy, northern Spain and central and eastern Europe. Thus the vocal style regions established in Spain and Italy by the earlier study were reflected in systems of assonance (Lomax and Trager, 1964).

Later that summer, Victor Grauer, composer and musicologist, collaborated with me on the development of a holistic descriptive system, later named *Cantometrics,* for evoking performance style from sound recordings. The structure of this empirical rating scheme is set forth fully in Chapter 2. That first summer Grauer and I tested it on a sample of more than 700 songs, taken from the world range of singing styles. Margaret Mead suggested that we create profiles of our song ratings, which could be arranged in groups by visual inspection. We quickly discovered clusters of profiles from which contrastive original master profiles could be assembled that made very good ethnographic and musical sense.

Hypotheses about the social function of song style structure were then developed in consultation with Conrad Arensberg of Columbia University:

1. Solo song characterized highly centralized societies, and leaderless performances were most common in societies with simple political structure.
2. Unified choirs occurred in highly cohesive societies and diffuse choruses in individualized cultures.

The confirmation of these early hypotheses appears in Chapters 6 and 7 of this volume. In general, a culture's song performance style seemed to represent generalized aspects of its social and communications systems.

These findings were presented in a paper to a joint meeting of the Ethnomusicological Society and the American Association of Anthropology in the winter of 1961. In their preliminary statement, they formed the basis of an application for a four-year grant from the National Institute of Mental Health, jointly sponsored by the Department of Anthropology and the Bureau of Applied Social Research at Columbia University. The proposal,

Folk Song as a Psycho-Social Indicator, called for a test of the cantometric
coding system on a large and representative sample of recorded songs from
around the world, and for confirmation of the postulated correlations between performance structure and social structure on a cantometric sample
for which rated ethnographic data were available. Parallel studies were to be
made:

1. In extending phonotactics beyond the border of the Indo-European
   language family;
2. In development of a technique for cross-cultural content analysis of
   song texts; and
3. On a pilot study of dance style.

The grant (No. MH–06842) was awarded with a beginning date of Febru-
ary 1, 1962, and has been subsequently extended to end in 1970.

From its inception, cantometrics has been a group enterprise employing
the special skills of musicologists, linguists, anthropologists, statisticians, pro-
grammers, and movement analysts. Team work in folk song research is vital
because song is a multileveled communication which combines the signals
carried by many systems into a single, evocative message. Elements of the
dance, of speech melody, of role playing, of social organization, of ritual
practice, and of emotive communication blend together in a performance so
that none of the components is individually perceptible. But in order to understand and classify a song style one must establish control over all the levels
of its complex message, and thus folk song research must employ a number
of disciplines and advance on several fronts at one time.

The best of songs rise like a cry from the heart of the singer to arouse the
sympathy of any culture member. This apparent simplicity is due to the sub-
ordination of all the expressive systems involved to some overriding cultural
need. Our working hypothesis has been that each system supports and reinforces the same central message in its own way. When the cantometric profiles made it possible to review 37 levels of song style at a glance, we could
see that individual songs of a profile cluster were no more than reflections of
one stylistic model. The inference was that within this stylistic model, just
as within a single song, many levels combined to support and reinforce a
single pattern. We began to find such patterns running through many songs
from many adjacent cultures and characterizing large culture areas. We
hoped to show that each pattern of sung communication symbolized the dominant patterns of social structure and communication style in that large area.
The possibility of finding such generalized behavioral models expressed in
song was a stimulating one.

For all these reasons the Cantometrics Project was designed to study several aspects of the sung communication concurrently. Although such an approach was bound to be clumsy and difficult in its early stages, it had certain built-in advantages. Patterns established in one subsystem of the sung communication can presumably be confirmed by those discovered in another subsystem. Our findings are encouraging in this respect: the distributions of song styles seem to be repeated in the distributions of dance styles.

The performance orientation of this research has given it a behavioral bias somewhat novel in both musicology and anthropology. The measurements or parameters making up the various rating systems were found in the recorded data; that is, the dimension of each measurement corresponds to the full worldwide range of some quality scored in song or dance. A great many rating ideas were tested in the course of assembling each descriptive system. Only those devices were retained on which expert coders achieved reasonable consensus and which continued to classify songs into manageable sets. In a very real sense, every page of this volume is a further elucidation of this primary research principle, as the following summary of the project demonstrates.

Cantometrics

The first version of the *Cantometric Coding Book* was written up in 1961 with the assistance of Robert Abramson, an able music theoretician of New York City. The result of many years of reworking and testing by Victor Grauer and myself, the final version, as presented in Chapter 3, represents a first attempt to crystallize a set of perceptive categories that the ordinary listener can apply to the classification of his musical experience. Grauer, chief musicologist of the project, and his assistant, Roswell Rudd, applied this system to a sample of more than 3,500 songs during a period of about two and a half years of full-time effort. The collection of tapes and long-playing records they rated represented what was then known of the folk music of the world's peoples. The development of this collection beyond the limits of my already large library required the better part of two years of correspondence and personal solicitation. Thanks to the generosity of various institutions in the Soviet Union, the collection now contains a selection of the song styles from the Baltic to the Bering Sea. The only large areas of the world not represented are China and the Gran Chaco, although, of course, many other musical territories are not thoroughly covered.

Orchestral Types

At the outset we decided to limit our study to song performance, on the ground that, while singing is a universal trait of culture, instrumental music seems to be a derivative system. Furthermore, the full rating of complex orchestral music would have at least doubled the time of our first experiment. We therefore confined our look at orchestras to a sketch of the social and rhythmic relationship of these instruments to the sung melody and to each other and to a roster of the instruments present in the accompanying ensembles. The classification system used was a modification of that developed by Sachs and Von Hornbostel (1961).

An inspection of the computer compilation of orchestral patterns encouraged us to expand this data bank. Together with Theodore Grame of Yale University, we devised a system to retrieve information about the structure, function, role, symbolism, and body relationship of instrumental ensembles from the ethnographic and musicological literature dealing with this subject. This bibliographic tool was applied to standard sources describing the orchestras of 775 cultures, a sample so distributed by area as to supplement the information already available in cantometric codings. The computer has assembled interesting maps of instrumental and ensemble distributions. One map shows, for example, that orchestras in which chordophones play the leading role occur most frequently in areas touched by the civilizations of the Orient and, further, that such ensembles are most frequent in cultures where severe sanctions are placed upon the premarital sexual activities of women. This supports a supposition of Sachs (1962) that the chordophone is a symbol of passive femininity. The full exploration of these data, however, still lies in the future.

Phonotactics

Theoretical linguists generally agreed that the system devised by Trager and myself for the comparative analysis of assonance could not be applied across linguistic family lines because it dealt with the logically noncomparable phonemic level. Phonotactic research was delayed until Fred Peng, a student of Haxey Smith, designed a componential system, based on vowel and consonant articulation areas, by means of which the relative frequencies of the sounds from all language families could be compared. This rating system, which enables the expert listener to assess the articulatory preference pattern in a song style, was applied to a sample of 300 songs from 30 cultures. The information was computerized and still awaits full analysis. One remarkable result has emerged, however—the level of complexity of a culture can be judged from the number of articulatory distinctions it consistently employs in its sung verse (p. 140).

Textual Analysis

It seems obvious that the themes and concerns of a culture will also emerge in song texts. Consequently, with the help of Joan Halifax, I developed a coding scheme for the identification and comparison of the concepts embodied in sung words. Such a rating instrument must take into account the fact that there is a broad variation in the semantic load carried by different song styles. On the one hand there are textually complex narratives like the Western European ballad, and on the other, the songs of primitive peoples, which frequently consist of repetitions of a few words or phrases and seldom contain a story structure.

To provide a means for measuring this difference and to seek the basic concepts in the sung poetry, I decided to apply some form of computer dictionary to the task of concept analysis. Experience had taught us that the principal communication of song resides in its redundancies—that the brevity and speed of its patterns of repetition restrict song to those bits of information which culture members agree are paramount in importance. In spite of the errors and the blurring of meaning inevitable in translations, therefore, one could expect to find in the redundant patterns of song texts statements about crucial cultural patterns.

Benjamin N. Colby, Pierre Maranda, and Elli-Kaija Kongas provided counsel and printouts of the computer dictionaries with which they were experimenting. The tool that Miss Halifax applied to a small sample of song in the pilot experiment (Chapter 13), was a stripped-down version of Colby's revision (Colby, 1965) of the Harvard General Inquirer System (Stone and Hunt, 1963). Since it produced such good results and since programs incorporating this dictionary already exist, we plan soon to treat song texts from a large sample that will parallel the other samples in the study.

Early experiments in the content analysis of song texts showed that in English language folk song a valid concept analysis of text can emerge from counts of only those words which receive the strongest stresses in a verse. An untrained listener, watching a good sound-volume meter, can match the score of an expert linguist in rating stress. This result was confirmed when scores for expert raters and for meter watchers were checked by an instrument especially designed to measure volume.

Cultural Data Bank

Conrad Arensberg, co-director, foresaw, when we first discussed preliminary cantometric findings, that the proper use of the cross-cultural data banks would produce verifiable correlations between style and social structure. We sought, therefore, to assemble a computer bank of comparative ethnography. To this end John Roberts of Cornell, Robert Textor of Stanford, Irvin Child of Yale, and John Whiting of Harvard generously contributed sets of punched data cards and rating sheets, as well as much good advice. From the opening of the project in 1962, a full-time ethnologist has always been a part of the staff. Monika Vizedom, Barbara Ayres, and Edwin E. Erickson worked under Arensberg to control the accuracy of the ethnographic data and the relevancy of its use in the research.

Since our first task was to set song style in its cultural context we made our first and largest cross-cultural match with data from the *Ethnographic Atlas* (Murdock, 1962–1967), which provides standardized ethnographic ratings for subsistence type, family organization, settlement type, etc. George P. Murdock sent ratings from many cultures which had not yet been published. Others, structured in the scheme of the *Atlas,* came from ethnographers who brought their song tapes to the experiment. Many more were derived from the literature by Barbara Ayres, under the supervision of Arensberg. After two years, the matched Murdock-Cantometrics sample for which both musical and ethnographic data were available reached the level of 233 cultures.

Many of the hypotheses tested on this sample were developed in conference between Conrad Arensberg and myself. Indeed, this project owes its principal intellectual debt to the insight and wisdom of Arensberg, although Monika Vizedom and Barbara Ayres implemented and contributed to the development of the anthropological postulates. However, it is to the erudition and statistical good judgment of Edwin E. Erickson, the staff ethnologist, and associate editor of this volume, that the technical evaluation of the numerical evidence is due.

The punching, correction, organization, and intercorrelation of all these data banks in the Columbia computer was planned and carried out by Norman Berkowitz, staff programmer. For the past four years Berkowitz has provided a steady output of accurate, well-designed, and easily read data displays of many types. His inventions, discussed by him in Appendix 2, crystallized all the many issues covered in this research.

Choreometrics

The elusive element in our study of musical style was rhythmic structure, and this problem led us into a study of the dynamics of body communication in the dance. Two seminar courses with Ray L. Birdwhistell of the Eastern Pennsylvania Psychiatric Institute had taught me that systems of body communication always operate in parallel with any signal that goes on the air. Indeed, the cantometrics research strategy was inspired by Birdwhistell's theoretical approach to the field of human communication. However, he was wise and generous enough to suggest that his own kinesic notation system was unsuitable for this cross-cultural study and that the Laban notation system might be the appropriate device. The Project was fortunate enough to enlist the interest of Irmgard Bartenieff, who has specialized in the shape-effort aspect of the Laban tradition.

Shape-effort provides a theory and a cursive script for recording the qualitative aspect of dancing and other movement. Martha Davis and Forrestine

Paulay, two advanced students of this system, have worked as co-raters, and during the last two years all of us together have made a first appraisal of the full range of movement style, cross-culturally, as it appears in filmed dances. Gradually, a system for the comparative rating of movement style, called choreometrics, has evolved, although progress, compared to the growth of cantometrics, has been very slow. No one has yet had the vision to assemble a representative filmed archive of dance style to match the Folkways Library or the World Library of Folk and Primitive Music (Columbia Records). Therefore, two years were required to find and view a fair sample of films and to test the preliminary rating parameters on the wide range of cultures. Furthermore, the complexity of the kinesic communication system, in which many aspects of the body play a part simultaneously, makes a rating system for dance style a far more complex design problem than is the case for singing.

Our research goals have also been more ambitious. We are comparing dance to everyday movement in order to verify the hypothesis that danced movement is patterned reinforcement of the habitual movement patterns of each culture or culture area. Moreover, since the study of the organization and level of synchrony of the singing group had proved so useful in classifying song, these aspects of the dance have been given a very elaborate treatment in the choreometric rating system. Thus we are now producing comparative statements about the level and kind of synchrony, as well as the social choreography of the dances studied. Hopefully, all three instruments will make it possible to compare and typify any filmed dance in such a way as to relate it to its social and cultural context. Already we know that dance style varies in a regular way in terms of the level of complexity and the type of subsistence activity of the culture which supports it. In addition we have found dynamic models of movement that characterize all behavior in large world style regions, paralleling those found in the song study.

In summary, when the term of the present National Institute of Mental Health grant comes to a close in 1970, we hope to have completed the development of five well-tested instruments for the analysis of the relation between style and culture.

Acknowledgments

The principal debt of the Cantometrics Project is to a generation of field workers who have taken the pains to record song and dance after having cajoled the temperamental artists of the world to perform for them. The assemblage of over 2,000 tapes and 400 long-playing records in the cantometric archives required the better part of three years and depended upon the generosity of more people than can be thanked by name here. Our first debt of gratitude is to Moses Asch, Director of Folkways Records, who contributed his recorded library of world song and opened his unpublished tape archive to us, thus providing something like one-quarter of all the songs examined. In the Soviet Union, Radio Moscow, the Moscow State Conservatory, and the Ethnographic Institute of Leningrad presented an essential résumé of Siberian, Asian, and Russian songs, toward which Edward Alexev, Anna Vasilievna Rudnyova, B. M. Dobrovolskii, Galina Zarembo, K. G. Tskhurbaeva, and V. V. Akhabadze made significant suggestions. Other important sources in Europe were Albert Lloyd, the Recorded Library of the BBC, The Norwegian Radio, Peter Kennedy, Svatava Jakobson, Diego Carpitella, Carla Bianca, the Musée des ATP in Paris, Claudie Marcel Dubois, Maguy Andral, Wolfgang Laade, John Andromedas, Alan Waterman, José María Arguedas, Paul Bowles, the National Archives of Rumania and Bulgaria, as well as my own collections from the United States, Great Britain, Spain, Italy, and the West Indies. Funds for travel to the Soviet Union came from the Wenner-Gren Foundation.

For Africa, the best-recorded of continents, the principal donors include: Gilbert Rouget, Norma McLeod, Roxanne McCollester, Alan Merriam, Nicholas England, André Lhote, Colin Turnbull, Stephanie Dinkins, L. Estreicher, David Ames, David Spock, David Sapir, Elizabeth Hopkins, Caldwell Smith, Robert Ritzenthaler, Ronald Guttridge, Pierre Gaisseau, Simone Roche, Melville Herskovits, Norman Whitten, and J. D. Elder. From Hugh Tracey's enormous archive in South Africa came the largest single contribution to the African sample.

For the Amerindian music of North America, recordings were from many sources, among them the Laura Boulton collection at Columbia University, the Archives of Primitive Music at the University of Indiana, Carmen Roy at the National Museum of Canada, David McAllester, José Helmer of Mexico City, Henrietta Yurchenko (the important collector of Mexican primitive songs), Kenneth Peacock, Warren d'Azevedo, Wayne Suttles, Frederica de Laguna, William Fenton, and Charles L. Boilés, Garreth Muchmore, Heloise Gray, William Sturtevant, Nicholas Smith, Ida Halpern, Lorraine Koranda, Jean Gabus, June MacNeish, and above all, from the wide-ranging surveys of Willard Rhodes.

South America, so varied and so little known, is represented by the collections of Charles Furlong, Harry S. Tschopik, the Instituto Linguistico Verano of Peru, Michael Harner, Simone Roche, Harold Schultz, William Crocker, Terence Turner, Helmuth Fuchs, Brian Moser, John Cohen, G. E. Dale, Bertrand Flornoy, Phillipe Luzuy, Edward M. Weyer, Jr., T. P. Rootes, G. Plaza, Juan Liscano, Clyde Keeler, Roberta Montagu, John Baroco, Henrietta Yurchenko, and has been especially enriched by the contributions of Isabel Aretz of the Institute of Folklore in Caracas.

The Pacific, where so much work still needs to be done, is represented by the work of J. Maceda and H. Conklin of the Philippines, Ivan Polunin in Borneo, Bernard Ijzerdraat in Indonesia, and Professor T. Kurosawa in Formosa. Australia, New Guinea, and Melanesia were analyzed from recordings of Anthony Forge, Colin Simpson, André Dupeyrat, Murray Groves, Nancy Bowers, Jeremy Beckett, Cherry Vayda, Jane Goodale, Ward Goodenough, Geoffrey O'Grady, Robert Glasse, Roy Rappaport, Louis Luzbetak, A. P. Elkin, and most especially the Australian Broadcasting Commission under the direction of Allen Simpson. Songs from the Insular Pacific came from Harold Scheffler, P. Henderson, the Templeton Crocker Expedition, Bruce Biggs, P. Rothschild, Chester Williams, Barbara Smith, Ted Schwartz, Margaret Mead, the Indiana Archive, Jim Spillius, and, especially, the South Pacific Commission with Alice Moyle.

Asiatic material came from many sources. Among them were Douglas Haring, Genjiro Masu, the American Himalayan Expedition, Serge Bourguignon, Fosco Maraini, Robert P. Austerlitz, Edward Alexeev, B. M. Dobrovolskii, P. Rubell, Radio Hong Kong, Edward Norbeck, the Japanese Music Institute, Dr. Wojbowitz, Georges Condominas, H. D. Noone, Ivan Polunin, the Cambridge Expedition to Southeast Asia, Christopher Byrd, Wolfe Leslau, Dr. Kiwi-Gerson, Ralph Solecki, S. Lubtchansky, Morton Klass, John Levy, the Indian Department of Anthropology, Peter Kunstadter, Laslo Vikar of Budapest, Alain Danielou, and Robert Garfias.

In a group research project a director's debts of gratitude are many. The project would never have got under way without the encouragement and intellectual guidance of Margaret Mead. Ray Birdwhistell's sophisticated views of communication inspired many of the approaches developed on the project. We have depended upon the sound advice and helpfulness of David McAllester at many stages of the work. Among linguists, George Trager, Haxey Smith, and Robert Austerlitz have given good counsel; linguistic research has been done in collaboration with Edith Trager, Roger Wescott, and above all, Norman Markel, who has served as linguistic consultant for several years. Other scholars in the humanities who contributed ideas and encouragement were Richard Waterman, Alan Merriam, Robert Garfias, Charles Seeger, Franklin Udy, Ted Schwartz, Robert Gardner, and most particularly, Norma McLeod. Arnold Semmel, Victoria Bordaz, and, particularly, David Brown of the Columbia Psychology Department, all made important contributions to the system of statistical validation. Donald Meisner designed the computer maps illustrated in the end papers. Kathleen Mullen and Ethel Raim carried out a year's analysis of melodic type. Jan Syrjala and Sandy Kirsh planned and maintained the high quality and unobtrusive audiovisual setup in the office. Dena Hirsh established the office routines and set up the primary data catalogs, and Linda Oldham saw the data through the punching stage. The talent, energy, and devotion of research assistant, Joan Halifax, solved problems in every aspect of research.

For the past five years the project has been generously endowed with funds from the National Institute of Mental Health and has greatly benefited from the counsel of Phillip Sapir, former director of research grants. My appointment as research associate in the Department of Anthropology at Columbia University has facilitated the research in manifold ways. Alan Barton and other members of the board of directors of the Bureau of Social Research, along with Clara Shapiro and Phyllis Sheridan, the Bureau's administrators, have made the daily operation of this project a pleasant and uncomplicated matter.

I am deeply indebted to Roswell Rudd, the brilliant modern jazz composer, who worked with patience for so long to produce our musical data bank. But I feel especially obligated to Victor Grauer and to Conrad Arensberg, close collaborators from the beginning of the research.

Alan Lomax
New York, 1968

TABLE OF CONTENTS

FOLK SONG STYLE and CULTURE

1

The Stylistic Method

Alan Lomax

A SONG style, like other human things, is a pattern of learned behavior, common to the people of a culture. Singing is a specialized act of communication, akin to speech, but far more formally organized and redundant. Because of its heightened redundancy, singing attracts and holds the attention of groups; indeed, as in most primitive societies, it invites group participation. Whether chorally performed or not, however, the chief function of song is to express the shared feelings and mold the joint activities of some human community. It is to be expected, therefore, that the content of the sung communication should be social rather than individual, normative rather than particular. The cantometric experiment has, in fact, shown that song style is an excellent indicator of cultural pattern.

So far as we know, every branch of the human species has its songs. Indeed, singing is a universal human trait found in all known cultures as a specialized and easily identifiable kind of vocal behavior. During this century, especially in the past twenty years, recordings of song have been made in every quarter of the globe in all sorts of cultural settings. Probably singing is the only human behavior which has been documented so generally and in a form so adaptable for laboratory research. A recording can be played again and again for judges, and their observations can be compared to those obtained from repeated auditions of other recordings. Thus a modern library of musical tapes provides ideal material for a comparative study of social communication. The cantometric system sets up a behavioral grid upon which all song styles can be ranged and compared. This grid was not designed to replicate the music, already accurately recorded on tape, but to rate it on a series of rating scales (loud to soft, tense to lax, etc.) taxonomically applicable to song performance in all cultures. Thus song can be compared to song, song to speech, and hopefully to other aspects of behavior.

The main findings of this study are two. First, the geography of song styles traces the main paths of human migration and maps the known historical distributions of culture. Second, some traits of song performance show a powerful relationship to features of social structure that regulate interaction

3

in all cultures. Neither of these ideas is new to the thoughtful humanist. However, the statistical confirmation is so strong as to indicate that expressive behavior may be one of the most sensitive and reliable indicators of culture pattern and social structure. Apparently, as people live so do they sing.

THE CULTURAL GREY–OUT

The work was filled with a sense of urgency. To a folklorist the uprooting and destruction of traditional cultures and the consequent grey-out or disappearance of the human variety presents as serious a threat to the future happiness of mankind as poverty, overpopulation, and even war. Soon there will be nowhere to go and nothing worth staying at home for. War is wasteful of lives, but only rarely and at its most dreadful does it eradicate a whole way of life. On the other hand, big government, national education, information networks, and a worldwide marketing system kill off cultures whose ways do not conform to those of the power center. Our western massproduction and communication systems are inadvertently destroying the languages, traditions, cuisines, and creative styles that once gave every people and every locality a distinctive character—indeed their principal reason for living. Tribes in New Guinea, dreaming that they will possess the endless wealth of the European, literally throw their culture into the sea and sit waiting for a new cargo to come in by ship or plane. Everywhere the pitchmen and the preachers persuade the innocent of the earth to laugh at or to forget the unified folkways of their forefathers, in exchange for broken speech, plastic saints, and novel vices. Meantime Telstar rises balefully on the western horizon.

The folk, the primitive, the nonindustrial societies account for most of the cultural variety of the planet. Though rich in the expressive and communicative arts, these folk communities seldom have the means to record, evaluate, or transmit their songs and tales except by word of mouth; and the noise of our hard-sell society is drowning out the quieter communications of these word-of-mouth traditions. Indeed, the bookish and literate West labels all expressive output not enshrined in print as inferior *per se*. Certainly any people without some technique for institutionalizing and fostering its traditions is at the mercy of societies with printing presses, schools, and broadcasting systems. Such a lack of knowledge-saving devices and educational institutions, however, has little or nothing to do with the universal or local value of a style of communication. Each style is a way of experiencing, transforming, knowing, and expressing life, sharpened by the genius of a people through many centuries, as it adapted itself to some special environment.

When a civilized European or Oriental celebrates the virtues of his heritage, he mentions its music, literature, art, science, and history. The education he bestows on his children consists largely of a grounding in these humane traditions, for with such reinforcements young people gain a sense of full-blown identity. In the end, a person's emotional stability is a function of his command of a communication style that binds him to a human community with a history. As our aggressive and economically motivated communication system smashes the tribal, local, and neighborhood communication worlds, whole generations are left with a sense of belonging nowhere and we, ourselves, losing our local roots, become daily more alienated.

The loss in communicative potential for the whole human race is very grave, for these threatened communication systems represent much of what the human race has created in its thousands of years of wandering across the earth. In them lies a treasure, a human resource, whose worth is incalculable, and which can never be replaced when it has been wasted and lost. Enumeration of some of the new expressive directions that have (without our understanding how) recently emerged from the cross-fertilization of styles, gives one a sense of the potency of tradition:

1. The effect of African sculpture on modern painting.
2. The bloom of jazz out of Europe and Africa in New Orleans.
3. The flowering of popular dance in South America from a cross of Latin, African, and Indian influences.
4. The birth of Israeli music from Arab and Central European streams.

The health and life-giving delight of each of these cultural hybrids stems from the merging of vigorous and independent parent styles. The geneticist tells us that a healthy genetic future depends upon the survival of the present gene pool with its variety of strains. So, too, healthy cultural development depends upon the survival of the world pool of cultural styles in all their variety. Folk and primitive arts, their flinty structure tested at the fireside across the centuries, have always strengthened the more effete traditions of the city. Though somewhat more narrowly dimensioned, these simpler traditions have a germinal vitality and staying power that much cosmopolitan art lacks.

Each of these communication structures, now being swept off the board, may be capable of seeding a whole new cultural development. Each becomes the beloved companion of the field workers and specialists who know it on its own terms. Even more important, however, each of these traditions can serve as a bridge of dignity and continuity for the people of a simple culture as they move across the stream of change into their uncertain future. A verse can recall a whole epoch; a turn in a tune can hearten a people through a generation of struggle; for, if the written word pre-

serves and expands knowledge, the multileveled symbolic structure of music
and art can preserve and expand a life-style. It is the purpose of this volume
to offer an explanation for this truism and to demonstrate how it may serve
the ends of humanity, as well as of social science.

THE SOCIAL BASE OF STYLE

The relationship of life to art forms the bond between the artist and his
audience, though the specific terms of this bond have been mysterious until
now. In the present study we translate life-style as "culture pattern," drawing our profiles of how people live from the field data of the anthropologist. Against his panoramic range of custom and ritual from every branch
of the human family we set forth the varied performing styles of song
and dance. Our recordings and social data represent the full spread of human achievement. Thus, when a steady pattern of difference in the economic
system or sexual mores is paralleled by some consistent shift of song performance across this range of two hundred and more cultures, we surmise
that the two patterns are interdependent. The charts, the statistical tables,
and the arguments in the forthcoming chapters all rest upon the inference
that if song performance and life-style vary together, one is the reflection
and reinforcement of the other. At a first level, then, our demonstrations
signify that features of song performance symbolize significant traits in
culture.

We find that song styles shift consistently with:

1. Productive range
2. Political level
3. Level of stratification of class
4. Severity of sexual mores
5. Balance of dominance between male and female
6. Level of social cohesiveness

Nothing in the established correlations, however, shows that song style
refers to any particular institution or the behavioral pattern of any one culture. Rather, song style seems to summarize, in a compact way, the ranges
of behavior that are appropriate to one kind of cultural context. If style
carries this load of social content, however, song can no longer be treated
as a wayward, extra, belated, though pleasant afterthought upon the serious
business of living. Song presents an immediate image of a culture pattern.
A man's favorite tune recalls to him not only some pleasant memory, but
the web of relationships that makes his life possible. No wonder, then, that
a song from home brings a rush of feeling to the heart and tears to the

eyes of a traveler. It reminds him of how his branch of the human family has stayed alive, loved, and perpetuated a culture on a particular terrain. Immediacy of recall is a normal symbolic function, but it is raised to a peak of rapidity and potency in song because of the condensation of, and the congruency among, all its levels.

The emotional urgency of the song performance, then, is a function of its direct connection with the humdrum but essential procedures of life. The resultant span of communication and the style that shapes it, however, have a status and continuity of their own apart from the cultural realities from which they stem and for which they stand. This concept cannot be too much emphasized since it rescues the reasonable man from the trap of cultural determinism. Any set of symbols can be manipulated and combined with others independently of their origins, and the outcome may be quite different from the starting point. For example, we have discovered that song style is, in many respects, a reflection of economic level, and yet the terms of this symbolic relationship are too complex to give rise to crude economic determinism. On the one hand the complexity of song texts seems to vary directly with the level of productive complexity. On the other the position of women in the productive system seems to control the level of integration in a song style. Each intersection of these two factors gives a different impression to the listener. Each one symbolizes a special pattern of social relationship essential to the smooth functioning of an economy and its work teams, a relationship which is dramatized and reinforced in song and dance style in unexpected ways.

These norms (presented not only in the chants of labor, but in love and ritual songs as well) have no connection in the ear of the audience or the mind of the performer with the droning tempo of daily labor. To a member of the culture they appear simply as the amusing and enjoyable sounds of life, arranged in a familiar and satisfying context. In fact, the performing arts acquire their quiet and unobtrusive authority in the lives of men precisely because they carry their message about social structure beneath the surface. They deal, not with any specific social interaction, but with the boundaries within which behavior must fall to be acceptable. The qualitative aspects of these behavioral ranges are what we speak of as the realm of style. A "style," for example a "song style," is the recurrent juxtaposition of a set of such qualitative formulas which define the precise limits for tempo, loudness, emphasis, interval width, etc.

Cantometrics finds, then, that no branch of the human family, no matter how well- or ill-equipped technically, fails to symbolize its social norms in a suitable song style. Each culture raises its voice in a way that speaks for its economy, its sexual mores, its degree of stratification, its ways of organizing groups, etc. Therefore the main song performance profile in a culture will match an important behavioral profile made up of many general features of social structure. Both song and social profiles are models for human behavior, the former organizing some sort of collective, public exercise in phonation, the latter a framework for relations between people in everyday life. We have found that a small number of song profiles accounts for most of our data.

Among Amerindians of North America, for example, it is common for most public singing to be done by groups of males in a harsh-voiced, forceful style, where strong voices are matched in a roughly organized, hearty unison with no singer more prominent than his fellows. The most frequent activities in Indian communities (hunting, fishing, making war, ritual curing) were carried out by associations of equal males, who joined together temporarily and by mutual consent, and conformed to some traditional plan of action, on their own accord and without a dominant leader. This way of singing and of getting things done certainly occurs in all cultures; it is simply more frequent in North America than any other model. One may say it is a characteristic "Indian style."

STYLE AND CULTURAL RENEWAL

Each song style we have studied thus portrays some level of human adaptation, some social style. Each performance is a symbolic reenactment of crucial behavior patterns upon which the continuity of a culture hangs, and is thus endowed with the emotional authority of the necessary and the familiar. Moreover, many levels of this symbolic behavior are brought into congruency with some main theme, so that a style comes to epitomize some singular and notable aspect of a culture, by which its members identify themselves and with which they endow many of their activities and their feelings. This is why an expressive style may become the focal point for cultural crystallization and renewal.

One aim of the Cantometrics Project is to provide descriptive techniques for the speedy characterization and classification of these life-giving culture-defining patterns. Our practical intent is that every communication style be a readily recognized entity, appreciated on its own terms by its carriers, its audience, and the administrators of communication and education who nowadays make so many of the decisions about what is to have a hearing and a chance to survive. The establishment of a clear connection between the art and the essential life-style of a culture endows the style with the double authority of necessity and history. The realization of its uniqueness, on the one hand, and its family connections, on the other, gives it resilience and conceptual strength. The discovery that each culture style is a part of some grand regional and continental tradition can lend the weight of history to a skein of songs that might otherwise be cast aside. The maps in Chapter 4, for example, delineate six world song-style regions. They also demonstrate a very high level of style unity among the many diverse cultures of Negro Africa and of aboriginal North America. Apparently two great, independent song- and dance-style traditions, continental in extent, have flourished in these areas for many millennia. Africans and Amerindians can thus legitimately view their contemporary communication styles as the outcome of aesthetic histories, as venerable and as self-consistent as those of Europe or Asia.

Perhaps enough has been said to indicate that the stylistic approach, defined in these pages, can bring more understanding of the expressive traditions of folk and primitive groups. One hopes that each style may be reestablished in its cultural space and begin again to develop along its own course, providing another rallying point for the maintenance of cultural variety. Such has certainly been a principal aim of the folklorists, musicologists, and ethnologists who patiently recorded the arts and life-styles of mankind. Unfortunately the major result of this scholarly effort has usually been the publication of books and articles in European languages which, like a good deal of research, have often been of more benefit to the researchers than to the people whose lives they closely concerned. Now, however, cultural feedback, through the use of field recordings published as discs and broadcast, and films projected and televised, has become an easy matter. Every culture has a mature and ripened heritage of speaking and singing styles that can immediately find a place on records, radio, film, and television. An "underdeveloped" people feels a renewed sense of significance when its own artists, communicating in genuine style, appear on the powerful and prestigious mass media or begin to use them for their own purposes. Experience teaches that such direct feedback of genuine, uncensored native art to its roots acts upon a culture like water, sunlight, and fertilizer on a barren garden; it begins to bloom and grow again. The direction, planning, and administration of this cultural feedback system will be facilitated by the recognition of style structures and style differences. Here is where style taxonomy will play a role in social planning.

THE EXPLANATORY FORCE OF STYLE

Comparative analysis of styles brings a new taxonomic device to the social scientist. Prior to the development of the cantometric coding book, no system existed for the transcultural classification of musical performances. With the aid of the system, two raters in two years analyzed over 3,000 songs representing the whole range of mankind's musical output. Computer manipulations of these ratings have produced a world map of folk song style that not only supports and enriches the conclusions of the cultural historians and musicologists, but also provides a unified way of looking at the story of mankind's musical growth. Indeed, this classification of singing behavior maps the great cultural traditions of mankind as efficiently, and perhaps as easily, as the data of linguistics, cultural anthropology, and archeology.

Late in the study, dance became the focus of a parallel investigation so that the validity of the stylistic approach could be tested in another realm of expressive behavior. An observational technique similar to that of cantometrics, but dealing with some qualitative aspects of movement, was systematically applied to the analysis of dance films from all the main regions of culture. The first stages of the work offer support to a theory of the Laban school (Laban, 1960) that dance epitomizes the movement of everyday life. Furthermore, styles of dance and, more broadly, movement seem to be distributed across the world map in large regions strikingly congruent with those of song style. It seems quite likely, therefore, that these two expressive patterns go hand in hand in culture and perhaps both may be manifestations of a stylistic spine that unites all the communication of a people. Moreover, we see that description of style brings order to the visual and kinesthetic patterns stored on film, as well as to the acoustic patterns stored on sound recordings.

In the study of style one is not concerned with the particulars or the specific contents of cultural events, but asks instead how people sing, how they dance, how they relate to each other. The rating systems record the relative speed, duration, energy, cohesiveness, sonority, sinuousness, complexity, number of body parts, etc., as outstanding and overall characteristics of a given stretch of behavior in a particular culture or culture area. The matching cultural profiles, in which the data of ethnography have been molded into rough measures of social interaction, deal with relative range of the productive system, level of stratification, severity of sexual sanctions, relative stability of community type, complexity of governmental structure, degree of female contribution to subsistence, and other features of community life which can be handled in scalar form. Put together these scales form the behavioral profiles which are like predictive propositions of the following kind: From the evidence of the tapes listened to or films observed or social relationships described, it is predicted that the members of a society will frequently conform in their song, dance, or everyday behavior to the most prominent pattern displayed on this rating line or profile of rating lines. In other words, the profiles produced by style analysis summarize habitual patterns, and we may compare cultures or musical styles with each other in terms of their relative positions on these qualitative grids. From these profile comparisons, the distributions of song and dance and culture are mapped. Furthermore, since the song profiles have been found to vary in regular and meaningful ways along the culture profiles, it is possible to elicit the social content of song performance and to begin, in some degree, to predict a song style from a culture style, or vice versa.

One validation of the stylistic method, then, is its efficiency in classifying and epitomizing culture regions. Moreover, the consensus tests reported on in a later chapter indicate that the qualitative judgment scales employed in characterizing song may attain a high inter-rater reliability. For me, however, the validity of the approach is demonstrated by the consistency of results of the multiple experiments described in this volume. Although the samples have not yet been brought into complete agreement, four different analytic techniques have been applied to four different kinds of expressive behavior across the same range of culture.

1. Cantometrics—to overall song performance style.
2. Choreometrics—to overall dance and movement style.
3. Phonotactics—to overall phonemic patterning in sung verse.
4. Concept analysis—to overall conceptual patterns of sung verse.

The classifications produced by the four systems overlap in remarkable ways. Dance and song style, analyzed at this level, seem to fall into the same general regions: Amerindia, Maritime Pacific, Australia, Old High Culture, Africa, and Europe. Each of the systems ranks cultures in the same series on scales of communication complexity that conform to a tested scale of productive complexity. The congruence of these four stylistic systems points to the existence of behavioral models that shape all the communication modes in culture.

The diagnostic power of style analysis, however, lies in its simplicity and directness. First of all, it deals with frequent and easily identifiable qualities in behavior which can be expressed in numerical terms and on which inter-rater consensus can be tested. Song is regarded as an act involving a group of a certain size whose behavior is marked by certain clear-cut patterns of redundancy. A political meeting can be described in much the same terms. In these descriptions one turns away from specific content and particulars to noting frequencies, especially those frequencies of such a high order that they are perceived as qualities which characterize the behavior of a person or culture. In this way all descriptions of human activity become comparable. Observations derived from one platform of stylistic observation, such as dance style, can be used to draw forth significance at another platform of observation, namely song or culture style.

Style is a potent culture classifier because it goes to the level where people actually experience and shape culture patterns. Culture is perceived and reacted to in terms of its tensions, its tempos, its "masculinity or femininity," its hungers, its "feel." The "feel" of things must be right in order for an interchange or an activity to proceed satisfactorily. The most important thing for a person to know is just how appropriate a bit of behavior or communication is and how to respond to it appropriately. The rules of suitable interaction in books of etiquette and social anthropology are only crude approximations of the patterns or models of repeated, learned behavior to which they refer (Sheflen, 1965). Human beings are constantly evaluating and recalibrating their experiences in terms of such learned models. A style is a summary of a range of such models. It is the critical focal point for the multiple calibrations that identify the member of a culture to himself and to his companions, and that pick out the familiar paths along which successful activity can proceed.

Style is thus the constant concern of everyone and provides highly sensitive, though approximate, scales of awareness on which all human behavior is constantly being assessed. Any culture member can immediately sense that something is stylistically wrong about a greeting, a cooking pot, a song, or a dance, without being able to explain why this is so. Everyone in a culture responds with satisfaction or ecstasy to the apropos and with scorn and resentment to the unseemly. We all have a very nice sense about what new or exotic patterns are suitable to us culturally, although some trained specialists —the artists and critics—have more skill at this than ordinary folk.

All these decisions are qualitative, immediate, and comparative; all are complex evaluations of the fit of stylistic patterns. In sum, then, the stylistic approach takes systematic advantage of the ways in which all human beings, everywhere, perceive and structure their experience and pattern their behavior. It is because these stylistic, epitomizing features of culture are the stuff of the expressive arts that song- and dance-style analysis proves to be such an effective way of classifying cultures.

2

The Cantometrics Experiment

Alan Lomax

OUR study began with the perception that there are powerful stylistic models shaping the majority of song performances in large regions of the world. Once a listener has heard Negro African, Indian, Oriental, Australian, or Polynesian songs he will seldom fail to recognize the style on a second encounter. Scholars know that melodies and song themes wander freely within several enormous regions, past language and culture barriers, without losing their essential form. However, when the Pygmies hoot "My Darling Clementine," when the Cherokee Indians chant "Rock of Ages," when the Kentucky mountaineer moans the Negro blues, or when Beethoven sets Scots bagpipe tunes for the symphony orchestra—when, that is, a tune moves from one style region to another, it is often distorted out of recognition by the new performance framework. Within these regions, despite many fascinating areal and cultural differences, song styles remain fundamentally similar and are so perceived by the people of the region.

The goal of our research was, first, to devise a descriptive technique that would locate these grand song-style patterns in the recorded data itself and, second, to find what cultural regularities underlie and are relevant to these far-ranging and powerfully formative styles. No summative characterizations of pan-Africa, pan-Amerindia, pan-Europe, or pan-Australia existed in the literature of musicology or ethnology. Such was the substantive problem.

From the outset song was seen to be the most highly ordered and periodic of vocalizations. In fact, song may be recognized and defined as more frequently redundant at more levels than any other kind of vocalizing. Most of the regularities of speech are carried over in song and are usually employed in some more formalized way in sung verse than in speech. Not only are the sounds, words, syntax, and forms of a language all touched by the peculiar regularities of poetry, but the redundancy introduced in song at the nonverbal level gives rise to meter, melody, harmony, and the singing voice. A review of some aspects of singing provides a notion of the effect of redundancy on the sung communication:

13

1. The degree of concert within the musical group is maintained at a constant and generally higher level than in any other type of phonation.
2. The social organization of the musical group is generally fixed in terms of numbers of members, spatial arrangement, orders of dominance, length of utterance, etc.
3. The behavior of the audience is usually governed by formal rules.
4. The text is generally marked by one or several forms of repetition.
5. The patterns of stress are handled in such a regular fashion that they can be abstracted and repeated separately as rhythm.
6. The length of the melodic segment and its subsegments are adhered to strictly throughout a song and frequently are standard for a culture.
7. Intonation patterns are so redundant that they can be abstracted and treated separately as melodies.
8. Pitch is precisely calibrated and a series of more or less exact intervals are established that may be abstracted as scales.
9. If ornamental devices occur, they conform to a small number of patterns.
10. Tempo is maintained steadily or controlled throughout a performance.
11. Volume is set at a notably loud or soft level, or contrastive levels are employed.
12. Some marked vocal stance is maintained throughout the performance, limiting itself to a range, a register, and to vocal qualifiers that define a "singing voice" preferred by the culture and different from the speaking voice.

The convergence of so much formalization and redundancy in the sung communication makes it a potent means of organizing and coordinating group behavior. The idiosyncratic is eliminated and a precisely controlled stretch of phonation is reiterated so that others may join in, either as active participants or as audience, assured of either performing or hearing the same message. As a matter of fact, song, among primitive people, is usually a joint communication, often combined with dance, that links the whole community in concerted action. Before a joint rendition of a song can take place there must be tacit agreement among the performers to abide by the musical formulas of their culture and of the particular song. Thus the performance will not be well done if the chorus comes in at the wrong moment, if the wrong voice qualities are used, or if there are departures from the melody and rhythm—in short, if many stylistic niceties are not abided by.

Even when a song is solo, it must meet the expectations of its audience to elicit a positive response. Always this response is a result of a particular cultural context. Not even the musical soliloquy departs from the standardized patterns of the public song style, for it may be immediately understood by any culture member who inadvertently overhears it. In fact, the sung soliloquy is only one of many techniques that the lonely and isolated individual employs to bring other human beings, at least symbolically, into his company.

This multileveled redundancy makes song acoustically louder or more penetrating than speech. Primitive song performances frequently consist of the whole of the society (or a large sector of it) vocalizing in unison in one giant harsh voice. This aesthetic formula still holds true, for example, in the Protestant church, where all the members of the congregation call out to God together across the infinite. Even where the performing group is small, its match of vocal stance, melody, and meter creates a sound that cuts through the normal hubbub of everyday and carries its message to the ears of all present. Very quiet music, because of precisely calibrated and repeated patterns, can be heard in a noisy room.

Music becomes socially louder than speech, in part because of its acoustic redundancies. Not only does this pattern of regularities provide a platform upon which a group can impressively display its unity of purpose to an audience, but, by regimenting levels of everyday interaction, it tends to knit its auditors together in a unified reaction that will inspire them jointly in work, battle, dance, worship, burial, initiation rites, and the like. Indeed, the prime function of song and music appears to be group-organizing. As a relatively rare communication, song turns up most frequently at the ritual points of human experience when groups of people must agree on a minimal program of feeling and action. In the rites of the life-cycle—at christenings, marriages, and wakes, the community-building, the culture-perpetuating needs of a society are dramatized. Behavioral norms crucial to a culture are then set forth and reinforced in such terms that the whole community can accept them and join in their restatement. Singing and dancing share a major part of the symbolic activity in these communal gatherings, and come to represent those roles, those modes of communication and of interaction which the whole community agrees are proper and important to its continuity. Song and dance style then symbolize and summarize attitudes and ways of handling situations upon which there is the highest level of community consensus. This is why we have found that the main posture used in dance is the body attitude that runs through a majority of everyday activities; this is why we have found high correlations between norms of song performance and patterns of social interaction.

Since singing seems to be a community-directed, group-oriented communication, musical situations can be differentiated in terms of the level of participation of those present. A group can relate to a song performance either by listening in relative silence or by participating at some level of coordination. This dichotomy came to underlie the cantometric research approach, which looks at song in terms of two contrastive models:

A. *The highly individualized and group-dominating performance,* in which a solo singer commands the communication space by presenting a pattern that is too complex for participation (in text, melody, rhythm, ornament, vocal technique, or in all five of these ways) ; often he is accompanied by a supporting orchestra which further enforces silence.

B. *The highly cohesive, group-involving performance,* in which all those present can join in easily because of the relative simplicity and repetitiousness of the patterns—for example, a nonsense refrain, set to an unornamented one-phrase melody in a simple and regular meter.

In their extreme form this pair of performance models looks like this:

Model A *Individualized*	Model B *Integrated, groupy*
Solo	Choral, multileveled, cohesive
Textually complex	Repetitious text
Metrically complex	Metrically simple
Melodically complex	Melodically simple
Ornamented	No ornamentation
Usually noisy voice	Usually clear voice
Precise enunciation	Slurred enunciation

The manipulation of this pair of simple models brought considerable order into the world of song. Model A is the style of exclusive solo dominance and is found all along the highroads of civilization from the Far East all the way west into Europe, or wherever political authority is highly centralized. Model B is the integrated style and has its center among the acephalous and tightly integrated bands of African Pygmies and Bushmen, but turns up in one form or another among very simple people in many parts of the world. Actually, all the singing styles of mankind can be described in terms of their positions on the grid defined by these maximal cases of individuation and integration. Shifts in a few parameters give rise to subordinate models that include most of the style types encountered early in the research. For example, two variant forms of Model A differentiate the two main regions of complex civilization, (A1) Western Europe and North America (Fig. 1) and (A2) the Orient (Fig. 2) :

The most integrated form of Model B seems to be the primordial style of Africa, for it is the form almost universally adopted by the aborigines of Africa, the Pygmies and the Bushmen. Solo song is a rarity among these tightly integrated hunting bands, as it tends to be among Africans generally. In fact, so accustomed are the little hunter-gatherers to group performance

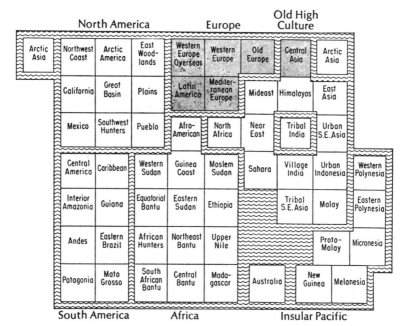

Fig. 1. World distribution of European strophic singing.

Model Al
Western Europe and
Colonial North America

Solo
Textually complex
Precise enunciation
Metrically simple
Melodically fairly complex—strophe
Somewhat embellished
Voice somewhat noisy

of music that not only do they perform habitually in polyphony and poly-rhythm and in magnificent concert, but it is usual for each phrase of the melody to be the joint responsibility of at least two voices. They also sing in yodel tone, the vocal position which laryngologists see as being the most wide open and relaxed in all dimensions, and cantometrics finds that African hunters perform at the peak of rhythmic and choral cohesiveness.

Model B1 (below) is most frequent among the Bushmen and Pygmies, but is common also among the Bantu speakers who have, since historic times, occupied the territory over which the little African hunters once ranged.

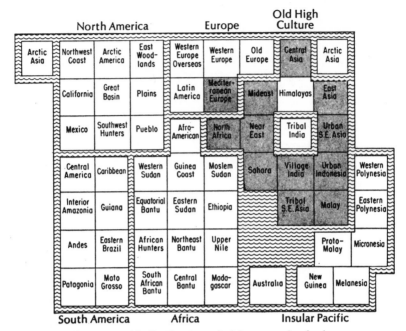

Fig. 2. World distribution of elaborate solo singing.

Model A2
The Orient

Solo
Textually complex
Precise enunciation
Metrically complex—Rpa
Melodically complex—tc
Highly embellished
Voice usually noisy
Narrow intervals

Even today Congo Pygmies are regarded by their Negro neighbors as master entertainers who can outperform them on their own drums and in their own dances. The replacement of the African hunter bands by Bantu gardeners and herders was recent and gradual. Moreover, close symbiotic contact was maintained between the two groups during this process. There was ample opportunity therefore for the Negro to receive a strong hunter imprint as the Bantus spread across the African continent. In any event one can hear songs that bear strong Pygmy-Bushman traces among many African groups.

Model B1
African Hunter

Choral
Highly cohesive and multileveled
Very repetitious
Slurred enunciation
Melodically simple—litany
Metrically simple, although multileveled
No embellishments
Clear-voiced—yodel tone

Besides Africa, two other large culture regions, Oceania and Central Europe, employ a form of the groupy Model B. In both, choruses perform in a cohesive and frequently multileveled fashion; in both, voices are relatively wide and free of noise. Yet melody, rhythmic pattern, and text may be complex in both, and enunciation is usually precise. The choruses in these areas achieve a high level of unity in spite of the noise level introduced by a heavy loading of text and precisely enunciated consonants; they are similar in being highly integrated and yet heavy with information.

Model B2
Oceania and Old Europe

Choral
Cohesive and multileveled
Wordy
Precise enunciation
Melodically simple or complex
Metrically simple or complex
Occasional use of embellishment
Clear-voiced

The model that accounts for much of the choral singing in the primitive world, especially in North America and round the arc of the Pacific Ocean, is non-cohesively performed in spite of a lack of specificity. The North American song performance style is often marked by considerable melodic and metrical complexity, as well as a heavy load of vocal noise.

Model B3
Amerindia

Choral
Individualized—one level
Repetitious
Slurred

Melodically complex
Metrically complex
No embellishment
Noisy

Operations with crude models of this type led directly to the construction of the cantometric coding system by Grauer and myself in the summer of 1963. A small but representative library of recorded song from every continent formed the test sample. We worked with a high-fidelity playback system, feeding two matched speakers, one for each rater. Each rating concept was tested on the entire sample as to whether it gave rise to steady and clear-cut consensus between the two judges across the whole range of world song styles and whether it produced a meaningful regional ordering of the whole sample.

Into this rating scheme we introduced such of the taxonomic concepts of musicology as we could apply in a purely auditory and comparative rating system. A number of ideas came from Nettl's (1956) survey of ethnomusicology, and scoring lines for vocal qualities were worked out with the help of Markel, the psycholinguist. The rating system encompasses those ranges we found represented in the recorded sample. We tried to give the same importance to all aspects of the musical events. Eight main levels are represented about equally on the coding sheet:

1. The social organization of the vocal group
2. The social organization of the orchestra
3. The level of cohesiveness of both vocal group and orchestra
4. The level of explicitness—text and consonant load
5. The rhythmic organization of vocal group and orchestra
6. The order of melodic complexity
7. The degree and kind of embellishments used
8. The vocal stance

Such an empirical rating system, although it does not touch upon every possibility in every type of musical performance, has certain practical advantages, because it takes regular note of a wide range of behavior. Even if several aspects of a performance are in free variation (when a culture exploits many points on a rating line with about equal frequency), there is usually a cultural focus on a set of other lines sufficient to produce a distinctive and stable performance profile. We found that the affinities between these stable profiles located telltale traces of cross-cultural similarity. In other words, the profiling system early taught us that the defining and diagnostic traits of song style were to be found where the communication system was most redundant.

The dichotomy between groupy and individual styles continued to be the basic structural element in the rating system. It governed the arrangement of the lines on the coding sheet so that "solo-exclusive" profiles (Model A1 and A2) would run on the left, somewhat individuated profiles along the center (Model B3), and cohesive profiles along the right of the coding sheet (Models B1 and B2).

In the majority of styles simplicity of structure, absence of ornament, low specificity, and damping-out of noise are associated with maximum cohesiveness and integration in the singing group. The opposite proposition is also generally true: that complexity of structure, pile-up of ornament, high specificity, and, usually, increase of noise are associated with extreme individuation in performance. Thus not all lines score an increase of trait from left to right. Rpa (parlando rubato), embellishment, glissando, melisma, tremolo, glottal shake, melodic form, phrase length, and number of phrases are all features which add to the complexity of the song and are scored high on the right. Tempo, volume, rhythm, and register seem to be independent of the individuated-cohesive dichotomy and thus the decision as to their direction was somewhat arbitrary (Table 1).

This is the outline of the rating system, described in detail in the coding book in the next chapter. It was applied at various times over a period of three years to three progressively larger samples of songs. In the first summer's work, Grauer and I rated about 700 songs from a small collection. Figures 3 and 4 reproduce two profiles from that period. Our working rule at that time was to stop coding in a culture when we ceased to find notable differences between the songs. In some cases, of course, we had only one or two songs from a culture. At the end of the period, we sorted the profiles by eye and drew master modal profiles for the main regional types as they emerged from this purely visual kind of statistics (Figs. 3–6). Although the sample has quadrupled in size and has twice been reorganized in its cultural spread since that first summer, the main characteristics of the regional types discovered then have not been drastically affected.

When the work was renewed about a year later, Grauer corrected the first coding run and increased the total sample to twice its size, adding a great many new cultures and culture areas to the list. This sample, when computerized and arranged within the confines of the Murdock culture area system, gave us our first statistically validated song regions. The results at this stage were so promising that it was decided to match the Murdock ethnographic cultural codings with a rated musical sample of at least ten songs per culture for more than 200 cultures, evenly distributed across the world culture map. This resulted in the discard of about half of the songs already coded. Another year was required to bring together a representative collection from many sources and to rate about 1,700 additional songs so that the final sample consisted of ten songs from each of 233 cultures. In a few cases

Table 1. *Summary presentation of the coding sheet showing its general structure.*
L = leader; C = chorus.

Individualized and little integrated	←			→	Groupy and integrated
1. Leader Chorus	Solo	L with C (little differentiation)	L with C (alternation of parts)	L with C (overlapping of parts)	Parts independent (leadership submerged in choral activity)
2. Relation of orchestra to vocal part	Solo	Simple accompanying relation		Heterophony	Orchestra has independent role
3. Relation within orchestra	Solo	Unison		Heterophony	Part independence
4. Choral musical organization	Solo	Unison		Heterophony	Polyphony
5. Choral tonal integration	Solo	Poor	to		Very good
6. Choral rhythmic organization	Solo	Poor	to		Very good
7. Orchestral musical organization	Solo	Unison		Heterophony	Polyphony, polyrhythm
8. Orchestral tonal concert	Solo	Poor	to		Good
9. Orchestral rhythmic concert	Solo	Poor	to		Good
10. Text part	Wordy		to		Very repetitious, nonsense
11. Vocal rhythm	Simple and regular meter		to		Irregular and free meter
12. Vocal rhythmic organization	Unison		to		Many independent parts
13. Orchestral rhythm	Simple and regular meter		to		Irregular and free meter
14. Orchestral rhythmic organization	Unison		to		Many independent parts
15. Melodic shape	Arched	Terraced	Undulating		Descending
16. Melodic form	Complex organization		to		Simple organization
17. Phrase length	Very long		to		Very short
18. Number of phrases	More than eight		to		One or two
19. Position of final	Bottom note in scale		to		Top note
20. Range of melody	Monotone		to		Two octaves and more
21. Average interval size	Monotone		to		A fifth or more
22. Type of vocal polyphony	Drone		to		Counterpoint

23. Embellishment......Much.........................to..............Little or none
24. Tempo...........Very slow.....................to..............Very fast
25. Volume...........Very soft......................to..............Very loud
26. Vocal rhythm.......Completely free...............to..............Strict tempo
27. Orchestral.........Completely free...............to..............Strict tempo
    rhythm
28. Glissando (gliding...Constant voice.................to..............Clearly separate
    between tones)   gliding   tones
29. Melisma...........One syllable to.................to..............One note per
    (note load)   many notes, frequent   syllable
30. Tremolo...........Much tremolo,.................to..............Little or no vocal
    (quavering   frequent   quavering
    attack)
31. Glottal effect.......Heavy and.....................to..............No glottal
    (guttural at-   constant (glottal
    tacks and with   ornamentation)
    embellishments)
32. Vocal register.......Very high falsetto..............to..............Very low deep-
    (voice placement)   chest register
33. Vocal width and....Very narrow, squeezed,........to..............Very wide, open,
    tension   and hard   and mellow
34. Nasalization........Constant and heavy...........to..............Free of nasaliza-
                      nasal sound   tion
35. Raspy.............Very harsh, noisy,.............to..............Clear and limpid
                      chesty sound   tone
36. Accent.............Many notes heavily............to..............Very relaxed attack
                      stressed (very forceful   (no notes strongly
                      attack frequent)   stressed)
37. Consonants.........Precise enunciation............to..............Most consonants
                      of consonants   slurred over and
                                                                      hard to hear

samples of less than ten songs were included when these cultures were needed to round out some poorly represented area or culture type.

If the reader consults the Cantometric-Cultural Sample at the conclusion of this chapter, he will get a first impression of the range of our recorded sample. Its limits pretty well represent the present situation of musical ethnography. Only in the past 30 or 40 years has it been possible to record music in the field with high fidelity, and only in the past decade have small portable recorders made this task a reasonable one. Recording has been done for all sorts of motives and by people of diverse interests. Sometimes the "best" recordings have been the work of inspired amateurs who were caught by their interest in the folk and did not know enough to interfere with what the people of a culture wanted to perform. In many other cases musical scholars or ethnographers of repute set up the microphones and recorded the songs. Thus in one way or another the music of great sectors of the human race has been put into acoustical storage. Although much of this material is poorly cataloged, badly labeled, and certainly difficult of access, it is invaluable as scientific data because:

24

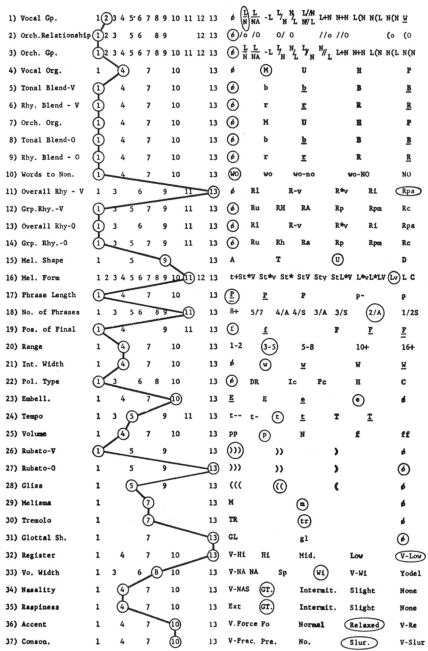

Fig. 3. Cantometric ratings and profile for a Pitjantjara (Australian) shaman song. Group: Pitjantjara; Language: Australoid; Location: Central Australia; Source: Vogue Contrepoint EXT. 1.056 B-2.

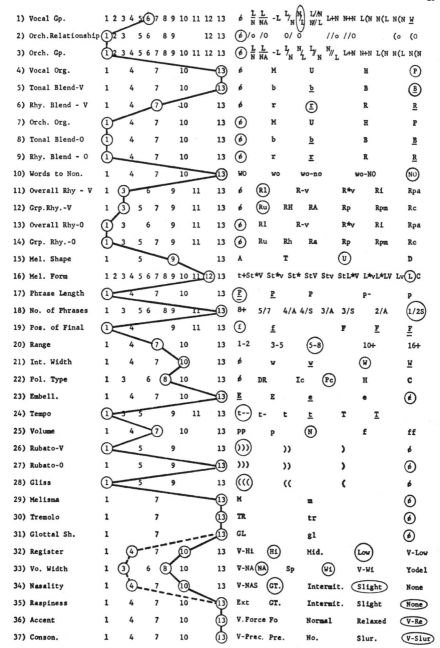

Fig. 4. Cantometric ratings and profile for a Vunun (Formosan) choral song. Group: Vunun; Language: Malayo-Polynesian; Location: Formosa; Source: Columbia KL 214-B 24.

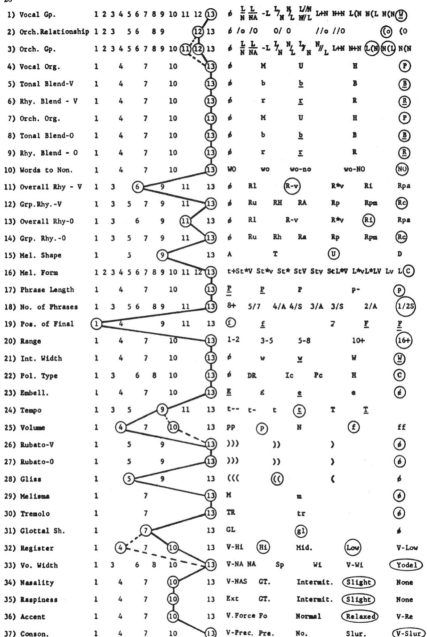

Fig. 5. Modal profile of African Hunter (Pygmy and Bushman) singing. The profile is drawn on the most frequent coding points.

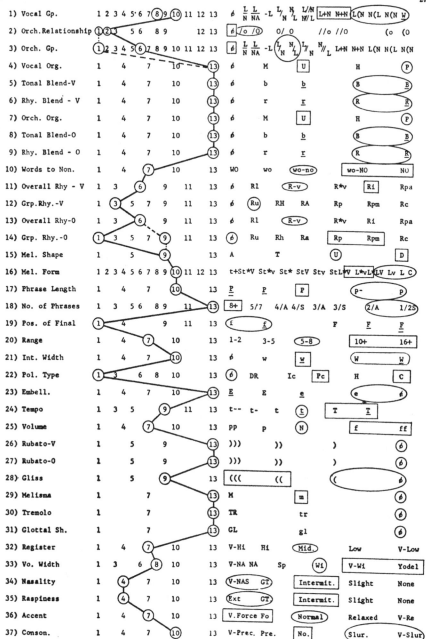

Fig. 6. Modal profile for Bantu African (south of the Sahara, including Afro-America) song style. The profile is drawn on the most frequent coding points. Rounded forms indicate primary modes, rectangular forms indicate secondary modes.

1. It may be repeated again and again by simply putting back the needle or rewinding the tape.

2. It is a full and unprejudiced report of what was in range of the microphone.

3. It is significant social behavior because, in most cases, a song is an often repeated stretch of communication passed on through the life of a people. As has been suggested before, song is a multileveled communication at each level of which there lies stored information for the student of culture and communication.

4. It is likely to be highly reliable data, providing the cultural source of the recording is defined. Not everyone in a culture is a virtuoso performer, but if a culture member sings at all, he has to sing in the style of his people because it is the only style he knows. It is in fact almost impossible for anyone really to change his singing style. It takes years for a non-European to learn opera; it has required half a century for Europeans to learn to perform American jazz. In the overall view of cantometrics, therefore, there is likely to be real ethnographic worth in any document rendered by a proper complement of performers who are genuine members of the culture named on the label.

The particular recordings that fall into one's hands may not come from the most secret ritual sources and may not be performed with all the fervor of which the culture is capable. Nevertheless, it is unlikely that, in an overall sense, they can be stylistically wrong. Song is so redundant and is so much a learned cultural artifact that, like other art, it is hard to fake successfully.

With considerations like these in mind, we could accept all field recordings that came to us from reputable sources as worthwhile and comparable data. Most of the samples were recorded by scientists who knew their people and could authenticate not only the style but the internal balance of the sample itself. Other batches of songs came from experienced amateurs or travelers. Only in the case of the Siberian collection, where we needed to fill an absolutely empty part of the map, did we accept recordings not made in the community itself. In that case the singers were natives studying in the Institute for Minority Groups in Leningrad and their recordings were made under the supervision of specialists in Siberian ethnology.

Experienced field folklorists despair of making exhaustive collections because human beings are too inventive. I have never managed to exhaust the repertory of a small area or even of one talented singer. Quite another intention animates this study. Because it was obviously impossible to represent the total song population of any one area, not to speak of the whole world, we took another approach. We felt sure that most collectors had recorded at least some of the everyday performance styles of the societies they visited.

Our study was designed, therefore, as a cross-cultural comparison of the public song performance style, because this is what we believe the important available data mainly consists of. Certainly we do not have much of the "shy" or the secret material. Yet this does not seriously affect the validity of our conclusions. I have never found that "secret" songs were stylistically different from music that was more generally performed. Furthermore, the coding system was designed to portray the gross stylistic patterns.

For reasons of this kind, as well as for purely practical considerations, we arbitrarily limited the number of songs per culture sample to ten. Where we could, we asked the collectors to give a balance of types. Where such response was not forthcoming, we split the sample space between the several kinds of performances in each batch. Only in the case of rather complex cultures, involving several subcultures, do we feel we missed representing the song styles of everyday. Here again, the design of the coding system was crucial. In most simple societies, a run of song profiles tends to converge on one or two models, and the coder is likely to become bored after analyzing the first half-dozen items. Even in cultures that are apparently more complex, profile similarity is usually very high.

We certainly wish that our sample were better. We know that we could have spent a century in improving it. Despite its limitations, however, we feel that it contains many of the important patterns of traditional singing style. The main cantometric profiles have not changed for several years. Only from little-recorded areas such as South America, Tribal Southeast Asia, Tribal India, and East Africa do new patterns continue to turn up. We would be most grateful to any of our readers who would send us new information for study in the Cantometrics Laboratory.

THE CANTOMETRIC–CULTURAL SAMPLE

Both cantometric ratings and cultural data (in the format of the *Ethnographic Atlas*) were assembled for the following 233 cultures. The names are those used by Murdock or, in the case of our additions, were made up to tag the community or the area from which the data came. The geographic layout represents a revision of the scheme employed by Murdock in the *Atlas*. Arctic Asia, Australia, and Tribal India have been separated, since their ties with the other six regions are unclear. Even though most cultures in circum-Mediterranean had some traits in common, we dropped this area because: (1) of the distinctive homogeneity of European song style and (2) of the powerful stylistic line that links the song performance styles of the Near East, the Middle East, and India with those of the Far East and South Asia. This vast world of ancient civilizations we have called Old High

Culture. It embraces the Malaysian sector of Murdock's Oceania, as well as the cultures of North Africa and the Sahara. The cultures lying north of the Pyrenees, to the north and east of the Apennines, in the Alpine center, and in Eastern Europe are grouped together for stylistic reasons into an area labeled Old Europe. The song sets from Colonial North America are clumped under Western Europe Overseas, while samples from former Spanish- and Portuguese-speaking colonies round the Caribbean and South America are included in Latin America. These overseas areas form part of the European region. Correlations were run on the 233 samples and tested on a Select Sample (S) and a Test Sample (T), both of which are explained in Appendix 2.

I. *SOUTH AMERICA*
  Patagonia
    1. Yahgan (T) [1]
    2. Ona (S)
  Andes
    3. Aymara (T)
    4. Quechua (Q'eros) (S)
  Interior Amazonia
    5. Amahuaca
    6. Bora-Witoto (T)
    7. Conibo (S)
    8. Jivaro (S,T)
    9. Campa (S,T)
  Mato Grosso
    10. Camayura (S)
    11. Trumai (T)
  Eastern Brazil
    12. Northern Cayapo (S)
    13. Caraja
    14. Kraho-Canela (S,T)
  Guiana
    15. Guarauno (S,T)
    16. Guahibo (S,T)
    17. Yaruro (S)
    18. Yekuana
  Caribbean
    19. Goajiro (S,T)
    20. Motilon (S,T)

Central America
    21. Tzotzil (S)
    22. Lacandon (S)
    23. Cuna (S,T)

II. *NORTH AMERICA*
  Mexico
    24. Seri (S)
    25. Tarahumara (T)
    26. Yaqui
    27. Huichol
    28. Pima (T)
    29. Papago (S)
    30. Totonac (S)
  Southwest Hunters
    31. W. Apache
    32. Mohave (S,T)
    33. Navaho (S,T)
  Pueblo
    34. Hopi
    35. Laguna (S)
    36. Taos (S,T)
    37. Zuni
  Eastern Woodlands
    38. Creek (S)
    39. Yuchi (S,T)
    40. Iroquois (T)
    41. Wabanaki (S)

[1] Two subsamples for purposes of statistical evaluation have been constructed within the main sample. The manner in which they have been drawn is explained in Appendix 2.

Plains
  42. Teton Dakota (S,T)
  43. Blood-Blackfoot (T)
  44. Cree (S)
  45. Kiowa (S)
Great Basin
  46. Flathead (S,T)
  47. Kutenai
  48. Washo (S)
  49. N. Paiute (S,T)
California
  50. Hupa (T)
  51. Pomo (S)
Northwest Coast
  52. Nootka
  53. Haida (S,T)
  54. Salish (S,T)
Arctic America
  55. Carrier (S)
  56. Slave (T)
  57. Alaska Eskimo (S)
  58. Caribou Eskimo (T)
  59. Atna

III. *OCEANIA*
Proto-Malay
  60. Paiwan
  61. Vunun-Tsos (S)
  62. Sajek-Tayal
  63. Murut (S)
New Guinea
  64. Fore
  65. Kakoli (T)
  66. Middle Waghi (S)
  67. Dani (S)
  68. Maring
  69. Abelam (S)
  70. Motu (S,T)
  71. Murray-Torres
Micronesia
  72. Palau (S,T)
  73. Ulithi

  74. Gilberts (S,T)
  75. Yap
Melanesia
  76. Choiseul (S,T)
  77. W. Nakanai (S)
  78. Manus (S,T)
  79. Usiai
  80. Kualong
Eastern Polynesia
  81. Cook Island (S)
  82. Mangareva (S,T)
  83. Maori (S,T)
  84. Hawaii
Western Polynesia
  85. Samoa (S)
  86. Fiji
  87. Tikopia (S)

IV. *OLD HIGH CULTURE*
Central Asia
  88. Kalmyk (T)
  89. Turkmen (S,T)
  90. Buryat (S)
  91. Kazak-Kirghiz
East Asia
  92. Amami
  93. Japan (S,T)
  94. Korea (S,T)
  95. Hakka (S,T)
Himalayas
  96. Tibet (S,T)
  97. Sherpa
Tribal Southeast Asia
  98. Pwo Karen (S,T)
  99. Mnong Gar (S)
  100. Lua
  101. Temiar Semang
Urban Southeast Asia
  102. Burma (S,T)
  103. Laos (S)
  104. Thai
  105. Vietnam (S,T)

170. Fon
171. Toma (S)
172. Susu-Mende
173. Yoruba (S,T)
Afro-American
174. Toco
175. Carriacou (S)
176. Haiti
177. Jamaica
178. Salvador (S)
179. United States Negro (S)
180. Colombia-Ecuador Negro
Moslem Sudan
181. Hausa (S,T)
182. Wolof
183. Fulani
Ethiopia
184. Amhara (S,T)
185. Afar (T)
186. Galla

VI. *EUROPE*
Old Europe
187. Basques (S)
188. Nuoro
189. Friuli (S)
190. Dragas
191. Strpci
192. Central Russia (T)
193. Georgia (S,T)
194. Osset (S)
195. Moravia
196. Cheremis (S,T)
197. Slovak (S)
Western Europe
198. Western France (S)
199. Lowland Scots
200. Hebrides (S)
201. Norway (S,T)
202. Dutch (T)
203. Irish (T)

Western Europe Overseas
204. Americans
205. French Canada
206. Anglo-Canada
207. Kentucky
208. Hillbilly (S)
Mediterranean Europe
209. Tras-os-Montes
210. Naples
211. Sicily (S,T)
212. Andalucia (S)
213. Castile
214. Kitos (S,T)
Latin America
215. New Mexico (S,T)
216. Tarascan
217. Puerto Rico
218. Quechua-Mestizo (Central Peru) (S)
219. Argentina
220. Chile
221. Maya (Yucatan) (T)

VII. *TRIBAL INDIA*
222. Abor
223. Gond (S,T)

VIII. *ARCTIC ASIA*
224. Yukaghir (S,T)
225. Ainu (S,T)
226. Tungus (T)
227. Samoyede
228. Chuckchee
229. Yakut (S,T)
230. Ostiak
231. Lapp (S)

IX. *AUSTRALIA*
232. N. Australia (S,T)
233. W. Australia (S)

3

The Cantometric Coding Book

Alan Lomax and Victor Grauer

CANTOMETRICS, a coined word which means a measure of song or song as a measure, is a method for systematically and holistically describing the general features of accompanied or unaccompanied song performances. With the cantometric system the listener can evaluate a song performance in ways that supplement the conventional measures of melody, rhythm, and harmony. The several systems of musical notation found in Western Europe, India, the Near East, and elsewhere make it possible to record various details of melodic and metrical movement and to reproduce them with accuracy. There are, however, many other expressive and social phenomena which shape all musical productions. For example, if the same tune is sung by culture A in a wide-voiced, well-blended unison and by culture B in narrow, harshly blended overlap, two different songs are likely to be perceived because of a shift in three performance controls. Such features of the musical event may be characterized as paramusical in relation to the melody, just as emphasis, speed, and vocal rasp are paralinguistic, and play an important qualifying role in the spoken event. Indeed, it was contact with the teaching and the writings of George and Edith Trager, Haxey Smith, and Ray Birdwhistell, all of whom had made important contributions to the study of the paralinguistic or non-verbal aspects of discourse, that stimulated the senior editor of this book to develop the present system.

The cantometric approach, however, is considerably more generalized than the method taught by Trager and Birdwhistell. It does not look at the sung event word by word, frame by frame, note by note, or unit by unit. It takes advantage of the highly redundant and formalized character of the sung performance in which a vocal stance, a group relationship, an approach to musical elaboration, or a kind of rhythm is maintained prominently and steadily throughout the event. It picks out the set of overall qualities which strongly characterize a performance and in terms of which it may be compared to another song. Our discovery was that each culture has a few favored ways of handling major paramusical controls and that these could be compared level for level with the same set of phenomena in the singing posture of other human communities.

The cantometric system operates with an intentionally coarse grid. It was not set up to describe musical ideolects or dialects or any one musical statement, but to point to differences in styles at the regional and areal levels. Its aim is not to mirror the flowing language of song and its shifting nuances, as a detailed notation or a recording does, nor to examine the internal tonal structure of a piece of music. It can, however, broadly characterize song performance style in such a way that the main families of sung performance may be recognized, their geographical distribution mapped, and their relationship to cultural continuity, acculturation, and the expressive arts perceived.

Two publications are planned to make this rating system available to others. A set of training tapes for each rating line is in the process of completion and will eventually be distributed to those who want to experiment with the present cantometric system. In addition, we have edited six long-playing records for Folkways Records which contain examples of a great variety of song styles and illustrate a great many cantometric coding sheets. When this recorded publication appears (Lomax and Grauer, 1968, in press), the student can learn the rating scheme as he listens to the record, check his own impressions against those recorded by the expert judges of the Cantometric Project, and so become adept in the cantometric rating scheme. However, if the student acquaints himself with the widest possible range of song styles now easily available in various recorded libraries, we believe he will fall into a listening pattern similar to our own. He will discover for himself the same or very closely similar ranges of acoustical experience which, when regarded comparatively, will roughly arrange themselves in the patterns that we have begun to describe in this first work.

We seem to be dealing here with some universals of communication which vary together and in an orderly way as the circumstances of human life and the necessities of human communication systems vary. A quality, like a phoneme, may have different meanings in different cultural contexts. It is nonetheless true that the relative frequency of a given quality across a range of cultures may have genuine significance, and there is no question that an outside observer can gauge such differences. Personal and social adjustment would both be impossible if human beings were not able quickly to shift their perceptive scales as they moved from one situation to another, for instance, from the desk where fine observation is essential to the swimming pool where cruder calibrations are more appropriate. In this sense, then, an ordinary but attentive listener can accurately evaluate, define, and locate a song on his scales of musical memory. The cantometric rating system attempts no more than to make this everyday experience considerably more systematic, especially in regard to cross-cultural comparisons. At first we were somewhat concerned because so many details of song had been left out of the rating scheme. With more experience we began to wish for an even simpler system.

The coding book that follows is a set of definitions and explanations that define the rating measurements used in the cantometric experiment. After some practice with it, a simple, unaccompanied song in a familiar style may be coded in a few minutes. Songs with multileveled rhythmic complexity or elusive melodic style may demand more time. Only a few of the parameters—those dealing with melody, rhythm, and harmony—require musical training. The nonprofessional coder can console himself with the thought that, even if he has to omit five or six of these coding parameters, his ratings will still be valid and useful for comparative purposes. Thus far we have been able to find no orderly relationships between melodic form, metrical structure, or harmonic style (code sheet Lines 11, 13, 15, 16, 17, 18, 19, 22) and aspects of social structure. Most of the correlations established in our research involve aspects of the musical event that listeners without specialized musical training can observe with accuracy.

The following general suggestions in using the coding sheet should be heeded. Since the system is designed to record readily identifiable acoustical phenomena, the coder must be willing to record his immediate but considered responses. He should not attempt to be analytical over and above the outlines of the coding book, nor should he attempt to read into a given performance what the performers really meant or really felt or perhaps failed to do. Prior expert knowledge of a song style may actually impede coding. Strong aesthetic bias makes good ratings impossible.

The cantometric system is usable only for the rating of accompanied or unaccompanied singing. Purely instrumental music is beyond the scope of this system. If we had attempted to code the contributions of the instruments in the orchestra to each performance, many pages would have been required for each item. Therefore, to set feasible limits on this study, we confined ourselves to song, the universal and primal mode of musical expression. The instruments present in the orchestras were, however, systematically noted in terms of the Sachs systems of classification (Sachs and Von Hornbostel, 1961), and a publication dealing with the distribution of orchestral types is in preparation.

"Song" is here defined as the use, by the human voice, of discrete pitches or regular rhythmic patterns or both. Vocal noises which do not employ discrete pitches and have no rhythmic regularity are not considered singing and are not rated by us. Thus, shouts, wails, and sobs should be ignored by the coder, unless they are performed in simple and musically understandable rhythmic patterns. If they do conform to such rhythmic patterns, they should be coded as part of the singing situation. The focus of this study is song, and the coder should ignore the activity of the instrumental accompaniment on all the lines save those which refer to it exclusively. Thus, when coding all but Lines 2, 3, 7–9, 13, 14, and 27, the coder should listen only to the singers and code as though no instruments were present (see Chapter 2 for coding sheet).

At the top of the coding sheet note the source of the performance being recorded, that is, whether on tape or on record. Following "Group or Song," set down the name of the song as known. The language and the dialect should be briefly indicated as "Language." Fill in "Location" with the name of the culture or the community where the song was recorded or heard. Use the space between the ruled lines for the geographical source of the recording, its setting, the function of the song, and other information that the coder judges to be pertinent. (Note: A second sheet provided the opportunity to record the composition of the chorus and orchestra in terms of the number, age, and sex of the performers; the age and sex of the leaders of the chorus and orchestra, if any; and the types and the numbers of the accompanying instruments.)

On the right side of the sheet there is a field of symbols, each of which is described in the coding book that follows. This symbolic field is quickly memorized and it is here that the rater can swiftly record his perceptions of the song he is listening to. In our experience it is best to begin by noting outstanding impressions. In other words, the easy coding should be done first, because as one's faculties penetrate the musical event in many directions, the more difficult judgments are formed almost unconsciously. When the ratings are complete, they should be transferred to the field of numbers on the left side of the sheet; this number field exactly matches the mnemonic coding field in all dimensions. When completed, these numerical ratings are ready to be punched and fed into the computer, or studied as profiles.

Perhaps the most crucial of the rating scales is Line 1 in which the rater notes the relation between song leaders and chorus he has perceived in the performance. Each point represents an ever more complexly integrated arrangement of the participating voices in the choir. The scale begins on the left with solo and ends on the right with a choral situation in which the parts are independent and tightly integrated. We represent every solo song with L (for leader or soloists) over N (for audience), because the presence of the social group is always assumed, even in the situation of the sung soliloquy. Singers do not perform outside the context of their musical-cultural pattern. Even when a man sings alone, he uses the musical language he has learned as a culture member. In describing choral performances we assume that there is some level of leadership even when we do not hear anyone beginning the song. Therefore performances of perfect social unison are represented as N over L.

The coding system described in the following pages is by no means complete. For instance, we discovered, after it was too late to make a change, that we needed a way of distinguishing between the rather vague antiphony of many primitive societies and the clearcut alternation so prominent in Western Europe. In the first case, the leader may sing an opening phrase or so alone and thereafter be submerged in the group sound, whereas in Western Europe the leader's part is not only singled out by a pause but by clearcut successive and regular alternation with the chorus throughout a performance. We cite this example in order to suggest that the student may add features to the system where he finds that they will be useful. He should be warned, however, against a lack of parsimony. Too many small distinctions may choke the classification system or change the level of classification.

The coding book follows.

Line 1. The vocal group.

The ratings on this line refer to the social structure of the singing group. They are arranged so that the degree of integration among the members of the group increases, roughly, as one proceeds from left to right along the line. Two symbols occur more frequently than any others: L—standing for a solo or leading part; N—for a group of two or more singers.

Most of the ratings in this line depend upon a clear recognition of the leader's part. Here the rater is advised to listen for the following cues, one or more of which may be observed: (a) often a leader's voice may be heard at the outset of a song and at the beginnings of sections; (b) the leader may sing more loudly, more frequently, or more forcefully than the rest of the performers; (c) the leader's part may stand out melodically or rhythmically; (d) the leader may employ other mannerisms which set his voice apart; (e) finally, the leader may be heard to urge on the other performers in various ways.

The coding points for the social organization of the singing group follow:

1. ∅ *No singers.*

2. $\dfrac{L}{N}$ *One singer,* whether accompanied by instruments or not. The N below the bar symbolizes a silent audience, whether actually present or not.

3. $\dfrac{L}{NA}$ *One singer with an audience* whose dancing, shouting, etc. can be heard. In practice we omitted this point and coded all solos $\dfrac{L}{N}$.

4. —L *One solo singer after another.* (Two or more singers alternate in singing a melody or split the melody between them in some way. Only one singer is heard at a time.) If any two singers' parts overlap con-

sistently, code L(N as well. If two or more singers alternate in leading a chorus, code −L and the appropriate choral situation (see below). If two singers both alternate and sing together, code −L and L + N or N (L (see below).

5. L/N *Social unison with a dominant leader.* Code here if a single dominant voice, a leader, stands out above the general effect of social unison. This dominant leader's voice is usually louder and more forceful than the others. Sometimes he imitates phrases or other parts of the melody. Sometimes he seems to spur the group on. *Social unison* is a simply organized group performance in which all participants sing the same melody and text all the way through a performance. Everyone sings at the same time. There is no alternation of parts. Although there may be some melodic and rhythmic deviations, the general effect is one of coordinated unity.

Note: In general, a "dominant" part is one that is either louder, more elaborate, more active, or longer than the others.

6. N/L *Social unison with the group dominant.* Code here if no dominant lead voice is steadily heard over the social unison. Sometimes a lead can be heard briefly above the group at beginnings of sections, but as soon as the group joins in his voice is submerged.

7. $\dfrac{L//N}{N//L}$ *Heterogeneous group.* Uncoordinated or casually coordinated group performance, rhythmically diffuse. In extreme cases, the singers do not seem to be aware of each other at all.

Two types of casually coordinated performances are coded here. In the first, the impression is of a group of individuals singing totally different things at the same time. In the second, all singers may follow the broad outlines of the melody or rhythm, but diverge radically on most details. Sometimes the effect is intentional; it may, in fact, be cultivated, the result of meticulous rehearsal and conscious control. The general impression, however, is one of discoordination.

In some cases one voice may stand out among the rest as leader, but this will not affect the rating unless there is a clearcut antiphonal relationship involved (see below). If antiphony *is* combined with this kind of heterogeneous group activity, code $\dfrac{L//N}{N//L}$ and either L + N, L(N, N(L, or N(N. Sometimes the total effect is so complex that it is difficult or impossible to judge coordination. Certain kinds of performances produce a diffuse effect but show evidence, in detail, of close coordination. In any case, where the coder cannot make up his mind as to whether the performance is uncoordinated or highly coordinated, he should code both L//N *and* W (see below).

8. L + N *Simple alternation: leader-chorus.* Code here all situations in which there is alternation between a solo voice and a chorus with a perceptible, if slight, pause between the two parts. The group may repeat the leader's part or respond with new material. The leader may join the chorus, or, indeed, may form the chorus by singing with one other person. In some cases there may be regular alternation; in other cases the leader may sing only once, with the chorus singing for the remainder of the piece. In any case, the leader must sing at least one complete phrase or subphrase alone.

If, however, the leader begins and the other singers *drift in* on the same phrase, L/N or N/L, rather than L + N should be coded. If there is occasional overlapping or if one part enters right on top of the "cutoff" of the other part, both L + N and L(N or N(L should be coded.

9. N + N *Simple alternation: chorus-chorus.* Two groups of two or more singers interact as described above. The same rules for double-coding apply.

10. L(N *Overlapping alternation: leader-chorus.* A more integrated alternation of leader and chorus. The leader and chorus parts overlap so that one begins before the other ends. In extreme cases the chorus may also be heard backing the leader during his part. However, the leader is dominant; his part is longer than that of the group and often more elaborate. The group's activity serves to support and contrast with the leader's part.

11. N(L *Overlapping alternation: chorus-leader.* The same case as L(N, except that the group dominates rather than the leader. Although it may sometimes support the leader, its part is very active. The group sings more than half of the time.

12. N(N *Overlapping alternation: chorus-chorus.* Two or more groups overlap as above. In those rare cases where the groups are radically different in size (e.g., two singers versus 20), N(N is still coded despite the fact that the smaller group may give the impression of leading the larger.

13. W *Interlocking.* The group is divided into two or more parts which are rhythmically distinct and melodically complementary. Often there is no perceptible leadership—each individual is equally important; but, as distinct from $\dfrac{L//N}{N//L}$, *there is a high degree of coordination between the parts.* Although some singers may be duplicating another part at the octave or in unison, the general impression is one of a group of individuals, each with his own part, interacting in such a way as to create a homogeneous texture.

If an individual voice can be heard in alternation with the rest of the group code both *W* and L + N, L(N, or N(L, whichever is most appropriate. When the situation is so complex that the coder cannot decide whether the singers are really well-coordinated or not, he should code both L//N and *W* (see above).

Line 2. The relationship between the accompanying orchestra and the vocal part.

The term "orchestra" refers to a single instrument or to a group of instruments, no matter how organized. It covers all the non-vocal sounds heard on the record, whether body-produced (clapping, stamping, and the like) or object-produced, by anything from two sticks to a symphony orchestra.

1. ∅ *Non-occurrence,* no accompaniment.
2. /o *A small orchestra* (one to three players), *accompanying the vocal part and subordinate to it.* One or more of the instruments may perform the melody.
3. /O *A large orchestra* (four or more players) *in the same relationship as* /o.
5. O/ *A large or small orchestra dominant over the sung part.* The orchestral part takes up more time and/or is considerably louder than the sung part.
6. O *The orchestra* (large or small) *plays interludes between passages.* It is *never* heard simultaneously with the vocal part.
8. //o *A small orchestra* (one to three players) *which seems unrelated or only casually related to the vocal part.* The effect resembles that described under $\dfrac{L//N}{N//L}$ on Line 1, and is the result, usually, of some lack of *rhythmic* coordination between instruments and voices. A number of situations are coded here: (a) the instruments may be out of phase with the singers or slightly faster or slower, so that there is a blurring effect; (b) they may alternately lag behind the singers and speed ahead of them; (c) they may play the melody of the vocal part, but in an individualized manner, as in certain types of heterophony; (d) the sung part may be in free rhythm while the accompaniment adheres to strict rhythm or vice versa; (e) the instruments may play long, drawn-out "drone" notes, with no rhythmic shape, as a background to a rhythmically active voice part; (f) the singers may be rhythmically with the instruments much of the time, but the coordination is so subtle as to be missed by the untrained listener; the crucial moments of the voice part—beginnings and ends of phrases, melodic peaks, strong

accents—do not coincide with the rhythmic patterns of the accompaniment.

Double-coding may be necessary when some of the instruments coordinate well with the singers and others do not.

9. //O *The same relationship as above, with an orchestra of four or more players.*

12. (o *An orchestra of one to three players in complementary relationship to the singers.* The instruments are basically well-coordinated with and subordinate to the vocal part, but provide more than a mere background for the voices (as in /o and /O). Here again a number of situations are coded. The orchestra may comment on the vocal part in a significant way. Some of the instruments may pick up the melody from the voices and take the foreground temporarily. In other cases, the orchestra plays a highly contrastive but well-coordinated foil for the voices, the instruments providing a large share of the total musical interest, but on a distinctly different plane from that of the singers. In sum, the effect of the (o situation is of continuous interplay between voices and orchestra or of two distinct musical planes (vocal and orchestral), linked by a strong rhythmic bond.

In some cases, the relationship between singers and orchestra will be so complex or ambiguous that it is difficult to tell whether or not there is real coordination between them. It may therefore be necessary to code both //o *and* (o.

13. (O *Same as* (o, *but for orchestras of four or more players.*

Line 3. The instrumental group.
Social structure of the orchestra alone (see also definitions under Line 1).

1. ø *Non-occurrence.* No instruments.

2. $\dfrac{L}{N}$ *One instrument.* An accompaniment on one instrument.

3. $\dfrac{L}{NA}$ *One instrument with an audience.* An instrumental accompaniment with an active audience that can be heard dancing, shouting, clapping—but not singing. In practice, this category was placed under $\dfrac{L}{N}$.

4. —L *Series.* Two or more instruments playing solo parts one after another.

5. L/N *An orchestra playing in social unison with one instrument clearly dominant.* The other instruments are subordinate to the leader, playing the same tune in the same way or in simple accompanying parts.

6. N/L *An orchestra in social unison with no dominating instrument.* No leading instrument can be heard. The leader's part is subordinate to the group or submerged by it most of the time. Here also code all unison group performances in which no leader can be heard.

7. L//N *Heterogeneous relationship, leader dominant.* Similar to $\dfrac{\text{L//N}}{\text{N//L}}$ on Line 1, but applied to the relationships among the instruments of the orchestra, and a single dominant lead instrument.

8. N//L *Heterogeneous relationship, leader subordinate.* The same musical situation as above, but either the leader is subordinate to the group or leadership shifts from one instrument to another.

9. L + N *Simple alternation: solo-group.* A simple antiphonal relationship between a lead instrument and an orchestral group (see L + N, Line 1).

10. N + N *Simple alternation: group-group.* An orchestra divided into two or more parts with an antiphonal relationship between them.

11. L(N *Overlapping alternation: leader-group.* Alternation between leader and group, but with overlap (see L(N on Line 1).

12. N(L *Overlapping alternation: group-leader.* The same, except that no one instrument is in the foreground more often than the others.

13. N(N *Overlapping alternation: group-group.* The orchestra is divided into two or more opposing groups, each of which acts as a unit. There is a good deal of overlap between units, as described on Line 1 for N(N.

COORDINATING FACTORS IN THE PERFORMING GROUP

Lines 1 through 3 serve to differentiate certain patterns of social interaction among the performers. In Lines 4 and 7, the type of musical coordination in the segments of the musical group is coded. Lines 5, 6, 8, and 9 are five-point scales along which the coder may rate the degree of integration, both tonal (Lines 5 and 8) and rhythmic (Lines 6 and 9), practiced by the singing group and the instrumental group. The degree of acoustic integration (or, in our terms, "tonal blend") is perhaps the performers' attempt to match or enhance one another's tone. On the rhythm lines the coder rates the degree of rhythmic coordination or simultaneity among the members of the group. A high rating on both tonal and rhythmic integration (or rhythmic blend) indicates that the members of the group are willing to submerge their individuality in favor of a group sound, in which all the voices unite, forming a single, transcendent "voice." A low rating would indicate that each performer maintains his individuality despite the fact that he is a member of a group. The degree of blend should not, of course, be considered an aesthetic judgment in any sense. These terms are simply measures of group coordination and integration.

Line 4. Basic musical organization of the voice part.

1. ∅ *Two or more singers who are totally unrelated musically.* Each singer has his own part and goes his own way. The effect may be similar to a mob scene.

4. M *Monophony.* Only one voice is heard at a time.

7. U *Unison.* Two or more voices singing the same melody in unison or octaves and conforming to the same rhythmic pattern.

10. H *Heterophony.* Each voice sings the same melody in a slightly different manner. The variation is usually rhythmic, with some voices lagging behind, others pushing forward, or with some voices more rhythmically active than others. There may be some melodic individuality, but it is only temporary and usually inconsistent. Some voices may deliver a more embellished or rhythmically varied melodic line against others which are less embellished and more straightforward, but all sing essentially the same melody.

    Simultaneous combinations of different tones may occur irregularly due to the variation of melodic detail in some voices. In such cases, H should still be coded since P (defined below) is reserved for songs in which such "chords" recur *consistently*.

13. P *Polyphony.* The use of simultaneously produced intervals other than the unison or octave. Two part "chords" are considered polyphony, as well as harmonies of greater complexity. Simultaneously produced intervals can also occur in *Heterophony* (see above). Therefore, polyphony should be coded only if one of the following situations is perceived: 1. if "chords" are heard often enough so that it is obvious that "part-singing" is taking place; 2. if "chords" are infrequent, polyphony is coded only if they recur in some consistent way; 3. in intermediate cases, the length of the "chords" is relevant—if they tend to last about as long as the important melody notes, it is likely that true polyphony exists; if they are ephemeral, the case is probably heterophonic. (See Line 22 for a breakdown into the six categories of polyphony; no polyphony; drone; isolated chords; parallel chords; harmony; counterpoint.)

Line 5. Tonal blend of the vocal group.

A Western choral director attempts to mold his choir into a single voice capable of producing a wide range of colors. To achieve such complete unity or blend, the singers must carefully match the way they attack, accent, color, and pronounce every sound. Only sustained rehearsal under a demanding director brings a group of Americans to this level of tonal blend, whereas in some cultures any group can achieve it with a sort of effortless and instantaneous empathy. In any case, the overall effect is that of a highly sonorous, unified group.

Elsewhere in the world there is, apparently, little desire to project this image of unity. In some cultures, singers seem to enjoy demonstrating their tonal independence of each other. The effect may resemble a noisy argument, where no individual yields to another. In less extreme cases, the chorus will produce a reedy unison in which individual voices stand out. The level of overall resonance is low. The effect is one of strongly maintained independence.

The present rating scale permits a judgment of this phenomenon in five steps from minimal to maximal blend—from a low to a high level of sonority, from maximal tonal individuation to tonal unity.

1. ∅ *No blend.* Only one person singing at a time.
4. b *Minimal blend.* Singers make no attempt to match one another in *tone.* Individual voices stand out. The effect is harsh and often noisy.
7. b *Medium blend.* The singers make some attempt to match voices. The total effect is less harsh than minimal blend.[1]
10. B *Good blend.* The group sounds resonant as a whole, with some harshness.
13. B *Maximal blend.* The singers match each other's tone in such a way as to present the effect of a single tone quality. Any harshness is the result of harmonic dissonance rather than poor blend. The total effect is highly resonant, clear, and unified.[2]

Line 6. Rhythmic blend of the vocal group.

The degree of rhythmic coordination among the singers is rated here. The coder must observe how the members of the group move together rhythmically. If all attacks and releases are precisely coordinated, the rhythmic blend is considered maximal. If, on the other hand, the group seems ready to fall apart, with individual voices discernible on all attacks and the movements from note to note invariably ragged, the rhythmic blend is considered minimal.

In the urban areas of Western Europe and the United States, large groups of singers can sing in tight rhythmic coordination only after many hours of rehearsal under a director who sets and maintains the rhythm for them. Groups in other parts of the world, however, seem to have little difficulty in achieving rhythmic blend. No leader is needed to mark the beat. Indeed, in

[1] b appears on the coding sheet as an underlined b.
[2] B appears on the coding sheet as an underlined B.

some cases, excellent rhythmic blend is achieved in music which has no beat at all; the singers follow one another precisely through the most subtle kinds of rhythmic nuance; on the other hand, there are cultures which seem to value what we would call "minimal blend" and employ complex artistic devices to achieve the desired ragged effect.

1. ∅ *Non-occurrence.* (a) No group. Only one singer at a time. (b) **A** group performance in which there appears to be no linking rhythmic principle. Every individual handles rhythm in his own way, so that the total effect resembles a mob scene.

4. r *Minimal rhythmic blend.* An extremely ragged and uncoordinated performance.

7. r *Medium rhythmic blend.* Much of the total effect is ragged, but not in the extreme.[3]

10. R *Good rhythmic blend.* Attacks and releases are generally well coordinated, but not really precise.

13. R *Maximal rhythmic blend.* Precise coordination at every rhythmic level.[4]

Line 7. The basic musical organization of the orchestra.

1. ∅ *Non-occurrence.* (a) No instruments. (b) A performance in which two or more instruments are perceived to be totally uncoordinated.

4. M *Monophony.* One instrument playing one note at a time, or in octaves.

7. U *Unison.* Here code the following cases and their variants: (a) A group of instruments playing the same melody in unison or in octaves. (b) An instrumental solo with simple percussion accompaniment— drum, rattle, sticks, clapping, etc. (c) Any untuned percussion ensemble unless it is playing polyrhythmically. In the latter case, code P.

10. H *Heterophony.* (See definition in Line 4, point 10.)

13. P *Polyphony or polyrhythm.* (See definition in Line 4, point 13.) Code here for the presence of harmony of any kind in the accompaniment, whether produced by an ensemble or on a single instrument, such as a guitar. Also code at this point cases of two or more percussion instruments playing polyrhythmically.

Line 8. Tonal blend of the orchestra.

This concept must be applied to orchestras in a different sense than choruses. An orchestra composed of several different kinds of instruments can hardly achieve the same degree of tonal unity as a chorus of voices. Conse-

---

[3] r appears on the coding sheet as an underlined r.
[4] R appears on the coding sheet as an underlined R.

quently, the measure of blend for orchestras is not uniformity of timbre, but rather the overall sonority of the ensemble. When the instruments are in tune with one another and play in a similar manner, so as to reinforce and maintain a consistent sonority, good blend should be coded.

Orchestras consisting exclusively of untuned percussion instruments are a special case since it is difficult to assess their overall sonority. If an ensemble of this type consists of instruments of the same kind only (such as clapping ensembles, or a group of people striking axes against wood), maximal blend is automatically coded. If untuned percussion instruments of different types are used, the criterion should be the degree to which they tend to sound as though they *were* of the same type.

If the entire "orchestra" consists of a single instrument, ø, or non-occurrence, should be coded on this line and the following one. This holds true even when the instrument is a polyphonic one, such as the guitar or piano, in which there is a certain element of blend between individual strings or other components.

1. ø *Non-occurrence.* No blend. Only one instrument at a time, or no instruments at all.
4. b *Minimal blend.* Little or no overall sonority. Instruments contrast in tone quality and do not reinforce each other.
7. b *Medium blend.*
10. B *Good blend.*
13. B *Maximal blend.* Total effect is highly sonorous; the overall sound is perceived as "rich."

Line 9. Rhythmic blend of the orchestra.
See Line 6.

1. ø *Non-occurrence.* (a) No instruments. (b) No group—one instrument only. (c) A complete lack of coordination of any kind.
4. r The members of a group follow the same rhythmic pattern, but with such ragged coordination as to produce a disunified effect.
7. r A group that plays together on the beat or follows the same rhythmic pattern with a moderate degree of coordination. Here code for the perception of lack of precision, raggedness, or slackness, if these effects are present but not pronounced.
10. R A group that plays together on the beat or follows the same rhythmic pattern or patterns in a cohesive fashion. There is clearcut coordination of attack.
13. *R* Here the orchestral group is completely linked together rhythmically.

Line 10. Words to nonsense.

The degree of repetitiousness in the text is judged here by the rater. He listens to the text as it is performed. He is not concerned with the meaning of the words or with his own ignorance of the language. He makes a judgment about the proportion of the text in the whole song which seems to be repeated or that consists of "nonsense material." Repetition of passages of text are of frequent occurrence in some song styles—in the form of refrains, choruses, burdens, responses, or lines sung over several times to fill out a poetic form. "Nonsense," if it appears in song, usually recurs again and again and thus is an important factor in rating repetitiousness. The term "nonsense material" includes a multitude of phenomena of high occurrence in song— nonsense syllables, nonsense words, vocal segregates, babbling, ululating, animal imitations, shouts, cries, moans, laughter, sobbing, grunting, and the like. Although accurate judgments cannot always be made about *which* of these phenomena occur in a song, attentive listeners can usually arrive at a good estimate of the proportion of the time nonsense takes up in the entire song. Such material often occurs in formally patterned ways and is usually clearly contrasted to passages of new text.

In coding this point, the chorus part is counted along with the leader's part, so that, for example, if a chorus always sings the same line in response to a fresh line from the leader, this case should be coded 50-50 or wo-no (see below).

1. WO *Words dominant.* Code this point if you hear a continuous stream of *different* sung syllables, words, and phrases, with little or no repetition or use of nonsense material. In such songs—epics, ballads, sung prayer, much Western song—text is usually of paramount importance.

4. wo *Words still dominant,* but there is some degree of repetition and/or use of nonsense.

7. wo-no *About half the text is repeated.* There is a substantial amount of repetition and/or nonsense which more or less equals the flow of unrepeated words.

10. wo-NO Considerably more than half the sung performance is accounted for by repetition and/or nonsense.

13. NO The text seems to be almost *entirely composed* of repetition of some sort or of nonsense.

Rhythm: Lines 11 through 14 summarize the rhythmic patterns of the singing group and its accompaniment:

Line 11: The kind of meter around which the rhythmic activity of the *singing* group is organized.

Line 13: The same judgments for the *accompaniment* as a whole.

Line 12: The way in which the members of the singing group relate to one another within the metrical framework.

Line 14: The same judgment for Line 12 applied to the rhythmic relationship among the accompanying instruments.

Line 11. Overall vocal rhythmic scheme.

In most musical styles, the performer or performers employ a single, overall rhythmic scheme, or "ground plan," which serves as a point of reference for the infinite variety of rhythmic detail possible within the scheme. Although a large number of such overall schemes are possible, we have, for simplicity's sake, chosen to divide them into five general categories. The categories on this line apply to the overall rhythm of the voices; those on Line 13 apply to the instrumental part.

1. ∅ *Non-occurrence.* No singers.

3. R1 *One-beat rhythm.* A series of equally accented single notes of about the same length.

6. R-v *Simple meter.* Code this point when any one simple meter, duple, triple, "simple" or compound—runs through the whole song. Thus, if the entire song is in 4/4, 3/4, 6/8, 9/8, 12/8, or any other similar meter, it should be coded R-v. However, R-v should *not* be coded if the accents within the measure are unevenly distributed in a consistent manner throughout the song (e.g., 9/8 divided into 2/8, 2/8, 2/8, 3/8).

9. R*v *Complex meter.* Here, as with R-v, one meter prevails throughout the song. In R*v, however, the measure cannot be evenly divided by two or three to form subunits of two or three beats each. Thus, R*v includes such meters as 5/4, 7/8, 11/16, etc. Also meters such as 9/8 and 12/8, although mathematically divisible by two or three, are coded R*v when the accent pattern within the measure is, in performance, distributed unevenly but consistently throughout the song. A subdivision of 12/8, for example, into 3/8, 2/8, 3/8, 2/8, 2/8, should be coded R*v, while a subdivision of the same 12/8 into the more usual 3/8, 3/8, 3/8, 3/8 is coded R-v.

11. Ri *Irregular meter.* Code as Ri all songs in which no one meter prevails throughout. A song that is basically in 3/4, but has one or more measures in 2/4, is coded Ri, as well as a song in which the meter shifts continually from measure to measure (e.g., 3/4, 2/4, 3/4, 3/4, 5/4, 3/2, etc.). Meter changes involving "Hemiola" effects only are *not* considered irregular. "Hemiola" effects depend upon the ambiguity possible in measures which may be divided evenly by two *or* by three, such as 6/8 meter. Since 6/8 meter contains six eighth notes,

they may be divided into two groups of three notes each, or three groups of two. Certain kinds of music employ this ambiguity to create a special effect, so that there can be measures of 6/8 divided into two groups of three, followed by a measure or measures divided into three groups of two. Because of conventions connected with the history of notation, six eighth notes divided into two groups of three are usually called "6/8," while the same number of eighth notes divided into three groups of two are called "3/4." When one kind of subdivision succeeds another, the time signature may therefore change from 6/8 to 3/4 or vice versa in conventional notation. This is not a shift in meter as we define it. The situation described above would be coded R-v, *not* Ri.

Care should be taken that a song in simple meter not be coded Ri merely because it is sung with some degree of rhythmic freedom. For example, a performer often loses the beat during the pause at the end of a phrase only to pick it up again with the beginning of the next phrase. An irregular pause of this type should be coded as rubato (see Line 26) unless all such pauses in a performance are of the same length. In the latter case, code Ri. But, so long as the phrases themselves are sung in the same duple or triple meter throughout, the song should be coded R-v regardless of whether the pauses between phrases tend to give the impression of Ri.

13. Rpa *Parlando rubato.* "Free rhythm," in which no regularly recurring beat can be distinguished. Rpa is often close to speech in general effect; accents and rhythmic patterns are grouped in meaningful ways, but without reference to a regular division of time into steady beats.

Note on technique of coding rhythmic lines: For coders who have difficulty understanding the technical definitions given above, the following procedure is recommended.

First try to locate *the beat;* that is, the regularly recurring pulse around which all the notes of a song group themselves (unless the song is in "free" rhythm, of course). Keep time with the music as you listen, marking the beat with swings of the arm—conducting. You may choose such a fast pulse that conducting becomes uncomfortable, as, for instance, if you try to conduct a fast waltz "in three." In that case, try another pulse that is twice, or, as in the waltz, three times as slow. On the other hand, you may adopt a pulse so slow that it is difficult to maintain an even beat. Then try doubling or tripling your pulse, until you find a beat that you can comfortably maintain and observe.

Rpa . . . If it is impossible to locate any pulse; that is, if the rhythm seems largely free and unrelated to a beat, so that in conducting you find yourself continually speeding up and slowing down without being able to relate your motions to any regular time pattern, Rpa should be coded.

R1 . . . Once the beat has been established, it should be fairly easy to determine whether R1, R-v, R*v, or Ri should be coded. If each note of the song contains the same number of beats (i.e., all notes are about the same length) and all the notes are stressed more or less equally, R1 should be coded. (This is rare in the vocal part but not uncommon in the instrumental part, where simple hand-clapping or the continuous beat of a drum forms the only accompaniment to the singers.)

As one "conducts" the song, the beats may seem to group themselves into larger patterns marked by accents or determined simply by the way the melody is phrased. Make a downward thrust of the arm on the beat where such patterns seem to begin (the "downbeat"). Move the arm sideways for all other beats (the "upbeats").

Ri . . . Count the number of upbeats between each downbeat—i.e., between each downward armstroke. If the number between each downbeat varies constantly or unpredictably, code Ri. If most of the downbeats occur regularly (that is, with the same number of upbeats between them), but *some* of them are separated by a different number of upbeats, Ri should still be coded.

R-v . . . If the pattern of up- and downbeats is adhered to throughout the song, code R-v or R*v. If the total number of beats in the pattern is two or three, or some multiple of these, such as four, six, eight, nine, etc., the meter is *simple* and R-v should be coded.

R*v . . . (a) If the pattern of beats between downbeats is regular, but is not one of those patterns included in the definition of simple rhythm, the meter is coded as complex. Patterns such as five or seven beats should be coded under complex rhythm. (b) It may be difficult to conduct the song. Though the downbeats recur regularly, the upbeats may be in some *complex* meter, such as 5/8 or 7/8. Such music, especially at fast tempos, can give the impression of two or three unequal beats per measure; it is perceived as a kind of *lopsided,* or *limping* effect. In this case, code R*v.

Care should be taken to distinguish between a simple meter, which is sung freely, and one of the more complex types of rhythm (R*v, Ri, or Rpa). Many folk and primitive singers treat simple meters with a good deal of freedom, almost as if they were Rpa. If one finds, when conducting the song, that the hand has to hesitate now and then or hurry to catch up with the beat, yet the movements of the arm remain on the whole steady and simple, with a regularly recurring downbeat, then meter should probably be rated as simple (R-v), but with some degree of rubato (see Line 26).

Some songs may be divided into two sections, each with its own rhythm. A parlando rubato introduction, for example, may be followed by a section in simple meter. Again, some singers may be singing parlando rubato, while others are simultaneously singing simple meter. In such cases double coding is in order.

Line 12. Rhythmic relationship within the singing group.

Singing groups coordinate their rhythmic activity in a number of ways. In some cases all singers or parts in a chorus may stick to the main rhythm. In others, there may be one or more contrasting rhythmic parts. This line provides seven descriptive categories for the various types of rhythmic relationships that link a group together within one of the overall metrical patterns already coded in Line 11.

1. ∅ *Non-occurrence.* (a) No singing group. Only one singer at a time. (b) No rhythmic coherence of any sort. Each individual is on his own and does not relate rhythmically to the others.

3. Ru *Rhythmic unison.* All voices move together with little or no rhythmic independence.

5. Rh *Rhythmic heterophony.* Similar to Ru, but one or more singers consistently deviates from the others in some way. Some may be out of phase with the others, may embellish the melody in an individual manner, or use more or less rubato than the others.

7. Ra *Accompanying rhythm.* The singing group is divided into two or more parts, one of which accompanies the other. The accompanying part has independent rhythmic patterns but these are subordinate to the main part—that is, they may be (1) less active rhythmically, (2) less active melodically, (3) softer, or (4) may occur intermittently. If the accompanying part is equal in importance and rhythmic activity to the main part, so that the accompaniment becomes, in effect, another melody, consider coding Rc (see point 13, below).

9. Rp *Simple polyrhythm.* All of the parts basically conform to a single pulse. However, there are moments when one of the parts will *temporarily* deviate from the basic pulse to create a new pulse in *conflict* with it. The conflict may last a moment or it may resolve itself only after several "measures" (as in much classical Indian music). In any case, this rhythmic conflict must only be temporary.

11. Rpm *Complex polyrhythm.* Two or more conflicting pulses are heard *simultaneously and more or less continually* throughout the song. For a fuller discussion of the problems set forth by Rp and Rpm, see explanatory note below.

13. Rc *Rhythmic counterpoint.* Two or more rhythmic patterns, equal to and distinct from one another, occur simultaneously within the same rhythmic framework, but *without* conflict of pulse. A Bach fugue is an example of this trait, although it can be found in primitive music. The principal trait to watch for is the presence of two or more independent and active parts *throughout* the piece.

Line 12. *Summary.* If all parts follow basically the same rhythm, so that they move together note for note, code Ru. If they follow the same rhythm in a very general way only, with much straggling and catching up between the notes, code Rh. If some parts are rhythmically distinct from others, code either Ra, Rp, Rpm, or Rc. When the rhythmic activity of all the parts relates in such a way that no conflicts of pulse occur, code Ra or Rc, depending on the relative importance of the parts. If one part stands out and the others seem to be accompanying it, code Ra. If two or more parts are equally important, code Rc. If conflict of pulse occurs between two or more parts, code Rp or Rpm. Rp is coded when the conflict is temporary, Rpm when the conflict is heard throughout most of the song.

Explanatory note regarding Rp and Rpm: On the whole, Western European art music is more highly developed harmonically than rhythmically. Much of its drama, motion, and subtlety depends upon the effect of harmonies and harmonic progressions. Though it does exhibit considerable rhythmic variety and invention, this dimension is considerably less developed in the music of the West than in certain other cultures. Even in so complex a work as a Bach fugue, where the composer has striven for the maximum amount of independence for each "voice" or "part," all of the voices usually conform to the same pulse and the same meter. Thus, when we say of such a work that it is in 4/4 time and that it should be performed at the speed of ninety-five beats per minute, we are referring not to just one part, but to all the parts; with only a few brief exceptions, all the parts are in 4/4 time and all move at the speed of ninety-five beats per minute.

Modern composers are working with more complex rhythmic relationships. This trend has its precedents in the polyphonic art music of medieval and Renaissance Europe, where one can also sometimes find compositions with highly complex rhythmic relationships. In other parts of the world, however, complex rhythmic organization of multi-part music is commonplace. We suspect that several different types of complexity exist, but we have singled out two types which we feel we can distinguish with relative security. In setting up these categories, we have been forced, because of the breadth of our sample and the vagueness of current concepts about this rhythmic situation, to develop a somewhat novel point of view.

Where there is a feeling of simultaneous rhythmic conflict in multi-part music, at least two of the parts will seem to be organized around different tempos. Moreover, the difference must be of such a nature that their juxtaposition creates a feeling of *conflict*. Such conflict-generating independence is often called "polyrhythm," or "cross-rhythm." We have been able to distinguish two varieties of polyrhythm, the first mainly characteristic of India, the second of Africa, although both are found elsewhere. The first type—frequently found in music of the Near East and Andalucia, as well as of India—is here designated as Rp.

Essentially, one can say that Rp is a type of polyrhythm in which all of the conflicts *depend on and relate to a single unchanging unit of beat.* Rp occurs when there is a *temporary* conflict of pulse. This differs from the Rpm category (see below) in that the conflict of pulse is always "resolved"; the secondary pulse always returns to the basic pulse. Illustrations of Rp:

or, even more complex:

In the above examples, the introduction of "triplets" means that the tempo of the lower part temporarily becomes ♩ = 60, while the upper part continues at ♩ = 90. Note that at the fourth measure the lower part returns to the original pulse and "resolves" the temporary conflict. Note also that in all the above examples, there is only one basic and permanent tempo.

The other kind of polyrhythm, characteristic of much African drumming and possibly of certain Pygmy-type group singing, we designate Rpm. Rpm is characterized by more or less *continual* conflict of pulse. There may be changes of pulse in any of the parts at any time, but there are few if any moments when these conflicts resolve themselves. One part may be louder than the rest, as in some cases of African drumming where one drummer functions as "leader," but the effect on the listener is of a texture made up of two or more independent parts, in more or less continuous rhythmic conflict. Illustrations of Rpm:

or, the same notated differently:

Of course, as with Rp, there must be true *conflict* of pulse, not merely difference. If the main part is moving at 60 beats per second and another part is moving at 120, for example, the ratio of 1:2 between the tempos is simple and there is no feeling of conflict. Ratios such as 2:3, 4:3, 5:2, etc., between the tempos of simultaneous parts are sufficiently complex to produce a feeling of conflict.

Line 13. The overall rhythmic structure of the accompaniment.

This line is rated according to the same symbols and definitions given for the singing group in Line 11. The coder should refer to these, making the adjustments necessary for coding instruments rather than voices.

1. ∅ *Non-occurrence.* No instruments.
3. R1 *One-beat rhythm.*
6. R-v *Simple meter.*
9. R*v *Complex meter.*
11. Ri *Irregular meter.*
13. Rpa *Parlando rubato.*

Line 14. Rhythmic relationship within the accompanying group.

In this line various types of interrelationship among the *instruments only* are rated, not between voices and instruments. The coder should refer to the definitions given for the singing group in Line 12.

1. ∅ *Non-occurrence.* (a) No accompanying group. (b) No rhythmic coherence of any sort.
3. Ru *Rhythmic unison.*
5. Rh *Rhythmic heterophony.*
7. Ra *Accompanying rhythm.*
9. Rp *Simple polyrhythm.*
11. Rpm *Complex polyrhythm.*
13. Rc *Rhythmic counterpoint.*

Phrase. The coding of Lines 15 through 18 depends on an understanding of the complex matter of "phrase." The *Harvard Dictionary of Music* defines a musical phrase as "a natural division of the melodic line, comparable to a sentence of speech . . . the term is used with so little exactness and uniformity that a more specific description can hardly be given." More specific definitions of the term do, in fact, exist in musicological literature, but they are so involved with the mechanics of European harmonic music that they are of little use in the phrase analysis of folk and primitive music. In the long run, the recognition of phrase structure is largely a matter of feeling tempered by certain more or less specific objective guides.

In the simplest sense, a phrase is a complete musical statement. It serves to break the song up into a series of recognizable melodic segments. Because of the division of a piece of music into phrases we are able to hear it as an entity composed of interrelated and understandable segments, rather than a

continuous unarticulated stream of sound, although such phenomena do occur in the musical idioms of some cultures. However, as stated in the *Harvard Dictionary of Music*, the musical phrase serves much the same purpose
as the sentence in speech—a large organizational segment which can be related to other important, similar segments to create a whole.

Listed below are some "cues" which we have found useful in determining
phrase:

1. The end of a phrase is often signified by a breath and/or a pause.
2. The end of a phrase is frequently marked by one or more long notes.
3. Often the end of a phrase is marked by an abrupt change of component
   or color: new instruments may enter or old ones drop out; the size of
   the singing part may shift from group to solo or vice versa.
4. It is sometimes best to consider the overall structure of the song before
   attempting to locate the specific phrases. Here the coder listens for the
   "stanza," the "strophe," or some large subdivision into which the performance is divided. Then he observes how this large unit seems to be
   subdivided. Once the coder has a clear idea of the number of phrases
   in one large segment of a song, he can then check to see whether or not
   the other large segments subdivide in the same fashion.
5. Linguistic cues can be very useful. If the coder understands the language, he can listen for the broad patterns of the verse, which often coincide with the phrase divisions in the music. Even without knowledge
   of the language the coder can listen for a rhyme scheme, or observe that
   singers will use special linguistic signals to mark off sections of the music—glottal stops, downglides, upglides, "swallowing" sounds, etc.

Using these criteria, the coder should be able to come to some conclusion
about where the phrases of a song begin and end. If this interpretation feels
right and follows some consistent pattern, it should be adopted for a first try.
If doubt remains, the coding can be revised later, when more experience
with an idiom makes the pattern clearer.

Now we come to the problem of phrase identity. Considered objectively,
any two phrases of any piece of music have some elements that are the same
and some that are different. When, therefore, can two phrases be considered
repetitions (or variants) of one another and when should they be regarded
as distinctly different? After experimenting with other approaches, we decided to regard the last note of the phrase as the principal criterion for
phrase similarity. *If two phrases have the same final tone, regardless of how
contrastive they may be in other respects, they are rated as variants of the
same phrase.* In this case the coder counts only one phrase. If, on the other
hand, two phrases have different final tones, they are rated as different
phrases, regardless of how similar they may be in other respects.

Exceptions may occur when there is some consistent pattern that overrides this rule. If one hears a series of phrases, each of which ends on the same note, and each phrase is strikingly different from all the others—as in the pattern A1, A2, A3, A4, A5—then each phrase is considered a variant of the other and the item is coded as having one phrase. If, however, there is a consistent pattern—such as A, A1, A2, A, A1, A2, A, A1, A2—then each phrase in each segment is considered different from the others and the form is considered to be A, B, C—A, B, C—A, B, C.[5]

All of the judgments for Lines 15 through 37 (with the exception of Line 27) pertain to the vocal part of the song only, regardless of whether or not there is an accompaniment, or whether or not the accompaniment dominates the song. This should be borne in mind especially in coding the lines pertaining to form (16 and 18), since an accompaniment may be organized in a completely different way than the voice part.

Line 15. Melodic shape.

The characteristic contours of the vocal line are described here in very general terms. While most of the other lines are scalar to some degree, this line did not lend itself to such treatment. Hence, the sequence of the four categories defined below is arbitrary.

1. A *Arched*. An arched phrase begins at a certain point, rises in pitch and then descends. We code at this point only if arched *phrases* occur prominently, *not* if the melody as a whole is arched.

5. T *Terraced*. The *entire melody* is characterized by a long descent interrupted by periods of leveling off and, in some cases, incidental rises. The melody begins high, moves downward through a phrase or two, then levels off. The next portion begins at the last pitch level or slightly above it, descending to an even lower point, where it once again levels off. This cascading descent proceeds throughout the song, so that the melody ends on or near its lowest point. If sketched, a profile of this kind of melody would resemble a terraced field or a tiled roof.

9. U *Undulating*. Most phrases have a wave-like shape. They move up and down through a number of peaks and valleys of varying heights. Also coded here are those rare cases in which the shape of the phrase is predominantly ascending.

13. D *Descending*. Most phrases descend gradually or abruptly.

Note: The decision to code T depends on an observation of the shape of the entire melody. For categories A, U, and D, however, we found that it was the shape

---

[5] Note: This type of song organization should be double-coded as both strophe and litany (see Line 16, point 9c).

of the *most typical or characteristic* phrases which determined our ratings. If all
the phrases conform to the same shape, there will be no problem. Since, however,
most strophic and through-composed songs contain more than one type of phrase,
the coder must decide which type is most characteristic of the song as a whole.
Usually this is simply a matter of observing which shape occurs most frequently
or is associated with the longest and most important phrases. If the coder cannot
decide which of these forms is most appropriate, the song should be double-coded
in some way.

Line 16. Melodic form.

On this line the range of formal possibilities is broken down into thirteen
general types, scaled roughly from simple to complex. We have chosen to
focus our attention on the simplest and most obvious formal distinctions.
(This series of definitions begins on the right, at Point 13.)

13. C *Canonic or round form.* Found only in certain types of polyphonic
    singing. The music is divided into two or more parts, each of which
    is rhythmically distinct. Each part is limited to one or two phrases re-
    peated over and over. Simple rounds or canons are included here, as
    well as the hocketing "bell chime" singing so common among African
    Bushmen and Pygmies.

12. L *Simple litany.* One or two phrases repeated over and over again in
    the same order with little or no variation: A A A A or AB AB AB AB.
    This rating is to be used even when such a form is preceded by one or
    two phrases of introduction.

11. Lv *Simple litany with a moderate amount of variation* in each repeat.

10. LV *Simple litany with a high degree of variation* in each repeat.
    Note: In many songs involving alternation between a leader and a
    chorus, the chorus sings the same phrase over and over with little vari-
    ation, while the leader varies his part continually. In such cases, if the
    leader's part is dominant, the song should be coded for a high degree
    of variation (V) ; if the leader has only a few notes to sing, the degree
    of variation is considered moderate (v) .

9. L* *Complex litany* is similar to L (simple litany) , but involves cer-
    tain complications, as in the following cases: (a) One or two new
    phrases inserted in the midst of an otherwise similar phrase pattern:
    ABABABACCAB . . . (b) More than one litany pattern occurring
    in the same song; i.e., another new phrase may appear after the pre-
    ceding one has been repeated several times. Such a pattern might be:
    AAAAAA . . . BBBBBB . . . CCCCCC . . . (c) In much African
    singing, a clear-cut litany is established and then a refrain, sometimes
    of one phrase, sometimes of more, may occur (see Line 18, page 62) .
    If the refrain seems to occur irregularly, as in AAARAARAAAAAR,

then code as complex litany. If it recurs regularly, as in AAAAR-AAAARAAAAR, code as a simple strophe (see St below). If, however, there are several (5 or more) consecutive repetitions of the same phrase, code both L* and St—AAAAARAAAAAR. (d) Litany pattern preceded by a short through-composed passage. (e) Any litany involving more complexity than the simple repetition of one or two phrases should be coded complex litany.

8. L*v *Complex litany with a moderate amount of variation* in each repeat of a section.

7. L*V *Complex litany with a high degree of variation* in each section.

Note regarding litany: In a leader-chorus pattern, a single phrase may be divided between the leader's part and the chorus part in the following manner:

Leader		*Chorus*
A (part 1)	followed by	A (part 2)
B (part 1)	followed by	B (part 2)

It is important to distinguish such cases from types in which the leader sings a complete phrase before the chorus comes in. The decision to code strophe or litany depends on this distinction. A test of this is to imagine the two parts sung by a single voice. The coder should then be able to perceive whether the chorus part sounds like a continuation of the leader's phrase or not. The pattern above would be coded as litany, since there are only two phrases (A and B). This pattern is common in West Indian sea chanties.

6. St *Simple strophe with little or no variation.* A series of three to eight (but not more than eight) phrases which are repeated, phrase by phrase, over and over, with no insertions of new material and no omissions or changes of order.

Such a complete "strophe" must be performed at least twice to be coded as a simple strophe. Thus, a song with the repeated pattern ABACD ABACD is coded as a simple strophe, but if the whole consists of two sections such as ABACD ABAC, it should be coded as St* (see below) because here the repetition is only partial. Similarly, a single, short pattern that is heard only once cannot be coded as a strophe, since there is no repetition of the whole pattern. Thus, a short song made up of only ABACD would be coded through-composed (see below), not St, even though it may seem "strophic." Exceptions are made when the coder knows that the recording is only an excerpt from a performance in which complete repetitions did take place.

Some simple strophes may appear to be more complex than they really are. Thus, in certain Amerindian songs, we have the phenomenon of incomplete repetition: ABCC ABC ABCC ABC. At first listening, the coder may be listening for the repetition of a four-phrase strophe and decide that, since the last phrase does not recur as before, the pattern is complex, not simple. By listening through carefully to the end, however, the coder will realize that the entire *seven*-phrase pattern *is* repeated without omissions and the pattern does form a simple strophe: ABCCABC ABCCABC.

5. Stv *Simple strophe with a moderate amount of variation.*

4. StV *Simple strophe with much variation.*

3. St* *Complex strophe with little or no variation.* St* is similar to, but more complex than, St. More is contained within the form than the regular repetition of three to eight phrases. Listed below are some basic types of complex strophes, which have turned up in our study:

   (a)   There are more than eight phrases before a full repeat.

   (b)   There is more than one refrain: ABA CD ABA EF . . .

   (c)   The refrain is not sung until the strophe has been repeated one or more times: ABA ABA CDE . . .

   (d)   The order of the phrases varies from strophe to strophe: ABAC AABC ABAB . . .

   (e)   Some of the phrases are more often repeated in one strophe than another: ABC AABC ABC ABC ABBC . . .

   (f)   A series of simple strophes followed *during the course of the same song* by a different series of simple strophes: AABC AABC AABC DEFE DEFE . . .

2. St*v *Complex strophe with moderate to great variation.*

1. tc *Through-composed.* A song that has no recognizable litany or strophic pattern, but instead is made up of a series of phrase groups in which consistently repeated sections seldom occur. Not every section of the piece need consist of completely new material; certain melodic motifs may occur throughout, but not in a regularly recurring order. tc is common in much Oriental music as well as in Western art music.

Explanatory note: Line 16 is an attempt to deal succinctly with the full range of melodic forms. It sets up two extremes. One, the most complex, is the through-composed (tc) category, in which many varied phrases are strung together in a fashion that, to some listeners, may seem to be almost formless. The other extreme is the simple litany form, defined here as a short tune composed of one or two phrases, which are repeated over and over again.

Most litany singing involves many repetitions of these brief sections. If a litany tune is sung one time, it leaves the listener "hanging in the air," with a feeling of incompleteness. This may be a Western attitude, but the fact is that litany tunes are seldom, if ever, sung only one time through. Normally a litany is repeated a number of times. This "ongoing" quality indicates, perhaps, one essential difference between litany and other forms.

A strophe, on the other hand, normally completes itself and *can* be sung once without leaving the impression that something else needs to be added or repeated. Another important characteristic of the strophic form is its sectional nature. The phrases are related in patterns of contrast and congruence that group themselves into larger units. In our definition of simple strophes, the *units do not exceed eight phrases,* and there is usually only one unit, which is then repeated. In complex strophes, however, the larger units, or sections, may be quite long and there may be several of them. Repetition takes place, but *not* always in the same sequence; the units may be shifted and internally altered to form an intricate pattern.

Through-composed songs are rarely divided into sections. Each phrase is succeeded by another to form a continuous chain. When larger sections *are* created, they are almost never repeated. Completely new phrases appear at various points in the middle and even near the end. The total effect is usually that of a gradually evolving form, rather than an interrelationship of clearly established sections.

Sometimes two forms may follow one another in the same piece. Often, for instance, a simple litany will be preceded by a through-composed introduction. In such cases, double coding is in order, unless the introduction is relatively short (see definition of L*).

Double coding may also be useful in ambiguous cases. Thus, for a piece that has a definite strophic pattern, but in which all of the phrases end on the same note, strophe and litany should both be coded. Some litanies have so much variation that they give the impression of being through-composed. If the coder cannot come to a satisfactory decision as to which is the proper choice in such a case, he should code both tc and LV.

Line 17. Phrase length.

A simple five-point scale is used. If all phrases in the song are about the same length, coding should present no problem. If *most* of the phrases are of the same length or if one phrase length seems most typical of the entire song, code for that and disregard the other, atypical, phrases. If the coder cannot decide which of two different lengths is most typical or frequent, he should code both. (Coding was done without a stop-watch for half the song sample. Then a test with a stopwatch was made and it was discovered that the principal coder had been rating length of phrase by ear in close approximation to the set of stopwatch measurements recorded in what follows.)

1. p *A very, very long phrase,* one that seems to run to the limit or beyond the limit of a singer's breath capacity (16 to 25+ seconds) .[6]

4. P *Longer than medium to quite long phrases,* a point intermediate between medium phrase lengths and frequent in p (10–15 seconds) .[7]

7. P *Phrases of average length,* normal for the familiar English ballad type (5–9 seconds) .

---

[6] p appears on the coding sheet as a double-underlined P.
[7] P appears on the coding sheet as an underlined P.

10. p— *Phrases of shorter than medium length* (3–4 seconds).

13. p *Short and very short phrases* (1–2 seconds).

Line 18. Number of phrases.

The coder should count the number of phrases that occur in the song *before there is a full repeat*. A song such as the following: ABC ABC ABC, would be considered to have three phrases. ABC ABC DE ABC ABC DE ABC ABC DE has a full repeat only after eight phrases, despite the partial repeat of the ABC section. Some songs, which in their entirety have such a pattern as ABC AB BC ABC BC, or ABC AABC, contain no full repeat and thus the "number of phrases" counted should be the total of all the phrases, in the first case, 12, and the second, 7. The exception to this rule occurs in complex litanies, in which the initial pattern of a frequently repeated phrase governs the coding decision. Thus a complex litany organized as follows— A A A A B C A A A A A B C—would be considered to have one phrase, since the initial pattern is a repeat of the single phrase "A."

Since phrase counting can be confusing, especially if there are many phrases in a song, we suggest the coder adopt and adhere to some straightforward method of keeping count. Raising a finger at the beginning or end of each phrase is one effective way to do this.

In Line 18, also code the presence or absence of "symmetry." If all phrases of a melody are of approximately the same length, code S for symmetry. If *even one* deviates from the standard pattern, code A for asymmetry. This code applies only to points (5) to (13).

The following are the available points:

1. 8+ There are *more than eight phrases before a full repeat.*
3. 5/7 There are *five or seven phrases before a full repeat.*
5. 4/A There are *four or eight phrases, asymmetrically arranged.*
6. 4/S *Four or eight phrases, symmetrically arranged.* All of the phrases are approximately the same length.
8. 3/A *Three or six phrases, asymmetrically arranged.*
9. 3/S *Three or six phrases, symmetrically arranged.*
11. 2/A *Two phrases, asymmetrically arranged.*
13. 1/2S *One or two phrases, symmetrically arranged.*

If a song is double-coded on the *Form* line (Line 16), it may also require double-coding on Line 18. For example, a song coded for both tc and LV on Line 16 might be double-coded as 8+ and 1/2S (or 2/A) on Line 18, since the double-coding on Line 16 indicates that the form can be looked at in two different ways. Double-coding on Line 18 can also occur if a song is divided into two parts, one of which has a different number of phrases from the other.

Note: The coding of Lines 19 through 21 requires a small amount of specialized musical training and ability. If the coder feels that he cannot make the proper judgments by ear, he should use an instrument such as a piano or guitar as a guide. Do not use a pitch pipe, since its range is too narrow to encompass songs whose range extends beyond the octave. If the coder is not familiar with the method of naming intervals used in Lines 20 and 21, he should consult a book on the rudiments of music.

Line 19. Position of the final tone.

This is determined by considering the relation of the final tone to the total range of the song (see Line 20).

In simple strophic or litany songs, the coder need only listen for the last note of a repeated section. In through-composed and certain complex strophic and litany songs, it is necessary to listen for the last note of the entire song. In polyphonic music there may be more than one final note. In such cases, the extreme notes of the last chord should *both* be coded.

1. f *The final tone is the lowest note of the song.*
4. ƒ *The final tone falls within the lower half of the total range.*[8]
9. F *The final tone is located at or near the midpoint of the total range.*
11. F *The final tone falls within the upper half of the total range.*[9]
13. ꜰ *The final tone is the highest note of the song.*[10]

Line 20. Range.

The coder should determine the total range of the song; i.e., the distance between the highest note and the lowest. Every note that is heard must be taken into consideration, even if it occurs only once. When both men and women participate, the following procedure is used. If women are singing an octave higher than men, their part should be considered as though it were actually in unison with the men. If there is alternation between a male soloist (or group) and a female soloist (or group), the female part should be considered as if it were an octave lower than it actually is. If, however, the song is polyphonic, the women's part is considered at its actual pitch, provided the part is unique and not merely doubling the men an octave higher.

If the song is divided into two sections which are highly contrastive in range (e.g., the first section is a major second in range, the second, a major tenth), it should be double coded for both traits. Similarly, in those rare cases where two songs are being sung simultaneously and their respective ranges are highly contrastive, the total range of each should be coded. If the differences in range are not highly contrastive in the above cases (e.g., one

---

[8] ƒ appears on the coding sheet as an underlined f.
[9] F appears on the coding sheet as an underlined F.
[10] ꜰ appears on the coding sheet as a double-underlined F.

is a fifth, the other an octave or a tenth) , the range of both combined should be coded.

1. 1–2 *A monotone to a major second.*
4. 3–5 *A minor third to a perfect fifth.*
7. 5–8 *A minor sixth to an octave.*
10. 10+ *A minor ninth to a major fourteenth* (an octave and a major seventh) .
13. 16+ *Two octaves or more.*

Line 21. Interval width.

The coder should listen for the kinds of intervals that occur in the melody of the song. Intervals sounded in chords are not considered. Intervals that occur between the end of one phrase and the beginning of the next are not considered.

Logically, the best way to determine the prominence of any kind of interval is to count the number of times it occurs. Since this procedure is time consuming, and, in fast music, almost impossible, it is suggested that the coder make a subjective estimate instead. Actual counting may be resorted to if no subjective decision seems reliable.

1. ø *Monotone.* No intervals occur. The song remains on approximately one pitch throughout. A polyphonic song should be coded "monotone" if each part stays at the same pitch level throughout.
4. w *Narrow intervals.* Intervals of a half step or less are prominent (though not necessarily dominant) in the song. Intervals found in embellishments should be considered as well as intervals between main notes of the melody. Even when whole steps predominate in the song, code w if smaller intervals are outstandingly important. When small intervals are prominent but thirds or larger intervals actually predominate, double-code for w and either W or *W*.
7. w *Diatonic intervals.* Whole steps predominate; half steps may occur, but not prominently. Thirds, fourths, or fifths may occur prominently, but not so often as whole steps and half steps.[11]
10. W *Wide intervals.* Intervals of a third occur more frequently than other intervals.
13. *W Very wide intervals.* Intervals of a fourth and a fifth or larger predominate.[12]

[11] w appears on the coding sheet as an underlined w.
[12] W appears on the coding sheet as an underlined W.

Line 22. Polyphonic type.

The use of simultaneously produced intervals other than the unison or octave. Two part "chords" are considered polyphony, as well as harmonies of greater complexity. Simultaneously produced intervals can also occur in *Heterophony* (see above, page 44). Therefore, polyphony should be coded only if one of the following situations is perceived: (1) "chords" are heard often enough so that it is obvious that "part-singing" is taking place; (2) "chords" are infrequent, polyphony is coded only if they recur in some consistent way; (3) in intermediate cases, the length of the chords is relevant—if they tend to last about as long as the important melody notes, it is likely that true polyphony exists; if they are ephemeral, the case is probably heterophonic. The line is arranged so that the degree of harmonic complexity and integration increases roughly from left to right.

1. ∅ *No polyphony.*
3. Dr *Drone polyphony.* One or more tones are held or repeated while the melody follows its own course. The drone part (or parts) need not necessarily remain on the same level throughout the song. The pitch of the drone can be shifted, while another part moves freely around it. Do not code drone polyphony when the drone effect is only a transitory one.
6. Ic *Isolated chords.* Chords occur in a texture which is basically unison. Two different chords rarely succeed one another. In some cases there may be only one chord in each section. If this chord tends to recur at the same point in each repeat, the song is coded Ic. If not, the song should not be considered polyphonic.
8. Pc *Parallel chords.* Two or more parts moving parallel to one another at intervals other than the octave or unison. The distance between the parts does not have to be maintained at exactly the same interval throughout, as long as the general movement is parallel.
10. H *Harmony.* Contrary motion occurs. Some parts move downward while others move upward. This may happen within the general context of parallel movement. As long as there is some significant amount of contrary motion, H should be coded.
13. C *Counterpoint.* Two or more parts which are rhythmically and melodically independent. In all other cases except drone polyphony, the parts move together rhythmically. In C, as distinct from Dr, the parts are active melodically. C is coded when at least two parts are rhythmically active and contrastive.

Sometimes two types of polyphony occur at the same time. Isolated chords or parallel chords may occur with drone polyphony. A chorus that is singing parallel chords may be in counterpoint with a leader singing a free melody, etc. In such cases, both types should be coded.

Line 23. The degree of embellishment used by the singer(s).

Embellishment is one of several devices used by the performer as a kind of qualification of or ornamentation upon the "basic" melodic line. Other forms of ornament which we have included in this coding system are tremolo (see Line 30) and glottal shake (see Line 31). Of the three here included, embellishment is closest to the melodic dimension, tremolo and glottal shake being more closely connected with vocal qualifiers.

An embellished melodic line contains two entirely distinct kinds of note value, the "embellishment" part being much more rapid and ephemeral than the melodic part. In conventional music notation, embellishments are generally written as "grace notes"—notes smaller in size than the notes delineating the "basic" melody line—and are given no definite time value.

The coder who is not familiar with notation should first try to identify the "basic" notes of the song. These are the notes which seem the most essential in the melody—if one of them were omitted, the shape of the melody would be seriously affected or destroyed. The coder should listen for any very rapid, relatively weightless notes that may be inserted between the basic notes. These are the embellishments. Their effect is to color the song in a special way. If they were omitted, the melody would lose much of its atmosphere and feeling but the overall melodic shape would not be altered.

Although embellishment may be found in intimate association with glissando (see Line 28), rubato (see Line 26), and melisma (see Line 29), remember that it should be coded without reference to them. In some styles embellishment and glottal activity are combined. In such cases the coder should record his judgment about the relative strength of each on the two lines. In some choral singing, all singers may not use the same degree of embellishment. The leader, for example, may sing with much embellishment, while the chorus uses none. In such cases, both degrees should be noted on the coding line.

    1. *E Extreme embellishment.*[13]
    4. E *Much embellishment.*
    7. *e A considerable amount of embellishment.*[14]
   10. e *Some embellishment.*
   13. ε *Little or no embellishment.*[15]

[13] *E* appears on the coding sheet as an underlined E.
[14] *e* appears on the coding sheet as an underlined e.
[15] ε appears on the coding sheet as a slashed e.

Line 24. Tempo.

Determining the absolute tempo of a song is a much more complex matter than setting a metronome. Before a metronome marking can be assigned, a song must be transcribed, and a specific note value chosen as the unit of beat. In many cases, however, the beat is ambiguous. With a song in 4/4 time, for example, one may not be able to decide whether the quarter-note or the half-note is the unit of beat. If the quarter-note value equals 120 beats per minute, the half-note equals 60. Thus a decision to use the quarter- rather than the half-note as the unit of beat would double the speed, as it is read from the metronome mark. Such a margin of error is too great for our purposes.

The solution we arrived at was to use a subjective scale from "very fast" to "very slow," with gradations between. Probably the surest way to get the feel of the tempo is to sing along with the record and make this experience the basis of judgment. Despite the apparent simplicity of this approach, it works quite well in practice, producing few difficulties for the coder and generally resulting in no more than one-point differences of judgment among different coders.

In some styles of singing, tempo changes occur. In such cases double coding is in order. If an item ranges through several tempi, the extremes only should be coded.

1. t— *Extremely slow.*
3. t- *Quite slow.*
5. t *Slow.*
9. *t Medium tempo.* The music moves at a neutral pace which sounds neither fast nor slow.[16]
11. T *Fast.*
13. *T Very fast.*[17]

Line 25. Volume.

As in the previous line, a subjective scale proved to be more useful than any conceivable objective technique. The precise degree of volume in any given recording is affected by so many factors that a decibel count would be meaningless unless every stage of both the recording and the playback were subject to the most rigorous control. On the other hand, the human-ear-plus-mind is capable of distinguishing loudness or softness as psychological effects, with scant reference to their measurable volume. Anyone who has had the experience of adjusting the volume control of a radio, phonograph, or television set knows how easy it is for the ear to determine the level of volume appropriate to a given sound-signal. It is this level of auditory aware-

[16] *t* appears on the coding sheet as an underlined t.
[17] *T* appears on the coding sheet as an underlined T.

ness that is required of the coder. He must distinguish from among five different broad levels of loudness the one that seems most appropriate to attribute to any given performance. If the degree of loudness varies sharply within a song, two degrees (the extremes) should be coded. If loudness varies, but not to any considerable degree, or only as the result of the natural differences between attack and production of a stable tone, or as the result of shortness of breath at the ends of phrases, etc., the coder should decide which level of volume seems most characteristic of the song as a whole and code for that volume only.

1. pp *Very soft.*
4. p *Soft.*
7. N *Mid-volume.*
10. f *Loud.*
13. ff *Very loud.*

Line 26. Rubato in the voice part.

This line permits the coder to record his judgment about how strictly tempo is maintained during a performance. A four-point scale ranges from no rubato (or strict tempo) to extreme rubato (or a rhythmic situation that is handled very freely). The coder must determine an underlying, steady beat and then the degree to which the performance strictly adheres to it or deviates from it. If there is strict conformity to the beat, code "no rubato." If there is a small amount of freedom—for example, if pauses of irregular length occur between sections or stanzas of the melody—we generally code "some rubato." If there is even more rhythmic freedom, code "much rubato." If there is no beat at all, so that the song has already been coded Rpa on Line 11, "extreme rubato" should be automatically coded.

If the song is in two parts which are contrastive in this respect, or if some of the singers use substantially more rubato than others, then double-coding is in order.

1.))) *Extreme rubato.*
5.)) *Much rubato.*
9.) *Some rubato.*
13. ø *No rubato.* Strict time.

Line 27. Rubato in the instruments.

The same as Line 26, but applied to the accompanying instruments.

1.))) *Extreme rubato.*
5.)) *Much rubato.*
9.) *Some rubato.*
13. ø *No rubato.* Strict time.

Line 28. Glissando.

This term is used to designate the effect created when the voice slides from one tone to another, passing through all the intermediate pitch levels. Listen for the number of tone changes that are accompanied by glissando and the degree of prominence of this effect in the whole performance.

  1. (((*Maximal glissando.* Glissando is *highly* prominent.
  5. ((*Glissando is prominent.*
  9. (*Some glissando.*
13. ø *No glissando.*

Line 29. Melisma.

The same syllable sung to (or stretched over) two or more basic notes of the melody. Thus, a song is very melismatic when each syllable is "stretched out" over several different pitches, as in the coloratura sections of many Italian operatic arias or in elaborate forms of Gregorian Chant. A song is non-melismatic or "syllabic" if it is sung mostly one note per syllable. The frequency of unarticulated pitch changes is a rough measure of the degree of melisma. Glottal shakes, tremolos, and embellishments should not be considered articulated pitch changes. Care should be taken to distinguish between embellishment and melisma.

  1. M *Most of the pitch changes are unarticulated.*
  7. m *Some of the pitch changes are unarticulated.*
13. ø *Syllabic.* All of the pitch changes are articulated.

Line 30. Tremolo.

A quavering or shaking in the voice that is heard as undulation between two closely adjacent pitches or tone colors. Tremolo is usually discernible only on notes that are held for an appreciable length of time. Thus, the coder is advised to listen for held notes and observe the degree to which undulations (if any) are used by the singer.

It is difficult to draw the line between vibrato and tremolo. For our purposes, any quaver of the voice which is audible as such is considered tremolo. If the undulation is so finely controlled and so narrow in pitch (as in normal vibrato) that it is heard as a constant aspect of the singer's voice quality *rather than* a quaver of the voice, it is not considered tremolo.

  1. TR *Tremolo is heavy throughout the song.*
  7. tr *Tremolo is present and noticeable, but relatively slight.*
13. ø *Little or no tremolo.*

Line 31. Glottal shake.

Code here for glottal stops, glottal trills, considerable amounts of glottal articulation, forceful glottal articulation, glottal stroke, and strongly emphasized, wide vibrato from deep in the throat. While tremolo is a wavering sustained tone, akin to the vibrato which appears to accompany much singing as an acoustic feature, the features coded as *glottal* seem to be the product of a noticeably more forceful activity in the pharyngeal or glottal area. Some singers actually manipulate their Adam's apple with their fingers to produce this effect. If in doubt, the coder should attempt to reproduce the sound. Such simulation will assist him in distinguishing between these intermittent, highly emphasized and forceful phonations, and others which would be tagged tremolo, embellishment, or normal vibrato.

   1. GL *Strongly characterized by glottal activity.*
   7. gl *Glottal activity present and noticeable.*
 13. ø *Little or no noticeable glottal activity.*

Note regarding Lines 32–37: There is no agreed-upon terminology to describe the qualities of either the speaking or singing voice, nor is there yet any body of accepted theory to explain or describe, either in acoustic or physiological terms, where and how these qualities are generated. This is an area where voice teachers, speech pathologists, psychologists, linguists, and laryngologists take diverse views.

Folk singers do not sing naturally, like birds. All singing is learned behavior. Every field collector discovers this anew as he reorients his ear and his preferences in order to enjoy and to study the singing style of a new culture. As one surveys the whole range of recorded data, it becomes evident that each culture area sets rigid standards for the voice qualities of its chosen singers, and that these vocal models seem to pattern and limit other dimensions of the musical systems they project. In broad and intensive listening, the student encounters a wide variety of vocalizing styles, discovering that he can place singers culturally by voice quality alone.

The recorded data indicate that voice qualities frowned on by Western teachers are important in the aesthetics of other singing styles. Rasp and nasality, qualities which are anathema to the European voice teacher, play an essential part in certain singing styles. Cantometrics, therefore, takes a more catholic and less pejorative view of the singing voice than is normal to most Western students of the voice. The scales were chosen after extensive discussion with a laryngologist and a psycholinguist. They are admittedly preliminary and impressionistic, but work by two coders has indicated a fair amount of consensus in most cases. Furthermore, their consistent application has produced classes of singing style which seem to conform to the distributions of other cantometric patterns and to culture areas. This is a field which clearly cries out for intensive, many-faceted research.

Perhaps the best practical coding approach is what Dr. Paul Moses, the voice pathologist, termed "creative listening." This means listening carefully, trying to reproduce the heard quality, locating it in one's own vocal mechanism, and *then* analyzing it.

Line 32. Register.

The coder must make a judgment about the "natural" placement of the voice of the performer and then decide whether the singer is sticking to the middle of his range, singing at the upper or lower end of it, or pushing it to one or both extremes. It is best to begin by using the rating scale in a fairly naive way, trusting one's first reactions in coding and gradually improving one's judgment by practice. Human beings constantly react to register in conversation. This facility of the inner ear has only to be made conscious to become a tool for the analysis of singing. Double-code when more than one register is used by one singer, or when two singers are using different registers.

1. V–Hi *Very high.* Usually falsetto in men.
4. Hi *High.* Usually head register.
7. Mid. *Mid-voice.*
10. Low *Low.* Usually sung "in the chest."
13. V–Low *Very low.* The singer is probably producing his lowest tones.

Line 33. Vocal width.

Vocal width has to do with a scale, ranging at the extremes from a very pinched, narrow, squeezed voice to the very wide and open-throated singing tone of Swiss yodelers. This quality is the product of a set of dimensions within the vocal apparatus which includes:

a. The distance from the outside of the lips to the back of the oral cavity.
b. The width of the opening of the throat.
c. The opening of the glottis.
d. The relative tension of the glottal region.

When all these dimensions are at their largest and most relaxed, the individual is breathing deeply and naturally with a wide-open mouth. At the other extreme there is maximum constriction of all vocal dimensions (vomiting or ventriloquism). Between these two extremes we code five degrees of vocal width or narrowness. The following definitions have grown out of experiments with "creative listening" (see above).

1. V–NA *Very narrow.* The most narrow, squeezed, thin, and tense voices. The vocal cavities are narrowed and constricted by raising the glottis, raising the tongue and pulling it back, and tensing the muscles in the throat.
3. NA *Narrow.* A markedly squeezed, narrow, and tense voice.
6. Sp *Speaking.* A voice that corresponds to a speaking tone normal for most English-speaking Americans, where intermittent, but pro-

nounced tenseness and narrowness often gives rise to a hard, grating quality.

8. Wi *Wide*. A relaxed, open-throated voice, usually evincing a considerable amount of resonance and richness. This latter quality can be obscured by nasalization.
10. V–Wi *Very wide*. A wide-open, resonant, often ringing or liquid voice.
13. Yodel. A distinctively liquid, wide-open, and extremely relaxed way of singing, often, but not necessarily, characterized by quick, wide, and apparently effortless leaps in pitch which pass from chesty tone to falsetto (or head tone) and back again.

Line 34. Nasalization.

Traditionally, nasal tone has been described as one produced by a speaker with a cleft palate or a bad cold, or as a sound produced when the soft palate drops and air is forced through the nose. The sound produced is "honky" or "twangy." Lately, however, investigators have realized that the sound of nasality can be heard when none of these conditions is satisfied. Certain kinds of intonation seem to activate the nasal passages in ways that are only perceptible to the ear. At any rate, twangy, honky, nasalized tone is a strong characterizer of some singing styles even in the absence of nasal syllables, probably because singing is normally louder and more forceful than speaking. When a wide sample of recorded song is examined, the absence of nasalization in some styles is also striking. For this reason we decided to code for "nasalization" in spite of the vagueness of the term. Although there has been considerable difference of opinion as to which of the five points to use, there has been good consensus on the presence of great nasality or its relative absence. Until further acoustic studies define the nature of the various types and degrees of nasalization, the coder must depend upon his ear and upon "creative listening."

In order to determine the degree of nasality it is suggested that the coder listen to long vowels such as *oh, ah, ee,* etc., which are not preceded or followed by a nasal consonant. If these seem to be nasalized, one can be sure that nasalization is present in some degree.

We have not attempted to distinguish between the degree of nasalization present in the language as spoken and sung. If we knew that a high degree of nasalization characterized the speech of the singers and also occurred in their singing as well, we still coded great nasalization. Where great nasalization shows up both in speech and in song, as in the case of much of French vocalization, this is simply a steady vocal signal in this culture, and perhaps an index to a certain emotional set.

1. V–NAS *Extreme nasalization*. Strongly nasalized throughout the performance.

4. GT. *Marked nasalization*, with clear-cut but not extreme nasality running throughout the performance.

7. Intermit. *Intermittent nasality*. Nasality which occurs irregularly but clearly in the voice, as is frequently the case with singers of African origin. This is also the midpoint in the line and may be coded for songs which seem to be neither marked nor slight in their degree of nasality.

10. Slight *Occasional touches of nasalization* which do not occur in relationship to nasal consonants. This situation is encountered, for example, in the singing of many groups of Central Europe.

13. None *Little or no nasalization;* that is, songs in which nasalization occurs only in connection with nasal consonants or in which nasal consonants tend to be eliminated and little or no nasalization is heard.

Line 35. Raspiness.

There is as yet no measure of the presence of the several familiar vocal qualities one calls hoarseness, harshness, grating, buzzing, etc., except in extreme or pathological cases. For this reason we decided to lump all these throaty, roughening voice qualities under one heading of "raspiness." We could just as well have spoken of "throatiness" or "harshness." Perhaps, with more precise work by the visible speech machine or some refinement thereof, we may be able to distinguish among several kinds of throaty noises.

Raspiness is frequently associated with extremely marked and forced vocalizing; however, it is quite possible to sing with enormous volume, as do Western opera singers, without introducing any degree of raspiness. On the contrary, a number of primitive peoples seem to use rasp in a relaxed way. Their intention may be to produce an animal-like growling or roaring sound, thus identifying with the animal world. Other singers use deep chesty vibrato, which produces the effect of rasp. This type of vocalizing may stand for the commanding masculine leader, the voice of authority, the tone of the chief or the military commander. It cuts through and dominates musical performances in which everyone is singing very loudly with a loud accompaniment. In many parts of the world, performers sing in a grating tone, forcefully emphasizing consonants. The result is clearer articulation, but often a noisier tonal image. Code for the presence of any or all of these qualities.

1. Ext *Extreme raspiness*. An extremely harsh, hoarse, raspy, grating voice.

4. GT. *Great*. Pronounced raspiness, less harsh than above.

7. Intermit. *Intermittent rasp*. A voice midway between pronounced and slight rasp.

10. Slight *Perceptible touches of rasp.*

13. None *Voices which lack rasp.*

Line 36. Accent.

Here code the strength of the attack on sung tones in a given sample. Certain singers—American Indians, for instance—force out the first note in every small phrase with great muscular drive. At the other extreme there are singers who use barely perceptible accents. Between these two extremes we code for three other degrees of relative force or relaxation of attack.

1. V–Force *Very forceful accent or attack,* with powerful accents falling on most notes or on the main pulses of the meter.
4. Fo *A markedly forceful attack,* with strong accents falling on the main pulses of the meter.
7. Normal *A moderate attack* which conforms to the main beat pattern of the meter, clearly outlining but not exaggerating it.
10. Relaxed *A relaxed, unemphatic attack*—a lazy handling of the accent pattern.
13. V–Re *Very relaxed, almost unaccented rhythmic motion* in which a flowing, sometimes understated, melodic line is produced.

Line 37. Enunciation of consonants.

Here code the degree of precision of enunciation of consonants as against the other extreme of the parameter—a slurring of all the syllables. In order to establish a sense of this parameter, the coder should speak or sing in the most articulately over-enunciated manner he can manage and then gradually diminish the distinctness of his pronunciation of each word until the syllables run lazily together with a minimum of clarity.

1. V–Prec. *Very precise.* Highly articulated enunciation, which generally characterizes the vocalizing of story-telling singers found in Europe and the Orient.
4. Pre. *Precisely or clearly articulated* enunciation of the consonants in the sung texts. Here one listens to the whole consonantal range and makes certain that all consonants are easily discernible.
7. No. *Normal.* A "normally clear" pattern of enunciation in singing. It must be remembered that clear enunciation in singing is bound to be less well articulated than in speaking.
10. *Slurred.* Consonants are hard to distinguish and syllables are run together to a considerable extent. A good deal of primitive singing is slurred.
13. V–Slur *Very slurred.* A condition in which consonants are absent from the text and/or in which syllables are run together so that they are virtually indistinguishable as such.

4

The World Song Style Map

Alan Lomax and Edwin E. Erickson

A PRIME aim of cantometrics, as a scheme of descriptive and systematic comparison, is the establishment of a structurally and historically meaningful taxonomy of the world's folk song styles. Early in the development of the research, when less than half the working sample of 2,557 songs had been coded, Lomax and Grauer discovered, from simple inspection of modal profiles, that cantometric descriptions of song style mapped the world in a way clearly congruent with the major cultural distributions. Proceeding from this discovery and from our ruling hypothesis, that song style reinforces and expresses the major abiding themes of culture, we set out to show that the patterning of similarities and dissimilarities among contemporary styles reproduces a faithful picture of world ethnohistory.

The taxonomy that has emerged from the coded descriptions of our song sample, though not yet in final form, generally meets this expectation. It consists of regional style units thousands of miles broad and, from a scrutiny of the available archeology and ethnohistory, millennia deep. Moreover, relationships within and between the regional units appear laden with historical detail, ranging from recent, well-documented events to very old and scarcely understood distributions of peoples and cultural features. In this chapter, we shall present the results thus far achieved as well as the logic and method of procedure.

METHOD

The basic units, both in exploration and in the taxonomy set forth here, are samples averaging about 40 songs apiece, drawn from each of the 56 culture areas into which we have divided the world, largely following Murdock (1962–1967). The samples, though by no means exhaustive, were presumed to be representative of the modes and ranges of style in their areas. For a given sample, that is, the modal attributes on each of the coded lines were taken to stand for the salient features of a dominant areal style, and the statistically significant dispersions around such modes were taken to express the range of variability in the style.

Any attempt to cast 56 multi-song samples, described in 37 ways, into a scheme of ordered relationship encounters the classic dilemmas of the taxonomist. How much of the available information is to enter the classification? How is the scheme to be made with sufficient detail to bring out significant variations, yet simple enough to be comprehensible? Distributions of small numbers of attributes do, in many cases, produce orderly mappings of song style. For example, songs combining wordy and precise text, embellishment, free rhythm, and long phrases can be shown to map, very specifically, the heartland of Eurasian civilization. Similarly, those combining repetitious and slurred texts, forceful and noisy vocalizations, and strophic melodic forms are confined largely to Amerindia. But no such small subset of attributes will map the entire world. The subsets just described, although they single out specific regions, are entirely useless in comparisons among regions where they do not occur.

The obvious way out of the dilemma is to use all, or most, of the available information and to introduce simplicity by folding that information into a scalar measure of similarity between pairs of style samples. This approach entails a systematic line-by-line comparison for each pair of style samples in the 56-member set of the distributions of attributes, calculating a percentage figure of similarity for each line comparison, then taking an arithmetic mean to form a single percentage score of similarity. With such scores, based on a single, universally applied yardstick calculated for every pair, it is possible to proceed to a mechanical clustering, grouping similar style samples in homogeneous sets, and separating sets that are relatively dissimilar.

Clearly, to calculate a similarity score between two samples of about 40 songs each, based on multistate measurements over many variables, is feasible only with a computer. Berkowitz gives a full technical description of his similarity program in Appendix 1. At this point, we shall offer only a description of its logic.

The comparisons of single song pairs and of pairs of song styles (i.e., multi-song samples) present different sorts of problems. In the first case, the similarity score can be computed simply as a function of absolute scale values (for example, Line 1, point 5; Line 2, point 13; . . . vs. Line 1, point 7; Line 2, point 9; . . .). In the second case, the comparison is more complicated. Looking at two hypothetical samples, one might note, for instance, that the first contains a predominance of diffuse choral performances (Line 5, points 4 and 7), the second a predominance of cohesive performances (Line 5, points 10 and 13). Almost certainly, however, there will be songs falling away from the modes in both styles. Consequently, the interstyle similarity measure must take into account ranges and relative frequencies. The comparison,

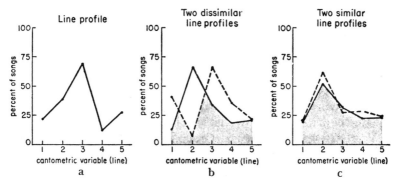

Fig. 7. Line profile and profile similarity. a: A line profile is the percentage distribution of a song sample on all attributes of the coding line. b: The dissimilarity of these two profiles is apparent in the predominance of the unshaded area between them. c: The basic similarity of these two profiles is apparent in the predominance of the shaded area shared by both. Line similarity is measured by: Common area under curves/Total area under curves. Total similarity is: The sum of line similarities/The number of lines compared.

then, is made on composite (or line) profiles—in effect, the graphs of relative frequencies of attributes over variables. Figure 7a illustrates a composite profile of a hypothetical variable in a hypothetical style sample. The abscissa on this graph represents the coding line (here divided into five attributes, or points) and the ordinate is marked off in percentage units. Thus, each point on the curve represents the percentage of frequency of the attribute over which it lies.

In Figure 7b and c, we have illustrated the logic of profile comparison. Here, music resumes its classic relationship to geometry, for in comparing song styles on a specific coding parameter, we are actually comparing sizes and shapes. It is easy to see that the two profiles in Figure 7b are far less similar to each other than are those in Figure 7c. In both cases, the similarity between profiles can be expressed as the ratio of the common area under the curves to the total area under the curves, that is, the ratio of the shaded area to the sum of the shaded and unshaded areas. Since the distributions are defined only at the points and the area under each profile is standardized to 100 percent, the computer merely evaluates minima at each point, then enters these in the formula for the similarity calculation. When all variables in the two styles under comparison are thus evaluated, the resulting scores are averaged to form the total similarity score.

The similarity program originally used the raw frequencies of every attribute on all 37 coding lines. Even though, in this form, the program yielded generally satisfactory statements of style similarity, it was apparent that, with a few modifications, the results could be markedly improved. Inspection of rank-order listouts and distribution maps indicated that certain lines produced little or no clustering on either a regional or a cultural-functional basis. Also, redundancies of measurement between certain lines tended to produce undue skewings (for example, Lines 26 and 27 of the coding worksheet: Vocal Rubato and Orchestral Rubato). To meet these problems we removed certain lines from the calculation. The remaining set of 27 lines on which the similarities presented here are based consists of the following:

1. Vocal Group, 3. Orchestral Group, 4. Vocal Organization, 5. Tonal Blend—Voices, 6. Rhythmic Blend—Voices, 7. Orchestral Organization, 10. Words to Nonsense, 11. Overall Rhythm—Voices, 12. Group Rhythm— Voices, 13. Overall Rhythm—Orchestra, 14. Group Rhythm—Orchestra, 16. Melodic Form, 16a. Melodic Variation, 17. Phrase Length, 18. Number of Phrases, 20. Range, 21. Interval Width, 23. Embellishment, 26. Rubato— Voices, 29. Melisma, 30. Tremolo, 31. Glottal Shake, 33. Voice Width, 34. Nasality, 35. Raspiness, 36. Accent, 37. Consonants.

Another problem arose from the extreme skewing of certain attribute distributions. Looking, for example, at the world distribution on Line 26, Vocal Rubato, one notes that this quality is rare, except in a very few styles. As the calculation was first conceived, the negative condition, "little or no rubato," so common around the world as to be virtually irrelevant, was given equal weight with its positive, and highly significant opposite, "much rubato." To correct for this sort of skewing, Berkowitz and Erickson modified the calculation by weighting the contribution of each attribute to the similarity score by a factor inversely proportional to the world frequency for the attribute. Thus, an overlapping distribution on a rare attribute counts for relatively more than one on a common attribute (for the precise method of weighting, see Appendix 1).

We have several approaches for the discovery of clusters and cleavages in the similarity matrix. One of our basic computer formats is the similarity wave which is a simple rank-order listout for each style sample of all similarities down to some cutoff point, such as the quartile (Table 2). This format facilitates a quick search for recurrent patterns of shared similarity. On the samples given in Table 2, for example, note the high similarity linking the Andes and Interior Amazonia and the high positions occupied in both patterns by Mexico and Guiana. In broader view, this four-member cluster forms the center of a pivotal stylistic nexus in Amerindia. An expanded version of the similarity wave, called *Total Similarity-Homogeneity Analysis* (TISHA) provides not only the rank-order listout for each sample, but also a summary statement of similarity to some bigger unit, for example, a hypothesized style region. Another program, called *Forcing Factors,* dissects the similarity

Table 2. *Sample similarity wave listout.*

Areas with profiles most similar to 105 Andes

Similarity (percent)	Areas
80	107 Interior Amazonia, 203 Mexico
78	115 Guiana
75	113 Eastern Brazil, 217 Northeast Coast
74	109 Mato Grosso, 117 Caribbean, 119 Central America, 407 New Guinea
73	307 Himalayas, 405 Australia, 301 Arctic Asia

Areas with profiles most similar to 107 Inner Amazonia

Similarity (percent)	Areas
82	115 Guiana
80	105 Andes, 113 Eastern Brazil, 407 New Guinea
79	203 Mexico
78	219 Arctic America
76	119 Central America, 205 Southwestern Hunters, 215 California, 217 Northwest Coast, 301 Arctic Asia

score and lists out, in rank order, the relative contribution of each cantometric line to the total similarity.

More recently, we have begun to experiment with factor analysis, using a correlation of mean-line scores, for the automatic extraction of style clusters. This technique has shown promise in application to cultural (as opposed to areal) samples within style regions. The new approach, though not yet fully worked out technically, appears to replicate, in greater detail, the style groupings described here for Amerindian areas. A summary of results is set forth briefly at the end of this chapter.

The cantometric taxonomy of world folk song is cast into several very large style regions. In the process of sorting the smaller culture areas into regions, using the similarity program and its adjuncts, there was more confirmation than discovery. Lomax and Grauer's early basis of regional classification was similar in outline to the one presented here; it was based on simple visual inspections of hand-drawn profiles. Their principal findings were: (1) a dominating style pattern linking the entire North African-Eurasian heartland from the Mediterranean to East Asia; (2) a distinctive North American Indian profile with clear traces in South America; (3) consistent and unique patterns in Australia, Polynesia, and New Guinea; (4) the remarkable contrapuntal style of the little African Hunters, closely akin to a highly homogeneous black African style tradition that reproduced itself in America; (5) three distinctive and equally stable European traditions—Old or Central and Eastern, Mediterranean (linked to the East), and West Europe with its spillover into the New World (Lomax, 1955–1956, 1962; Grauer, 1965). As the sample grew and geographic gaps were filled in and the similarity program was developed, the clusters found by the computer largely confirmed and refined this early taxonomy. The statistical approach on which the final regional taxonomy is based, however, provides a powerful confirmation. Moreover, it brings into relief a wealth of detail, an intricate multileveled pattern of relationships which, because of its complexity, could never have been discovered by ear.

The final establishment of style regions was made in three steps. The first sorting placed the areal style samples within what might be called their "great traditions," as defined in the early Lomax-Grauer classifications. In most cases, this was merely a matter of retaining Lomax's revision of the geography in the *Ethnographic Atlas* (see Chapter 2 for revised classification). Next there were regroupings across obvious style gradients. Thus, for example, Indonesia, Malaysian Borneo, and the Philippines were moved out of the Insular Pacific and into the great Afro-Eurasian style set, in conformity with both ear judgments and similarity patterns. Finally, every area was subjected to a simple test by a scrutiny of its similarity wave to determine whether or not most of its top quartile similarities were with other areas in the region to which it had been assigned. An area failing this membership test was either shifted to an adjacent region, if it met the criterion there, or it was held aside as an isolate.

THE STYLE REGIONS

The resulting classification yielded six large regions, all macro-historical units, and three troublesome but interesting isolates:

1. *North America* and
2. *South America* (bounded at the Isthmus of Tehuantepec).
3. The *Insular Pacific*, drawn to exclude *Australia*, which could not be sorted statistically and was therefore held aside as an isolate.
4. *Africa*, from which we have excluded most of what the *Ethnographic Atlas* designates as circum-Mediterranean, except for Ethiopia and the Moslem Sudan, but in which we included Madagascar and Afro-America.
5. *Europe*, a single style region from the Caucasus to the Atlantic, excepting the Lapps, but including overseas Anglo-America, French Canada, and Ibero-America.
6. *Old High Culture*, the name coined for the great Afro-Eurasian region embracing the style continuity discovered by Lomax (1959, 1962).

Spreading from North Africa to East Asia and Malaysia, this region of early civilization and empire includes all the principal zones of influence at its margins, as well as the enclaves of tribal peoples not fully integrated to their national borders. It is touched by the broad musical style heritage. Two areas within the geographic boundaries of the region failed all membership tests and therefore joined the list of isolates: Arctic Asia (including, on the compelling grounds of style similarity, the Lapps) and Tribal India (consisting only of the widely separated Abors and Muria Gonds).

To set forth the relationships within and among style regions, we have designed a highly schematized world map, on which each of the 56 areas, grouped into the six grand style regions, is represented as a labeled box. One of these maps, using the following manner of construction, was prepared for each region and each isolate:

1. A computer search was made over the top quartile of similarities for each of the component areas of the region under study, to determine which of the 56 world areas were represented. The frequency of appearance of each of these areas was then calculated as a percentage of the number of areas within the region.

2. A cutoff was then established. In all but one case this was set at the minimum percentage registered for any area lying within the region.

3. Those areas, both within and outside the region, meeting the minimum percentage criterion (i.e., lying at or above the cutoff) were considered to be significantly similar in style to the region, and the boxes representing them were shaded and labeled with their percentage figures. The map thus constructed expresses the style homogeneity of the given region: the higher the percentage figures within the region and the less frequent the occurrence of shaded boxes outside the region, the more uniform and self-contained is its style.

Throughout what follows, stylistic affinities among and within regions are discussed largely in historical and distributional terms, with little direct attention to the cultural settings in which the styles have developed and diffused. This frame of reference is only a matter of convenience and does not represent the sum of our thinking on the nature of interstyle relationships. In later chapters of this volume we show that the most diagnostic traits of song performance are representations and reinforcements of essential aspects of social structure. Each style, then, necessarily symbolizes a specific way of life and flowers out of, or diffuses into, those areas where it is an appropriate statement of the everyday behavior of the majority of its carriers. Since we do not yet understand how whole song styles vary with whole culture patterns, we do not discuss the matter in this volume, although we can see that style and culture vary together as wholes. From this point of view, the historical process of style and trait diffusion is the result of the spread of social and economic systems or of their powerful influence upon other cultures.

NOTE ON MODAL PROFILES

The profile of South America that appears in Figure 8 and those on subsequent pages permit a quick, visual appraisal and comparison of regional styles. On the righthand side of the field, where the ratings are entered by the coder, we have circled the most frequent trait and boxed the next most frequent. On the number field to the left, the profiles link those points which, taken together, compose the main singing style of the region. These profiles not only follow the dominant modes down the cantometric scale of measurements, but also match the principal patterns that the listener hears.

In a technical sense, what has been circled in the righthand symbol field is often a modal range rather than a modal point and these divide the lines into the attributes used to make correlation runs. Thus, the circles and boxes mark either modal points or ranges. On all lines where less than 75 percent of the sample falls at the mode, the next most dominant point or range is set in a box. Dotted lines indicate alternate modes of performance, but the main profile ordinarily represents the main performance style in the region, whether solo or choral, accompanied or unaccompanied.

In Appendix 3, the reader interested in the numerical data from which these profiles were sketched can find the summodal profiles in which the percentage of frequencies for all points on all parameters are given.

South America

Figure 9 illustrates the homogeneity and out-of-region links of South America. The region shows its historical unity in a general style that, though somewhat heterogeneous in its components, links clearly with those of North America and Arctic Asia. Patagonia, Central America, and some other areas show a low order of relationship within the region, and equal or higher relationships occur widely across North America and Siberia. Moreover, the similarity pattern reaches into the Pacific.

The map illustrates a pattern of relationships in close accord with the known or inferred outlines of history. It establishes the unity of Amerindia as a distinctive world region whose traces have persisted over more than 10,000 years of settlement in a vast area. It indicates Siberia as the point of contact between the New World and the Old and, rather more diffusely, implies the existence of a very old and generalized circum-Pacific historical nexus. Internally, the picture is one of specialized local styles, weakly similar

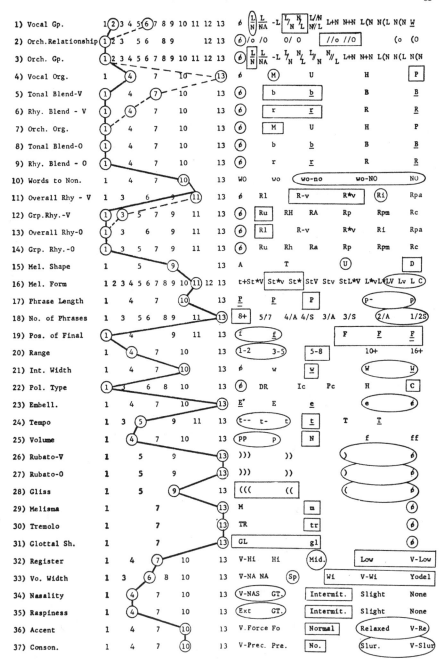

Fig. 8. Modal profile for South America: 230 songs. The solid line to the left sketches the main performance profile. The dashed line outlines the principal choral profile. In the symbol field on the right, the mode on each parameter is circled and the second area of activity on that parameter is set in a box. The reader may note a strong overall resemblance to the North American profile, except that polyphony is important in South America, brief melodic forms are more common, and North American song style is more forceful.

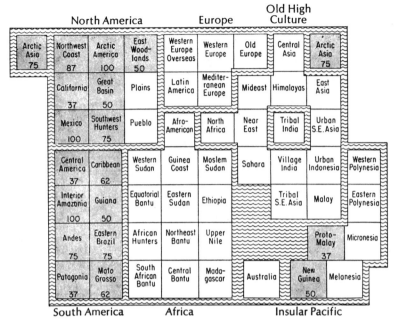

Fig. 9. Homogeneity mapping for South America.

to each other in the general frame of Amerindian unity. It is a pattern entirely consistent with the variety of cultural and ecological specializations, spanning the range from Andean empire builders to tropical horticulturists and Fuegian hunters. The pattern also appears to reflect in its diffuseness the physical barriers to the intercommunication of peoples posed by the Andean ranges and the tropical forests.

The regional profile of South America (Fig. 8) is in part a product of a number of dissimilar modes of song performance. There are certain features, however, that link it to North America and to the performance styles of many other primitive cultures. Chorally, the principal mode is acephalous unison, poorly blended in its tonal and rhythmic aspects; it is the product of a very raspy, harsh-voiced, glottal vocal attack. As in most of the primitive world, song texts consist largely of repetition and nonsense syllables with laxly articulated consonants, singers employ little or no embellishment or melisma, and use scales in which wide intervals of a third or more are prominent. Rhythmic organization, as in North America, runs to irregular meters with rhythmic unison in the chorus, set to a one-beat accompaniment, often loosely related to the voice part. Melodic formulas, however, are often simpler than in the north; brief one- or two-phrased litanies predominate, except among the Ge-speakers, whose melodies are often complex strophes or through-composed. Polyphonic singing, which is frequently diffusely organized counterpoint, occurs in South America especially along the eastern slopes of the Andes. In this area, too, one encounters an unemphatic, soft-voiced, subdued, feminine-sounding style, with a frequent use of harmony. Such singing can be heard in the backwoods of highland Peru (Q'eros) and from the Campa of the eastern Andean slopes, through Venezuela and Colombia, into southern Mexico among the Tzotzil. Otherwise we have coded this subdued, polyphonic, highly "feminized" style only in Tribal Oceania. It seems to be an ancient and specialized trans-Pacific model found along the paths that connect the cultures of the Andes with the civilizations of Mexico.

North America

The North American map (Fig. 10) shows an almost perfect homogeneity of style. The only significant links beyond its borders are in Eastern Brazil and Mato Grosso, reflecting the general Amerindian interconnection that appeared on the South American map. Further, the intra-regional similarity level is considerably higher than it was in South America. The generally high style homogeneity seems consonant with a history of long intrahemispheric isolation, combined with a relatively free passage of peoples and cultural traits across the whole continent.

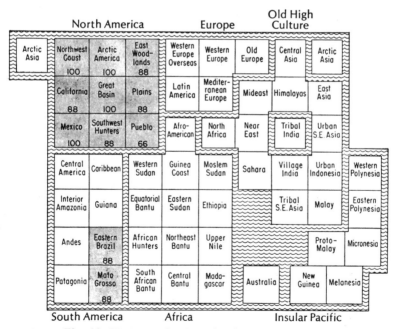

Fig. 10. Homogeneity mapping for North America.

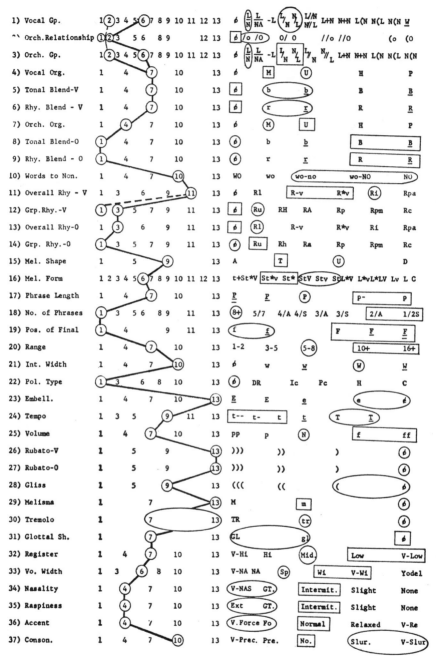

Fig. 11. Modal profile for North America: 374 songs. The dashed line indicates the importance of solo singing in North America—about 30 percent of this sample. Note the similarity to South America. The principal North Amerindian traits are: a strong preference for strophic songs with long phrases, a wider range, a more forceful and aggressive singing style, a more frequent use of accompanying orchestra, and a steady attachment to unison choral organization. In the rhythmic lines, 11–14, an attempt is made to indicate the two main rhythmic types: (1) choruses in irregular meter and rhythmic unison accompanied by a one-beat orchestra in rhythmic unison, and (2) solo in irregular meters, unaccompanied or accompanied by one instrument in a one-beat pattern.

A majority of North American Indian songs (Fig. 11) are sung in poorly blended unison, accompanied in unison by one or two simple percussive instruments. Texts run to repetition of chains of nonsense syllables, imprecisely enunciated. The rhythmic formula is irregular vocal meter, chorally organized in rhythmic unison, set to a steady one-beat accompaniment in the orchestra. Melodic forms are the longest and most complex employed in any large region of primitive culture. The strophe is the most frequent form, with complex strophes of many phrases quite common. As in much hunter-gatherer music, intervals of a third to a fifth are frequent and there is little ornamentation of any sort. The singer sticks strictly to the rhythm and to a syllabic style, with, however, some considerable use of quavering and glottal shake, the latter feature being a principal stylistic link between Amerindian and Siberian singing. This is the most masculine of song styles; it is low in register, and loudly and forcefully enunciated in a harsh nasal tone.

The Insular Pacific

The pattern illustrated in Figure 12 seems appropriate to a maritime world settled by a variety of widely spaced waves of migration. In cantometric terms, the region is quite homogeneous, considering the distance spanned by the far reaches of Formosa (here represented in Proto-Malay), Hawaii, and

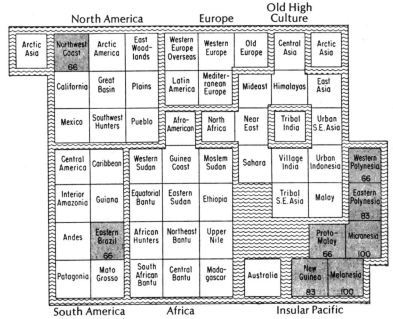

Fig. 12. Homogeneity mapping for the Insular Pacific.

New Zealand. Its underlying stylistic unity is further underscored by the fact that the New Guinea sample clearly belongs in the set, being connected to other parts of Oceania in a consistent network of high similarity; it is heavily freighted with songs from the highlands at the center of a large landmass far removed from the general maritime pattern.

In a generally high array of regional similarities, Micronesia and Melanesia appear to form a centroid. The similarity between these two areas is at the top of the regional distribution, and their average similarity to the rest of the region is also the highest (Fig. 13) ; this is especially true of Melanesia. Thus, our evidence suggests the existence in Melanesia and Micronesia of staging areas or pathways for the movement of peoples into the farther Pacific. Considering the archeological evidence developed by Shulter (1961) that Melanesia lay athwart the early principal lanes of Pacific voyaging, the structure of scores assumes at least a conjectural relevance (Table 3).

Table 3. *Intraregional similarity scores (in percent) of the Insular Pacific.*

	Proto-Malay	New Guinea	Micro-nesia	Mela-nesia	E. Poly-nesia	W. Poly-nesia
Proto-Malay	—	78	79	82	69	66
New Guinea	78	—	79	84	75	72
Micronesia	79	79	—	84	75	74
Melanesia	82	84	84	—	77	75
Eastern Polynesia	69	75	75	77	—	82
Western Polynesia	66	72	74	75	82	—

Only two areas outside the region, both Amerindian, met the criterion for inclusion on the Insular Pacific map. Nevertheless, the broader patterning of similarity outside its geographic boundaries merits brief consideration, for in detail it either reflects known history or is historically suggestive.

Documented history shows up in a strong statistical similarity (seconded by the listener's ear) linking the region to the area we have called Old Europe. Old Europe includes all of Eastern and Central Europe and, most noticeably, Moravia and other west-central areas from which the Euro-American religious singing drew strong influence during the eighteenth and nineteenth centuries. Protestant hymnals laden with four-part songs of Old European origin traveled with missionaries throughout the South Seas, and especially to Polynesia, where they were enthusiastically received by the Polynesians and gave rise to the hymene and hula styles of today. Statistically, the Old Europe similarity gradient reflects the historical priorities of missionary endeavor. Eastern and Western Polynesia bear by far the greatest similarity, scoring 81 and 79 percent, respectively; indeed, they are more similar to Old

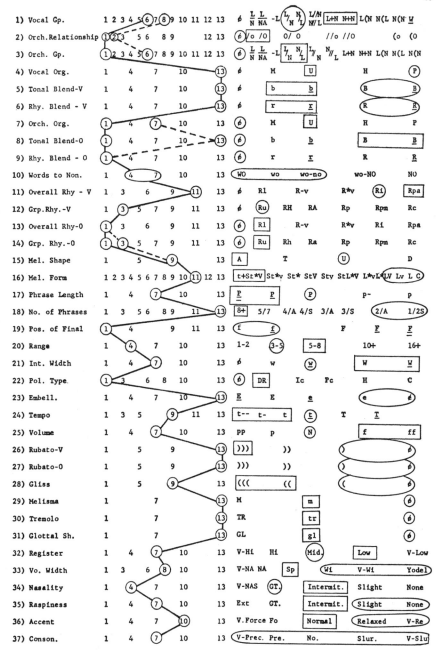

Fig. 13. Modal profile for the Insular Pacific: 309 songs. In this predominantly choral area, alter nation does not seem to be quite so important as simple unison, although a majority of choruses sing in parts and in good concert. Our sample was mostly unaccompanied. The accompaniments we did find were, most frequently, percussive—hand clapping or sticks. When only one type of percussive instrument is present in an orchestra, it is usually scored for good tonal blend. Note the presence of through-composed melodic forms sung to complex rhythms in conjunction with good tonal blend.

Europe than they are to the rest of the Insular Pacific. The similarity level drops progressively from Melanesia (74 percent), to Micronesia (70 percent), to New Guinea (69 percent), to Proto-Malay (64 percent).

Beyond the well-documented history of the peripatetic hymnal, the Old Europe similarity trace in the Insular Pacific responds to a further, though not contradictory, explanation. Codings from many of the most distant reaches of Oceania indicate that certain features common to the Old European style were almost surely present before contact with European explorers in the eighteenth century. The song traditions of Oceania and Old Europe share a distinctive cluster of traits—textual complexity plus precise enunciation plus cohesiveness plus polyphony—major features of Middle European folk hymnody (Lomax, 1962). This commonality of style pattern explains the ease and rapidity with which the pagan Polynesians adopted Protestant hymn style.

More suggestive than demonstrably historic is a cluster of high similarities placing most of Oceania in a very general but consistent circum-Pacific distribution with Amerindia and the tribal fringes of East Asia—Arctic Asia, Tribal Southeast Asia, and Malay. Top quartile similarities for areas in the circum-Pacific occur frequently throughout the region, except in Polynesia. Amerindia is most strongly represented in the top quartiles of Proto-Malay and New Guinea; the Asian tribal fringe appears most prominently in Proto-Malay and Micronesia.

Another line of similarities is indicated along the old Malayo-Indonesian track across the Indian Ocean. Madagascar, the Upper Nile, and the Western Sudan appear in the top quartiles of half the Insular Pacific sample. By far the strongest African resemblance is found in Polynesia.

Table 4 shows the most important patterns of similarity linking the Insular Pacific to Amerindia, Tribal Asia, Africa, and Europe. The search for significant similarities has been made, in this case, over the top third of ranked similarity scores for each of the six areas of the Insular Pacific. Thus,

Table 4. *Principal similarity links of the Insular Pacific. This table shows the number of areas represented in top third of similarity scores.*

	Amerindia	Tribal Asia (Arctic Asia, Tribal Southeast Asia, Malay)	Africa	Europe
Proto-Malay	7	2	3	—
New Guinea	8	1	4	—
Micronesia	3	3	4	2
Melanesia	5	1	6	2
Eastern Polynesia	2	0	11	4
Western Polynesia	1	0	11	3

for example, seven areas in Amerindia fall into the top third of the Proto-Malay similarity wave, whereas only one Amerindian area lies in the same range for Western Polynesia.

The Pacific regional profile, reflecting a diversity of traditions and influences, is not so crystallized as that of North America (Fig. 11). Nevertheless, there are a few salient and widespread features which contribute to the distinctiveness and unity of the regional style. Most performances are choral, with well-blended polyphony or unison as a principal mode. Polynesians employ little melodic ornamentation, and singing voices are usually relaxed and wide, with a lower level of nasality and rasp than in other regions. This constellation of features marks the style, in cantometric terms, as cohesive.

Other outstanding and widespread traits of the regional style are, in world perspective, generally correlated with social complexity as defined in Chapter 6. These include frequent use of antiphonal forms of choral organization (almost as common as unison) and precisely articulated, word-heavy song texts, especially in the maritime area. Frequently, too, the melodies are complexly organized. One specific song form, the genealogical chant common to the maritime areas, incorporates all these features. These chants served an important function of social regulation and demanded an accurate recall of the names, attributes, and histories of ancestors; this demand was met most effectively in a wordy and precisely articulated text, delivered in a carefully controlled recitative.

In one way, the singing of Oceania stands in marked contrast to that of other regions: many choral performances, though set in irregular or free rhythm, are nevertheless performed in excellent concert. The only other area in the world where choruses commonly sing in free rhythm, yet in good concert, is Old Europe. It seems likely that this peculiarity, along with a shared preference for text-heavy, polyphonic performances with drone chords, facilitated the adoption of the Central European hymn style, especially by the Polynesians.

Africa

The remarkable homogeneity illustrated in the African map is interrupted only by the African Hunters (Pygmies and Bushmen), whose low representation in the quartile lists (15 percent) required that they be excluded (Figs. 14 and 15). Even this departure from the general homogeneity, however, is more apparent than real, for although the African Hunters appear low in the statistical ranks, their own quartile list is completely dominated by African areas. Thus, their song style stands out as very specialized (hence the low score pattern), but completely African. As Grauer (1965), in a dis-

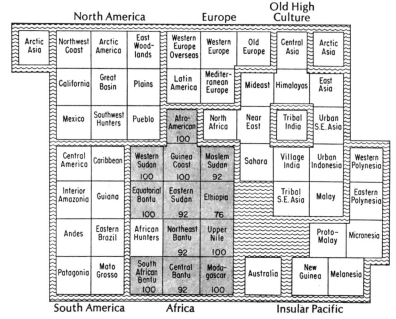

Fig. 14. Homogeneity mapping for Africa.

cussion of African Hunter singing pointed out, most of the specializations are extreme variants of features that characterize the broader regional style. Thus, the Pygmies and Bushmen, statistics notwithstanding, show up as prototypical Africans (see also Lomax, 1955–1956, 1962).

Even more dramatically than in Oceania, the similarity pattern evokes a picture compounded of known events and plausible historical inference. Let us follow some of the specific traces.

First, if there is a song-style centroid for Negro Africa, it encompasses the Guinea Coast and the Equatorial Bantu. From these two areas, 86 percent similar to one another, style similarities flow to the South African Bantu and to the Central Bantu with little perceptible gradient. A mean similarity of 84 percent links the Equatorial Bantu, the Central Bantu, the South African Bantu, and the Guinea Coast; it lies in the top one percent of the world distribution of 1,540 paired scores. The Eastern Sudan also joins the cluster at the same high level of similarity.

This striking uniformity of style, covering perhaps one-quarter of the continent, and linking large numbers of Bantu-speaking people to the southern coast of the bulge and adjacent portions of the Sudan, may well be an important historical marker. Murdock (1959) has marshalled a long bill of linguistic, botanical, and cultural evidence for an explosive spread of Bantu

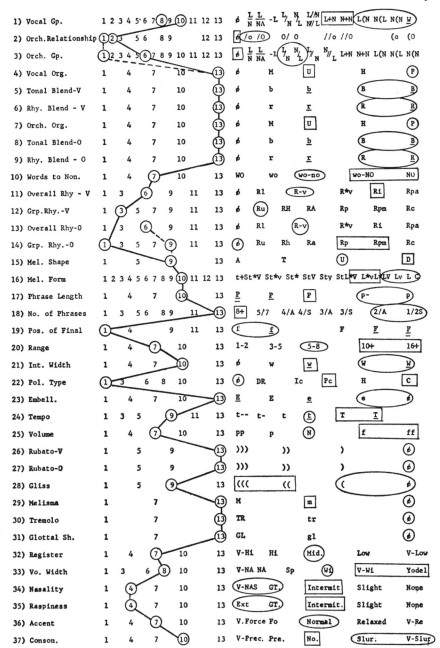

Fig. 15. Modal profile for Africa: 666 songs. The alternate dashed line indicates that many songs in Africa are unaccompanied. Most performances are both accompanied and choral, however, with overlap the most important form of organization. This profile leans strongly to the right side of the sheet, where factors that increase musical integration are scored.

speakers early in the Christian era from a homeland near the Cameroon-Nigerian border, close by the territory which cantometrics finds stylistically central in Africa.

Another similarity trace links the Guinea Coast to Madagascar, with a score of 86 percent. Ethiopia and the Northeast Bantu also join this cluster, though at a somewhat lower level. Here again, cantometrics may have caught the song-style echoes of an important distribution, the transcontinental reverberations of the East Indian maritime trade. The eastern and western ends of this cluster mark the terminals of a trans-Sudanic trade route, along which, according to Murdock's reconstruction, yams, taro, bananas, and other important food crops frcm Malaysia reached West Africa.

To these two linked clusters the remaining areas of Africa attach themselves in various ways. The Western Sudan clearly belongs with the Guinea Coast-Madagascar-Ethiopia-Northeast Bantu cluster. The Moslem Sudan lies between the two clusters.

The Upper Nile is most similar to the South African Bantu, suggesting, perhaps, a style trace following the lines of East African pastoralism. The African Hunters join the Guinea Coast-Eastern Sudan-Bantu set. Finally, Afro-America shows close similarities throughout the continent, but most strongly with the Guinea Coast and the Equatorial Bantu, whence the majority of American slaves were carried off by the slavers.

Looking at the pattern of similarities beyond the area (none of which met the criterion for inclusion on the map), we find that only Western Polynesia (in the upper quartile of 60 percent of the African areas), Eastern Polynesia (30 percent) and Tribal India (30 percent) show any degree of affinity. Here, apparently, is the other end of the trans-Indian Ocean link noted in the discussion of Oceania.

It seems likely from the distribution of trans-Indian Ocean similarities that these connections may be accounted for, at least in some part, by the maritime trade of Malayans, Indians, and Arabs. It was noted above, for example, that Madagascar and the Western Sudan, which are on the hypothesized diffusion route for the Malaysian crop assemblage, are similar at or above the top quartile to half of Oceania. More specific support arises from the ranking of African similarities to Tribal India and Village India, lying at an important terminus of the maritime trade (Table 5). The upper half of the regional distribution is occupied exclusively by the areas lying on or near the hypothesized transmission route.

The regional profile is dominated by the style features of the Bantu-African Hunter core. The major approach to song is choral and antiphonal, with the characteristic use of overlap, so that at least two parts are frequently active at the same time. A well-blended, rhythmically tight, often polyphonic choral performance is the norm in most areas. The major vocal style is clear and unconstricted, but with playful and intermittent use of high register, yodel, nasality, rasp, and forcefulness.

The melodic line is almost entirely free of ornamentation. Rhythm is strictly maintained, as in most primitive styles and in most well-blended styles as well. Consonants are slurred over and texts are highly repetitious. The outstanding melodic form is the litany of one or two brief phrases, although complex litanies employing more than one refrain are also characteristic and frequent. The common ranges lie between a fifth and an octave formed usually of diatonic intervals, although songs with wider intervals are also frequent.

Table 5. *Ranking of African similarities to Tribal and Village India.*

Similarity (percent)	Tribal India	Similarity (percent)	Village India
83	Ethiopia	76	Northeast Bantu
77	Western Sudan	74	Western Sudan
76	Northeast Bantu-Guinea Coast	72	Ethiopia
75	Madagascar	71	Moslem Sudan
		70	Madagascar-Guinea Coast

Everything contributes to an open texture, inviting participation fostered by a rock-steady beat, and by clear, liquid voices singing one note per syllable. The rhythmic formula is a playful use of simple four-square meters with rhythmic unison in the chorus, but in the orchestra independence of parts gives African music its most unusual characteristic—polyrhythm, or metrical conflict between two or more levels in the orchestra—frequent elsewhere in our sample only for India. Vocal polyrhythm, quite rare in our sample, occurs as an important feature of the specialized African Hunter style. The overall impact of the African style is multileveled, multiparted, highly integrated, multi-textured, gregarious, and playful-voiced.

Old High Culture

The most remarkable discovery of the cantometric coding system is the stylistic homogeneity of the vast Afro-Eurasian heartland, which includes more than half the world's population. The statistical map (Fig. 16) shows a somewhat lower homogeneity than was the case in Africa; but, given the approximate reaches of this great tradition, from Marrakesh to Manila, it is impressive that the least typical areas show high similarity to more than half the assemblage.

Looking first beyond the regional boundaries, only Australia and Mediterranean Europe show strong affinities to Old High Culture. The Australian similarity to Old High Culture turns up in the North Australian sample

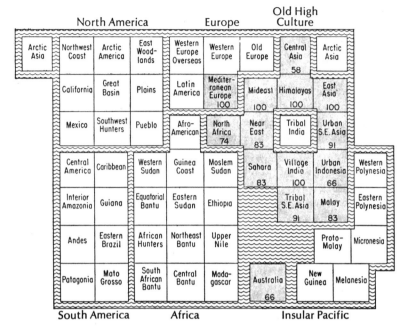

Fig. 16. Homogeneity mapping for Old High Culture.

which comes from an area known to have been visited often by traders from Malaysia (Berndt and Berndt, 1964). On the other hand, Mediterranean Europe, the ancient center of the Greco-Roman metropolis, and later for many centuries widely Islamized, shares as much of the Old High Culture tradition as it does that of Europe. This clear identification of boundaries is compelling evidence for the unity of the tradition.

Further evidence of unity is apparent in the internal structuring of similarities. Three of the four areas polling high similarities through the entire region were East Asia, Village India, and the Mideast. These contain most of the ancient centers of religion, empire, and trade. Their societies dominated much of the region for centuries without challenge until the beginning of the Western European expansion, scarcely 500 years ago. From such entrepots, stylistic patterns and influences appear to have been continuously received from and distributed to the peripheries of the region. The position of the Himalayas, at the top of the distribution, may reflect a centrality of location, for the area is flanked by India, East Asia, and Southeast Asia.

Probably even before the eastward wanderings of Alexander the Great, waves of conquest and steady flows of trade have linked the world of Old High Culture from one end to the other. Song styles and singers moved along the Bactrian Trail and the Sabean Lane, accompanying such other fine com-

modities as silks and wines. With them moved orchestral styles and instruments, both important factors in the structure of the song style. By the beginning of the Christian era the Indian and Chinese trade of Rome was so
well developed that Pliny the Younger could complain of a balance of pay-
ments deficit. Superimposed on this steady flow were the occasional marches
of troops and missionaries which brought the Turks to the Mediterranean
and Islam to Morocco and the Philippines.

More than a conquest or an exchange of bills of lading was involved in this
massive integration of styles. The existence of elites and powerful organized
religions throughout the region provided an indispensable framework for
musical specialization, within which novel styles could be consciously selected and adapted to local tastes. The nearly universal existence of temple-
dwelling gods, god kings, and conquering kings seems to have called forth a
common pattern of bards, chants, and epics.

Both the flow of styles and their adaptation to local use are illustrated by
the case of Indonesia which has a pattern of similarity reaching to Urban
Southeast Asia, East Asia, Village India, and the Mideast. For millennia, as
the target of repeated bombardments by traders and missionaries, Indonesia
has been the heir to diverse traditions. Absorbing the specialized aesthetic
contexts of temples, courts, and theaters, the Indonesians have created a rich
synthesis of local styles and, apparently, elements from the styles of distant
empires.

The cantometric profile for Old High Culture (Fig. 17) shows a widely
shared and a highly distinctive pattern. Probably the most important theme
is "exclusive and elaborated dominance" where a solo performer, accompanied by an orchestra (frequently playing in heterophony), sings a precisely enunciated, long, and complex text. The length, wordiness, and precision of the text is combined with a complex, multiphrased melodic structure, extreme ornamentation, frequent use of rubato, and a constricted vocal
style, all of which effectively prevent participation by others. Such, apparently, has been the style long employed by plowmen in harvest songs, and
by priests and bards for the praise of gods, great beauties, and princes. Within
this stylistic framework, great virtuosos and aestheticians developed scales and
musical systems, poetic forms, and refinements of instrumental structure and
technique. (For a fuller explanation of the relation of this style to a complex
productive and social system, see Chapters 6, 7, and 8.)

The normal choral style of this mainly monophonic region is an antiphonal, but poorly coordinated, unison. Here, too, one occasionally comes upon
the use of subtly organized choral heterophony, in which the members of a
highly skilled group follow the lead voice at a respectful distance, as Oriental
instrumentalists often follow the orchestral lead. The songs of Old High Culture are frequently grave and serious in tone, an effect produced by the com-

98

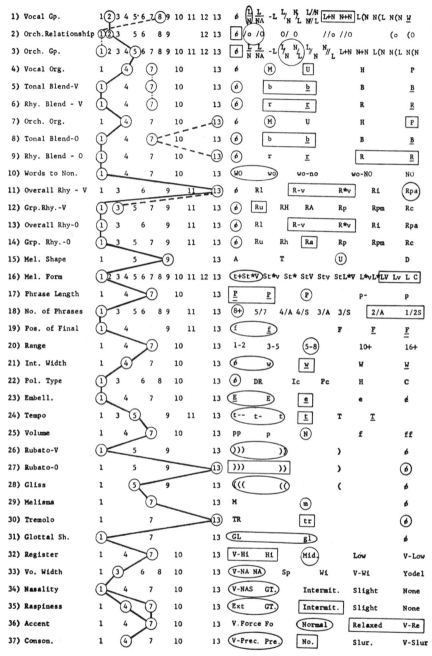

Fig. 17. Modal profile for Old High Culture: 422 songs. The solid line outlines the main style of Old High Culture, which is solo-exclusive and elaborate. The dashed line indicates two other less frequent situations: alternation in poorly organized unison, and an orchestral organization which is frequently multileveled and in good rhythmic concert. This profile leans more strongly to the left than any other in the set.

bined use of intervals of a second or less, slow tempo, and embellishments, melismas, glissandos, and glottal tremolo.

Europe

Given the ample base of historical unity and long and close intercommunication, the perfect internal homogeneity shown by the European region (Fig. 18) holds little surprise. The statistical evidence is strongly seconded, both in the listener's ear and in the coding profiles, by a list of distinctive and broadly shared attributes.

Although no other world area met the 100 percent mapping criterion, several did appear in the quartile lists of three or four European areas. Central Asia, marginal in its Old High Culture setting, shows a high order of similarity with 80 percent of the European assemblage. This pattern seems plausibly explainable by a long history of culture exchange beginning with the spread of horse culture east from Scythia and the subsequent seesaw of conquest and migration back and forth across the vast plains that stretch from the Tien Shan to the Pripet Marshes. At the 80 percent level we also find aboriginal Mexico with its strong affinity to Latin America. Western Polynesia and the Western Sudan lie at the same level. Madagascar and Eastern Polynesia come in at 60 percent.

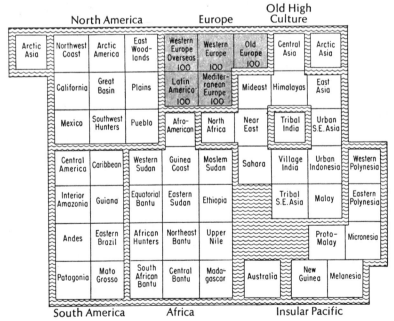

Fig. 18. Homogeneity mapping for Europe.

100

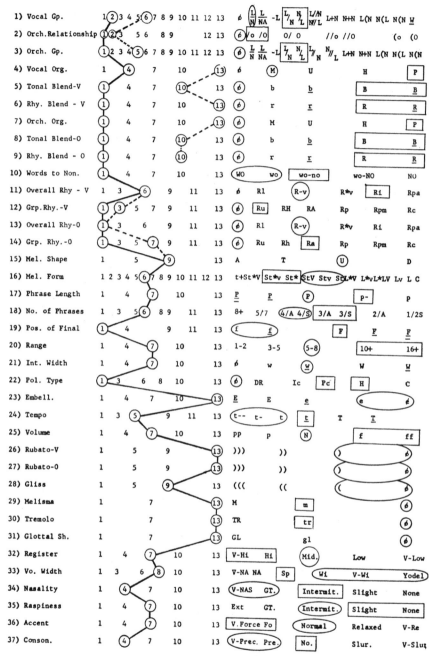

Fig. 19. Modal profile for Europe: 383 songs. The solid line traces the course of the main type of European song—solo, unaccompanied performance of foursquare strophes in simple meter. The dashed line shows a second type—simple group organization in polyphony with good tonal blend. Accompanying orchestras are likely to be multileveled and in good concert, with one or more parts in an accompanying relationship (see Line 14). This profile most strongly resembles Old High Culture.

We are not certain whether European song is the northern branch of Old High Culture style or the modern survival of some very ancient European model (Lomax, 1955). The profile (Fig. 19) shows one dominant type rare elsewhere in the world: the unaccompanied solo singer, performing three- or four-phrase, symmetrical strophes, with phrases of medium length and diatonic intervals, to simple meters. Song is rendered with little embellishment and in a forthright manner so that the precisely enunciated text is clearly understood. The clarity and simplicity of this European model contrasts with the rhythmic, melodic, textual, and orchestral complexities which enrich the sung poem in much of the Orient, often to the point of obscuring the message.

Two other style types show up dimly on the profile, marked off by the secondary modes. The first is the well-blended polyphonic song of Central and Eastern Europe, sung in a relatively noise-free, clear vocal style. The second is the European version of the Old High Culture embellished solo, where rhythmic freedom, melismas, and a high-pitched, nasal delivery color the complaints of the Mediterranean world, as they do to a considerable extent even among the ballad traditions of Western Europe.

Australia

In Australia (and the other isolates) only a single area enters the homogeneity test, and the map shows an all-or-nothing distribution. The Australian pattern specifically places the area squarely in both Amerindia and Old High Culture (Fig. 20). The profile shows strong traces of both song types (Fig. 21). On the one hand, the resemblance to the principal Amerindian style appears in the frequent occurrence of male group performances rendered in a poorly blended unison, with noisy, nasal, and emphatic delivery, often with an instrumental accompaniment. The rhythmic framework is also similar—often an irregular meter in the voice part is organized into rough rhythmic unison by the chorus and accompanied by a one-beat rhythm. There is often another accompanying level in the orchestra, however, a feature shared with cultures higher on the complexity scale. This is an assertive and masculine style that seems from the Amerindian evidence to be appropriate to hunters. On the other hand, an affinity to Old High Culture perhaps appears in a frequency of wordy and elaborate songs unusual for primitive cultures. Moreover, narrow intervals, narrow voices, vocal rubato, melisma, and tremolo color many solo performances with a feeling reminiscent of that so familiar in the Orient.

Tribal India

The Tribal Indian sample is so small that any remarks about style can find only scanty support in the evidence. As far as the Abor and Muria Gond cod-

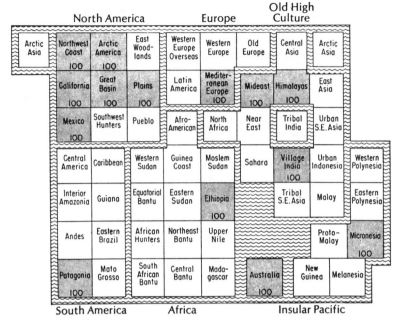

Fig. 20. Homogeneity mapping for Australia.

ings can be considered valid, certain features do stand out in its profile (Fig. 22). There is a strong preference for well-organized antiphony. Texts are frequently quite wordy and often precisely enunciated. There is some use of embellishment, but little rubato. Litanies or three-phrase strophes are sung in simple meters; and wide intervals, a feature of much primitive song, are common. The vocal style is noisy and yet moderate. Finally, there is some preference for polyphony in the chorus and polyrhythm in the orchestra.

The profile characteristics of Tribal Indian singing place the style about halfway between Africa, on the one hand, and the broad circum-Pacific distribution, on the other. The homogeneity map reflects this widespread pattern (Fig. 23). In other respects this profile can be viewed as an early model for circum-Mediterranean song styles.

Arctic Asia

Given the position of Arctic Asia at the apex of the great circum-Pacific arch, the similarity pattern illustrated in Figure 24 offers considerable support to our hypothesis of a generalized, but consistent, style stratum linking Amerindia to the Insular Pacific and primitive Asia. With the exceptions of Tribal India and Ethiopia, the areas represented in the top quartile list are circum-Pacific.

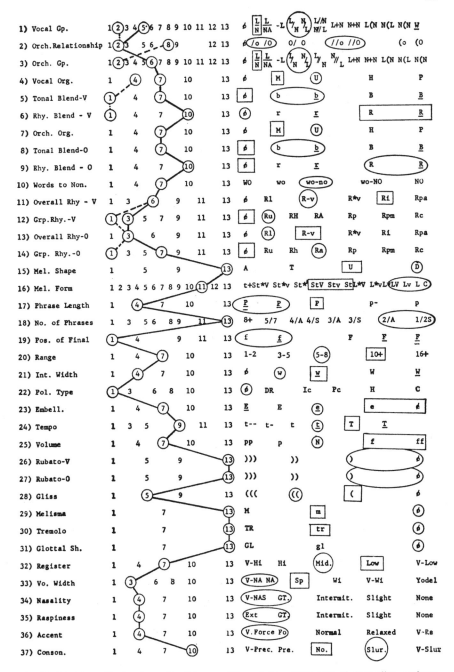

Fig. 21. Modal profile for Australia: 32 songs. The relative uniformity of Australian performances from all parts of the continent made coding of a large sample unnecessary. The solid line traces the main style: simple group in poorly blended unison, accompanied by an orchestra in good rhythmic concert and with one part frequently in an accompanying relationship (see Line 14). A second solo type, often ritual chant, is traced in the dashed line. The Australian profile resembles those of Amerindia in choral and rhythmic organization. Other features are characteristic of Old High Culture; namely, long phrases, narrow intervals, embellishment, and narrow, constricted vocalization. One unusual feature is the dominance of descending melodic shape (most common elsewhere in Africa) in which the main trend of most phrases in the melody is downward.

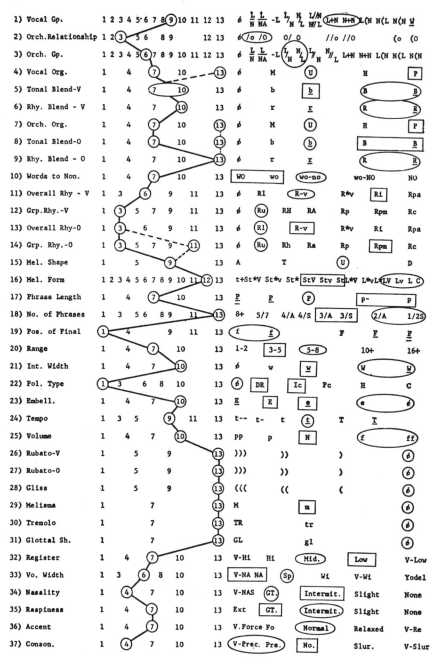

Fig. 22. Modal profile for Tribal India: 19 songs. The songs in this group come from two contrasting groups—the Gond and the Abors—and can no more than hint at the style patterns that would emerge from a comprehensive look at this area. It is interesting that the main style pattern is so strongly reminiscent of Oceania on the one hand and of Africa on the other. The Indian cultures coded here stand at approximately the same subsistence level as the cultures of these two regions.

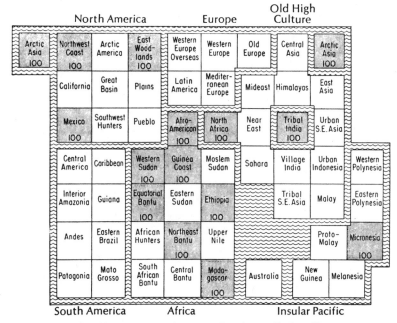

Fig. 23. Homogeneity mapping for Tribal India.

Although the regional profile (Fig. 25) shows a style compatible with this distribution, it is also one of the most homogeneous in the world. From Kamchatka to Lapland there is little departure from the pattern. The typical song is a highy guttural solo chant of a one-phrase melody, usually in irregular rhythm—the whole almost identical with the main profile for South America. The Siberian songs we have examined are characterized by slurring and repetition of text, by nasality, and by the strongest preference registered in our sample for glottal shake and tremolo. Intervals are extremely wide and melodies are often simply constructed of one or two short phrases encompassed within a narrow range—a type common in the primitive Pacific. Here and there, however, for instance in the songs of the Yakuts, features normally associated with Old High Culture appear. Principal among these qualities are embellishment, rubato, melisma, occasional traces of precision in articulation, antiphonal choral style, multi-phrased forms, and slow tempos.

AMERINDIA—A CLOSER LOOK

Recently we have begun to study style relationships over smaller samples of songs, drawn at the cultural rather than the areal level, with three general aims in mind:

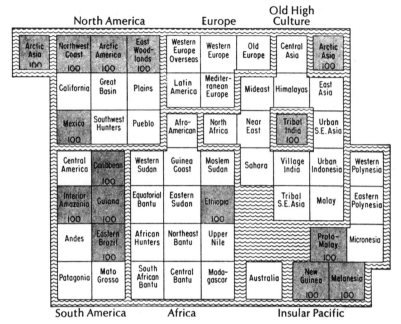

Fig. 24. Homogeneity mapping for Arctic Asia.

1. to test the stability of cantometric codings in smaller sets of songs;
2. to produce a taxonomy based on stylistic traits of cultures, not culture areas; and
3. to explore further the taxonomic dimensions of the coding system.

This approach, though still in an early phase, has yielded a provisional ordering of Amerindian styles which deserves a brief exposition.

In contrast to the procedure followed in the worldwide study of areas no preordering was imposed on the culture-level sample. Rather than establish, then validate, an *a priori* scheme, we sought to extract the clustering of styles directly from a factor analysis of the statistical measures of likeness.

A further change was in the base of the similarity score. If the cantometric coding lines are scaled measures of underlying variables, then it should be possible to characterize styles in terms of the central tendencies exhibited by their songs over each of the lines. This characterization has proved its utility in the summary descriptions provided by the modal profiles exhibited throughout this book. In order to explore the taxonomic sensitivity of the whole line as opposed to its individual coding points, we adopted the correlation between mean profiles as the measure of similarity. As a first step in the new comparison, mean coding positions over the 30 vocal lines were calcu-

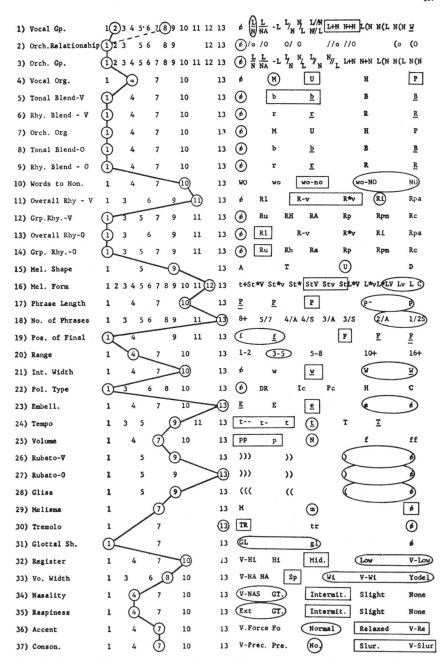

Fig. 25. Modal profile for Arctic Asia: 92 songs. This style is remarkably consistent all the way across Siberia to the camps of the Norwegian Lapps. In most respects it can be viewed as an ancient, worn-down prototype from which Amerindian style could have developed. It is certainly closer to the South Amerindian profile than to that of North America. The predominance of solo singing may be a result of the fact that many of the Siberian songs were collected away from a village; and yet we know that most Lapp singing is in solo.

lated for the 59 cultures in the Amerindian sample and standardized, for each line, to a grand mean of zero and a variance of 1.00. For every pair of 30-line profiles thus derived, product-moment correlations were calculated to form a Q (subject-by-subject) matrix, which was factored (see Appendix 2).

Basically, the effect of factor analysis, as applied to the comparison of profiles, is the definition of a few "average" or "ideal" profiles to which the much larger number of cultural profiles can be related. Each cultural profile can be characterized in terms of its likeness or contrast to each of the "ideal" models, and a clustering of styles emerges, defined by the distribution of high congruences. (A basic text on factor analysis is Harman, 1960; for specific applications in numerical taxonomy, see Sokal and Sneath, 1963.)

Ten factors with latent roots of 1.00 or more were extracted from the 59-row Q-matrix. Simply put, ten distinct and significant "ideal" profiles were found to account for most of the style variability in Amerindia. The method used was that of principal factors (Harman, 1960), which yields a set of mutually uncorrelated factors extracted in order of their contribution to the total variance in the matrix. Normally, such a factor structure is transformed by the rotation of axes to produce the optimal clustering. At the time of this writing, experiments with various kinds of rotation are still under way. The results described here are derived from the principal factor solution.

Of the ten significant factors, the first two, accounting for nearly half the total variance, were found to be directly interpretable in terms of the Amerindian style classifications presented earlier in this chapter. Table 6 shows the grouping of cultural style samples on each of the two "ideal" profiles implied in these factors. The degree of congruence to the "ideal" profiles is expressed in factor loadings (the correlations between variables and factors). For ease of reading, only those loadings at or above the median have been listed in the table.

It is clear from the distribution of loadings that the two factors replicate, culture by culture, the classification derived earlier for the areal samples. The two American continents are shown to be distinct from one another, yet interlinked by broad traces of similarity.

Factor 1 has abstracted the forthright, emphatic, masculine style of America north of Mexico. The top of the loadings distribution, dominated by the Western Apache and the Plains and Plateau tribes, confirms the earlier hypothesis that this distinct regional style is basically one of hunters. Nevertheless, the style is broadly distributed across North America, and especially east of the Rockies. Somewhat surprisingly, the singing of the Taos, Hopi, and Iroquois gardeners also shows strong congruence to the style, although their performances lack some of the typically harsh edges of noisy, unblended choralizing. Other features common to the regional profile

Table 6. *Cultural style placements on Amerindian Factors 1 and 2*
(Principal Factors Solution).

Culture	Factor 1	Factor 2	Culture	Factor 1	Factor 2
Ona		.63	W. Apache	.90	
Yahgan	(no high loadings)		Navaho	.52	
Quechua		.73	Mohave	.58	
Aymara		.56	Taos	.83	
Bora-Witoto		.71	Zuni	.49	
Conibo	(no high loadings)		Laguna	.64	
Jivaro		.45	Hopi	.82	
Campa	(no high loadings)		Creek	.56	
Amahuaca	(no high loadings)		Iroquois	.79	
Trumai	.40	.41	Wabanaki	.45	
Camayura	.50	.44	Yuchi	.31	
Kraho-Canela	.24		Cree	.87	
Caraja		.52	Teton-Dakota	.86	
N. Cayapo	.44		Kiowa	.85	
Yaruro		.46	Blood-Blackfoot	.75	
Guahibo		.51	Flathead	.77	
Guarauno	(no high loadings)		N. Paiute		.55
Yekuana		.34	Washo		.61
Goajiro		.68	Kutenai	.70	
Motilon		.51	Hupa	.47	
Lacandon		.57	Pomo	.42	.57
Tzotzil		.35	Haida	.39	.54
Cuna		.49	Salish		.46
Huichol		.68	Nootka	.53	
Papago	(no high loadings)		Caribou Eskimo		.49
Pima	.22	.39	Alaska Eskimo	.73	
Yaqui		.59	Carrier		.42
Seri		.76	Slave	.51	
Tarahumara		.64	Atna	.25	.46
Totonac		.43			

are irregular meter, unison chorus, forceful delivery, and strophic melodic structure. These apparently form, in the hemispheric perspective, a sufficiently distinctive framework of style to submerge the differences in vocal attack. In the case of Taos, too, ethnologists and musicologists have long noted strong flavorings of Plains features both in singing and in other aspects of the culture pattern (Tschopik and Rhodes, 1951). The linkage with South America, apparent in the areal survey, shows up here in the relatively low, but above median, loadings of the Trumai, Camayura, and Ge-speaking peoples of Eastern Brazil. As was demonstrated earlier in this chapter, this principal North American style is extremely homogeneous and specialized. Except for the Eastern Brazilian connection, all cultures with a more than average congruence to the master profile lie north of Mexico. Homogeneity is reflected, too, in the large number of high loadings; more than a third of the cultures above the median of the distribution show loadings of .70 or more.

Factor 2 has abstracted a style model that is principally, but not exclusively, South American. As was apparent in the broader view, the South American style is much less self-contained regionally and much more heterogeneous in its components than that of North America. Only three of the loadings lie at or above .70, and the geographic trace is extremely broad. Within this low level of unity, however, certain features appear with some frequency—most notably the rather soft-voiced feminized vocalization and the polyphony described for the South American profile. Heterogeneity of regional style also shows up in the five South American cultures whose mean profiles show little similarity to either of the factor models. Significantly, these cultures lie at the edges of the more focused historical continuities: at the mouth of the Orinoco, in the Chilean archipelago, and at the uppermost reaches of the Amazon on the Andean slope.

The style unities abstracted in factor analysis of mean profiles dimly reflect some important lines of ethnohistory. First, the distribution on Factor 1 indicates that the focus of North American style unity lies chiefly to the east of the Rockies in what was a vast and essentially unified archeological province (Griffin, 1967). Similarly, the strong and exclusive ties of the Great Basin cultures with the South American-Mexican set strongly suggest the ancient desert culture continuity. In South America, the sharp division of the eastern Brazilian styles from the general regional clustering bears overtones of the archeological discontinuity separating that region from the tropical forests of the Amazon and Orinoco Basins (Altenfelder Silva and Meggers, 1963).

Given the sparse sampling of cultures, especially in South America, the results presented here must be considered tentative. Nevertheless, the general outlines of relationship coincide broadly with those of known ethnohistory with a frequency far in excess of random expectation. It seems possible, therefore, to conclude that song styles bear distinct and durable traces of history. Moreover, the replication of the results of the areal study, based on comparison of all coding attributes, suggests that the cantometric system, considered as a set of scale measurements, is an effective device for the characterization and comparison of styles. (The taxonomy of Amerindian song styles is being treated in greater detail in a doctoral dissertation by Edwin E. Erickson.)

5

Consensus on Cantometric Parameters

A. CONSENSUS TESTING

Alan Lomax and Joan Halifax

THIRTEEN of the cantometric scales have been tested for inter-rater reliability, mostly those features of the system, such as tempo, loudness, forcefulness, etc., for which no musical expertise is required. We plan eventually to test the musical parameters with musically trained judges.

A computer program ordered all the ratings from the 3,525 songs in the cantometric sample into a large dictionary by line and by trait. A typical page of this volume titled *very fast tempo* lists the recorded sources of the 300 songs in the tape archive which cantometric judges had rated as "very fast." An unambiguous example was selected from this page along with an equally clearcut and thus very contrasting example of *very slow tempo,* in order to make the extremes of the tempo clear to the listener. Brief excerpts of these two examples were then copied on tape. This was the first step in preparing the training tape for tempo. A quotation from the script of the tempo tape will demonstrate how the remainder of this training tape was structured.

> "There are six levels of tempo. You will first hear the two extreme levels: Level 1—very slow and Level 6—very fast (excerpts 1 and 6 presented). Here are the six levels of tempo in order: Level 1—very slow (excerpt); Level 2—quite slow (excerpt); Level 3—slow (excerpt); Level 4—moderate (excerpt); Level 5—fast (excerpt); Level 6—very fast (excerpt). Rate the following 12 songs for level of tempo on your coding sheet."

Twelve previously rated excerpts illustrating the six levels of tempo were then presented in random order with a pause after each to allow the trainee to note his rating of the excerpt. After the judges had registered their scores on a rating sheet, the investigator read out the cantometric ratings on each example, so that the raters could recalibrate their judgments to cantometric standards.

111

In the second part of the test, the raters were played a tape containing brief excerpts of 50 songs and asked to record their ratings for tempo. Inexperienced judges were used; all were either high school or college students in Gainesville, Florida. Except for one test, at least six judges rated each parameter. It was the first time they had heard songs from every culture area and song style in the world. As a precaution against contamination of the tests by the bias of the Cantometrics staff, this experiment was carried out under the direction of Norman N. Markel in the Communication Sciences Laboratory at the University of Florida.

Inter-rater reliability for tempo, by these inexperienced judges, turned out to be 96 percent. The statistical formula used was Ebel's technique of interclass correlations (Guilford, 1957). Three parameters, accent, precision, and nasality, have been tested on two sets of judges. Consensus varied by no more than two percent within the three pairs of tests.

Similar testing procedures have been applied to the 12 other parameters of the cantometric rating system which are common to both spoken and sung communication. The results of consensus tests obtained in the manner described above show a mean reliability of 84.7 percent, a comparatively high figure (Table 7).

Table 7. *Inter-rater consensus.*

Parameter	Cantometric line number	Reliability (percent)
1. Tonal Blend	4	92
2. Wordiness	10	89
3. Embellishment	23	80
4. Tempo	24	96
5. Volume	25	88
6. Melisma	29	83
7. Glottal	31	85
8. Pitch (Register)	32	95
9. Vocal Width	33	65
10. Nasality	34	76
11. Vocal Noise (Raspiness)	35	78
12. Accent	36	90
13. Precision (Consonants)	37	86

A number of interesting conclusions may be drawn from this experiment. The first concerns the structure of the training tapes themselves. Tapes in which each parameter was elaborately explained in the words of the cantometric coding book produced lower inter-rater reliability than tapes which simply displayed the parameter with only the briefest identifications of the dimensions. In the latter case, the raters could calibrate their ear responses directly to the scale presented on the training tape.

Second, the comparative difficulty of the raters with judgments about nasality and vocal width may be due to the special psychological and cultural implications the qualities have for many Americans. Nasalization is such a steady feature of some American dialects that some speakers may not become alerted to it unless an extreme or exotic kind of nasality is presented to them. In the tests run in Florida, student judges consistently rated American pop singers lower on nasality than the more experienced cantometric raters.

Third, the redundancy and formality of the sung communication, in which most qualities tend to be held steady, makes observation of overall presence or absence of a quality easier than in speech. For instance, traits such as slowness or emphasis tend to be used in a more extreme fashion and to be adhered to more steadily in singing than in speaking.

Fourth, the training tape, by displaying the extremes of some aspects of human vocalization, can bring the listener to a vivid awareness of a voice quality or characterizer. Recordings of heightened use of voice qualities can be found in any library of world song style.

In conclusion, it seems that when the listener experiences the whole range of the formal use of a voice quality, as demonstrated on a training tape composed of songs, he learns to rate the relative presence of this quality with good reliability. Thus, voice qualities can be measured far more reliably than before seemed possible. Some of these traits seem to vary by culture area. This approach, then, offers a valid way of characterizing culture in a paralinguistic fashion.

B. THE PARALINGUISTIC FRAMEWORK

Norman N. Markel

COMMUNICATION through the vocal-auditory channel is the focus of attention for a large number of investigators in a wide spectrum of disciplines. It engages the interest of the most clinical as well as the most objective of specialists from the "hardest" to the "softest" sciences. But, in the formidable array of scholarly investigations of this channel of communication, only a few concern themselves directly with the question of what the message on this channel has to say about behavior in general.

A large part of the problem is that the level of these studies almost precludes insights into human behavior. The more the investigators have moved away from the biological foundations of vocal-auditory communication, the more difficult it becomes to make generalizations about all human beings or to see each individual or each culture in terms of variations of the fundamental behaviors which they all share.

In the preceding paper we have presented the results of tests on a number of paralinguistic parameters in folk songs which indicate that cantometrics is an exception. These demonstrations show that if one has chosen the right level for a look at the vocal-auditory channel of communication, insights and statements about human behavior are automatically generated. It is apparent that on the right level one can remove the curtain of culture and perceive aspects of vocal communication which he has been taught to ignore or keep at an extremely low level of awareness. Further, when one has used a measuring device that can be placed across the world, deviations, variations, or ranges of human behavior automatically display themselves. It is then only a question of the ingenuity of the investigator to interpret the meaning of the deviations.

Every vocal-auditory message that goes on the air can be categorized as voice set, voice quality, vocalization, or language (Trager, 1958). There is no residue; the total vocal act can be accounted for. Vocalizations are modifications of language and can only be measured in juxtaposition to language. In order to make statements about vocalizations, one must know the linguistic structure of the language in question. Voice quality and voice set provide the background in which language and vocalization take place. The term "paralanguage," as it is currently used, refers to voice set, voice quality, and vocalization, but does not include language. In the paralinguistic framework of cantometrics we examine voice quality and voice set. It is important to note that all categories are concerned with various aspects of exactly the same physical material—the mechanical changes in air pressure initiated by air being expelled from the nose or mouth of a speaker. The quality of the airstream being expelled by a speaker is a function of biological activities from the surface of the lips to the bottom of the stomach, but all differentials in the airstream can be accounted for as either linguistic or paralinguistic phenomena. One can visualize a series of concentric circles. The smallest and innermost circle is language; around language is vocalization; around both vocalization and language is voice quality; and surrounding and encompassing all these is voice set. The heuristic value of this visualization is the fact that language is depicted as the innermost circle, in a sense the narrowest and most limited category of vocal phenomena. It is true that language has categories within it—phonemes, morphemes, function classes, and so on—that include all of the units of the descriptive linguist. There is a strong tendency to feel that nothing could possibly be left over after a complete linguistic analysis of a language has been accomplished. But in the context of the total vocal process, language occupies only one small area of concern. The more one moves into this inner circle of language, the more difficult it becomes to make meaningful interindividual or intercultural statements.

Within the theoretical framework in which we are operating there are available only two reasonably workable, relevant techniques of analysis: acoustic and perceptual. An acoustic analysis consists of the translation of the air waves set into motion by the act of speaking into electronic information and the kymographic recording of this information. Perceptual analysis consists of the translation of the air waves into psychological categories.

Some feel strongly that anything analyzed by the human brain is, by definition, non-scientific, but the important scientific issue is not who or what analyzes the raw material under investigation but the reliability of the measurements. The question of reliability is essentially this: can another investigator using the same procedures come up with the same measurements of the raw material? The results of our consensus studies indicate that our measurements of the paralanguage in folk songs are reliable. A particular reliability score means that if another group of trained judges rated the same material, the correlation between the ratings for the two groups would be at the level of that reliability score. Such correlations would be statistically significant beyond the .001 level of confidence and there is, therefore, no question that the parameters of paralanguage which we have measured in folk songs can be rated reliably.

It is important to note that the raters in our consensus studies were individuals with no specialized training in linguistics, music, speech, or any related field. They were trained with our training tapes to rate paralinguistic parameters in folk songs. This fact has three important implications: first, any investigator interested in pursuing this line of research may replicate our procedures exactly, without first obtaining highly skilled research personnel or expensive equipment; second, the paralinguistic parameters tap a basic level of vocal-auditory communication; and third, these paralinguistic parameters are meaningfully valid measures when applied cross-culturally.

6

Song as a Measure of Culture

Alan Lomax

WE HAVE shown in Chapter 4 that song style, considered in cantometric terms, defines the culture regions familiar to ethnologists and historians of culture. The taxonomic efficiency of cantometrics stems directly from the modesty of its aims and its methods. Cantometrics does not operate with minimal units or structural principles, nor does it pretend to exhaustive descriptions. Its variables correspond, we believe, to the ways in which ordinary people make up their minds about the general tone of any conversation or any piece of music they hear. The individual's survival, his sanity, indeed his ability to interact moment by moment with his fellow human beings depends, not only upon his knowing the meaning of words and his correct use of grammar, but even more on his response at a very subtle level to many qualitative aspects of the act of phonation. In effect he is continuously holding up a set of multiple scales to every bit of speech or song and rating its relative level of loudness, degree of forcefulness, tension, nasality, and the like. There is a good deal of variation among individuals on these paralinguistic ranges, and even these idiosyncratic patterns shift from situation to situation. Any listener, however, can orient himself instantly to these changes, judge them on a score of scales, and evaluate the output as familiar or new. Indeed, all human transactions depend upon a constant interflow of signals between individuals adjusted by such delicately shifting calibrations. In this context it is easier to understand the successful application of such crude tools as the three- to five-point cantometric paramusical rating scales to the extravagances of human song.

Markel's consensus testing (Chapter 5) demonstrated that a group of naive listeners can put aside ingrained biases and learn to make judgments about even the most exotic song styles. In reacting to our test songs, drawn from every part of the world, Markel's judges—most of them middle-class college students from Florida—had to form new and much broader perceptions of such qualities as nasality, vocal constriction, and vocal blend. That they did so, and with such high consensus, speaks for a panhuman capacity for making sensitive qualitative judgments. This faculty explains the success

117

of the cantometric grid in pulling out the broad frameworks for song performance employed by the various branches of mankind.

The cantometric coding sheet enables the listener to arrange his ear judgments of song performances on pre-defined scales. Thus he can describe a
song as a function of a set of relative ranges of behavior. These sets of ranges
are combined in cultural profiles and the notion of song style emerges. A
song style is an agreement by members of a culture to conform their vocal
behavior to a certain model. The function of song style seems to be to produce social consensus at a minimal level, so that a group of individuals from
a culture can phonate together in concert or take pleasure in listening to a
long stretch of phonation performed by others. Thus the content of song
must touch upon those concerns and those modes of behavior which the
members of a culture feel are both satisfying and valuable.

A cantometric style profile sketches the framework that the performers
and the audiences in a culture agree is suitable for making music. If a performer ignores this framework it will not matter whether he sings the words
and the tune correctly; his audience will find a dramatic way of expressing
its disapproval, booing, beating, or even killing him. No grand opera audience, for instance, would tolerate singers who rasped, nasalized, performed
in unison and with poor blend, out of tempo, with an orchestra of drums and
rattles—all of which are conditions essential to many stirring Amerindian
chants. Plains Indians may have as little regard for the coloratura trilling of
a European soprano as have opera lovers for the emphatic Amerindian style.
An anthropologist friend of mine who did work among the Kiowa Apaches
found one infallible way of overcoming the tendency of his Indian friends
to stay too late in the one-room house where he was living with his young
bride. When he put a record of Galli-Curci on the phonograph, the visiting
Indians would rise, one by one, and slip away into the Oklahoma night.

Since these performance styles link cultures stably in large culture regions,
the question arises as to what aspects of culture these constant features of expressive behavior represent; what communications about culture are going
on the air through these channels? Consider, for instance, the inter-regional
variation on seven of the main cantometric coding points (Table 8) :

Since these patterns seem to vary by regions, their variance may depend
not so much on localized cultural structure as on norms of conduct and
cultural traditions that have shaped behavior across vast stretches of time
and space. Therefore, the search for the meaning of song is not only culture-
oriented, it not only rests upon the assumption that song style is learned behavior, but it becomes a search for the grand regional traditions of cultural
style as well as song style.

The tools employed in cantometrics cross-cultural research include a number of data banks. First and foremost is the huge *Ethnographic Atlas* com-

piled by Murdock, containing rated information on over 1,100 cultures. To this Barbara Ayres and others added codings from many community studies, especially in Europe, so that the sample could reflect the rich and complex folk traditions of the western world and its colonies in the Americas. The final match between ethnographic and cantometric codings was 233 cultures, fairly evenly distributed across 56 of Murdock's 60 culture areas. A list of the cultures in this sample appears at the end of Chapter 2. The reader may see for himself where it is strong and where it is weak. It is across this range of 233 peoples that we have studied the co-variation of musical and cultural forms. In addition, we have set up two special test samples in which obvious

Table 8. *Percent frequency of cantometric traits by world region.*

	Polyphony	Good tonal blend	Repetitious text	One-phrase melody	Wide singing voice	Precise articulation	Wide melodic intervals
South America	28	11	58	58	35	6	64
North America	8	17	69	26	35	5	79
Arctic Asia	13	0	52	72	50	14	64
Australia	6	3	22	44	10	13	3
Pacific	41	47	27	58	58	33	32
Africa	49	61	34	63	69	8	48
Tribal India	26	52	21	59	11	53	58
Old High Culture	6	5	7	36	17	57	24
Europe	28	28	7	19	51	50	21

cultural and historical duplications have been systematically eliminated. (The cultures in these subsets are identified in the sample list by S and T.) Most of the correlations to be presented on the following pages have been tested both on the large sample and on the subsets. (See Appendix 2 for an account of these tests.)

Beyond the broadly ranged ethnographic data of the Murdock *Atlas*, we have studied song style variation across the codings of Udy's *Organization of Work; a Comparative Analysis of Production among Non-Industrial Peoples* (1959), and Child and associates' ongoing investigation of child rearing (Barry, Child, and Bacon, 1959). Although the cultural match is much smaller (56 for Udy and 32 for Child) than with the Murdock sample, these more specialized perspectives have added depth to our view of music in its cultural setting.

The ordering of the multileveled cantometric data banks in relation to those from Murdock, Udy, and Child, occupied Berkowitz for the better part of two years. Out of his work came a new computer language that could correlate variables of any degree of complexity and test for their relationship in a number of ways. Berkowitz' device, which when perfected delivered several thousand correlation tests within a few months, is explained in Appendix 1. It enabled me to evaluate every conceivable match of song style and culture feature within the space of a very few weeks and to build these into clusters of dependable, tested relationships.

The assumption that gives significance to these relationships, established between song style and social structure, is that every cultural system has an internal congruence reflected in its expressive and communications systems. The rigorous work of Birdwhistell, McQuown, Trager, and Hall has shown that all levels in any communication, whether verbal, intonational, kinesic, para-kinesic, or situational, must bear a complementary relationship to each other, so that an ongoing signal at one level reinforces and perhaps qualifies, but does not contradict and cancel out a signal at another level. When the opposite situation obtains, participants are caught in what Bateson terms the "double bind"—as, for example, when parents induce a psychotic condition in a child by denying love and giving it at two different levels at the same time (Arieti, 1955). The very horror and rarity of this aberrant and injurious use of the normally dovetailed, multileveled communication system emphasizes the fact that there is usually harmony and reinforcement between the levels of any communication act.

It stands to reason, therefore, that one should discover that each of the style profiles sketched by cantometrics has an internally consistent structure and, at the same time, that this consistent pattern should recur elsewhere in the total cultural structure. Arensberg made the same point in another way at the American Association for the Advancement of Science symposium:

> "To find similarities or dependencies between singing styles and cultural customs and institutions, we must remind ourselves that all traits of culture whether, for example, singing styles, hunting, or clans, are—as S. F. Nadel defined culture—'patterns' or recurrent regularities of the behavior of human beings with or upon or in respect of one another. As such, we must look for a way of comparing and contrasting them. Such a way can be found within the canons of the scientific method, by treating them not for their attributes alone, but by redefining them in terms of the operations of description used to describe them and by reordering the patterned arrangements they show in the order of their occurrences.
>
> "In this way, since similarity of pattern can be shown to link culture traits of quite different content and a search can be conducted for the correlates of the personal and interpersonal production of song style which correspond point by point with those of non-singing customs, those of singing can also be compared and connected. Thus, for example, if some men hunt in ephemeral, male-led teams and bring their kill

to women, does their singing style take the same form and arrangement of their behavior vis-a-vis one another as men, women, and as givers and receivers? Thus, for example, if the structure of one's society is one of command and deference, of waiting and obedience before royal pomp and decision, does the style of one's songs show similar patterning of human relationships?

"The search for the patterning of interpersonal relationships in the social space of a culture's activity other than song guided us in our effort to search out the cultural correlates of song, on the old assumption of cultural anthropology that cultures are somehow integrated and ordered wholes. The novelty of our procedure is that by describing both singing and non-singing customs in terms of human interpersonal behavior, we were enabled to perceive an identification of their common forms. Such common form of interpersonal action and experience in cultural institutions and in singing disclosed many strong and surprising correlations. Song style is an integral part of each culture; it repeats its basic and common form of human relationships."

A SCALE OF SOCIAL COMPLEXITY

The most striking early observation in cantometric research was that many stylistic factors vary directly with complexity. The song styles of simple cultures differ in consistent ways from the song styles of technically more advanced societies. In order to measure these relationships, various arrangements of the material in the *Ethnographic Atlas* were tested. It soon became clear that cantometric measurements are as reliable (in the sense of replicability and specificity) as scales built up from other sorts of cultural data. Even more important, however, was the finding that the economic measurements produce the most dependable and understandable arrangements of cantometric data.

An extensive series of correlations revealed that: (1) many basic attributes of song style varied with the main subsistence activity of a culture; and (2) certain factors of song performance were good indicators of the level of complexity of the main productive processes of a culture, especially of the organization of its work teams.

Song is a kind of universal human behavior and so is work. Every person in every culture throughout history has usually been involved in the everyday, year-round food-producing activities of his culture. He has belonged to some kind of work team or was being trained for membership in one. The Yale studies show that child-rearing techniques vary decisively with the productive aims of societies. Roberts and Sutton-Smith prove that the kind of games a society plays also vary with subsistence type in the same directions that Child and his associates had already established. It was foreseeable, therefore, that song style would vary with productive type. Since the cantometric sample was twice as large and much more varied than that of any previous cross-cultural study, however, it was possible to test the relationship between economy and style on more refined scales than in earlier research.

Arensberg and I devised three-point, five-point, eight-point, and 18-point scales of subsistence types, each of which parsimoniously classified the economies of the world. The rules for this system, which produces productive classes from the whole Murdock sample, will be published in another study, but its validity was tested in two general ways: (1) whether each scale consists of stepwise systematic increases of productive range, and (2) whether it clusters cultures which are actually similar.

Of the several approaches to classifying subsistence types, the following five-point scale is the most effective. It is a classical nested hierarchy in which each higher term in the scale includes the ecological and technological resources of the term below, plus one more:

A FIVE-POINT SCALE OF SUBSISTENCE TYPES

1.   X — *Extractors:* major dependence on gathering, hunting, and/or fishing.
2.   IP — *Incipient Producers:* simple agriculture without animal husbandry prior to European contact.
3.   AH — *Animal Husbandry:* cultures depending on animal husbandry (involving pigs, sheep, or cattle, prior to European contact) and often agriculture, but without the plow or large irrigation works.
4.   PA — *Plow Agriculture:* cultures combining plow agriculture with animal husbandry.
5.   IR — *Irrigation:* agriculture, animal husbandry, the plow, and sizable irrigation works.

Later pages show that this scale proved to be an efficient way of ordering many cantometric variables. Those that had to do with the complexity, density, and specificity of the message increase along this scale in an orderly fashion, indicating that the more complex and productive the economic system, the more information-filled its songs are likely to be. The presumption was that, at any one production level, the song team and the work team operated at a similar level of complexity in communication. The following model illustrates this point:

Complex producers. Complex briefing for tasks; text-heavy and explicit songs.

Simple producers. Tasks understood; little or repetitious and non-explicit songs.

We hold, then, that the norms regulating the activity of work teams provide part of the formal structure for the output of the song team, or that both are governed by the same rules. Such a link between the norms of work and the norms of song implies that song style is a reflection and reinforcement of the way a culture gets it work done. Both models represent the way a culture arranges all behavior in the patterns crucial to its survival. Since the five-point production scale establishes an orderly and stepwise relationship between economies and songs—from simple through middling level to complex—both factors seem to be indicators of evolutionary development and the scale becomes a measure of complexity. However, we went on to test the scale on other social variables in order to prove (1) that it was, indeed, a measure of social complexity, and (2) that increase of productive range brings more complex arrangements into play in social structure.

The following correlations demonstrate the value of this scale as a complexity measure by showing its relationship to many of the features of community structure and the norms that govern interpersonal relationships.

Figure 26 shows that community size and settlement form, two principal indicators of community type, are related to the level of subsistence. Typically, extractor communities tend to be small—with populations of 50 or less up to 300 or 400. Most incipient producers live in settlements of at least 100 inhabitants, and there is an increase in the size of the largest settlements at this level. The modal size for the category of cultures that know animal husbandry, but not the plow or irrigation, is about the same as for incipient producers, but more large communities occur at this level than at the two previous ones. Plow agriculture and irrigation share the top of the scale for very large communities. In sum, the size of the largest community per culture tends to increase with rising subsistence complexity.

Figure 26 (right) shows the way the settlement type relates to productive range. One can see that most extractors are nomadic, and that most incipients live in stable settlements. Even so, no real modal settlement type can be fixed for these simple producers, for probably the broad range and differential distribution of settlement types here reflects a wide range of ecological possibilities at this productive level. The settlement type in animal husbandry varies across the whole range as well, but there is a striking shift toward stable and compact settlement, a tendency that becomes firmer with the introduction of more efficient agricultural techniques such as plowing and

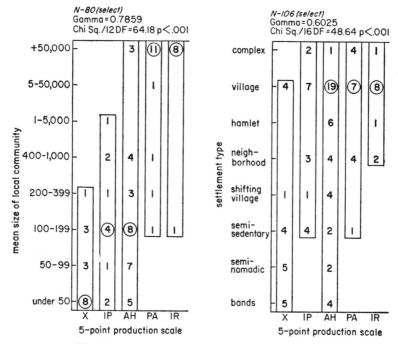

Fig. 26. Complexity: Community size and form.

At left: Community size is clearly a function of productive complexity. Note the steady rise of median size (indicated by circled numbers). Statistical split: X/IP/AH/PA/IR vs. under 50/50–399/400–5,000/more than 5,000.

At right: The incidence of stable settlement patterns rises with productive complexity. The modal settlement type per scale category is indicated by the circled numbers. In the case of Extractors (X) and Incipient Producers (IP), the ecological adaptations are apparently so varied that one cannot identify a truly modal settlement type. Statistical split: X/IP/AH/PA/IR vs. bands/semi-nomadic/semi-sedentary, shifting village/neighborhood, hamlet, village/complex.

irrigation. Stable and compactly ordered settlements do become more numerous as the productive process grows more complex. We have been unable to find whether there are styles typical of one form or another of the community, but the split in this correlation between nomadic or settled is, as we shall see in Chapter 7, of major effect on choral organization.

Murdock, revising the earlier scale of Swanson (1960), tags the cultures in his sample for the number of orders of control and government, both within and beyond the local community, on two scales from 0 to 4. Hierarchies of control *within* the local community might consist of (1) the nuclear family,

(2) the extended family, (3) the clan settlement, and (4) the village. In Europe, one might find four sovereign organizational levels *beyond* the local level: (1) the parish, (2) the district, (3) the province, and (4) the nation. The majority of primitive cultures at the extractive level are politically self-contained and thus score zero for extra-local hierarchies. Most of the agricultural societies of Africa have no more than one or two levels, such as the district chiefdom and the court of the king and his council, beyond the village. Only in Europe and high-culture Asia are scores of three or four for extra-local hierarchies common. The reader will note, therefore, that the five-point productive scale has a direct relationship to the increase of political complexity (Fig. 27, left). The extractors and incipients are generally politically autonomous. The range is wide at the animal husbandry level, but the mode is somewhere between zero and two levels of authority beyond the village. In plow agriculture, there are generally three levels of extra-local authority; but with irrigation, four levels of authority become frequent for the first time. This development of political controls accompanies population growth, increasing stability of settlement, and expanding productive range. Tribes come together in loose federations for truce-making and peace-keeping and then into states of increasing size. Bonds of blood and reciprocity are gradually superseded by political controls that impinge more and more on the internal affairs of the local community.

The relationship of Murdock's taxonomy of class stratification to the five-point productive scale also takes a step-wise form (Fig. 27, right). Among extractors and incipients there is a general absence of significant class distinctions dividing free men, although there may be some respect shown to individuals who distinguish themselves as hunters or shamans. Class structure emerges with the increase of productive range, community complexity, and political control, although at the level of animal husbandry most social distinctions are based on a simple differential in wealth or upon a dual system where a hereditary aristocracy with ascribed noble status is embedded in a lower class of commoners. This dual system becomes the norm in Negro Africa at a middle level of social development. With the vastly increased range of social complexity that accompanies the introduction of the plow, irrigation, and other agricultural techniques, social relations stiffen and a complex, layered class system develops. Blood, wealth, land, privilege, and social connections order society into a number of social classes correlated in large measure with the status of occupation.

As political centralization and stratification increase in society, the structure of the work team is directly affected. One of Udy's principal findings concerns what he terms custodial work teams, or teams in which the membership is compulsory and enforced by the authority structure of the culture.

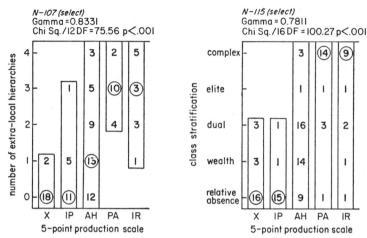

Fig. 27. Complexity: Political development and class stratification.

At left: Political development: The number of political agencies impinging on community life increases directly across the production scale. The median number of extra-local hierarchies per scale category is indicated by the circled numbers. Statistical split: X/IP/AH/PA/IR vs. 0/1/2/3, 4.

At right: Class stratification: Social structure becomes more rigid and complexly stratified with increase of productive complexity. The modal form of class system per scale category is indicated by the circled numbers. Although most societies in the Animal Husbandry (AH) category show some form of stratification, no real mode can be identified. Statistical split: X/IP/AH/PA/IR vs. relative absence/wealth/dual/elite/complex.

"When centralized government is introduced into a society, there is a tendency for all types of production to be carried out by custodial organizations, by virtue of preemption of control of resources by the political authority. . . . Considerable evidence can be brought to bear on the theory that under conditions of centralized government, custodial organization tends to be generalized to all types of production, by virtue of centralization of control over resources. . . ." (Udy, 1959)

In other words, as stratification and centralization increase with productive range, participation in the principal work activity tends to become compulsory. Furthermore, the preemption by managers or owners of the land of the goods produced by labor also sharply increases. Udy has demonstrated a strong relationship ($P < .001$) between these two tendencies, and we have charted this shift toward centralization of the control of wealth along a four-point production scale. (In this case, the Udy-cantometric samples at the levels of plow agriculture and irrigation were both too small and we were forced to combine them.) Looking at Figure 28, one sees that with the onset of the simplest agriculture, there is an increase of 40 percent in the incidence of control of the usufruct by the "bosses" over the frequency of this arrangement in extractive societies. This steep increase continues and reaches 95

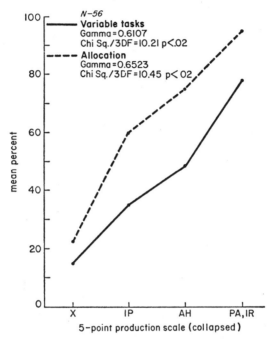

Fig. 28 Complexity: Organization of work.

Variable tasks: The frequency of complexly organized tasks increases directly with productive complexity. Statistical split: X/IP/AH/PA, IR vs. Median.

Allocation: With greater complexity, the control of work products increasingly is centered in management and ownership. Statistical split: X/IP/AH/PA, IR vs. Median.

The graphs on this and the following pages are representations of trends in relationships, usually between one ordinal and one continuous variable. Throughout, we will be presenting the statistical evaluation of these relationships based on:

1. The chi square distribution, which indicates the order of probability that the relationship would have occurred by chance (e.g., P < .001 states a 1 in 1,000 probability that the relationship occurred by chance).

2. Gamma, also known as the Index of Order-Association, which is a measure of strength of unidirectional relationship (see Appendix 2).

3. N indicates the number in the sample.

percent among the complex agriculturists who, in the Udy sample, are either European feudal or imperial Oriental societies. There is no question that one result of improvement in productive techniques is that control over the goods shifts from the hands of producers to those of the director or entrepreneur.

A look at one other characteristic of work team organization will conclude the test of the five-point subsistence scale. This is a Udy rating concerned with the variability of the workload and structural complexity of the teams. Udy defines this condition as follows:

> "If persons are regularly added to or subtracted from an organization, the process involves a variable workload; if not, the workload is constant. Variations in workload are closely related to task differentiation, in that the latter 'sets the stage' for the former, through reassembly of the organization at the start of each new task. . . ." (Udy, 1959)

He notes that agriculture, especially in fixed fields, is characterized by sharp swings in workload, and that, while tasks with a constant workload usually involve few processes, those with variable workload generally have a more complex structure. Oscillating workload and task complexity place fixed field agriculture in sharp contrast to the extractive modes of production. The relationship between production type and workload variability, illustrated in Figure 26, stands at a level of $P < .01$.

COMPLEXITY IN SONG AND SOCIETY

The five-point production scale is a reliable cross-cultural measure of general social complexity, since it has a demonstrable relationship to six other independent and powerful measures of cultural development: size of community, stability of settlement, government controls, stratification, exploitation, and task complexity. Those cantometric variables, therefore, which relate in a scalar way to this one measure may be thought of as representations of the complexity or statements about the complexity of the whole social structure.

Text load, precision of enunciation, interval size, degree of embellishment, number of phonetic elements, and number of instrumental type are the song variables, among others, closely tied to this complexity scale. A are measures of the number, the variety, and the clarity of the symbolic uni employed as well as the sheer amount of information typically carried in given performance style. In general, song styles from complex cultures a: dense with information, while songs from simple economies carry less i formation load.

The most potent indicator of complexity on the cantometric coding sheet is the parameter which is coded wordy (or text-heavy) to the left of the line and completely repetitious (or nonsense-filled) to the right, with three points in between (Chapter 3). Apparently, even without knowing the language, raters find it possible to agree on whether a singer is constantly introducing new strings of syllables, whether he is mostly repeating the same words or lilting a stream of nonsense syllables over and over.

Five familiar American folk songs serve to illustrate the five distinctions on this line:

1. Let the first stanza of the lumber ballad, *Young Monroe,* stand for wordiness (Wo):

> Come all you jolly fellows, wherever you may be,
> I hope you'll pay attention and listen unto me,
> Concerning a young lumberjack so manly true and brave,
> 'Twas on the jam on Gerry's rock he met his watery grave.

2. In the ballad of *John Henry* the last line is repeated once in every stanza and therefore the coding is wordy with a small amount of repetition (Wo-no):

> John Henry was a little baby.
> You could hold him in the palm of your hand.
> The very first word that poor boy said:
> I'm going to be a steel driving man, Lord, Lord,
> I'm going to be a steel driving man.

3. The Negro ballad of *The Grey Goose* represents those songs that are about half text and half repetition or nonsense (wo-no):

> Last Monday morning, Lord, Lord, Lord,
> My daddy went a-hunting, Lord, Lord, Lord,
> He went to the big wood, Lord, Lord, Lord,
> And the hound dog he went too, Lord, Lord, Lord.

4. And for a song that is almost all repetition (wo-No):

> I'm a poor lonesome cowboy,
> I'm a poor lonesome cowboy,
> I'm a poor lonesome cowboy,
> And a long way from home.
> I ain't got no mother,
> I ain't got no mother,
> I ain't got no mother,
> To mend the clothes I wear. etc.

5. Finally, for the category of all repetition and nonsense, where so much of the primitive world lives, there are few songs in English. Here, for instance, at (No) we would rate the refrain of the familiar:

> Amen, hallelujah!
> Amen, hallelujah!
> Amen, amen, amen!

We have purposely refrained from making this measurement of semantic load too precise, having discovered that the scale derives its taxonomic power from gross differences in level, rather than from the fine distinctions that would emerge from an exact count of words or syllables. So long as the raters were within one point of each other on the coding line or their judgments fell on the same side of the midpoint, the cultural, regional, and functional profiles in which we were interested kept their consistency. Figure 29 shows that wordiness varies directly along our scale of productive complexity.

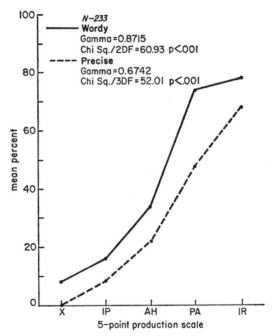

Fig. 29. Wordiness of song text and precision of articulation: the five-point production scale. Wordiness and precision of sung text become more frequent with growing complexity. Statistical splits: Wordy—X, IP/AH/PA/IR vs. Median; Precise—X, IP/AH/PA, IR vs. Median.

Moreover, text load has been shown to have a similar relationship to other facets of social complexity like political development, stratification, and community size. As the social net that holds the human community together becomes larger and more tightly woven, every individual act demands greater explanation, discussion, and rationalization. Seen thus, the appearance of the ballad, a factual and understated account of events—late in the evolutionary series and only in Western Europe—becomes the more understandable.

Along with sheer verbosity, precision of enunciation appears also to be related to social complexity. At the lower end of our production scales, among simple producers, singers most frequently slur over the consonants that divide the text into syllabic bits; at the upper end, syllables are carefully marked or fenced by bounding consonants.

As it is laid out on the coding sheet, the parameter measuring precision expresses a range somewhere between the verbal prissiness of a Parisian shopkeeper, coded on the left, and the unintelligibility of sounds run together by the extremely relaxed use of teeth, tongue, and glottis, coded on the right. Our best example of precision in song is the performance of a Basque bard projecting his ironic verses into the farthermost corners of a noisy barroom. The liquid, virtually non-consonantal flow of an African Pygmy chorus is an example of extremely slurred enunciation.

The ethnographic distribution of precise singing offers support to the notion that this trait reflects the communication demands of societies with complex orderings. Of all style regions, Oceania scores highest for precision, even above the Orient or Europe. Ethnologists such as Beaglehole (1947) and Mead (1949) have remarked that Polynesians attach great value to early mastery and felicitous use of language. The Maori, for example, send their children to school to learn genealogical chants from an adept, whose duty is to teach them to pronounce the traditional poems with such exactness and clarity that they acquire a magic power. The status of every Maori and, indeed, of every Polynesian is based on his inherited position. His very life has sometimes hung upon his recall of his genealogy. Captured in a battle, he might be spared by his enemies if he located a relative among them somewhere on his family tree. One imagines that the cultivation of a remarkable and precise memory was fundamental to the Polynesian feats of navigation which depended in the end only upon what had been learned by rote from those who had sailed that way before. Such factors, perhaps, make precision of enunciation especially functional in Polynesia. Around the world, however, heavy loading of exactly articulated bits of information in a song style indicates a high level of productive complexity.

Wordiness and precision form the compound variable of explicitness which also shifts with the level of social complexity. As illustrated in Figure 30, the sharp rise in the mean frequency of explicit songs along the five-point

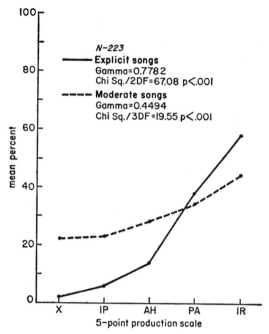

Fig. 30. Explicitness and moderate delivery:
the five-point production scale.

Both explicitness (wordiness and precision of
sung text) and moderate delivery (mid-volume
and normal accent) increase directly with productive complexity. Statistical splits: Explicit–
X, IP/AH/PA, IR vs. Median; Moderate–X,
IP/AH/PA/IR vs. Median.

production scale evokes an evolutionary picture of increasing specialization
of roles and growing complexity of the technical and social demands made
on the individual. In the explicit song, information and meticulous delivery
come together in the form of complicated, particularized instruction.

Clarity of message as a principle of style appears, further, in the mode of
delivery. Complex cultures show a strong preference for moderation, with
the level of volume and stress kept close to the mean for normal speech. In
complex societies, the most frequent stance of leaders is instructive and di-
dactic. The strategy of leadership is therefore likely to be one of moderate
presentation, neither too loud and forceful nor too quiet and relaxed. On
the basis of this hypothesis, we are not surprised to find that songs delivered
in mid-volume and normal accent occur more frequently at the upper end of
the complexity scale (Fig. 30). This is not to say that other more flamboyant

modes of delivery are not encountered among the virtuosi of High Culture Europe and Asia, but the dominance of quietly persuasive, expository style does appear to be a reasonably late development.

Wordiness, precise articulation, mid volume, normal accent, and solo delivery form a constellation (explicit and moderate solo) especially appropriate to complex cultures. Indeed, songs combining all these attributes hardly occur in our sample except at the upper ranges of the production scale (Fig. 31).

The principal discovery in cantometrics is that a culture's favored song style reflects and reinforces the kind of behavior essential to its main subsistence efforts and to its central and controlling social institutions. Thus, if the main productive roles and the chief models of leadership are expressed

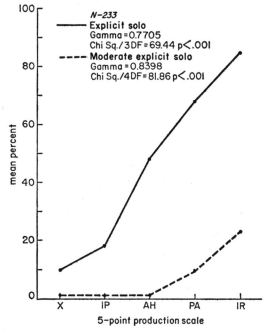

Fig. 31. Explicitness and moderate delivery in solo singing: the five-point production scale.

Explicit solo: The frequency of wordy, precise, solo singing increases directly along the production scale. Statistical split: X, IP/AH/PA/IR vs. Median.

Moderate explicit solo: Wordy and precise solos sung at mid-volume and with normal accent are absolutely diagnostic of social complexity. Statistical split: X/IP/AH/PA/IR vs. Median.

in forceful, masculine, aggressive, and repetitive behavior, the song style will be strongly canted in that direction. The principal examples of such songs in our sample come from the aboriginal hunters of Australia and North and South America. When the American Indian hunter steps before his people, he thrills them and is expected to thrill them by playing this forceful and aggressive role.

In our own society, made up of technicians, office workers, scientists, arbitrators, and supposedly reasonable people in every walk of life, audiences are often deeply moved by performers who address them with restraint and moderation. Perhaps this urban preference for the explanatory tone of voice played a decisive role in a recent revolution in popular music. Before the young urban white groups of England and the United States took over rock-and-roll, this style was marked by repetitiousness and by extremely forceful and loud delivery. This kind of rock-and-roll was never popular with the whole white urban audience, especially the serious critics. When, however, such singers as the Beatles and Bobby Dylan introduced complex texts, precise enunciation, and a moderate delivery, rock-and-roll grew to be acceptable to the urban audience, including the white upper-class elite.

As society grew more complex and leadership more exclusive, the solo bard began to hold the center of the stage. He preempted the communication space as the priests and kings seized and held the wealth and power of the human community. The bard, exercising exclusive dominance and enforcing passive attention through long songs, represented the dominant leaders and helped to train the audience to listen for long periods without replying. More than that, the bard, whether sacred or secular, addressed himself to the powerful leaders who more and more directed the life of ever larger social units. The priest linked the devout with the divine father through long, chanted prayers in which the deity is praised, cajoled, and made vivid. At court the bard celebrated the deeds of the ruling families, especially the king, in songs of praise; and these praise songs kindled the patriotic fervor of vassals and henchmen alike. Presently there appeared the epic composer with his lyre or lute, prepared to chant the history of a people or a dynasty in poems that lasted for hours, holding his audience enthralled, like Westerners at a symphony concert. The bard was an early information specialist, storing the traditional knowledge of his group with the help of the redundant devices of poetry. Although his mnemonic techniques were later replaced by writing and other forms of information storage, the leaning toward the specific and the explanatory style remains the keynote of all learning thereafter. Later, in Europe, came the ballad maker, who capsuled his narrative and restrained his poetic flights to please the sober, hard-working folk of the West.

The distribution of this individualized, moderate-voiced, explicit song style is confined to the complex cultures of Europe and Old High Culture. Cantometrics can separate these two regions from one another by introducing two further distinctions, one for each style, each representative of its region's strongest bent. Western Europe shows a clear preference for simple and compactly organized melodic forms. Most Oriental bards employ some form of embellishment, either melodic or rhythmic. The distribution of these two late-developed explanatory styles is demonstrated in Figure 1.

The opposite set of qualities, much repetition (generally of nonsense syllables) and slurred enunciation of consonants, are marked characteristics of the songs of primitive producers, especially at the extractive level (Fig. 32). These two indicators of non-explicitness often combine in songs of primitive extracting economies with another related feature—the frequency of large or

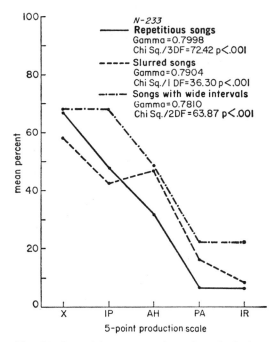

Fig. 32. Repetitious text, slurred articulation, and wide melodic intervals: the five-point production scale. With some variation in trend, the incidence of repetition of text, slurring, and wide melodic intervals decreases rapidly with productive complexity. Statistical splits: Repetitious— X/IP/AH/PA, IR vs. Median; Slurred–X, IP, AH/PA, IR vs. Median; Wide intervals–X, IP/AH/PA, IR vs. Median.

wide melodic intervals. Songs were rated by the coders as wide (W, *W* on Line 21) if intervals of a third, fourth, fifth, or larger were frequent and important. The preference for large intervals can be seen as a looser and more open-ended way of defining and splitting up musical space than if smaller intervals are sung. The striking occurrence of wide intervals in the songs of most extractor groups may symbolize a less confining, freer, more wide-ranging approach to the use of space (social and/or ecological) for the individual who lives in a simple society where access to land, food, privilege, sex, status, and other life resources is open to all members of the community on more or less equal terms (Diamond, 1960, 1963). Figure 33 points to an increasing preference for narrow intervals with a rise in productive complexity. Strikingly enough, prominence of very narrow intervals (minor seconds and less) turns up in cultures whose members are confined spatially or restricted by a system of rigid status differentiation in their free use of productive and social resources, notably in the area of Old High Culture, and among the authoritarian Australian Aborigines.

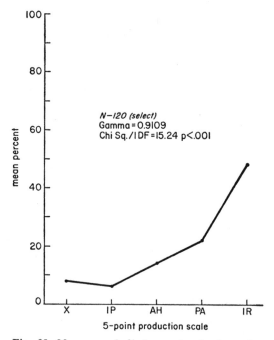

Fig. 33. Narrow melodic intervals: the five-point production scale. The use of narrow melodic intervals is frequent only in more complex societies. Statistical split: X, IP, AH, PA/IR vs. Median.

There are several ways, therefore, in which songs of simple producers seem less explicit and less articulated than songs from more complex economies. Frequent repetition of the same text and a high proportion of nonsense syllables, vocal segregates, cries, and the like, establish group consensus at a minimal level and might be said to permit a member of the group to fantasize freely during a song performance. I am told by ethnologists who have worked with Kung Bushmen and the Mbuti Pygmies of Africa that in a song that lasts a half-hour or so, there may be only one phrase of meaningful text; all the rest consists of yodeled and hooted vowel sounds. The non-specificity of the text is reinforced by a tendency to slur across consonants or omit them entirely, thus leaving the verbal line empty of another order of markers and definers, so that vowel sounds flow uninterruptedly into each other. Finally, musical intervals may be thought of as consisting of leaps from one pitch level to another, each leap being confined by boundaries of varying dimensions. Among simple producers, more wide leaps are employed in the sung communication than by the singers of complex cultures. Fewer markers and distinctions exist, and thus the bits in the communications stream are fewer, larger, and less frequently bounded.

Figure 34 (solid line) shows that songs defined by the traits of repetition, slurring, and wide intervals are seldom found except among collectors, hunters, fishers, and incipient producers. A Westerner may sing to himself in the bath or as he absentmindedly goes about his private life in this rum-tiddy-de-da style, but rarely so for a public audience. Nonsense songs like "Ja-Da" occasionally make the hit parade, but their very rarity indicates the strong preference of western culture for songs with a heavy load of information. As we have seen, the incidence of non-explicit song texts represents an equally powerful tendency. These two trends might be summarized as follows: Simply organized cultures achieve group consensus by restricting content and specificity to a minimum, while complex cultures bring about group consensus by increasing content and carefully defining this content with a multiplication of distinctions and articulations. The occurrence of these two opposing approaches to song performance arranges the cultures in our sample along a scale of increasing social and economic complexity in a decisive fashion. Here song style may be a direct reflection of the complexity of the productive process. Udy has applied a measure of work complexity to a sample of 100 pre-industrial societies. His conclusion, in summary, is that, "In total degree of complexity, tillage and construction are more complex than hunting, and hunting is more complex than fishing or collection" (Udy, 1959). As tasks grow more complex, plans, briefing, coordination, and work flow must be set forth ever more explicitly and fully; the appropriate and pleasing performance by the singing team in such a society is likely to be information-heavy.

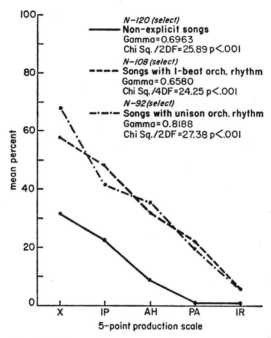

Fig. 34. Non-explicit text and orchestral simplicity: the five-point production scale. Non-explicit songs (those with repetitious text, sung
with slurred articulation) occur only at the lower
end of the complexity scale. The incidence of orchestral unison and one-beat orchestral rhythm
decreases with complexity. Statistical splits: Non-
explicit—X, IP/AH/PA, IR vs. Median; One-
beat orchestral rhythm—X/IP/AH/PA/IR vs.
Median; Orchestral unison—X/IP, AH/PA, IR
vs. Median.

It appears, then, that one of the functions of the sung communication is to
define and reinforce the level of specificity which most efficiently organizes
interaction in a given society. The members of a simple culture are so familiar with the behavior patterns traditionally required of them that most
situations can remain non-explicit; thus the individual is left free of verbal
restraints. In complex cultures, action plans are more complicated and full
of alternatives; group members need lengthy briefing and extremely explicit
indoctrination in order to bring about effective joint interaction. In such
communications the length of the text might be said to be a measure of the
relative importance of what leaders and specialists have to say, as compared
to what the led and the non-specialist may contribute. Furthermore, the
specificity of the text, though it sharpens the statement, at the same time

suggests a total preemption of the communication space by the thoughts, ideas, feelings, and needs of the leader. If the song "works," the members of the group are persuaded by the virtuoso to follow him and conform to the pattern he has elected.

Not only do the songs of simple producers tend to be non-explicit, but they are frequently simple in the rhythmic aspect of their structure, as well. Perhaps the easiest rhythm to follow in an orchestra is an undifferentiated, steady, one-beat meter; and the simplest way of organizing the orchestral group is for every instrument to play in unison with others. Figure 44, page 155, indicates that the number of types of instruments in a culture's orchestral roster provides a rough measure of the level of social stratification in that culture. Thus it is not surprising to see that the rhythmic plan uniting the instruments of an orchestra is also an indicator of social complexity. One-beat meter is heard almost exclusively among extractors or early producers, and rhythmic unison is the major principle of orchestral organization in such societies. The combination of these two features rarely occurs except in simple economies. On the whole, rhythmic plans for the orchestra grow increasingly more complex as one moves up the scale of general social complexity (Figs. 35, 36).

It is interesting to note that the two most complex forms of organization of orchestral rhythm—counterpoint and heterophony—though strongly associated with complex modes of production, do not bear as decisive a relation to this factor as those we have just noted. Here, as elsewhere, aspects of orchestral complexity seem to be indicators of the levels of political control and stratification in society (Table 9).

Table 9. *Orchestral counterpoint or heterophony with production scale.*

Percent counterpoint or heterophony in orchestral accompaniment		X	IP	AH	PA, IR
	Median	3	2	10	18
		27	19	71	31

Chi sq/3 df = 15.57; gamma = .4984; P < .01; N = 181.

Apparently, then, there are a number of easily observable indicators in song performance that signal the level of the social and technological complexity of the culture. All of these indicators measure the size and number of the bits in various aspects of the song stream:

1. Verbal complexity
2. Number of sharply enunciated consonants
3. Size and number of intervals
4. Number of different kinds of beats in the orchestra
5. Number of rhythmic parts in the orchestral plan.

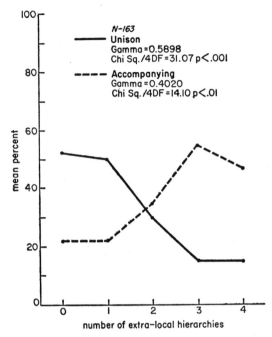

Fig 35. Rhythmic organization of orchestra and political development—I. The unison and the accompanying modes of orchestral rhythmic organization are clear definers of simplicity and complexity. Note the nearly perfect opposition of trend across the scale and the equality of incidence at the middle level. Statistical splits: Both Unison and Accompanying—0/1/2/3/4 vs. Median.

All these relationships stand up to statistical tests of a very high order and indicate that a song performance may be taken as a measure of the level of explicitness essential to most situations of public interaction in a culture.

PHONOTACTICS AND SOCIAL COMPLEXITY

This conclusion has been confirmed by another experiment in the Cantometrics Project called "phonotactics"—a word coined by Edith Trager. In 1961 Trager and I found that song styles and culture areas can be defined and differentiated merely by a systematic count of the different types of vowels used in typical folk songs and by a statement of the proportional use of the various vowel areas (Lomax and Trager, 1964). In an extension of

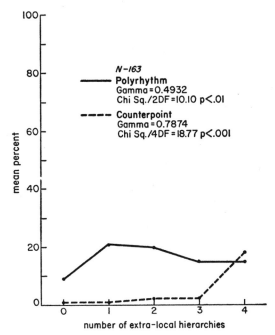

Fig. 36. Rhythmic organization of orchestra and
political development—II. Orchestral polyrhythm
is somewhat more frequent at the middle level of
complexity than at the upper and lower levels.
Orchestral counterpoint occurs only at the upper
level. Statistical splits: Polyrhythm—0/1, 2, 3/4
vs. Median; Counterpoint—0/1/2/3/4 vs. Median.

this experiment, Dr. Fred Peng and I devised a way to estimate the differential use of vowel and consonant areas cross-culturally. In this system,
vowel formation is seen as a three-dimensional set of components: (1) high,
medium, and low; (2) front, central, and back; and (3) rounded, and unrounded. Out of this set of components, 18 "vocoids" were established to record cross-cultural vowel usage. (Vocoid: a coined word meaning a vowel
area such as high front and unrounded or high front and rounded.)

Consonantal sounds are broken down in a somewhat novel manner. The
first dimension, the articulator, is regarded as being divided into three areas:
front, mid, and back. "Front" here refers only to the lower lip; "mid" to
both the tip and blade of the tongue; "back" to the back of the tongue and
to the rest of the vocal organs. The second dimension of consonant sounds,
the point of articulation, is also regarded as being divided into three areas:
front, mid, and back. But "front" here refers to both the upper lip and the

upper teeth; "mid" to both the alveolar ridge and the hard palate; "back" to the soft palate, the pharyngeal region, and the glottis. The third dimension of consonantal sounds, the manner of articulation, is regarded as having four classes: stops, fricatives, nasals, and laterals.

A clarifying note about the distinctions used in coding: the term "stop" here includes not only pure stops, but also the first sound of any affricate. This approach is based on the definition of an affricate as a stop followed by a fricative. The term "nasal" here includes only nasal "contoids"; nasal vocoids are not considered or coded. (Contoid: a coined word meaning a consonant area such as front front stop or front front fricative.) The term "lateral" includes all the liquid consonants as well as the lateral fricatives, or all sounds that are laterally produced.

Thus considered, the entire consonantal field is coded in terms of a set of the eleven most frequent combinations of the three determinants of contoids just discussed:

1. Front front stop
2. Front front fricative
3. Front front nasal
4. Mid front fricative
5. Mid mid stop
6. Mid mid fricative
7. Mid mid nasal
8. Mid mid lateral
9. Back back stop
10. Back back fricative
11. Back back nasal

Peng devoted six months to the analysis of the vocoid-contoid fields in a sample of 300 recorded songs, ten each from 30 cultures well distributed across the larger cantometric sample. This cultural sample may be inspected in Figures 37–40. His method was most direct. He first determined the field of vocoids and contoids that appeared to define the linguistic space in a recorded song. Second, through many repeated playings of the recording, he estimated by ear the percentage of the contribution of each component to the total percentage for the whole performance. He entered his estimates on a standardized coding sheet which made it possible to draw profiles or graphs showing the relative importance of the various phonotactic components. This facilitated comparison and contrast among songs and song styles.

Granted the reliability and consistency of Peng, the only expert coder, the evidence from even a small number of songs has considerable validity. Each song contains hundreds, sometimes thousands, of sounds. If a culture shows a strongly biased phonotactic pattern, the likelihood is that this tendency represents features of genuine importance to that song style. The data are admirably suited to computer manipulations.

When profiles were drawn for the song samples of cultures, culture areas, and production types, we found, on the whole, that the phonotactic profiles of complex cultures tend to be smoother than those of simpler cultures. In other words, simple cultures generally employ fewer components in song than do complex cultures. Thus phonotactics affirms the relationship between specificity and social complexity established by the Cantometrics Project.

This general notion has been refined by further tests. All indicate that, however the phonotactic data are manipulated, the number of consonantal distinctions increases with cultural complexity, whereas this relation is weaker in regard to vocoids. Perhaps the most useful as well as the most convincing phonotactic measure of cultural complexity is the mean number of contoid types per cultural song sample. This measure, as might be expected, turns out to have a highly positive relationship to the degree of explicitness (wordiness plus precision) present in the songs of each culture (Fig. 37). Actually the cantometrics coders were registering their perception that a sizable variety of consonantal sounds were present in the song stream when they set down a high rating for precise enunciation. Thus, the fact that an independent judge who is a trained phonetician scored for consonantal variety, where cantometric raters found explicitness, confirms the cantometric scores and strengthens the impression that this measure is a valid one. It should be recalled that all the non-expert judges were listening impressionistically to song in languages with which generally they had had no previous acquaintance. The fact that the ratings of the expert phonetican confirm those of the non-expert cantometricians supports the reliability of all three scales.

Another scale of measurement rests on the assumption that the vocal regions in which the contoids are shaped have a relationship to some order of complexity. More consonantal distinctions in more languages are formed at mid-position (alveolar ridge and hard palate) than in front (lips and teeth), and more in front than in the back of the throat near the glottis. In another attempt to test the relation of consonantal differentiation to cultural complexity, we made, for each song sample, a weighted index reflecting the relative importance of the three contoid regions. In calculating the index, we assigned weights of 0, 1, and 2, to back-, front-, and mid-contoids, respectively, then summed the weighted proportions of each per cultural song sample, and divided by 3. This produced a measure of presumed consonant complexity for each culture which was then tested against the degree of explicitness per culture. Again, an extremely high relationship was found to exist between level of consonant complexity and explicitness. Examination of

144

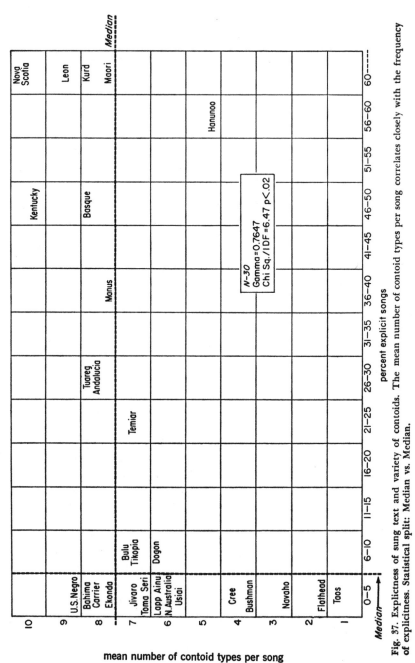

Fig. 37. Explictness of sung text and variety of contoids. The mean number of contoid types per song correlates closely with the frequency of explicitness. Statistical split: Median vs. Median.

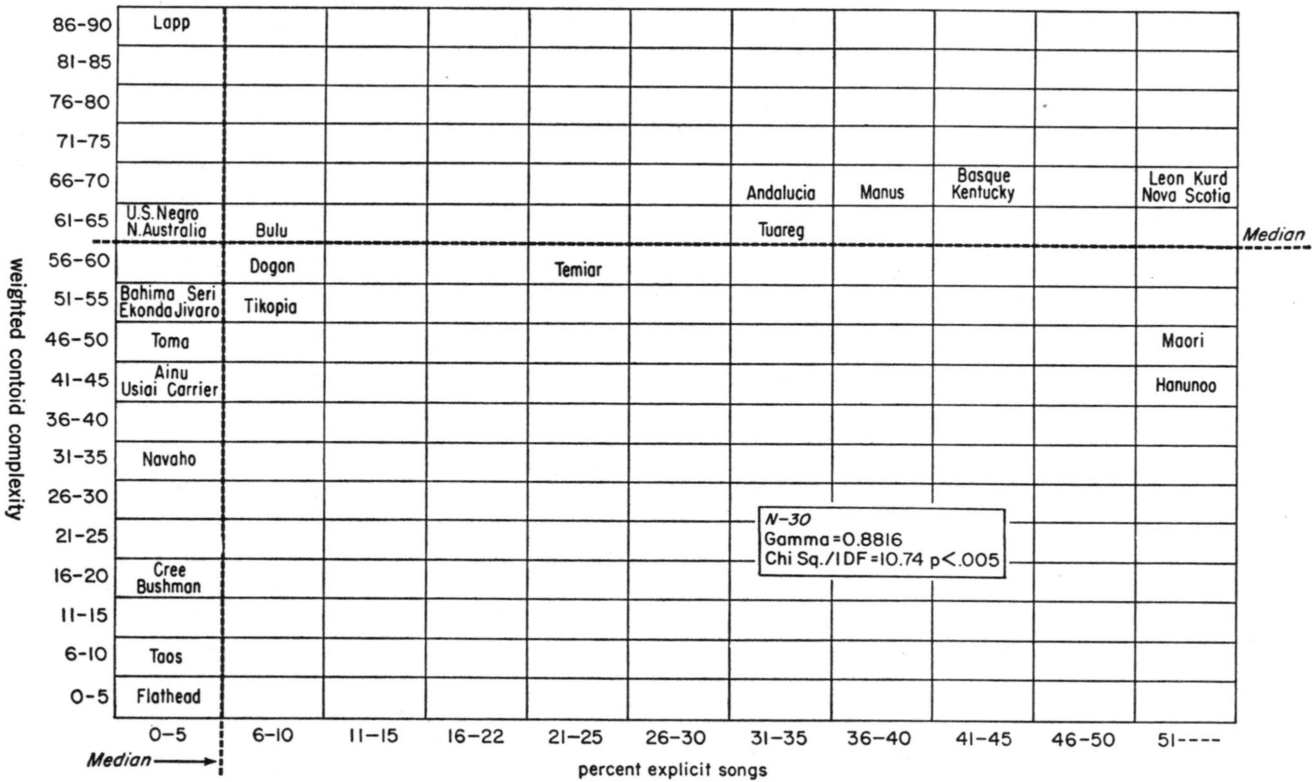

Fig. 38. Explicitness of sung text and weighted contoid complexity.

weighted contoid complexity	0-5	6-10	11-15	16-22	21-25	26-30	31-35	36-40	41-45	46-50	51----
86-90	Lapp										
81-85											
76-80											
71-75											
66-70							Andalucia	Manus	Basque Kentucky		Leon Kurd Nova Scotia
61-65	U.S.Negro N.Australia	Bulu					Tuareg				
56-60		Dogon			Temiar						
51-55	Bahima Seri Ekonda Jivaro	Tikopia									
46-50	Toma										Maori
41-45	Ainu Usiai Carrier										Hanunoo
36-40											
31-35	Navaho										
26-30											
21-25				Cree Bushman							
16-20											
11-15											
6-10	Taos										
0-5	Flathead										

N-30
Gamma=0.8816
Chi Sq./1DF=10.74 p<.005

Median ———→ (weighted contoid complexity)

Median (percent explicit songs)

percent explicit songs

Fig. 38. Explicitness of sung text and weighted contoid complexity. Complexity of articulation is closely correlated with explicitness. Statistical split: Median vs. Median.

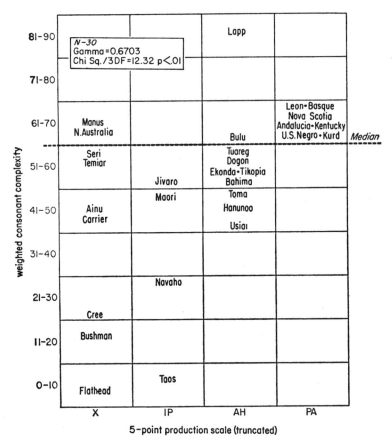

Fig. 39. Weighted contoid complexity: the five-point production scale
(truncated). Complexity of articulation is rare at the lower end of the
production scale. Statistical split: X/IP/AH/PA vs. Median.

Figures 38 and 39 shows that in most cases cultures occupy the same relative
position in the two fields of correlation. This means that, as far as songs are
concerned, there is a distinct relationship between explicitness, the number
of consonantal distinctions used, and the location of these distinctions in the
mid- and front-enunciatory regions.

Explicitness in song texts has already been established as a sign of cultural complexity. It was, therefore, no surprise to find that, if the mean number of contoid types is calculated per subsistence type, this mean increases
along the five-point subsistence scale. No marked difference shows up between the number of contoids used by extractors and incipients, but there is
a clearcut rise at the animal husbandry and plow agriculture levels. The

weighted index of consonantal complexity, differentiating among the three kinds of contoids, shows a somewhat better correlation (Fig. 39).

This sharpening of statistical contrasts results from the lower level of complexity scored for the four incipient producers in the sample, including three Amerindian groups, who characteristically fill their songs with nonsense syllables having initial back consonants like *He Ye He Ya*, etc.

Reference to Figure 39 will show that all the complex cultures cluster together at a high level of contoid complexity. It is unfortunate that the plow agriculture sample, with but one exception, Basque, includes only Indo-European languages. Thus the relation of phonotactic complexity to a high level of social complexity has not been tested on a representative range of language families. But the correlation is strong enough to indicate a clear association between back consonants and productive simplicity, and front- and mid-consonants and productive complexity.

The same tests, when applied to vowels, show a much weaker relationship between the number of types of vowels found in the songs of a culture and its position on the productive complexity scale. As shown in Figure 40, little if any relationship links social complexity and the mean number of vowels

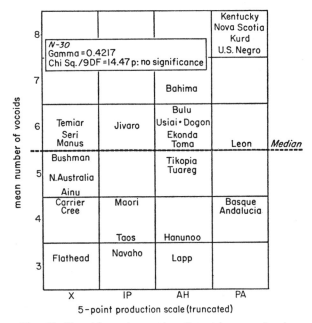

Fig. 40. Vocoid variety: the five-point production scale (truncated). There is little, if any, relationship between vocoid variety and productive complexity. Statistical split: X/IP/AH/PA vs. Median.

per culture. Perhaps the most interesting point to note in this display is that, on the whole, the cultures which employ more types of vocoids employ more contoids. The position of the cultures in both the vowel and consonant diagrams is remarkably similar. Generally, however, vowels do not seem to increase with the degree of specificity of sung communication in the decisive fashion of consonants. Figure 40 also shows that the number of vowel areas employed in the songs of a culture does not increase with its complexity. Some plow agriculturists are more narrowly selective in their use of vowels than many simpler cultures. Songs from these complex cultures often use a narrower vowel range than those of the simpler peoples, as shown in Table 10, where it appears that six out of eight plow agriculturists in the sample

Table 10. *Number of vowel types against truncated complexity scale.*

	X, IP, AH	PA
Cultures with 7–10 vowels which occur more than 20%	12	2
Cultures with 3–6 vowels which occur more than 20%	11	6
P not significant		

employ no more than six vowels more than 20 percent of the time in their songs.

Table 11 shows that in cultures where there is more than 20 percent dependence on hunting, the mean number of contoids is lower than in cultures where hunting is less important. Thus the number of contoid types seems to increase with productive complexity. On the other hand, if a culture knows animal husbandry or plow agriculture, it is more likely to employ more consonantal markers than if it follows a simpler subsistence plan (Table 12). Here again, specificity seems related to social complexity.

In a look at the relationship between front-, mid-, or central- and back-articulation areas in relation to the complexity scale, we see in Table 12 that in regard to vocoids there is no relation between vowel area and complexity. In my opinion, part of this effect is due to Peng's decision to treat the glides [y] and [w] as [i] [a], and [u] [o], respectively. The high incidence of vocables such as *"Ya Ye"* in primitive music ups the percentage of high front vowels enormously. Turning, however, to the lower half of Table 12 which shows the spread of contoid types in relation to the complexity scale, it appears that mid-contoids form, even with our small sample, an interesting index for complexity. This conclusion is all the more arresting since it is likely that mid is the last and richest area in the speech-learning process, because this is

Table 11. *Contoid variety and subsistence.*

	Dependence on hunting		
		0–10%	20–50%
No. of contoid types used per culture	10–11	16	4
	7, 8, 9	2	8

Chi sq/1 df = 6.96; gamma = .8824; P < .01.

	By subsistence type		
		X, IP	AH, PA
No. of contoid types used per culture	10–11	5	15
	7, 8, 9	8	2

Chi sq/1 df = 6.02; gamma = .8462; P < .02.

the area in which more types of discrimination are possible than in other buccal zones. Back-articulation is high among primitive producers and drops off sharply with complexity. It has a high peak in the IP category because three of the four IP cultures are Amerindian, with songs that tend to be heavily loaded with syllables containing back consonants such as [h] and [k].

Table 12. *Phonation areas versus social complexity.*

	Vowels			
	X	IP	AH	PA
Front	43	41	42	46
Central	29	31	30	24
Back	26	27	26	29
	Consonants			
Front	22	11	26	26
Mid	31	29	42	52
Back	47	60	32	22

Several general hypotheses of importance to the development of language and the nature of poetry may now be suggested.

1. Mid- and, to a lesser extent, front-articulation increases with social complexity. In other words, the areas that are richest in articulatory possibilities and permit most subtle enunciatory discriminations are used more frequently in complex than simple cultures.
2. Buccal closure, associated strongly with front- and to a lesser extent with mid-enunciation, also increases with social complexity. This phenomenon may be connected with another finding that a narrow and squeezed vocal delivery is more typical of complex cultures than of simple, particularly at the level of plow agriculture (Table 13).

Table 13. *Vocal constriction and subsistence.*

Percent narrow voices	X, IP, AH	PA	IR
	35	9	13
Median			
	51	11	1

Chi sq = 13.20/2 df; gamma = .4935; P < .01; N = 120.

3. Back-articulation, often emphasizing one back-contoid to the virtual exclusion of the others, shapes the song styles of many simple producers, particularly the game producers of North America. Most Indian performances in the phonotactic sample are by North American males, and the attack is almost always loud, forceful, and aggressive. Thus certain back-contoids may be representations of masculinity and aggressiveness. In a later chapter, Erickson demonstrates that harsh, guttural vocalizing is strongly associated with childhood training for independence.

SONG AND SOCIAL LAYERING

Turning back to the cantometric data, two features that might be called para-musical are now considered: (1) embellishment or the degree to which small, passing, decorative notes are added to the main melody; and (2) free rhythm, coded when no regularly recurring beat can be distinguished; in effect, the sung rhythm becomes so complex that it approximates the metrical irregularity of speech (Fig. 41). Spanish *cante hondo,* Jewish cantellation, Indian ragas, Japanese geisha songs, and many Oriental song types are frequently heavily embellished and metrically free. Both these features add vastly to the complexity of a sung melody. Both appear prominently at the most complex productive levels. When rubato and embellishment come together in a song, we term it "elaborate." In order to pinpoint the relation between this elaborate style and social complexity, we introduce another scale of production types, this one with eight points.

Eight-Point Scale of Subsistence Types
1. C — *Collectors;* major dependence on food gathering.
2. G — *Hunters and/or fishers;* principally.
3. IP — *Simple agriculture;* without animal husbandry.
4. CA — *Simple agriculture;* with animal husbandry, prior to European contact.
5. HF — *Horticulture with fishing;* tree cultivation with animal husbandry and ocean fishing.
6. PA — *Plow agriculture.*

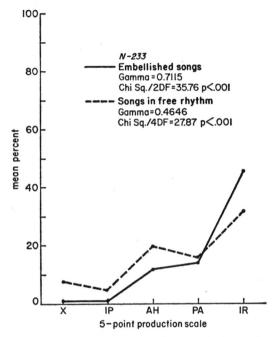

Fig. 41. Embellishment and free rhythm: the five-point production scale. Both embellishment and free rhythm vary directly across the production scale with a strong concentration in the IR category. Statistical splits: Embellishment—X, IP/AH,PA/IR vs. Median; Free rhythm—X/IP/AH/PA/IR vs. Median.

7. PC — *Full, nomadic pastoralism;* at least 70 percent dependence on animal husbandry.
8. IR — *Irrigation agriculture.*

The normal order of this scale, when used as a measure of increasing productive range, appears elsewhere in this book. In this instance, however, the scale has been rearranged to show that one special feature of stylistic complexity (elaborate singing) appears more frequently among complex pastoralists (PC) and irrigationists (IR) than elsewhere on the production scale. In other cases, the scale is reordered as a means of emphasizing the relation of yet other measures to other subsistence systems.

We found elaborate songs primarily in a specialized group of complex producers in the intertwined pastoral and agricultural societies of the Old High Culture region (Fig. 42). This was a highly stratified world, where the fate of every individual depended upon his relationship to the superstructure

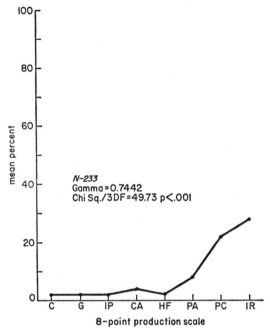

Fig. 42. Elaborate songs: the eight-point production scale. In the closer perspective of this production scale, elaborate songs (those with embellishment and free rhythm) appear to be concentrated in the irrigation societies of Old High Culture and on its pastoral periphery. Statistical split: C, G, IP, HF/CA, PA/PC/IR vs. Median.

above him, where he was confined within a system of rigid social stratification, and where his survival depended upon his command of a system of deferential etiquette with which he could appeal up through the system. The Oriental bard, weaving his complex song poems in praise of the emperor, the gods, or the unattainable beauty of the loved one, has long been the musical spokesman for this world. His output is elaborate, deferential, and suitable to a society made rigid by layers of privilege.

To characterize the deferential society, a layering scale of social rigidity was developed. It sums the Murdock scores per culture for the presence of a number of extra-local political hierarchies, of complex class and caste systems, and of slavery:

Layering (An additive score, compiled from Murdock's scales for caste, class, slavery, and number of extra-local hierarchies)
   a. The number of extra-local government levels: 0/1/2/3/4.

b. Class: Complex-4. Elite-3. Dual-2. Wealth-1. Absence-0.

c. Caste: Complex-3. Ethnic-2. Occupational-1. Absence-0.

d. Slavery: Any score-1.

These several systems of stratification and control increase the social distance between the members of a society and give rise to elaborate systems of etiquette and to deferential behavior of all sorts. Special forms of address, names, postures, forms of speech, accents, invocations, gifts, flattery, and a thousand other devices have been used by the lower orders of stratified societies to protect them in their dangerous approach to their powerful social superiors. The severity of the rules of these deferential systems mounts in direct ratio to the power and the social distance of the higher-ups. As can be seen in Figure 43, there is a strong relationship between increase of layering scores and elaboration in song style. If song is a reinforcement for generalized behavior, the more radical, extreme, and rigid the system of social dis-

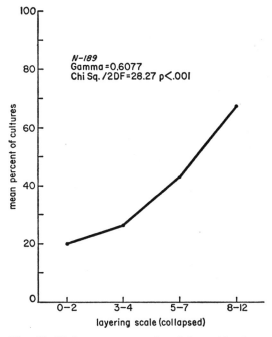

Fig. 43. Elaborate songs and social stratification. The ordinate represents the percentage of cultures with any incidence of elaborate songs. Clearly elaborate singing varies with the degree of social stratification. Statistical split: 0–4/5–7/8–12 vs. Median.

tance, the more intensively a system of musical deference or elaboration must be employed.

The Udy study of work teams gave us information on two other good measurements of rigid and tyrannical social controls—the importance of forced labor (among serfs, slaves, tenants, and peons) and the number of non-productive bosses in the work situation. Both turned out to be strongly associated at $P < .001$ with the presence of elaborate songs, again pointing to societies in which deferential behavior was socially necessary.

Another measurement of increased social formality is orchestral complexity. Instrumental music differs from song in being produced outside the body; melody is usually produced by the fingers (literally manipulated). The sung communication is instrumentalized and thus becomes less personal than that which rises within the body and pours out through the throat, shaped by the lips and tongue. The cantometrics ratings include information on the number of distinct types of instruments in the accompanying orchestras of the 233 cultures (see list of types).

INSTRUMENT TYPES (adapted from Sachs)

1. *Musical bows.*
2. *Zithers*—tube, stick, board, raft.
3. *Keyboard zithers.*
4. *Lutes*—plucked and bowed.
5. *Lyres, pluriarcs.*
6. *Harps.*
7. *Horns*—straight, curved, convoluted.
8. *Ribbon reeds.*
9. *Clarinets.*
10. *Oboes.*
11. *Bagpipes.*
12. *Flutes*—whistles, panpipes, mouth organs, harmoniums, accordians, organs.
13. *Bull-roarers and other free aerophones.*
14. *Clappers, cymbals, percussion sticks.*
15. *Gongs.*
16. *Xylophones, metallophones, lithophones.*
17. *Bells.*
18. *Slit drums.*
19. *Rattles.*
20. *Scrapers, rasps.*
21. *Jew's harps.*
22. *Mbira, sansas.*
23. *Friction drums.*
24. *Stamped idiophones.*
25. *Rubbed idiophones.*
26. *Drums*—all struck membranophones of any shape.
27. *Friction drums.*
28. *Kazoos.*

Accompanying orchestras with an average of two instrument types are found in societies with a low level of layering, that is, 0–4. On the other hand accompanying orchestras of about four or more different types of instrument score 5 or more on the social layering scale (Fig. 44). Other tests of orchestral complexity find weak or no relationships between this factor and other complexity variables such as government, population size, and subsistence range. Formal, instrumental presentation of music appears to be an indicator of increasing social rigidity. Thus the spread of the symphony orchestra across the United States during the past half-century probably symbolizes the gradual rise of a rich and powerful elite in American communities.

The key to understanding the performance situation, however, and its relationship to social structure is to be found in the social organization of the singing group. We have only begun an examination of this question in cantometrics, but we have already discovered that the relation between leader and led in song performance varies directly not only with societal complexity (Figs. 45, 46) but, more specifically, with the level of political complexity (Figs. 47, 48). This may be the most significant correlation established in our study. The sung communication differs from speech in that

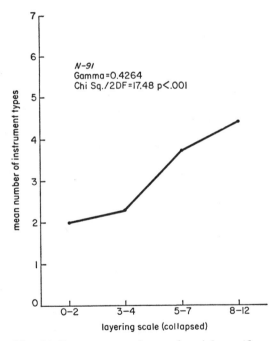

Fig. 44. Instrument variety and social stratification. Mean number of instrument types per style sample appears as a correlate of social stratification. Statistical split: 0–4/5–7/8–12 vs. Median.

usually a collective produces it or responds to it, or both. Song implicitly and constantly represents the human community and depends upon a high degree of formalization and redundancy to produce and maintain consensus, both as to the rules of its performance and the rules of its reception. The primary conditions of any performance, no matter what its "musical" content, are:

1. The size of the vocal group, one or many;
2. The interplay, if any, between the leader and the chorus;
3. The degree of dominance of the leader, if any;
4. The level of organization within the group.

Line 1 in the cantometric coding sheet sums up a few of the major leader-group relationships that we found in the data and that we felt we could continuously and reliably attribute to the recordings. Five conditions have turned out to be the means for sorting out, with considerable reliability, five levels of political development that are strongly associated with the same number of levels in the complexity scale:

1. *Interlocked.* A number of distinct paths or roles perceived in the singing group. Everyone present is singing so independently in melodic, rhythmic, and/or harmonic terms that it is impossible to ascribe a dominant role to any part. The effect may be one of integrated, contrapuntal unity, or extreme heterogeneity and diffuseness. This maximally individualized and leaderless style occurs most frequently among cultures dependent on collecting. Such cultures do not have authoritarian leaders; in fact, they frequently have no leaders at all even at a local level. Interlocking reappears throughout the evolutionary series wherever part-independence emerges as a central musical value, such as in the contrapuntal music of Bach and his contemporaries. In our study this type is strongly associated with female singing groups, or groups in which women play an important role. Perhaps it is more than idle speculation to suggest that this style, where everyone phonates at once, suits the feminine group which, in most societies, is essentially egalitarian. Most women are mothers or wives and, in these all-important respects, are equals. In assemblages of women, it is normal for all to speak at once. Thus interlock may represent the first, or one of the earliest and most egalitarian, models of all human interaction—the basic interaction model of the feminine society.

2. *Simple social unison.* Here again the social organization is essentially leaderless. Someone may initiate the song, but his part is soon swallowed up in the activity of the group and all members of the group adhere to the same path. Every member plays the same role throughout the performance. Simple tribal societies, where the leaders have little actual authority, favor this mode of performance. North American Indians, Australian Aborigines, and New

Guinea Highlanders all structure their singing activity in this way, as do many societies in which males dominate ritual life. Considerable discipline and conformity are enforced by social unison, for all participants must agree that for a considerable length of time, sometimes for hours, everyone follows the same melodic and textual pathway without notable departures from the main rhythmic pattern. Our research indicates that this was an early communication discovery, probably more associated with male than female performance and with dominance rather than with independence. Social unison tends to drop off in frequency in more complex social contexts, but it still remains the most important device for ordering joint activity. Thus the British barroom singer unifies his group with "All together, boys!" and 50,000 Nazis sear the memory by screaming "Sieg Heil" in one great jungle roar.

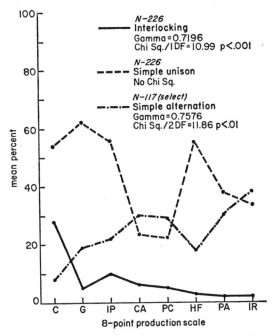

Fig. 45. Leader differentiation: the eight-point production scale—I. Interlocking occurs rarely, except among simply organized gathering peoples. Similarly, unison is characteristic of simple producers and Pacific horticulture. Simple alternation appears among game producers and plays an important role thereafter. Statistical splits: Interlocking—C/G, IP, CA, PC, HF, PA, IR vs. Median; Unison—no evaluation; Alternation—C/G, IP, CA, PC, HF, PA/IR vs. Median.

3. *Overlap.* Overlap is a fashion of arranging the alternation of parts of leader and chorus so that the two overlap to some degree. The leader and the chorus may sing two different patterns at the same time. Frequently, for instance, an African performance begins with the two parts just touching and, as the excitement of the performance grows, the chorus will encroach more and more upon the leader's time, until at last both are singing without letup in exciting rhythmic relationship to each other. Not only does this way of making music open up tremendous choral possibilities for Africans, but one is tempted to compare it to the way in which actions of the village chief are embedded in the reactions of his tribal council and his fellow villagers. Even in the vast kingly assemblies of the Zulus, the king reached decisions in public while the whole tribe voiced its approval. At the village level, of course, this assent can be moderated so as to redirect the course of events in a litigation, a dowry dispute, or a sorcery trial.

4. *Simple alternation.* Simple alternation was coded whenever the leader had a clearcut, separate melodic bit to sing followed by a pause and some response from a chorus. In the primitive world, even this degree of leader independence tends to appear only when one extra-local political hierarchy exists, as in the tribal confederations of the Iroquois or the peoples of the Plains. This type continues to increase in importance throughout the evolutionary series, becoming, for instance, the most common way of organizing a chorus in Western Europe. Usually in a complex culture there is regular alternation between the leader's part and the chorus's part and the two parts supplement or complement each other in some way. The dominance of this way of differentiating the leader's part almost always indicates the presence of at least one or two levels of extra-local political control.

5. *Solo and explicit.* Solo singing is common in almost every culture except for the Mbuti Pygmies, where Turnbull records it only for women singing lullabies (Turnbull, personal communication). Many primitive people yodel or lall nonsense syllables in a truly non-explicit style, so that these solos are as non-specific as their choral singing. Thus most of the reindeer herders of Boreal Eurasia, from the Chukchees west to the Lapps, chant liquid strings of glottalized vowels including few words but with some central image in the mind of the singer and his listeners. All this solo performance in non-idiosyncratic independence is found among people whose lives are not severely constrained by a tightly organized society. However, as social differentiation increases along with alienation and exclusivity of leadership function, there is usually a concomitant rise of explicit solos on the complexity scale. The relationship between explicit solos and increasing complexity is extremely tight, indicating that such exclusive control of the communication space by one voice represents the increasing importance of exclusive leadership with developing complexity. Thus, apparently, differ-

entiation of leadership in society and in song appears step by step as subsistence systems become more highly developed.

Leadership differentiation in the song-performing group is tied up, not only with a general increase of complexity, but with particular stages of political complexity as well. Even with the rough scales we have employed at this stage of cross-cultural research, it may be surmised that this element of performance style reinforces the order of political development in the culture from which it comes. In Figure 47, a scale of increasing political development is drawn from Murdock (Coult and Havenstein, 1965), a scale that begins with absence of any political integration and ends with states of 100,000 population or more. The five levels of performance style relate to

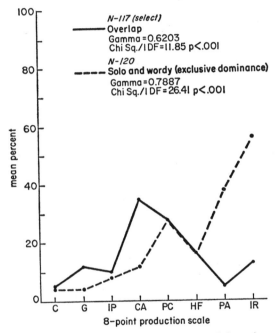

Fig. 46. Leader differentiation: the eight-point production scale—II. Neither exclusive dominance nor overlap are very important at the simpler end of the subsistence scale. Overlap is especially marked at the middle levels, whereas exclusive dominance maintains a steady increase across the scale, with sole deviation of trend in the HF category. Statistical splits: Overlap—CA, PC/C, G, IP, HF, PA, IR vs. Median; Exclusive dominance—C, G, IP, CA, PC/HF, PA, IR vs. Median.

this scale of increasingly complex governmental types in a remarkably step-wise way, considering that the two measures were designed independently of one another.

The acephalous performance style that we term "interlock" is found in our sample only in societies with total absence of political integration, even at the local level—further evidence that this may be one of the earliest, if not the primordial fashion of organizing joint communication. The sound of some groups performing in this way sometimes resembles a flock of birds chattering in the trees or a herd of mammals on the march. Social unison with undifferentiated leadership is also important at this totally nonauthoritarian level, but reaches its peak of frequency in autonomous tribal communities where populations are still small and no extra-local confederation yet exists (Fig. 47).

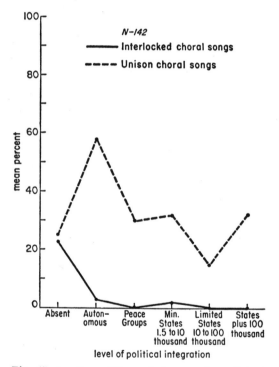

Fig. 47. Leader differentiation and political complexity—I. Interlocking choral organization appears to be most typical of the leaderless society. Unison becomes prominent at the next level, the simple autonomous tribe. No statistical evaluations.

In relationship to this political scale, overlap, where the leader is embedded and closely tied in with the supporting chorus, is found at a simpler level than in Figure 46. Overlap becomes prominent at the level of "the peace group . . . where the basis of political unity depends upon reciprocal trade relations, defensive military agreements, or a common cult or age-grade organization," rather than on political control. This political level is very common among the simpler cultures of Africa. If one takes the view that most African villages are linked by descent ties and common bonds of religious affiliation rather than by the intensive political organization which sometimes overrides these original bonds of affiliation, then the African emphasis on overlap, with its essentially egalitarian structure, is more understandable. This overlapped or embedded interactive structure has been continued (on both the political and musical levels) in the United States, where, until recently, the most significant organization in Negro life was the church, always headed by a powerful male leader. No matter how powerful the preacher might be, however, his tenure depended upon day-to-day contact with his deacons and his congregation, just as the success of his sermons could be judged by the rhythmic response evoked from his congregation.

In the majority of cases of full alternation in our sample, there is always a slight but respectful pause between the leader's part and that of the chorus. Most of our codings represent a situation of considerably more differentiation than does overlap, where the leader and group are not separate. Figure 48 shows that full alternation assumes maximum importance in states of a moderate size. In large states where political organization has always depended upon a powerful, centralized government and a strong leader of some kind, be he premier, president, emperor, khan, lama, or god, the solo wordy style which stands for exclusive dominance reaches its peak and supersedes all other performance types.

All these ways of molding the song performance can probably be found at every political level. Each one is a panhuman possibility. Each one is a discovery in organizational technique that, once made, can never be totally lost. Each represents an emphasis on or bias towards some way of handling joint activity adapted to the culture or situation in which it functions. Even the free-wheeling, anarchic interlock situation, which seems to have best suited the female collecting teams of early mankind, re-emerged in Western Europe as the dominant method of organization in the choral music of Bach and other polyphonic composers. We must leave until later the task of discovering the relationship of the egalitarian Pygmy bands of the Congo to the setting in which Bach and his fellow composers worked. For the present, it is enough to have demonstrated that the leader-chorus relationship varies decisively, steadily, and understandably with political complexity and that both seem to scale in an evolutionary fashion.

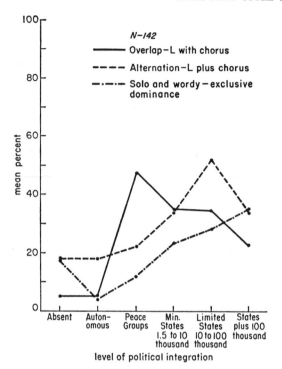

Fig. 48. Leader differentiation and political complexity—II. Overlap and alternation are important at the middle and upper levels of political complexity, respectively. These situations reflect the emergence of an increasingly defined and powerful leadership. Exclusive leadership increases steadily with political complexity. Note the general co-trending of alternation and exclusive dominance. No statistical evaluation.

This new notion that the ordering of performers in musical organizations may be an index of relative political complexity deserves one further test. It has been observed that orchestral complexity reflects formal societal structure, in that the number of types of instruments in the largest orchestra points to the area's level of social stratification there. If we look at Line 14 in the cantometric coding system, where the level of complexity of rhythmic organization in accompanying orchestras is scored, we find another representation of increasing levels of political complexity. In this case, the social measurement is derived from Murdock where he records the number of levels of government beyond the local community level as an indicator for increasing governmental complexity. Figure 35 shows a steady correlation between the complexity of rhythmic organization and political organization.

The simplest mode of organizing rhythm is for every instrumentalist to play the same metrical pattern with little or no independence; we term this situation *rhythmic unison*. This condition (see the solid line in Fig. 36) is most frequent in societies with one or no extra-local level of control. The next order of rhythmic complexity, where one or more parts accompany the leading part in a subordinate fashion, is seldom encountered in autonomous societies, but becomes frequent in societies of two or more extra-community political levels. Much of Africa, where the village is subject to one and usually two levels of authority, favors polyrhythm (solid line in Fig. 36) with two or more parts in rhythmic conflict. Finally, rhythmic counterpoint, the favorite device of European classical music, in which two or more rhythmic parts of equal importance remain active throughout the selection, is found almost exclusively among societies which are politically very complex (dotted line in Fig. 36).

When the human community sings, then, it seems to make many statements about the levels of complexity that strongly affect every aspect of its life—subsistence, stratification, government, leader differentiation, and general specificity. In performing a song, the human being reminds himself of the kind of community he comes from and its level of achievement. One function of song seems to be to reinforce the various levels of complexity that underlie all behavior. The cantometric parameters that seem to speak for orders of cultural complexity so strongly affect the outcome of musical performance that any alteration of them drastically shifts its effect. If this be true of an art once thought to be so spontaneous, so abstract, so idiosyncratic, what must we surmise about the communication of more mundane systems such as the spoken and written language? Their substructure too must be related in crucial but as yet unseen ways to social structure. The tools of cantometrics will certainly not serve to measure differences between very similar cultures or among situations within the same cultural setting, but the success of the present experiments suggest that such measurements might be contrived. At present we must be content with a further clarification of some general functions of sung communication systems.

COMPLEMENTARITY

It has been observed in foregoing pages that the arrangements that link members of orchestras seem to reflect formal social structure. On the other hand, the arrangements between singers have rather to do with a more personal, face-to-face relationship. The most important of these is the inter-action of males and females and here, not surprisingly, we discover that the cantometric profiles are most revealing. This is just as true of the mass of songs from the primitive world, which have little to do with love and fre-quently little to do overtly with sex, as of the songs of Western Europe, which are concerned with virtually nothing else but the romantic theme.

The feminine imprint turned up, however, far from any such sentimental setting—in the world of work, in the principal subsistence activity of a so-ciety. The best way we found for estimating the feminine contribution to publicly recognized social activity such as song performance was to see what proportion of the main food-producing task women carry out in a culture. On the whole, where women are excluded from the main food-getting job, they are likely to stand at the edge of the assembly ground and watch the rest of life's activities a bit passively. Such is the role of women in most hunt-ing societies, in the purdah societies of the Orient where women are hidden away in the family, and even in Western Europe where women work in the circle of the house and garden, while men move out through the fields to make the harvest and down the roads to market with the animals. It was not until the Western European woman began to go into factories that she be-gan to win legal equality. Among most gatherers, many incipients, and the majority of cultivators, however, where women bring back most of the plant food into the village, do the cooking, and mind the babies and the house, all of life has a somewhat feminine touch and the voices and bodies of women thread through the principal rituals.

Murdock provided information about the relative contribution of each sex to six subsistence activities and thus we were able to define each culture as being dominantly masculine or feminine in regard to its principal sub-sistence activity. Three states were identified in the six Murdock rating points: (1) M and N, where males perform most or all of the principal sub-sistence tasks; (2) D and E, where female participation is about equal, though sometimes differentiated; and (3) G and F, where females perform most or all of the main subsistence tasks. In practice, throughout the study, M and N has proved to be contrastive to D and E, and G and F. Each of these latter states points to the existence of a complementary relationship between males and females because, wherever women take the economic initiative at least 50 percent of the time, they also find ways to take initiative in other sectors of behavior—and the males must accept this. Our social con-trast, then, is between generally complementary and noncomplementary cul-tures, as defined by the level of importance of women in production.

Predicting female initiative in many sectors of behavior in complementary societies, we sought traces of such initiative in song-performance style. The first clue was provided by the discovery that multi-partedness of vocal rhythmic organization increases steadily in importance along the complementarity scale (Fig. 49). If we inspect the distribution of rhythmic counterpoint, in which there are two or more independent and active parts throughout the performance, we find this trait confined almost exclusively to the most complementary societies. It is hard to resist the notion, therefore, that independence of singing parts in the chorus stands for the existence of two independent roles in simple social orders: the male role with its clearly recognized complement, the female role.

This brings us to the question of vocal polyphony. Polyphony is defined in cantometrics as the use of simultaneously produced intervals other than in unison. In effect what this means is that there are at least two active tonal levels in a performance, an upper and a lower one. Since female voices, the world over, operate about an octave higher than male voices, I take the

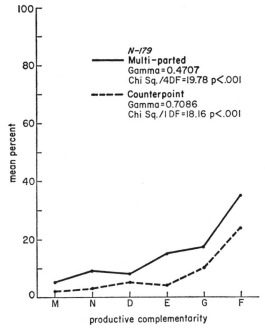

Fig. 49. Rhythmic organization of chorus and productive complementarity. Multi-parted and counterpoint rhythmic organization assume importance only in societies where women are major contributors to subsistence. The trend is especially marked in the case of counterpoint. Statistical splits: Multi-parted—M, N/D/E/G/F vs. Median; Counterpoint—M, N/D, E, G, F. vs. Median.

presence of two parts to be a simultaneous communication of male and female roles; and the effect is the same whether the chorus is all-male or all-
female. Given the function of a symbol—to stand for something else—the
upper voice part can and does represent the feminine, whether women are
actually present in the chorus and doing the singing or not. The hypothesis
then is that, if there are two levels in a vocal performance, one is likely to
stand for the feminine. This theory of polyphony is strongly supported by
the relationship between polytonal choral singing and a complementary subsistence relationship established in Figure 49.

Counterpoint (see solid line, Fig. 50) was once believed to be the invention of European high culture. In our sample it turns out to be most frequent among simple producers, especially among gatherers, where women
supply the bulk of the food. Counterpoint and perhaps even polyphony
may then be very old feminine inventions. The negative side of this idea

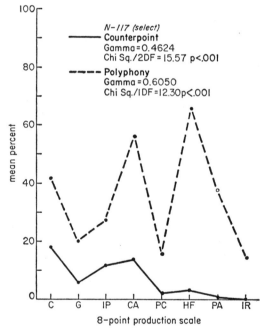

Fig. 50. Polyphony and counterpoint: the eight-
point production scale. On this production scale
counterpoint and polyphony are concentrated in
those categories where women are significant contributors to production. Statistical splits: Counterpoint—G, PC, HF, PA, IR/CA/IP, C vs. Median; Polyphony—G, IP, PC, PA, IR/, HF, CA
vs. Median.

is also substantiated in cantometric findings. Among Amerindian hunters and fishers, where most performances are dominated by males, vocal unison by far outweighs all other performance modes and polyphony scarcely occurs.

Subsistence complementarity is at its maximum among gatherers, early gardeners, and horticulturists. Among gatherers, women generally bring in the major part of the food. In early hoe agriculture women outweigh or equal men in productive importance, probably because it was they who domesticated the plants and even the animals. In such societies women are not so likely to be shut away from the public center of life; not so often are they passive witnesses of social events, but active participants at or close to the center of the stage. It is in such societies that we find the highest occurrence of polyphonic singing (see peaks on dotted line, Fig. 50). In Figure 51, we learn that polyphony is closely related to the level of complementarity, in-

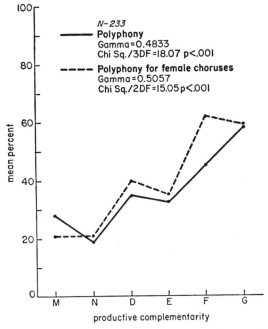

Fig. 51. Polyphony and complementarity. Both polyphony in general and polyphony in female choruses rise in direct proportion to the degree of feminine involvement in subsistence labor. Statistical splits: Polyphony—M, N/D, E/F/G vs. Median; Polyphony for female choruses—M, N/D, E/F, G vs. Median.

creasing steadily as the level of complementarity increases. This relationship
has been tested exhaustively and has been further confirmed by the discovery of a step-like increase of female choruses singing in polyphony. Vocal
polyphony, then, may be viewed as a communication about the recognized
importance of the feminine role in culture. This hypothesis does much to
explain its cross-cultural distribution. Vocal polyphony is far more important among the root-gardening tribes of South America, where women do
most of the agricultural work, than among North American hunters and
maize cultivators. Trans-culturally, root crops tend to be woman's work.
Among the North American Indian, polyphony is frequent, as far as we
know, only among the collectors of California. Polyphony is more common
among tribal than complex cultures of Asia and Oceania, for at the tribal
level women have a more crucial role not only in agriculture but in animal
husbandry. Polyphony is more often employed by Africans and Afro-Ameri-
cans than in the folk communities of Europe and America. It is practiced

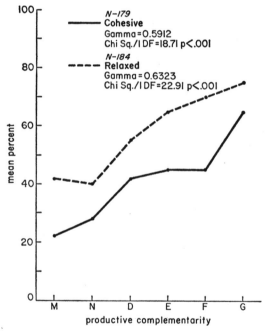

Fig. 52. Choral cohesiveness and vocal relaxation: Productive complementarity. Tonal cohesiveness and tonal relaxation both vary with the
degree of feminine contribution to subsistence.
Statistical split: Both Cohesive and Relaxed—
M, N/D, E, F, G vs. Median.

far more in Eastern Europe, where teams of women have traditionally done heavy work in the fields, than in Western Europe.

There are two stylistic features, relaxed voices and maximal tonal unity, that seem to provide the performance framework for vocal polyphony. Choruses that match their timbre so that the sound is cohesive and sonorous more frequently produce polyphony. There is an association between these two features and polyphony at far better than the .001 level. In fact, harmony depends on a very delicate meshing together of the upper partials of the voice, a difficult matter if the vocal delivery is constricted or noisy instead of clear and relaxed, so that individual voices can blend and melt together.

The fact that relaxed, clear vocal performance and cohesive choruses are both more frequent in complementary societies (Fig. 52), fortifies our hypothesis about the relationship between polyphony, the most integrated of choral forms, and complementarity, in which women are not forced to keep silent or inactive and where, therefore, one would expect less tension, less repressed anger, and more ease in everyday interaction. Vocal tension, as represented in songs sung in tight voices and with strong nasality, is notably lower in those societies where women are responsible for 50 percent or more of the central subsistence task (chi sq/1 df $= 13.72$; gamma $= .5034$; $P < .001$; $N = 233$).

The question arises then: What are the social conditions which favor the highly unified choruses found in Africa, Central Europe, Polynesia, and the Pueblos, and rarely elsewhere? This problem will be dealt with at length in the next section of the report.

7
Social Solidarity

Alan Lomax

ONE of the most fascinating and sometimes disturbing of social phenomena is the concerted activity of the mob, the army, or the choir that seems to feel and act as one person. Such group solidarity has to be trained into soldiers, orchestras, and teams in Western Europe and North America, but is often spontaneously achieved in other culture areas. Indeed, it is with joint and sometimes rhythmically synchronized effort that much of the work of pre-industrial societies gets done and that many of the sacred and ritual occasions of the human and social life cycles are celebrated.

The facility with which members of a collective act in concert and nicely coordinate their actions—their level of "groupiness"—is a significant feature of any social profile. Extreme groupiness lies at one end of a scale, and individuation or social diffuseness at the other. Most anthropologists would agree that Negroes and Polynesians operate in large, integrated groups more often than do the people of other world areas. In highly individuated cultures, like the Eskimo and our own, task responsibility is likely to remain the concern of the individual or of a small coterie of specialists working together on a voluntary or salaried basis.

The aim of this essay is to supply a measurement of solidarity or groupiness and to arrange a large sample of cultures along a scale from highly individuated to highly groupy, from diffuse to cohesive. The basic data come from ratings of 2,557 songs on Line 5 of the cantometric coding sheet, a rating scale for tonal cohesiveness in choral performances. In making this judgment the rater must decide whether a group of singers match their vocal qualities so as to sing "with one voice," or whether many separate voices can be heard, producing a somewhat harsh or strident choral effect. The consensus tests discussed in Chapter 5 indicate that inexperienced judges can easily be trained to achieve a 91 percent level of consensus in rating this aspect of song performance. We presume this means that members of our culture are constantly judging the relative cohesiveness of group activity.

In order to achieve what we call "good blend" or tonal cohesiveness, a singer has to conform his pronunciation of vowels and consonants, use of

170

pitch, rhythmic attack, and certainly many other aspects of phonation, to a model shared by the group. Tonal unity is achieved among Anglo-Americans only by intensive rehearsal of carefully chosen personnel under the restrictive guidance of a director. Yet a casual assembly of comparative strangers in other cultures can immediately form a harmonious choir of voices that seem to melt together into a big, unified, colorful sound. I have recorded this spontaneous choralizing not only among Negro singers, but at singing gatherings in the Hebrides, among the Basques and other northern Spaniards, notably among the longshoremen of Genoa and in the northern part of Italy, and at the wine-drenched, symposium-like banquets of the Georgians in the Caucasus. In all these settings, where a high level of tonal cohesiveness is achieved, idiosyncratic vocalizing disappears, thus increasing the blended power of the chorus. Each chorus member, by submerging his individuality in the collective intent, adds his complement to the structure of the whole sound. Perhaps his sense of satisfaction comes from helping to produce a sound as grandiose as the society itself.

Teamwork of any sort demands that idiosyncracies and personal conflicts be subordinated to the requisites of a common goal. Most music-making and dancing are the outcome of teamwork; indeed, it might be argued that a principal function of music and dance is to augment the solidarity of a group. Singing the same melody, dancing to the same rhythm, even utilizing the same pitch or the same levels of accent or any of the shared regularities of behavior essential to song or dance performance arise from and enhance a sense of communality. Such activity represents a decision that a certain stretch of communication is of central significance to the group producing or attending it. Thus every performance demands and brings about group solidarity in some degree.

Those areas that seem "most musical" in the popular estimation—Central Europe, Africa, and Polynesia—are also renowned for their highly coordinated group singing and dancing. In other words, Africans, Polynesians, and Central Europeans are seen as having an extraordinary talent for music, precisely because they are adepts at cohesive kinesthetic behavior. Twelve of the fourteen culture areas falling above the first quartile in regard to tonal cohesiveness lie within Africa, Oceania, or Central Europe (Table 14).

INTERPERSONAL SYNCHRONY

At first glance it would seem impossible that any group of individuals could delicately calibrate the manifold levels of phonation essential to produce a unified choral sound—the syllables, intervals, glides, attacks, releases, levels of emphasis, many voice qualities, etc. Nevertheless, singing

Table 14. *Percent distribution of tonal co-*
hesiveness by area, first quartile of 56 areas.

	Tonally cohesive
African Hunters	87
Equatorial Bantu	80
Western Polynesia	77
Central Bantu	72
Guinea Coast	70
Eastern Sudan	68
Tribal India	68
South African Bantu	67
Afro-American	66
Upper Nile	64
New Guinea	59
Pueblo	59
Old Europe	58
Eastern Polynesia	58

with blended voices, like marching in step, is found on all six continents, some individuals and societies being more given to it than others. As we shall see in what follows, singers in some cultures are already tuned in on shared channels of communication and locked into a multileveled system of interchange.

When a movie of a human encounter is studied at slow speed, any viewer will be impressed by the paralleling of posture, imitation of gesture, and synchronous or mirror-like behavior he sees. At normal speed the subjects may not seem to be actively engaged with each other, yet when narrowly inspected at slow speed, the scene will bloom with covert interchanges between the actors, linking them in a sort of bodily flirtation. Toes waggle up and down in synchrony below the table, as if dancing to the same beat. Insensibly the participants assume the same posture. Movements beginning on one side of a scene seem to spread across the surface of the communication pool and rock all the individuals to the same rhythm. Between singers and musicians the level of synchrony reaches such a peak that, in slow motion, their bodies seem like reeds waving in the current of a river.

The fact is, of course, that the film analyzer takes us into the communication world that Birdwhistell has been describing during the last decades in his work on kinesics. Birdwhistell wrote (1959a):

"The term 'communication,' as used in this discussion, is a term related to the dynamic, patterned interaction of the membership of a social group. As such, communication is constituted from the learned and patterned utilization of the various sensory modalities. . . . Thus, an individual does not communicate; he engages in or becomes part of communication. . . ."

He also wrote (1968b, in press) :

"The social performance of a given member of a society is by definition incomplete; task accomplishment is dependent upon continuative, coordinate parallel or complementary individual or sub-group behaviors. . . ."

Birdwhistell (1968b, in press) speaks of the essential interconnectedness of all human beings as the base line for adaptability and continuity. "The individual incorporates part of a pattern which requires the activity of several organisms to gain completion. . . ." In personal communications he has pointed out that at least 90 percent of the exchange along all the channels in any moment of human interconnectedness consists of signals that maintain the communication context and secure the base line of the conversation.

In everyday Western behavior, this supportive stream of imitative, context-establishing signals stays below the level of awareness, since it consists of tiny movements of low amplitude and brief duration. When vocal or physical synchrony of a grosser sort intrudes on social intercourse outside the contexts of drill, dance, music-making, and the like, Westerners tend to break off contact and become embarrassed. If voices or gestures are matched too obviously, Westerners call the speech sing-song and see the behavior as monkey-like and foolish. Children, artists, dancers, Negroes, and other "inferiors" are permitted more latitude in this respect.

Recent experiments by Condon, a student of Birdwhistell, have shown, however, that beneath this level of restraint, all of us are bound together in an eternal pattern of synchrony, far more regimented and precisely tuned than the Rockettes. Condon and Ogston have painstakingly analyzed interaction on sound film taken at 48 frames per second, twice the standard speed. At this level, they have discovered the units and the patterns of change that structure the conversational interaction of people. They report in brief:

"Intensive analysis revealed harmonious or synchronous organizations of change between body motion and speech in *both* intra-individual and interactional behavior. Thus the body of the speaker dances in time with his speech. Further, the body of the listener dances in rhythm with that of the speaker. . . .

"From the analysis of the sound film, we see that as a person talks . . . his body moves in a series of configurations of change which are precisely correlated with that serial transformation of 'phone into syllable

into word' of speech. Kinesic segmentation in general seems to coincide
with the etic [externally and universally comparative] segmentation of
speech. Further analysis, focusing on interactional behavior, revealed
a startling and relatively continuous harmony between the body motion configurational change patterns of speaker and listener" (Condon
and Ogston, 1966).

Condon demonstrated that when one person begins to speak, his listeners
fall into perfectly matched synchrony with his body, as it underlines, cross-
references, and emphasizes his utterance. The level of synchrony between
the speaker and everyone present is matched only at the moments of most
perfect cohesiveness in song and in dance. This remarkable discovery suggests that micro-synchrony is the essential base line in all communication,
without which no speaker could be understood by others or, for that matter, make sense to himself. Micro-synchrony must link the biological system
of the mother to that of the child before birth and thereafter bind the
individual to all his human surroundings. Perhaps it is this model, reappear-
ing at a grosser level of behavior with units of one to several seconds in
duration, that gives rise to the joint cohesiveness of dance and music, and
the feelings of unity and deep satisfaction these arts produce in man.

COHESIVENESS AND WORK TEAMS

Table 14 shows that gross synchrony figures more prominently in the
behavior patterns of some culture areas than in others. It may be assumed
that this groupy behavior style is generally supportive in aim, constantly re-
affirming links between group members, damping out conflict, and raising
the level of group coordination. Thus societal continuity in these groupy
cultures seems to depend on a high level of visible synchronous behavior.
The level of coordination of the singing group, then, reflects and reinforces
the level of synchrony essential for the continuance of the whole society and
should be discoverable in the relatively higher level of groupy behavior in
other aspects of social organization. Thus the degree of vocal blend should
prove a reliable index of social cohesiveness in general.

In the search for loci of social cohesiveness we looked first at main subsistence type, the variable that proved so powerful a mediator between social form and song style in the study of complexity. If good vocal blend is
run against this five-point complexity measure, the peak shows up at the
center among cultures of moderate complexity, rather than among either
simple or complex producers (Fig. 53).

We located groupy musical behavior first on production scales, then

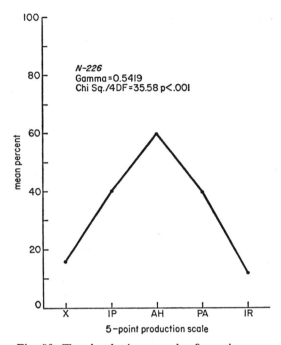

Fig. 53. Tonal cohesiveness: the five-point production scale. Tonal cohesiveness appears most prominently at the middle levels of complexity. Statistical split: IR/X/IP/PA/AH vs. Median.

tested the elements of social structure typical of these economic levels for independent correlations with musical groupiness. In order to define more precisely the productive levels connected with cohesiveness we turned to the eight-point production scale, developed by Arensberg and Lomax. As it appears below it, too, is a scale of social complexity. This arrangement of the subsistence levels correlates with such complexity indicators as mean community size (gamma = 0.81, chi sq/14 df = 100.21, P < .001) and number of extra-local hierarchies (gamma = 0.73, chi sq/2 df = 62.64, P < .001).

1. (C) *Collectors.*
2. (G) *Hunters and fishers.*
3. (IP) *Incipient producers.*
4. (CA) *Cultivators with domestic animals.*
5. (PC) *Nomadic pastoralists.*
6. (HF) *Horticulturists with specialized fishing and domestic animals.*
7. (PA) *Plow agriculturists.*
8. (IR) *Irrigation agriculturists.*

If each of these subsistence categories is assigned its percentage of cohesive cases and the scale is then reordered in terms of increasing song
cohesiveness, the mean curve in Figure 54 results. Game producers, irrigationists, and nomadic pastoralists seldom sing cohesively. Some incipient
producers, collectors, and plow agriculturists employ good blend some of
the time. The gardeners of Africa, New Guinea, and the Insular Pacific
usually sing cohesively; indeed, the strength of the correlation between
choral cohesiveness and the HF–CA set points to this as the economic level
where one might expect to find the conditions conducive to groupy behavior.

The distribution of cohesiveness in relation to geography and economic
function calls for a complex explanation. It does not seem to be a result of
specific regional style traditions in Africa and Oceania, for example. In order to rule out the possibility of regional biasing, we ran the same correlation on the 120-culture test sample which provides a more equal balancing

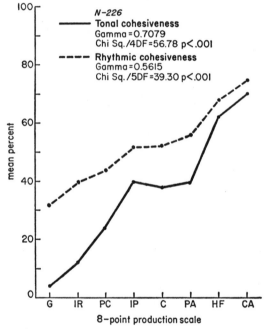

Fig. 54. Tonal and rhythmic cohesiveness with
cultivators and horticulturists. With some variation in trend both tonal and rhythmic cohesiveness rise in similar fashion across the eight-point
production scale. Statistical splits: Tonal—G, IR/
PC/IP, C, PA/HF/CA vs. Median; Rhythmic—
PC/G, IR/IP, C, PA/CA/HF vs. Median.

of world regions and eliminates the more obvious historical duplicates. Most of the correlations in this paper have been tested on both samples. Here, as shown in Figure 55, the relationship held at the same level of significance; indeed, the HF–CA set assumed a unique place on the mean curve.

A number of other measurements confirm the impression that HF–CA cultures have a strong preference for cohesive behavior. The rise of the mean for good rhythmic coordination in the chorus, for example, follows the same path as the mean for tonal blend. The gardeners again top the list (dashed line, Fig. 55).

In the same band of cultures one finds an even more homely groupy tendency, the preference for singing together in large collectives. In field work among folk Negroes the collector discovers that singing does not begin

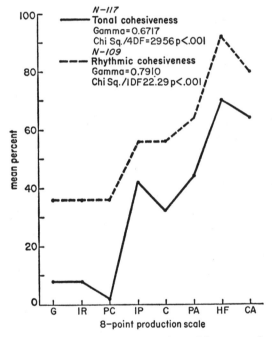

Fig. 55. Choral cohesiveness with cultivators and horticulturists. The correlation in Figure 54 between tonal cohesiveness and agricultural economies of mid-complexity is confirmed by the select sample. The mean curve of rhythmic cohesiveness closely matches that for tonal cohesiveness. Statistical splits: Tonal–G, IR/PC/IP, C, PA/HF/CA vs. Median; Rhythmic–G, IR, PC, IP, C, PA/HF, CA vs. Median.

until the right group has assembled in a familiar shape around the right leaders. Preliminary study of film shows that the social shape of the chorus in a culture reproduces and reinforces the most frequent patterns of social structure, but here we can report only on size. The cohesive cultures are also those which perform in large groups. Cultures in HF, CA, and C categories are far more likely to have choirs of 13 or more members than cultures of other subsistence types (Table 15). The people of gardening cultures tend to sing in very large choruses (21–50) and choruses of three or more are far more frequent in CA, HF, and C cultures than elsewhere in the subsistence series (Tables 16, 17).

Table 15. *Large choruses (13+) and production type.*

	G, IR, PC, IP, PA	C, HF, CA
Above median	49	63
Choruses of 13+		
Below median	80	34

Chi sq/1 df = 16.01; gamma = .5031; P < .001; N = 226.

Table 16. *Very large choruses (21–50) and production type.*

	G, IR, IP, C	PC, PA	CA, HF
Above median	10	11	35
Choruses of 21–50			
Below median	78	42	50

Chi sq/2 df = 21.22; gamma = .5496; P < .001; N = 233.

Table 17. *Choruses of three or more and production type.*

	All Others	CA, C, HF
Above median	39	71
Choruses of 3 or more		
Below median	97	26

Chi sq/1 df = 44.92; gamma = .7433; P < .001; N = 233.

The cultures that keep turning up above the median for musical cohesiveness (Table 18) are predominantly:

1. the mixed gardening and animal husbandry societies of Africa, Tribal India, New Guinea, Melanesia, Micronesia, and Polynesia;
2. the settled village agriculturists of the Pueblos, Eastern Woodlands, and the Kraho of the Xingu River;
3. the open-field, corporate villagers of Middle and Eastern Europe;
4. the African gatherers.

Table 18. *Percent tonal cohesiveness: Cultures above median*
(Median frequency = 34 percent).

91–100				
Afar	Bambara	Basoga	Basque	Bemba
Binga	Bulu	Chagga	Choiseul	Cook Island
Diola-Fogny	Ekonda	Fiji	Georgia	Haida
Hehe	Hopi	Kraho	Lala	Lozi
Luba	Luvale	Masai-Arusha	Mayogo	Mbuti
Mende	Moravia	Nandi	Ndau	Osset
Palau	Pari	Sajek-Tayal	Samoa	Shona
So. U.S. Gen.	Strpci	Taos	Toco	Toma
U.S. Pop	Vunun	W. Nakanai	Xhosa	
81–90				
Azande	Baule	Bushmen	Carriacou	Chopi
Creek	Fore	Fulani	Fut	Hebrides
Laguna	Luo	Mamvu	Mangareva	Maori
Merina	Motu	Slovakia	Tanala	
71–80				
Dani	Dinka	Jamaica	Murut	Nuer
Tadjik	Topoke	Yoruba	Zulu	
61–70				
Abor	Bara	Cheremis	Dutch	Friuli
Gond	Iban	Middle Waghi	Papago	Pima
Sakalava	Yuchi	Zuni		
51–60				
Central Russia	Colombian-Ecuadorian-Negro	Dogon	Dragas	Kakoli
Nuoro	Salish	Sotho	Tarascan	Ulithi
41–50				
Hillbilly Salvador	Maring	Naples	N. Mexico	N. Paiute
34–40				
Abelam	Java	Jivaro	Motilon	Tandroy
Turkey	Tzotzil	Unguja	Wabanaki	Washo

One thinks of Africans, Polynesians, and East Europeans as outstandingly gregarious, sociable folk who move through life in shoals. The work bees and singing crews of Slavic Europe; the age-grade teams, guilds, and village corvees of Africa; and the fishing parties and permanent rotating work associations of Oceania stand out among all mankind's organizations for a high level of groupiness or solidarity. These large, permanent, rhythmically coordinated teams perform crucial and onerous subsistence tasks such as clearing and breaking land, weeding and harvesting crops, and transporting goods on water and land. In them work becomes the occasion for feasting, drinking, dancing, making merry, and strengthening social bonds.

This pleasure-oriented, community-binding way of getting the work done was certainly one of the crucial discoveries at an early stage of settled agriculture. It seems to flower among village gardeners and then tends to disappear among more complex agriculturists, except in Eastern Europe. An examination of the cross-cultural data pertaining to these specialized producers will point out some social factors that give rise to cohesiveness.

First, it should be no surprise that the economic factor, subsistence type, produces the strongest correlations, not only with cohesiveness in singing but with various groupy forms of social organization. The procurement, distribution, processing, and consumption of food have always been the focus for most human activity. Prior cross-cultural studies of child-rearing (Barry, Child, and Bacon, 1959), games (Roberts and Sutton-Smith, 1962), and religion (Swanson, 1960) show that the major economic activity of the human community shapes or foreshadows its behavioral patterns, its institutions, and its approach to education. The children of hunters are trained for independence and assertiveness, and children of agriculturists are trained for compliance and obedience. Most hunter social structure is diffuse, while the development of agriculture brings with it an increase in social density and stability. High mobility and individualized skill are valuable personality traits for the hunter, since the life of the extractive community depends on an almost random search of the environment for a food source over which the culture has no control. Hunting parties bring together a group of equal, highly rational specialists in loosely bonded, temporary teams. Except in rare situations, such as the buffalo-hunting cultures of the Plains and the salmon-fishing villages of the Northwest, small populations and small, impermanent work parties are the rule in extractive economies:

Larger and more permanent associations develop with the onset of agriculture. In some cases, as among the Pueblos, the Iroquois, the Creeks, and the Kraho of the upper Xingu, a sufficient supply of game and a fairly high level of agricultural productivity support bigger, more stable settlements. But most such incipient-producer economies, prior to the development of a full-fledged animal husbandry, remain small and often migratory (Fig. 26).

The domestication of animals greatly increases access to the environment, since foraging animals can convert inedible resources—grass and the like—into meat, milk, and hides. Consequently, when domestication of animals is added to gardening, communities grow larger and more stable (Fig. 56) as do the operating social groups within them (work gangs and ritual teams, for instance). Population growth, however, puts a strain on the inefficient slash-and-burn agricultural system, so that societies at the CA level usually become expansionist. New groups bud off from the core village to take control of land held by extractors or by less aggressive gardeners. Blood ties are cherished in these new villages and the social ties of mixed garden-ing-herding peoples follow the lines of real or imaginary kinship, and are likely to be face-to-face and lifelong. The Murdock *Atlas* demonstrates a striking increase in the occurrence of large, structured kin groups in CA and HF societies (Table 19).

Table 19. *Large, structured kin groups and production type.*

	CA–HF	IP, PA, PC	C, G, IR
None	9	46	31
Lineages or ramages	74	40	28

Chi sq/2 df = 40.14; gamma = .5700; P < .001; N = 228.

Not only does economic level regulate the size of the community and the groups that compose it, but the nature of each task complex influences the shape of the teams that do the jobs, the teams that bring and distribute the food, and the teams that confirm these activities. If level of tonal cohesive-ness reflects the willingness of the members of a culture to coordinate their activities and affirm the value of grossly unanimous behavior, groupy work-team structure should be found where cohesiveness is high. Udy's classic cross-cultural study supplies the data on the organization of work. It em-braces 150 cultures, well distributed throughout six main culture areas, with good representation in the C to HF categories (in terms of the eight-point scale), but very few plow agriculturists or irrigationists. In spite of this, his evidence contributes to our view of social solidarity.

Table 20. *Work team characteristics and production type.*

	Tempo-rary	Volun-tary	Spe-cific	Terri-torially recruited	Perma-nent	Custo-dial	Diffuse function	Socially recruited
(G) Hunters	×	×	×	×				
(G) Fishers	×	×	×					
(C) Collectors	×	×						
(IP) Incipients					×	×	×	×
(AH) Animal husbandry					×	×	×	×

Table 20 summarizes Udy's data about the relative structural permanence of work teams at various subsistence levels. Extractive teams tend to be temporary in composition; voluntary in membership; specific in function, i.e., recruited for the accomplishment of one task only; and territorially re-cruited, that is, composed of the skilled personnel present, frequently in-

cluding strangers from outside the group. On the other hand, incipient cultivators (IP) and cultures that practice animal husbandry along with agriculture (CA, HF) operate with teams which are permanent in composition;
custodial, i.e., with forced recruitment; diffuse in function, i.e., organized
to perform several successive tasks such as land clearing, weeding, and harvesting; and recruited from a homogeneous social group of some sort (a
tribe, for example). Note that in these terms the teams of collectors seem
a little less diffuse than game-producer teams. In all the correlations that
follow between the structure of work teams and solidarity factors, this contrast in the stability of institutions in extractive and agricultural societies
will be reinforced. IP, as a category, appears in Table 20 as more stable

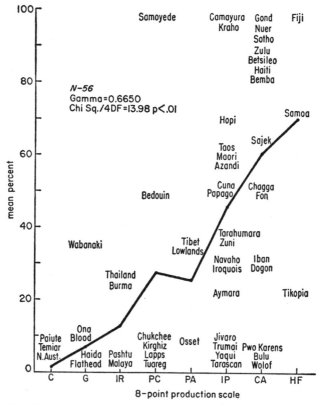

Fig. 56. Stable work teams: the eight-point production
scale. This distribution of cases shows a high frequency of
stable work teams in IP and especially HF and CA cultures,
as opposed to all others. Statistical split: C, G/IR, PC/PA/
IP/CA,HF vs. Median.

than it does in later correlations because the Udy sample is more heavily weighted with stable village cultures than is the Cantometric-Murdock sample.

Udy presents an analysis of the social base of the work teams he discovered. Of these structural types, the following were defined by us as more likely to be stable than unstable: (1) teams composed of the members of large or extended families; (2) family teams with a permanent contractual or reciprocal relationship to other family teams or to agencies in the community, such as community work associations; (3) large, contractual agencies such as guilds or community help groups; (4) compulsory or non-compulsory corvees where participation and authority are community-based. Figure 56 shows that such teams occur far more frequently in simple agricultural societies (IP, CA, HF) than at any other subsistence level.

An even stronger relationship exists between the percentage of stable teams found in a culture and the incidence of cohesive vocalizing per culture (Table 21). Where stable work teams exist, i.e., where members of a community come together for productive activity on a year-round, lifelong basis, choruses of a high degree of empathy are most likely to develop.

Table 21. *Stable work teams and cohesive singing.*

		Percent cohesive singing	
		Below median	Above median
Percent stable work teams	Above median	6	17
	Below median	21	8
Chi sq/1 df = 11.03; gamma = .7630; P < .001; N = 52.			

Unstable teams were defined as being small, purely voluntary or, on the other hand, held together principally by compulsion. Thus we lumped together the teams Udy describes as: *voluntary associations,* hunting and fishing parties; *small family teams with no reciprocal element; agencies directed by an individual,* like small business in our society; and *compulsory or exploitative situations* such as serfdom, tenancy, slavery, or peonage, where an esprit de corps would not be expected to develop, since both the system of authority and the system of rewards lie outside the team membership. In this latter case, it was felt that customary association under compulsion does not ordinarily produce a high order of cohesiveness. Table 22 shows that cohesive performance occurs far less frequently in societies where most work organizations are unstable.

Russian serfs and the American Negro slaves seem to be exceptions to the general rule indicated in the correlation, for both are reputed to have sung

Table 22. *Unstable teams and median cohesive singing.*

| | | Percent cohesive singing | |
		Below median	Above median
Percent unstable teams	Above median	19	7
	Below median	9	19

Chi sq/1 df = 9.05; gamma = .7028; P < .001; N = 54.

cohesively, even though they worked under compulsion. In the Russian case, the exploitative economic system overlies another social pattern—the village of large families; knit together by the council of village elders. Similarly, the Negro bondsman quickly filled the social vacuum of the slave quarter and the rural slum with the large grandmother family, the community work association, and the neighborhood religious cult.

Table 23. *Unstable teams and production type.*

		C, G	IR, PC	PA	IP	CA–HF
Percent unstable teams	Above median	6	7	3	6	3
	Below median	2	3	0	11	15

Chi sq/4 df = 15.61; gamma = .6609; P < .01; N = 56.

Table 23 shows that unstable teams are more frequent in very simple economies (C or G) or in very complex economies (IR, PA); that relatively few unstable teams are found in the CA–HF set; and that one-half of the incipient teams are unstable. This last finding puts some distance between full cultivation with domestication and the simpler and essentially less securely based incipient systems.

The relationship between unstable work teams and diffuse choral performance is not quite so strong as that between stability and cohesiveness (Table 24). If, however, solo performances are lumped with poorly blended

Table 24. *Unstable teams and level of choral diffuseness.*

		Below median	Above median
Percent unstable teams	Above median	7	15
	Below median	20	10

Chi sq/1 df = 6.17; gamma = .6216; P < .02; N = 52.

Table 25. *Unstable teams and individualized performance.*

		Percent unstable teams	
		Median	
Percent individualized performances	Above median	9	16
	Below median	22	9

Chi sq/1 df = 6.85; gamma = .6259; P < .01; N = 56.

choral performances under individualized singing, a better correlation emerges (Table 25). This view of song performance seems legitimate, since the search is for matching behavioral features in work teams and singing teams. In many complex economies choral folk song performance is comparatively rare. Solo singing stands for the individual worker on his own or in his relation to his patron.

We feel justified in assigning solo singing to the non-cohesive category because of the negative relationship between the percentage of solo singing and the percentage of stable work teams. Table 26 shows that solo singing is more likely to be found in cultures where unstable teams are the rule.

Table 26. *Unstable teams and solo performance.*

		Percent stable teams	
		Median	
Percent solo performances	Above median	21	7
	Below median	11	19

Chi sq/1 df = 8.60; gamma = .6765; P < .01; N = 58.

Diffuse and individualized song performance seems to represent three types of work situations: the voluntary and temporary teams of simple, band-organized societies; the permanent and compulsory teams of highly stratified societies; and the individual or small family teams of much of plow agriculture. Both stable work teams and good vocal blend are found among mid-level producers, such as Zuni, Kraho, Samoa, and Bemba, with low to moderate social superstructure. Groupiness in communication style, then, seems to rest on non-compulsory, community performance of common tasks. We now turn to other aspects of the social fabric for traces and sources of the same tendencies.

COHESIVENESS AND SOCIAL STABILITY

Arensberg suggested that some types of formal social organizations, as recorded in the *Ethnographic Atlas,* might set up a framework of stable interpersonal experience in the community and thus be mirrored by groupy singing behavior. Many factors and combinations of factors have been tested in the past several years to implement this idea. On the whole, the finding is that the formal categories with which ethnologists have described community and family organization cross-culturally have little or no interactional content. Although in some cultures a clan, a village, or a large family may be a closely knit web of human relationships, in other settings the same terms denote diffuse institutions more loaded with conflict than with contact and support. Nevertheless, a review of the evidence supports the general thesis that a tendency to groupiness found in the singing style of a culture will show up at various points of its social structure.

Earlier it was demonstrated that large corporate kin groups such as lineages, ramages, and clans increase decisively at just that point in productive development where cohesive singing is most common and where stable work teams endow everyday experience with a sense of group solidarity (Table 27).

Table 27. *Corporate kin groups and production type.*

Corporate kin groups	C, G, IP, PC, PA, IR		HF–CA
	Presence	62	74
	Absence	83	9

Chi sq/1 df = 34.72; gamma = .8334; P < .001; N = 228.

In the moderately stratified gardening societies of Africa and Oceania, the lineage or ramage gives a member status and social identity, helps him to find a mate, provides him with a protective and supportive kin group scattered throughout his territory, and deals with questions of inheritance of both property and perquisites. The appearance in the social fabric of such permanent, supportive, face-to-face human networks should be accompanied by an increase in cohesive singing. The relationship is positive but weak (Table 28).

A test of this correlation on the select sample, moreover, does not confirm it (P > .10). These large-scale kin groups are especially typical of Oceanic and African social structure and when the representation of these areas is reduced in the select sample, the correlation between large kin group and cohesiveness collapses. In all likelihood these large, supportive kin groups do contribute to the groupiness of African and Oceanic society.

Table 28. *Corporate kin groups and cohesive choruses.*

		Lineages or ramages	
		Absent	Present
Percent cohesive	Above median	36	73
	Below median	53	59

Chi sq/1 df = 4.69; gamma = .2912; P < .05; N = 221.

However, a corporate kin organization may be split by such factors as distance, wealth, nomadism, and extra-lineal allegiances, so that the unifying effect of the kinship organization is diffused. We therefore tested for the emergent solidarity of the corporate kin group within stable and nondivisive social settings.

In the next correlation, those "toppy" communities, in which either a complex or elite caste system or many levels of extra-local governmental authority split the community, were eliminated from the stable set along with those cultures that are partially or wholly nomadic and therefore intrinsically unstable. We asked whether cohesive singing would more frequently occur in stable and "non-toppy" communities than elsewhere. For the large sample the relationship is extremely strong, at the P < .001 level. In the select samples it polls at the P < .05 level. Thus the African or the Oceanic villager, living in daily contact with his lineage kin group and not split away from his community members by caste or governmental authority, does indeed experience solidarity. In the rest of the world, however, this relationship does not guarantee a seamless experience (Table 29).

Table 29. *Large kin groups in non-toppy, non-nomadic societies and cohesive choral performance.*

			Presence of lineage, ramage or clan for non-toppy, non-nomadic cultures	
			No	Yes
Full sample	Percent cohesive	Above median	18	61
		Below median	42	42

Chi sq/1 df = 12.96; gamma = .5443; P < .001; N = 163.

			No	Yes
Select sample	Percent cohesive	Above median	11	30
		Below median	23	22

Chi sq/1 df = 5.29; gamma = .4807; P < .05; N = 86.

The *Ethnographic Atlas* (Col. 38) provides information about age-grade societies in which adolescent boys, because of extended common residence and training experience, might be expected to develop a unified approach to song performance and other matters. Two cases were tested: T, complete segregation in bachelor dormitories; and P, partial segregation, sleeping away from natal families at night in a bachelor hut. The relationship between segregation and cohesive singing is positive but weak (Table 30).

Table 30. *Segregation of adolescent boys and cohesive choral performance.*

		Segregation	
		No	Yes
Percent of cohesiveness	Above median	42	31
	Below median	59	21

Chi sq/1 df = 4.47; gamma = .3493; P < .05; N = 153.

An even weaker relationship turns out to exist between cohesiveness and large families. In the test only those families scored by Murdock as both large and extended were counted (Table 31).

Table 31. *Large extended families and cohesive choral performance.*

		Large extended families	
		Below median	Above median
Percent of cohesiveness	Above median	43	13
	Below median	51	8

Chi sq/1 df = 1.79; gamma = .3168; P < .20; N = 115.

Several other factors, presumably productive of a stable framework for interpersonal experience, were run with cohesive singing:

1. The clan-organized or segmented communities (Murdock: Column 19—S, C, or P).
2. Settlements of moderate size (Murdock: Column 30).
3. Stable settlements (villages, hamlets, neighborhoods, or towns) (Murdock: Column 30—V, H, N, or X).
4. Combinations of these factors (Table 32).

Two or three varieties of social settings exist in which a feeling of solidarity and an ability to act or sing together with empathy or cohesiveness

Table 32. *Selected social indicators and cohesive choral performance.*

1. The relationship to the clan and segmented community is also weak.

		All others	Clan and segmented communities
Percent of cohesiveness	Above median	58	47
	Below median	77	31

Chi sq/1 df = 1.43; gamma = .2331; P < .30; N = 113.

2. In stable settlements, the relationship seemed strong but negative: cohesive performance was very unlikely to be found in migratory and transhumant communities, but only somewhat likely to be found in stable settlements (villages, hamlets, neighborhoods, towns).

		Unstable settlements	Stable settlements
Percent of cohesiveness	Above median	9	41
	Below median	22	31

Chi sq/1 df = 6.76; gamma = .5275; P < .01; N = 109.

3. In clan-organized communities that form stable settlements, good blend is about twice as frequent as individualized singing.

		All others	Clan organization occurring in stable communities
Percent of cohesiveness	Above median	28	20
	Below median	42	9

Chi sq/1 df = 6.89; gamma = .5385; P < .01; N = 99.

4. When all the factors are taken together in a social stability index, where each positive score counts one, the relationship with cohesive performance is not as strong as in case 3. The factors are: 1. large extended family; 2. clan organization; 3. stable settlements; 4. moderate size.

		Social stability index/cohesiveness	
		Below median on index	Above median on index
Percent of cohesiveness	Above median	43	14
	Below median	53	7

Chi sq/1 df = 3.30; gamma = .4228; P < .10; N = 117.

develop at the same time. The first is the large, permanent, community work team, with sufficient organizational spine to carry it through the years, but without the excess of authority or caste division that would lend a coercive or non-egalitarian, patronal condescension to its usual festive gatherings. The second situation is the group of clan brothers dwelling within a small stable community. The third is the lineal kin group functioning within a non-nomadic and non-stratified social web. Age grades, extended families, and various combinations of the institutions already cited may sometimes contribute to the institutional framework of the cohesiveness we find in singing organizations.

PERSONALITY FACTORS AND SOLIDARITY

Thus far we have explored only the social surroundings of a phenomenon which is essentially a way of sharing an experience or an emotion and must be based on personality-shaping factors. Cohesive choral performance demands that the individual conform precisely to the joint tones and rhythms of a singing group, just as participation in routine cultivation demands a high order of conformity to the style and traditions of the agricultural work group. The singing-dancing chorus fills out the calendrical rituals and brings the aid of the gods to the village, just as community work teams such as the African *dokpwe* or the West Indian *coumbite* prepares the land of the villagers for planting. The individual in all these organizations must have long experience of matching his bodily and vocal styles to the traditional patterns of the group. His childhood training should prepare him for the degree of conformity that the traditions of his community call for.

The Yale child-rearing studies, based on systematically rated data drawn from the ethnography, have demonstrated that childhood training for compliance is imposed by most agriculturists, but that hunters and fishers encourage their youngsters to assert themselves. In other words, the child of hoe cultivators learns obedience and respect for his elders and their traditions; he is prepared to attend his corn and pumpkin patch under their guidance, to live within the bounty-bringing calendar of his forebears, and to elicit the sympathetic help of others by his mild manner. Meanwhile, the son of the hunter or fisher is given laughing praise for sassing his father, setting his own bedtime, stealing or refusing food, running off to visit his neighbors, and generally behaving in the independent, exploratory, and assertive fashion that will later stand him in good stead while on the trail of wild animals or setting out from land in some flimsy boat.

Unfortunately, the cantometric co-sample with the Yale Child Training Study is very small (Barry, Child, and Bacon, 1959). In the course of her work on the project, however, Ayres found a significant relation between childhood training for compliance (as scored by Barry, Child, and Bacon, 1959) and cohesive singing, and the contrastive correlation of assertiveness training scores with individualized singing. The reader will note that the cultures in Table 33 occupy familiar quadrants.

Table 33. *Childhood training pressures and diffuse choral performance.*

		Childhood training pressures (compliance/assertion score) [1]				
		Assertion ($\leq$ 0)		Compliance ($\geq$ 0)		
	Above median	Manus Jivaro W. Apache Hupa Bali Camayura Tikopia		Navaho Aymara Dakota Ulithi		
Percent diffuse choral performance		N. Paiute 8		4		
	Below median	Maori 2 Tanala		11 Sotho Zulu Nuer Zuni Samoa Hopi	Yoruba Chagga Masai Azande Papago	

Chi sq/1 df = 4.95; gamma = .8333; P < .05; N = 25.

[1] The compliance/assertion score is a numerical scale expressing the degree to which, in the judgment of the raters, the dominant training pressures in a given society lie toward compliance or toward assertion. A positive score indicates a balance of emphasis on compliance training; a zero or negative score indicates a balance on assertion training (Barry, Child, and Bacon, 1959).

When individualized performances (solo as well as poorly blended choruses) are set over against cases of good blend, a more positive relationship emerges. The kind of training children experience does seem to affect the way the people in the culture sing together. One of the outcomes of compliance training is a bent for cohesive singing, just as training for assertion and independence leads to diffuse performance style. The strength of this relationship is demonstrated in Table 34.

In the layout of cultures in Table 35, cultures from HF, CA, and IP categories fill up the positive quadrant where good blend and compliance cases are counted. The same names appear time and again throughout this exposition, for the presence of cohesiveness in song means that this norm will pervade many sectors of social activity.

Table 34. *Childhood training pressures and
level of cohesiveness.*

		Assertion	Compliance
Percent cohesive performance	Above median	2	12
	Below median	10	4

Chi sq/1 df = 7.14; gamma = .8750; P < .01; N = 28.

Table 35. *Childhood training pressures and choral cohesiveness.*

	← Assertion		-0.5 to +0.5	Compliance →	
	< -5.0	-5.0 to -0.6		+0.6 to +5.0	> +5.0
90–100				Chagga (CA) Masai (CA)	Hopi (IP) Azande (CA) Samoa (HF)
80–89			Tanala (CA)		
70–79	Maori (IP)				Yoruba (CA)
60–69				Zuni (IP)	Sotho (CA)
50–59				Papago (IP)	Zulu (CA)
40–49				Ulithi (HF)	
30–39			Tikopia (CA) N. Paiute (C)		Nuer (CA)
20–29					
10–19	Jivaro (IP)				
0–9	Ona (G) Bali (IR) W. Apache (IP) Manus (G)		Hupa (C) Camayura (IP) Cuna (IP)	Navaho (IP) Teton (G) Dakota (G) Yahgan (G)	Aymara (IP)

(Left axis label: Percent cohesive choruses)

Chapter 8 demonstrates a strong relation between childhood training for assertion and a cultural preference for harsh or raspy singing. Although women sing with more rasp than men wherever they dominate subsistence or ritual activities, in most cultures males perform in harsher, heavier, noisier voices than women. Transculturally, rasp seems to be a masculine and assertive input in song and it would be generally agreed, I believe, that males in most cultures speak in a harsher and more assertive way than women though no data have been gathered on this. Raspy singing, then, is one aspect of phonation generally associated with masculine training for assertion. The irregular acoustical features of vocal noise militate against the production of good blend. If every noisy singer maintains his own idiosyncratic noisy style, poor blend or individualized singing will be the result. This negative relationship between vocal noise and good blend is set forth in Table 36, where it can be seen that with an increase of rasp, cohesiveness decreases.

Table 36. *Relationship of cohesive to raspy singing.*

		Percent cohesiveness		
		Little	Median	Much
Percent raspy singing	Above median	70		42
	Below median	44		70

Chi sq/1 df = 12.91; gamma = .4523; P < .001; N = 226.

A singer coming from a culture in which compliance training is emphasized would be motivated to damp out his vocal assertiveness to produce a noise-free tone, so as to blend with that of his comrades. Where unabashed male dominance is highly functional, however, a group of equal males should be expected to rasp away together in a noisy chorus. We found, indeed, that vocal noise is most common in extractive cultures (especially among game producers) where men actually dominate most public occasions and where political controls are minimal (Table 37). The effect of uninhibited mas-

Table 37. *Noisy singing and production type.*

		C, G, IP	CA, IR, PC, PA, HF
Percent noisy	Above median	26	33
	Below median	16	45

Chi sq/1 df = 6.27; gamma = .3706; P < .05; N = 120.

culine assertiveness thus seems to account for much of the poorly blended singing among simple producers. After the CA level, raspy singing becomes relatively less frequent. Increasing complexity tends to normalize voice qualities (Chapter 6).

Two other voice quality factors, nasalized tone and narrow or squeezed tone, have an even stronger negative relationship to good vocal blend. In Table 38 the reader can see that tonal unity is rare whenever the voice production is either very nasalized or narrowed. A pinched and nasal tone pervades many of the sounds of pain, deprivation, and sorrow. When we whine, wail, weep, moan, or scream, we pour in one of these two qualities, which narrow, block, or muffle the voice. Psychoanalysts know that fear of

Table 38. *Relationship of cohesive to nasal and narrow voice.*

		Percent cohesiveness	
		Median	
Percent nasality	Above median	83	29
	Below median	31	83
Chi sq/1 df = 49.74; gamma = .7691; P < .001; N = 226.			
Percent narrowness	Above median	78	33
	Below median	36	79
Chi sq/1 df = 34.31; gamma = .6767; P < .001; N = 226.			

punishment for sexual misdemeanors produces severe anxiety and tension in the individual. The voice, especially the singing voice, seems to be a remarkably accurate indicator of the cultural level of this tension. It is as if one of the assignments of the favored singer is to act out the level of sexual tension which the customs of the society establish as normal. The content of this message may be basically painful and anxiety-producing; but the effect upon the culture member may be stimulating, erotic, and pleasurable, since the song reminds him of familiar sexual emotions and experiences. Thus the shrieking vocal style of a culture which offends the stranger may melt the heart of the local resident.

In an earlier work (Lomax, 1959) I held that the relative severity of a culture's sexual code determined the degree of tension to be heard in the voices of its favored singers. This impressionistic hypothesis has now been tested and confirmed on the Murdock-cantometric sample, using the codes given by Murdock (Col. 78) in regard to the relative severity of restrictions placed on female sexual activity prior to marriage. A bi-modal index was fashioned from the Murdock six-point scale, as follows:

Permissive and Protective

1. T — Trial marriage, where monogamous premarital relations are permitted with the expectation of marriage if pregnancy results, promiscuous relations being prohibited and sanctioned (penalized).
2. A — Premarital sex allowed and sanctioned only if pregnancy results.
3. F — Premarital sex freely permitted and not sanctioned even if pregnancy results.

Restrictive

1. E — Early marriage in which the girl's choice of a mate is made for her in infancy.
2. P — Premarital sexual relations prohibited, but only weakly sanctioned, and not infrequent in fact.
3. V — Insistence on virginity at the time of marriage, with severe sanctions on premarital sex.

In Figure 57 three vocal sets are correlated with this two-part scale: narrow voices, nasalized voices, and wide, relaxed voices. Where feminine premarital sexual activity is restricted or severely sanctioned, narrowing and

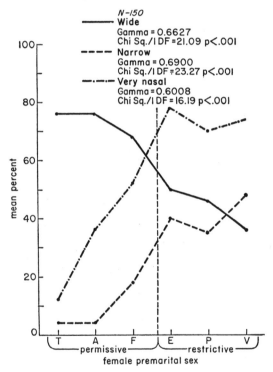

Fig. 57. Vocal qualities and sexual restrictiveness. Wide voices occur far more frequently in sexually permissive societies than in those which impose heavy restrictions. The frequency of narrow voices varies almost linearly with sexual restrictiveness. The trend for nasality is even more dramatic; at the restrictive end of the scale, nasality is absolutely dominant. Statistical split: For Wide, Narrow, and Nasal—T, A, F/E, P, V vs. Median.

nasality, both signs of tension, become prominent and constant features of a culture's singing style, and relaxed vocalizing is relatively uncommon. Where sexual standards for women are permissive and there are rules that pertain in the case of pregnancy, narrowing usually does not occur, nasality tends to be absent, and the singing voice is open and relaxed. It is most notable that the least tense situation—marked by absence of narrowing and nasality—is trial marriage, where the girl's social future is guaranteed and pregnancy is rewarded by marriage. That this provision for feminine security tends to reduce tension is further underscored by the contrast between points A and F. The A situation is permissive and yet sanctions or rules of some sort do exist that express the society's concern about the fate of the girl if she becomes pregnant. Here there is no narrowing, but a good deal of nasality. Nasality seems to increase when society demands too much independence of its children too early in life. In the A situation the girl is on her own in some degree; but in F cultures, where there are simply no rules that apply to sex, the girl is totally on her own, and thus less secure. The vocal tension in this situation approaches that of the restrictive set.

In many cases of early marriage a girl is exploited sexually by an older man prior to menarche; in all cases she has no freedom of sexual choice, having been betrothed in her infancy or, occasionally, before her birth. Note that this restrictive condition produces almost the same degree of vocal tension as the two cases, P and V, in which a girl is penalized if she is discovered to have indulged in premarital intercourse. The punishment for the violator of these codes becomes doubly severe, of course, if the girl becomes pregnant. Note the steady drop in vocal relaxation in V—insistence on virginity —the situation in which there is the maximum of tension surrounding sexual practices, because a woman's body becomes a focus for masculine and for family honor.

Sanctions that restrict women's premarital sexual activity actually represent the imposition of masculine control upon the opposite sex. Such sanctions usually arise in complex societies where a small coterie of powerful males dominate not only the productive and political systems but the ritual life of the community, as, for example, among the Plains Indians. In the purdah world of the Mediterranean and the Near East, the honor of the males of the line depends upon maintenance of the precious innocence of their women; and women are moved like pawns in the social chess game of the dominant males. The psychological and physical torment that women have been subjected to in this region varies from culture to culture, principally in its degree of cruelty. Only yesterday any Sicilian father might drive his daughter into the streets and, in order to live, into prostitution, for some real or fancied deviation from the code of perfect feminine modesty. And even today in modern Sudan, most girls are subjected to a labiodectomy and clitoridectomy between the ages of 9 and 12. The resulting infibulation seals up the vagina so effectively that an operation must be performed to make the Sudanese bride, a warranted virgin, available to her husband. The punishment for illicit affairs in such an environment falls most heavily upon the female and, if she is not killed outright, is eventually passed on by her to her mate and to her offspring. Thus we hear, in the high wail of the muezzin, appealing for mercy from Allah, and in the piercing silver tones of the cafe singers, a restatement of the pain, fear, and erotic hysteria of women.

A cross-cultural survey by the editor of the *Ethnographic Atlas* demonstrated that sexual sanctions increase in severity as population grows denser (Murdock, 1964). Our finding is essentially the same—a dramatic rise in the restrictions placed on female premarital sexual activity among complex producers, particularly in the irrigation cultures of the Orient (Table 39).

Table 39. *Premarital sex restrictions on women and production types.*

	IP, AH	X	PA	IR
Restrictive	28	12	23	12
Permissive	53	10	11	1

Chi sq/3 df = 21.44; gamma = .5831; P < .001; N = 150.

The inhibitory rules placed on erotic life by complex producers are paralleled by a rise of narrow or tense-voiced singing, especially at the level of irrigation agriculture (Table 40).

Table 40. *Vocal narrowing and production type.*

		X, IP, AH	PA	IR
Percent narrow voice	Above median	35	9	13
	Below median	51	11	1

Chi sq/2 df = 13.20; gamma = .4935; P < .01; N = 120.

Among simple producers, straightforward, noisy assertiveness, together with nasally expressed complaint (induced by overtraining for assertiveness), can be heard in the majority of performances. This "masculine" vocal style, of course, militates against good choral blend (Table 41).

It seems then that all three indicators—raspy, nasal, and narrow—are the product of masculine dominance and their level varies by subsistence type. With any one of these noisy factors in the voices of the singers, the level of tonal blend drops sharply. That dependence is expressed in Table 42, where "noisy" means either nasal, narrow, or raspy.

Table 41. *Raspy plus nasal/production type.*

		C, G, IP	CA, IR, PC	PA, HF
Percent raspy and nasal	Above median	49	50	17
	Below median	23	60	34

Chi sq/2 df = 15.96; gamma = .4224; P < .001; N = 233.

Table 42. *Noisy performance and cohesiveness.*

		Percent noisy Median	
Percent noisy	Above median	80	30
	Below median	34	82

Chi sq/1 df = 42.57; gamma = .7309; P < .001; N = 226.

The relationship between noise level in the singing voice and the co-hesiveness of a chorus is acoustical, as well as cultural. Any sort of noise disturbs the relationship between the partials that make up the tones. Sono-grams of various kinds of noisy voices show that many elements extraneous to the harmonics can muddy the clear and orderly layout that exists between them. Such acoustical irregularities in individual voices are difficult to match, of course, and are almost certain to clash and produce harsh choral effects.

The conditions which work most strongly against solidarity of the sing-ing groups are two varieties of masculine dominance: direct assertiveness and control of feminine sexuality, both symbolized by the introduction of disturbing and idiosyncratic noise into vocalizing. On the other hand, there is a type of voice production that closely ties in with a permissive, nonaggressive, nondominant, security-building attitude toward feminine sexuality—the wide, clear, and relaxed voice. Most of the great choirs in the C–HF–CA set, where we have found maximal cohesiveness, sing in this bell-like vocal style (Table 43).

Table 43. *Vocal width and production type.*

		IR, PC, G	IP, PA	C, CA, HF
Percent wide voices	Above median	15	30	68
	Below median	48	43	29

Chi sq/2 df = 35.10; gamma = .5928; P < .001; N = 233.

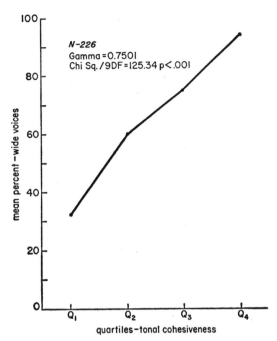

N-226
Gamma = 0.7501
Chi Sq. / 9DF = 125.34 p < .001

mean percent — wide voices

quartiles — tonal cohesiveness

Fig. 58. Vocal width and tonal cohesiveness. Vocal width and tonal cohesiveness are very nearly
linear functions of one another. Statistical split:
Quartiles vs. Quartiles.

Finally, the link between wide, relaxed vocalizing and good tonal blend
seems to be one of the closest and most powerful in our study, approximating
a straight-line relationship (Fig. 58).

COHESIVENESS AND COMPLEMENTARITY

Relaxed vocalizing not only stands for permissive sexual standards for
women, but for another basic source of feminine independence as well—the
importance of women in basic subsistence. Arensberg and I term this a complementarity indicator, on the ground that where women take a leading,
recognized part in the central activity of a society, such as supplying the
main source of food, they assume, at least in this respect, a complementary,
or more or less equal, interactive relationship with men (Chapter 6). In
such situations women are likely to initiate interaction in public activities crucial to the whole society about as frequently as men. Comparatively
speaking, one would expect to find an easier and more relaxed atmosphere

Table 44. *Vocal tension and productive complementarity.*

		M, N	D, E, F, G
Percent narrow and nasal	Above median	30	17
	Below median	14	35

Chi sq/1 df = 12.01; gamma = .6304; P < .001; N = 96.

in such a society than in one where women had, for one reason or another, to remain more passive or socially inert; and this appears to be the case, as illustrated in Table 44. Vocal tension (narrow, nasal vocalizing) is far higher in non-complementary societies, where men perform all or most of the main subsistence tasks. On the other hand, wide, relaxed voices seem to be the norm in complementary societies.

Although choral cohesiveness depends upon many factors, positive and negative, a relaxed singing style is the most crucial of them all. People tend to sing in wide voices in societies where women are most secure in their productive and sexual roles and where, therefore, they are freest to relate fully to the males. If conflict arises between a man and a woman in such an even-handed culture, both parties are likely to have more avenues for the resolution or the acting out of the problem, and thus the reduction of inner tension, than in societies where either sex must repress and deny these needs. In such societies singers will not need to express themselves overassertively in rasp, or appeal for sympathy in nasality, or express sexual tensions by vocal narrowing. It will be no surprise, therefore, to find that of all the cultural conditions for good vocal blend, complementarity is the most crucial. Table 45 shows that vocal solidarity is far more likely to occur in complementary than in non-complementary societies, at a P < .001 level.

It seems, then, that where feminine labor is crucial in production—namely in many collecting societies, among the settled incipients of the Americas, in almost all the gardening societies of Africa and Oceania, and among the villagers of Old Europe—tension between the sexes is reduced, voices are relaxed, and vocal solidarity emerges. This condition is of less effect in societies

Table 45. *Choral cohesiveness and productive complementarity.*

		M, N	D, G, E, F
Percent cohesiveness	Above median	24	64
	Below median	54	37

Chi sq/1 df = 18.80; gamma = .5900; P < .001; N = 179.

which are either so migratory, so diffusely organized, so male-dominated, or so split with stratification that the whole community scarcely ever acts together in any unified way. In other words, some degree of social stability must underlie the sexual complementarity of a community before its people can truly act and sing with full-blown solidarity. Both these conditions are fulfilled in most of the cultures in the HF–CA set, a majority of which are both stable, complementary, and sexually permissive.

Confirmation and further illumination of this distribution of cohesiveness has emerged from a more recent and, as yet, incomplete cross-cultural study of movement style. Films of dance and of everyday life from more than fifty cultures have been rated for a number of gross stylistic features. The data indicate that the distribution of a high level of synchrony in movement turns out to parallel that of cohesiveness in singing; the African and Oceanic gardeners, the Central Europeans, and the African gatherers seem to carry out joint activity with a higher level of gross synchrony than do the people of other regions and cultural traditions. The remarkable ability of these peoples to calibrate and coordinate their voices in song is a consequence of the fact that their bodies are already synchronized. Their cultures permit them to fall unselfconsciously into synchrony. The spontaneous and delicate tuning together of voices so that the overtone series of a group of individuals blends together in a unified stream of organ-like purity seems to be a function of bodies long trained to move in unison, not only in dance, but in work and in everyday life. The films show us these cohesively inclined people dancing beautifully together, walking in unison, paddling in incredible synchrony, even splitting conversation into a supportive and matching leader-response pattern where the phrases of two speakers mirror and complement each other like the steps of a pair of dancers.

It might be argued, then, that vocal cohesiveness is simply one aspect of a preference for gross paralleling or imitative behavior in a tradition and thus that the complex setting of culture pattern and role we have offered in the foregoing pages is superfluous. Yet this would leave the preference for gross synchronous behavior without a cultural explanation. Cohesiveness has been located on several levels of human behavior and we are now in a position to form a useful theory concerning it.

The degree of choral cohesiveness in a singing style, for which we already have a dependable five-point scale from no blend at all to maximal blend, seems a good measure of the degree of the stability and, especially, the complementarity of a culture pattern. It is probably safe to assume that the institutions of stable and complementary societies depend for their functioning success upon a high input of gross synchronous paralleling in bodily intercommunication. Such behavior has the effect of damping out interpersonal conflict and increasing the level of unity on a given occasion. In other words, the level of vocal cohesiveness represents a society's dependence upon a continual feed of empathy-producing, conflict-reducing, unifying parallel behavior in interpersonal interaction.

We know that the classes of cultures in which gross synchrony is reduced show one or several of the following characteristics:

1. Masculine aggressiveness
2. Diffuse organization
3. Rigid stratification
4. Masculine dominance of production
5. Repressive control of feminine sexual freedom

Apparently any one of these tendencies, all of which cluster around some form of masculine predominance, represses gross synchrony. Here "to repress" probably means to cut down the frequency of gross paralleling in intercommunication, or to reduce the frequency, amplitude, and duration of the synchronous behavior permitted by the culture as a constant feature in the stream of communication. In Line 5 of the cantometrics coding sheet dealing with level of tonal blend, we have a measurement of culture type in terms of the permitted frequency, amplitude, and duration of grossly synchronous behavior.

For the present we might conclude that the more even-handed and permissive a culture, the more it is given to gross synchrony in public communication, and that the symbolic effect of this tendency is to fill the subliminal communication stream with positive sexual affect. Two African Hunter societies, the Kung and Mbuti, have been thoroughly reported on in recent years. There, imitative mirror behavior is at its peak in song, dance, and behavior. In both cultures, although hunting is important, the daily collecting activity of the women brings in the bulk of the food. This subsistence balance is reflected in the egalitarian, supportive, and affect-loaded male-female interaction pattern. Cantometrics scores the performances of these little African nomads as being the most integrated and the most cohesive of all singing styles. The dance study finds them employing every type of synchrony-producing behavior at the most extreme level. Turnbull (1961) reports that the Mbuti use dance, song, play, or straight-out imitative behavior to resolve conflict. One day, for example, Turnbull made a crutch for a lame girl, but she was too ashamed to use it. When the other Pygmies saw her problem, they all made crutches and playfully hobbled about the camp until, after a few days, the lame girl lost her feeling of being different.

Total sharing of all food and possessions is a fundamental principle among these little pacifist peoples and is understood by them as a way to forestall conflict. A story from Thomas's (1959) remarkable account of the Kung

Bushman illustrates this idea. Stronger, warlike Negro tribes have pushed the Kung back into the Kalahari Desert where game, food, and even water are normally in short supply. One day, after a long hungry time, a hunter of one group killed. As the meat was being prepared another Bushman band appeared at the edge of the camp and sat watching, silently and enviously. The group decision was to give almost all the meat to the strangers so that no envious feelings would develop and endanger the future relations of the two groups.

This anecdote points to the resolution of one of the mysteries of anthropology and of human development. The African Hunter bands stand at the bottom of the social stability scales we have devised, yet in actual interaction, they can achieve a level of varied synchrony in song and dance that no other culture matches. In Turnbull's view the binding element in Mbuti society is that every Pygmy is ready to share with every other Pygmy and willing to support him emotionally whenever he needs support. In other societies such support comes only from a special group, such as the lineage, the team, the clan, or the family, and, in our Western society, only when it is especially solicited and even paid for. Among the Mbuti the support comes unbidden to everyone present in the form of tuned-in, interlocked synchrony of voice, of hand outstretched with food, and with naked, dancing, frolicsome, bodily synchrony. In the Pygmy culture we find social solidarity in its earliest and purest form in playful, affect-filled, mirror behavior. When we reflect that the peak in mirror interaction is sexual intercourse, the act of love itself, we may surmise that social solidarity is a generalization of the act of generation. A further task, then, is to find and nourish this cohesive element in the many specialized patterns of social solidarity that the human race has developed. We now have a dependable measurement of social solidarity as an aid in the search.

8

Self-Assertion, Sex Role, and Vocal Rasp

Edwin E. Erickson

CANTOMETRICS began with the hypothesis that song styles, whatever else their cultural function, provide a clear reflection of the personal perspective in societies—the ways in which people assert their presence, relate to one another, and express some of their most broadly shared anxieties. A corollary to this general proposition is that the most important differentials in sex role will also be expressed in singing behavior. The evidence thus far adduced supports both the major hypothesis and the corollary.

It is a matter of common observation that, transculturally, men, far more often than women, occupy the positions of leadership and specialized competence, and that they are far more self-assertive in public. In gross outline these differentials are clearly apparent in our codings of male and female song performance. Wordiness of song text, for example, has been shown in Chapter 6 to be strongly associated with the level of differentiation both of leadership and technical competence. Similarly, the solo singer asserts himself by total dominance of the communication space. In most cultures where there are sex differences in degree of text wordiness and frequency of solo performance, they lie heavily on the side of the men. By contrast, women are somewhat more likely than men to sing in interlocked choral groups, where leadership and individual voices are submerged in the collective vocalization (Table 46).

Table 46. *Sex differentials in song leadership.*

	Number of societies in which		
	Men sing more	Both sexes sing equally	Women sing more
Wordy text	66	112	16
In solo	100	71	26
In interlocked groups	10	4	21

Beyond such general attributes, we have sought more specifically to locate expressions of the personal perspectives and major sex roles in the area of vocal qualities. In Chapter 7, Lomax demonstrated that vocal noise, in the sense of any departure from a clear, relaxed tone, is expressive of the individual and his concerns, and that in tightly cohesive societies such noise tends to be damped out in song performance. Rasp, defined loosely as harsh guttural vocalization, appears to have an especially strong association with social diffuseness and personal assertiveness. We have hypothesized (1) that rasp, whenever it appears as a prominent feature of singing style, is the universal sound of self-assertion; and (2) that the differential importance of rasp in male and female song performances reflects the differential patterning of sex roles in the society.

The first hypothesis appeals strongly to the ethnographic intuition. In the world distribution of raspy singing styles, there is a heavy concentration of hunters and gatherers, with a distinct fall-off among cultivators and horticulturists. We find steady rasp prominent in Amerindia and less prominent in Polynesia and most parts of Africa. Exceptions to this broad outline are equally suggestive. Among the few hunting and gathering peoples falling below the world median for sung rasp are the groupy, intersupportive African Pygmies. In Amerindia, similarly, there is an interesting contrast between the lone, spirit-questing, and raspy Plains hunters and the communal, relatively non-raspy Pueblo peoples.

The search for the cultural correlates of sung rasp and its sexual differentials was twofold. First, we studied their distributions in the institutional settings, coded in the production scales and in the *Ethnographic Atlas,* that seemed likely to reflect varying levels of social diffuseness, culturally sanctioned self-assertiveness, and sex role contrast. Second, we studied both the cantometric distributions and the institutional settings against a background of cross-cultural variation in child-rearing practices, in order to add a dimension more directly related to the values and the observable modes of interpersonal behavior.

In the latter task, we have drawn on both data and findings from the socialization studies of Child, Whiting, Bacon, Barry, and others. The data banks from these studies contain numerically coded information drawn from ethnographic sources by trained raters, on infant nurture, later childhood training, training emphases, and the conflicts and anxieties of the rearing process, in a sample of about 100 societies. The variables that were most relevant to this exploration of rasp were:

1. The relative emphasis placed by society on training in each of six areas of behavior: responsibility, nurture, obedience, self-reliance, achievement, and general independence. Each of these emphases is

scored separately for boys and girls on an ordinal scale running from 1 to 14.

2. The compliance-assertion score, a composite of the scores for training in responsibility, obedience, self-reliance, and achievement. A positive rating implies a dominant pressure toward compliance.

Unfortunately, the cantometric sample and that of Child and associates share only 32 cultures, most of them non-literate, scarcely touching the upper end of our complexity scales. Direct comparisons of song styles and child-rearing styles must therefore be seen as more interesting than conclusive, even though, in the present case, the co-trending of the two styles is fairly consistent. On the other hand, we have been able to discover considerable covariation of cantometric and child-rearing parameters along the same institutional scales, although in separate sets of societies; this covariation provides an indirect support for the hypotheses of association.

Barry, Child, and Bacon (1959) have demonstrated a close and highly significant correlation (.94, P < .001) between intensity of food production and the degree of socialization pressure towards compliance. Their sample comes almost entirely from the X, IP, and AH levels. In the range of societies covered by them raspy singing, if it is an indicator of assertiveness, should trend in much the same way as training pressures for assertion. When it was placed across the truncated production scale, the distribution of rasp showed a weak relationship in the predicted direction (gamma = 0.405, chi sq/2df = 7.47, P < .03). But when the distribution of rasp in male performances only was set on the same scale, the relationship strengthened considerably (Table 47). When female rasp was scrutinized separately, it showed no significant correlation to production type.

Table 47. *Raspy singing (male performances) and assertion training: five-point production scale (truncated).*

	X	IP	AH
Percent of cultures above median for rasp in male performances (mean score)	69	61	34
Percent of cultures with dominant pressure toward assertion (C/A score zero or negative)	82	42	28

Associations:

Male rasp (median) to production scale (X/IP/AH); gamma = .561; chi sq/2 df = 13.73; P < .005; N = 160.

Assertion training (median C/A score) to production scale (X/IP/AH); gamma = .721; chi sq/2 df = 20.78; P < .001; N = 63.

C/A = Compliance-assertion.

A closer inspection of cases offers further, though impressionistic, support for the hypothesis that the distribution reflects the function of sung rasp as assertive self-projection. Hunting societies typically put a high premium on masculine assertiveness. Quite possibly, this premium is reflected in our find-ing that in the above-median range for male rasp, hunter societies outnum-ber collector societies by about eight-to-one as compared to two-to-one in the whole sample.

Another bit of confirmation is provided by a negative relationship, in the cantometrics-Child co-sample, between rasp in song performance and train-ing for compliance, although the small number of cases compels caution in acceptance. When the frequency of extreme rasp per culture is ranged against the C/A (compliance-assertion) score, a statistically significant correlation emerges, suggesting that an atmosphere encouraging conformity is a negative condition for sung rasp. Again, if the comparison is limited to rasp in male performance, the relationship improves (Table 48).

Table 48. *Raspy singing and training for compliance.*

| | Compliance-assertion score (sample median = +2.5) | |
	Below median (Assertion)	Above median (Compliance)
Above median	Ona Camayura Yahgan Tikopia Bali W. Apache	
Percent extreme rasp	Masai Manus W. Australia N. Australia	Chagga Aymara Zulu Navaho
At or below median	Jivaro N. Paiute Hupa Cuna Chukchee Maori	Ulithi Yoruba Sotho Teton-Dakota Papago Nuer Hopi Azande Zuni Samoa Fiji

Rasp (both sexes)	Rasp (males only)
N = 31	N = 32
Gamma = .641	Gamma = .669
P < .03 (Mann-Whitney U, 1-tailed)	P < .01 (Mann-Whitney U, 1-tailed)

In studying sex differentials in rasp, we excluded from the sample those cultures in which this quality appears less than 50 percent of the time in both male and female performances, as a means of minimizing the effects of possible coding error. We excluded also those for which we lacked adequate codings in the *Ethnographic Atlas*. In the resulting subset of 76 cultures, raspy singing appears as a strongly masculine quality; male performances are dominantly raspy in 50 percent of the cases, as compared to 16 percent for female performances.

We sought a social base line in the division of labor in major subsistence tasks, an area which has produced much order in other cantometrics distributions. Specifically, we took it as a working hypothesis that women are more likely to enjoy opportunities to exercise social initiatives and to assert themselves in societies where they make a significant or predominant contribution to subsistence than in those societies where males dominate strategic production. The classification of modes of subsistence labor division employed here distinguishes three states, in descending order of the importance of female labor:

1. Feminine dominance or equal and undifferentiated role in main subsistence teams (Murdock code F, G, or E).
2. Equal but differentiated contributions by men and women (D).
3. Male dominated (M, N).

At least for the subset of societies under consideration, the hypothesis seems well supported by the joint distribution of labor division modes and sex differentials in sung rasp (Table 49).

Table 49. *Raspy singing and division of subsistence labor.*

	Percent of societies in which sung rasp is		
	More important in male performance (N = 38)	About equal for both sexes (N = 26)	Female performance (N = 12)
Masculine domination (M, N)	66	50	33
Equal, differentiated (D)	10	11	—
Feminine or complementary (F, G, E)	24	39	67

Gamma (Labor division split M, N, D/E, F, G) = .492; chi sq/2 df = 7.15; P < .03; N = 76.

From left to right on the sex differential scale, the frequency of masculine-dominated modes declines steadily, while that of feminine and complementary modes rises. The case of equal but differentiated subsistence roles shows up as distinctly masculine, possibly reflecting a general tendency for the man's role to be the dominant or indispensable one in the task structure.

The Child codings vary in much the same way across the range of labor division modes. Table 50 presents the percentage of cases per category in which there is strong emphasis (a rating of 11 or more) for either boys or girls in training for the three areas of assertion.

Table 50. *Socialization pressures for assertion and division of subsistence labor.*

	Division of labor (Percent of societies, rounded to nearest 5)		
	M, N	D	E, F, G
Self-reliance			
Boys	65	35	40
Girls	15	0	10
Achievement			
Boys	50	40	40
Girls	15	20	45
General independence			
Boys	40	10	25
Girls	0	0	10

In every training area, the frequency of high pressures on boys is greatest in the M, N category, and the sex differentials are highest there. At the other end of the scale, except for self-reliance training, the frequency of great pressures on girls for assertion is greatest in the E, F, G category, and the sex differentials are lowest. The masculine bias of the D mode is supported, too, for even though the frequency of strong emphasis on male assertion is lowest in that category, the sex differentials are uniformly high.

Inspection of the sex differentials in rasp against analogous differentials in the Child data failed to produce a significant correlation. In the few cases where there was joint information, however, a pattern consistent with the hypothesis did emerge. Table 51 presents the relationship of the rasp differ-

Table 51. *Sex role in rasp and in independence training.*

Score differential (Boys' scores minus girls' scores)	Sung rasp	
	More important in male performances	Equally or more important in female performances
0–1	2	4
2	5	3
3–5	7	2

ential to sex differences in training pressures for general independence. At least in this small sample a large sex differential in emphasis on training boys for independence is clearly a positive condition for a masculine predominance in raspy singing.

The generally low level of statistical confirmation presented throughout this paper is due in part to the lack of an adequate co-sample with the Child scorings. More fundamentally, however, it seems to reflect the nature of the institutional variables. The two hypotheses—rasp as assertion, and sex differentials in rasp as a reflection of broader sex roles—must be tested against the visible public behavior of people. The social parameters available to us, however, do not afford direct descriptions of the behavior itself, but rather describe the institutions in which the behavior is presumed to be lodged in most cases. The fact that, notwithstanding the necessary indirection of approach, a consistent statistical case has emerged nevertheless encourages a tentative acceptance of the hypothesis.

9

Effects of Infantile Stimulation on Musical Behavior

Barbara Ayres

EARLIER chapters have demonstrated the important influence exerted by social and psychological factors on many aspects of musical performance style. The present chapter will focus on the effects of physiological factors on two additional aspects of musical style, range, and accent. The chapter supports the inference that the physiological processes involved are influenced by cultural factors.

Some years ago Levine and his colleagues at Ohio State University began a series of experiments designed to study the effects of early trauma on adult personality and behavior. During the experiments a group of infant rats was subjected to a series of mild electrical shocks. At maturity the animals were placed in a transparent box and their behavior observed for signs of emotional disturbance. Much to the experimenters' surprise the shocked animals displayed little urination and defecation and explored the box freely while a group of non-shocked controls crouched in the corners of the box where they urinated and defecated frequently. The experimenters concluded that the shocked animals were much less emotionally disturbed by the testing situation than were those who had not experienced the experimental trauma (Levine, 1960). Numerous subsequent studies have confirmed the finding that stimulation, either by shock or by handling, if it occurs prior to weaning at approximately 21 days, increases exploratory behavior and reduces emotionality in adult animals.

A number of other changes in behavior which persist into adulthood have also been discovered. When presented with water following a period of deprivation, shocked or handled rats approach the source more quickly and consume a greater quantity (Lindholm, 1962; Spence and Maher, 1962). When attacked by another rat they counterattack more quickly and are more aggressive (Levine, 1959). They require fewer trials to learn an appropriate avoidance response (Levine, 1956). Of particular interest is the greater

211

tendency of shocked or handled animals to engage in exploratory behavior. They enter an unfamiliar "open field" more quickly, traverse a larger area of the field, and approach a light source more closely than non-handled controls (Denenberg, Carlson, and Stephens, 1962). When tested in the open field over a number of days their emotional reactivity, as measured by frequency of urination and defecation, declines from session to session, while that of controls tends to remain at its initially high levels (Denenberg and Smith, 1963). These observations have led Levine to conclude that ". . . one of the major consequences of handling in infancy may be the endowment of the organism with the capacity to make responses more appropriate to the demands of the environment, including appropriate responses to stress" (Levine and Mullins, 1966).

These changes in behavior are linked with important changes in the animal's adrenal stress response system. Animals which have been shocked or stressed during infancy react with a minimal adrenal response to relatively minor changes in their environment, and their adrenal response to distinctly threatening or noxious stimuli develops rapidly and appropriately and subsides quickly following removal of the stimulus. By contrast, animals that have not been stressed during infancy respond to minor changes in their environment with a large output of adrenocorticosteroids and their adrenal response to stress develops more slowly and persists over a much longer period (Levine, 1960, 1962). These experiments indicate that non-stressed animals are hyper-reactive to novel stimuli and that they chronically experience abnormally high levels of circulating stress-response hormones.

These differing patterns of adrenal stress response have important physiological consequences. Stressed animals are longer and heavier at maturity and they mature more rapidly than their controls. They show superior ability to survive food and water deprivation and exposure to pathogenic agents (Levine, 1960). They suffer less cardiovascular and gastrointestinal damage as a result of immobilization and food and water deprivation (Weininger, 1956; Weininger, McClelland, and Arima, 1954).

Although these experiments were conducted with laboratory animals there is no *a priori* reason why similar effects should not be observed in human subjects, since the biological mechanisms involved are not species specific. In fact, Landauer and Whiting (1964) have produced cross-cultural evidence that an increase in stature is related to infant stress in human populations. These investigators found that in societies where infant-care practices include painful stimulation of the infant before age two, adult males are, on the average, two inches taller than in societies where such practices occur after age two or are absent. They interpret their findings as due to the growth-inhibiting effects of corticosteroid hormones. In a more recent study, Whiting (1965) has shown that menarche occurs earlier in societies where female infants are subjected to similar forms of stress. The fact that human subjects show physiological reactions to infantile stimulation similar to those observed in laboratory animals increases the probability that similar effects may also be seen in human behavior. Infant stress should produce adults who are bolder, more exploratory, and who have less tendency to avoid novel stimuli.

The cantometrics codings provide interesting data on which to test this hypothesis. Indeed, it would be difficult to imagine a type of behavior more likely to reflect the influence of psychological and physiological factors (Lomax, 1962). From among the 37 aspects of musical performance style coded by cantometrics, there are two, range and accent, in which the type of behavioral predisposition predicted by the stress hypothesis would seem most likely to be reflected. Range is defined as the distance between a song's lowest and highest notes. This measurement seems analogous to the measurement of exploratory behavior in the animal experiments. If musical space is thought of as the total range of notes which the average human voice is capable of reproducing, then the extent to which that space is utilized by the singers of a culture should provide a measure of exploratory behavior. On this assumption it was hypothesized that songs from societies where infant stress is present would be characterized by wider range than songs from societies where infant stress is absent.

The second cantometrics variable which seems likely to be related to stress is accent. Defined as the forcefulness with which notes or syllables are attacked by the singer, this variable should provide a measure of relative boldness vs. timidity similar to the measures of emotionality and aggressiveness in the animal experiments. On the basis of this assumption, it was hypothesized that songs in societies where infant stress is practiced will be characterized by more forceful accent than songs in societies where infant stress is absent.

These hypotheses were first tested on a small sample of 25 societies using the Landauer and Whiting ratings of infant stress. Stress was defined as any piercing of the nose, lips, or ears; circumcision; scarification; inoculation; cauterization; or persistent and vigorous molding, shaping, or stretching of the head, limbs, or body (Landauer and Whiting, 1964). These practices occur at various ages in a large number of societies and, since the animal studies found this to be an important variable, the age at which any of these practices was first reported was also recorded. This information on infant stress was obtained from the ethnographic accounts of infant and child care practices in each of the societies. When the hypotheses were tested on the small group of societies for which both cantometrics and stress data were available, the results were positive and statistically significant, but the sample was small and not geographically well distributed. It was decided, therefore, to enlarge and improve the sample by obtaining stress ratings on a number of additional societies from the cantometrics sample.

In order to obtain these new ratings a number of the Landauer and Whiting cases were re-rated for stress, and the reliability of the two sets of judgments established. Once this had been done, all of the societies in the Human Relations Area Files that were included in the cantometrics sample were coded for infant stress. Ethnographies were consulted for a large number of additional cases. During this process three additional types of pain stress were encountered which were added to the original list of Landauer and Whiting. These were tooth evulsion, clitoridectomy, and damage to internal tissue which results in bleeding. Data from over 100 societies were examined in this process. A substantial number of these societies (43) were dropped from the sample because of inadequate information: either the sources contained conflicting reports, or the age of stress was not clearly specified, or the stress applied to one sex and not the other.

In order to insure that the societies in the sample would be historically independent, no two were included which were members of the same linguistic subfamily. Murdock's linguistic classification was used for Africa, circum-Mediterranean, East Eurasia, and North and South America, while that of Dyen (1964) was used for Insular Pacific. Exceptions were made to this rule in four cases in order to increase the size of the sample. In each instance one of the two societies was rated "stress present" and the other "stress absent," thus eliminating the possibility of joint diffusion of both factors. When data were available for two or more societies from the same linguistic subfamily and their stress scores were similar, the case which had the more doubtful information or which appeared to be a poorer match with the unit of cantometric sampling was eliminated. The result was a sample of 48 societies, 10 from Africa, 9 from South America, 8 from Insular Pacific, and 7 each from circum-Mediterranean, East Eurasia, and North America.

Because the original cantometrics ratings applied to individual songs, it was necessary to average the ratings for each society in order to obtain scores that could characterize the society as a whole. A minimum of ten songs from each society was rated, but in many cases this number was considerably larger. Every effort was made to obtain a sample of songs that would be representative of the various types of song found in each society. These cantometric judgments were made without knowledge of the stress data or hypothesis.

The scale used in rating *range* was defined as follows:

1. A monotone to a major second
2. A minor third to a perfect fifth
3. A minor sixth to an octave
4. A minor ninth to a major fourteenth
5. Two octaves or more

Mean range scores in the subsample were distributed almost exactly like the scores for the entire cantometrics sample of 233 societies. Median scores for each of the major geographical regions were: Africa, 3.3; Insular Pacific, 2.6; circum-Mediterranean, 3.0; East Eurasia, 2.9–3.3; North America, 3.0; and South America, 2.6. The median for the entire sample was 3.1, indicating an average range of about one octave.

Accent was defined as the amount of muscular force used by the singer in producing accented notes or syllables. For purposes of statistical analysis the original five-point rating scale was collapsed to three points as follows:

1. Forceful accent—very forceful or markedly forceful attack with strong accents falling on most of the notes or on the main pulses of the meter
2. Moderate accent
3. Relaxed accent—relaxed, lazy, almost unaccented rhythmic motion

Table 52. *Relationship between infant stress and range.*

Stress before age 2, present vs. absent, $P < .005$ (Fisher's Exact Test). The Kung are omitted from this table because their hocketing style makes range an inappropriate measure of average behavior.

Mean range		Birth–2 weeks	2 weeks–2 years	2–6 years	6–15 years	Not before 15 years
			Age of earliest stress			
Wide	4.2		Yankee			
		Javanese				
	4.0		Masai			
	3.8		Shilluk, Irish			
	3.6	Burmese, Hupa, Lau	Zuni, Okinawa			
	3.4	Azande, Amhara	Thai, Zulu	Chagga		
	3.2	Lakalai	Bambara	Tikopia	Mende	
	3.0	Navaho, Hausa, Salish, Yoruba			Fon	
	2.8	N. Cayapo		Ainu	Camayura, Semang	Aymara
	2.6			Kurds, Yap, Atayal	Wolof, Witoto	Slave, Palau, Goajiro
			Tuareg	Gond	Fore	
	2.4	Jivaro, Nookta	Paiute		Trumai	Chukchee
	2.2			Amahuaca		
	2.0					
	1.8					
				Yaghan		
Narrow	1.6					

Table 53. *Stress and range by major geographical regions.*

Mean range	Africa (P : N.S.)		Cir.-Med. (P : N.S.)		E. Euras. (P = .029)		Ins. Pac. (P = .014)		N. Amer. (P : N.S.)		S. Amer. (P : N.S.)	
	Prs.	Abs.	Prs.	Abs.	Prs.	Abs.	Prs.	Abs.	Prs.	Abs.	Prs.	Abs.
Wide 4.2			✕									
4.0	✕						✕					
3.8	✕											
3.6			✕		✕✕				✕			
3.4	✕						✕		✕			
3.2	✕	✕	✕		✕							
3.2	✕	✕					✕					
3.0	✕	✕	✕					✕	✕✕			
2.8						✕					✕	✕
2.6				✕✕		✕		✕✕✕		✕		✕✕
2.4			✕			✕✕		✕	✕		✕	✕
2.2									✕			✕
2.0												
1.8												
Narrow 1.6												✕

The median score for both the cantometrics sample and the subsample on this scale fell between 1.9 and 2.0. Median scores for geographical regions were: Africa, 1.8; circum-Mediterranean, 1.9; East Eurasia, 2.0; Insular Pacific, 2.1; North America, 1.6; and South America, 2.1–2.2. The scores on range and accent are slightly, though not significantly, related.

RANGE AND INFANT STRESS

The relationship between infant stress and range is presented in Table 52. It can be seen that societies where infant stress is practiced before age two have songs with wider range than societies in which stress occurs after age two or is absent. The difference between the two groups of societies is significant beyond the .005 level.

In order to be sure that this relationship is not a result of joint diffusion of the two variables within one or more geographic regions, the relationship was tested within each region separately (Table 53). If the association between the two variables is repeated in widely separated geographic areas of the world between which there has been a minimal amount of borrowing and contact, it indicates that the two factors are functionally rather than

Table 54. *Relationship between infant stress and accent. Stress before age 2; Present vs. Absent; P = .025 (Fisher's Exact Test).*

Mean accent		Age of earliest stress				
		Birth–2 weeks	2 weeks–2 years	2–6 years	6–15 years	Not before 15 years
Weak	3.0					
						Goajiro
	2.8				Fore	
	2.6				Kung, Witoto	
	2.4	Javanese Salish	Okinawa		Trumai	Chukchee
			Thai	Chagga, Ainu		
	2.2		Zulu, Paiute Irish, Zuni			Palau
	2.0	Burmese		Amahuaca Yaghan, Gond	Semang, Fon	Aymara
		Cayapo, Jivaro, Azande	Tuareg		Camayura	
	1.8	Lau	Shilluk	Tikopia		
		Amhara	Yankee		Mende	
	1.6		Bambara			
		Hausa, Hupa, Navaho			Wolof	
	1.4	Lakalai, Yoruba		Yap		Slave
	1.2		Masai	Kurds		
		Nookta				
Forceful	1.0					

historically related. Such a test also clarifies the effect of genetic factors since geographic regions tend to be genetically somewhat homogeneous. Although the samples are small within each region, except for South America, the relationship is in the predicted direction. In East Eurasia and Insular Pacific the relationship reaches statistical significance.

ACCENT AND INFANT STRESS

Table 54 presents the relationship between infant stress and accent. Although in the predicted direction and significant, much of the variance in accent is not related to infant stress practices. Part of this variance can be accounted for by variations in type of rhythm. In some societies a large proportion of the songs are characterized by a type of rhythmic organization which is not based on the use of regularly spaced accents. The cantometrics codings refer to this as "free rhythm." The presence of free rhythm may tend automatically to lower a society's score on strength of accent. Since free rhythm and stress are not related, this factor may be controlled and the hy-

Table 55. *Infant stress and accent in societies with no more than 20 percent free rhythm. P = .007 (Fisher's Exact Test).*

Mean accent		Stress before age 2	
		Present	Absent
Weak	3.0		
			X
	2.8		
	2.6		X
			X
	2.4	X	X
			X X
	2.2	X	
		X X	X X
	2.0		X X X X X
		X X X	X
	1.8	X X	
		X X	X
	1.6	X	
		X X X	X
	1.4		X X
	1.2		
		X	
Forceful	1.0		

pothesis retested. When this is done by removing from the sample all societies which have more than 20 percent of their songs coded as free rhythm, the relationship between stress and accent becomes much stronger, reaching the P = .007 level of significance (Table 55).

Although the data strongly support the hypothesis that infant stress leads to an increase in boldness and exploratory behavior, the relationship between the two variables may be due to the action of a third, unknown variable which is related to both factors. One such variable, suggested by the Landauer and Whiting study, may be stature. Tall individuals may have wider range and more forceful accent either because they are physically larger and stronger or because physical size increases their psychological feeling of boldness.

This possibility can be tested by comparing the data on range with data on adult stature. The Landauer and Whiting study provides data on mean adult male stature for twenty societies in the present sample, and Gunders

Table 56. *Relationship between stature, stress, and range.*

Stature	Short < 65.5"		Tall > 65.5"	
Stress	Present	Absent	Present	Absent
Fisher's Exact Test	P = .021	P = .021	P = .016	P = .016
Mean range (Wide) 4.2			×	
	×			
4.0				
3.8			×	
3.6	×			
	×		×	
3.4			×	
	×	×	×	
3.2			×	
				×
3.0			× × ×	
		×		
2.8		×		
		× ×		
2.6		×		×
		×	×	
2.4		×	×	
2.2				
2.0				
1.8				
		×		
(Narrow) 1.6				

Short vs. Tall   P : N.S.

and Whiting (1967) provide data for six additional societies. When range and stature are plotted as in Table 56, it can be seen that the relationship between the two variables is far from significant. In order to control for the effects of stature on range, both short and tall societies were further subdivided according to the presence or absence of infant stress. Although the number of cases in each group is small, there is a strong relationship between stress and range in both groups of societies. It can be safely concluded that the effects of stress on range are quite independent of its effects on stature.

During the process of analysis, it began to look as if a second uncontrolled variable might be affecting the relationship between infant stress and range. It appeared that societies with wide range were socially and technologically more advanced than those with narrow range. Naroll (1956) has shown that community size is a good index of cultural complexity. Murdock, in Col. 31 of the *Ethnographic Atlas,* gives data on community size for 37 of the societies in the stress sample. In order to explore this association, scores on

Table 57. *Relationship between community size, stress, and range.*

Community size	Small < 200		Large > 200	
Stress	Present	Absent	Present	Absent
Fisher's Exact Test	P = .004	P = .004	P = .003	P = .003
Mean range 4.2 (Wide)			X X	
4.0	X			
3.8			X X	
3.6			X X	
3.4	X X X			
3.2			X X X	X X X
3.0	X		X X X	X
2.8	X	X X		X
2.6		X X X X X X X		
2.4	X	X X		
2.2		X		
2.0				
1.8		X		
(Narrow) 1.6				

Small vs. Large Communities   P = .008 (2-tailed)
Stress Present: Small vs. Large Communities   P : N.S.
Stress Absent: Small vs. Large Communities   P = .004

community size were compared with the cantometrics ratings. As Table 57 indicates, there is a strong relationship between community size and range. If, however, the effects of stress are controlled, this relationship holds true only in societies where stress is absent. What is more significant in the present context is that the relationship between stress and range is significant in both large and small communities. Whatever the reason for the association between community size and range in small communities, this association does not account for the relationship between range and stress. There are probably physiological limits to range which cannot be exceeded comfortably by the average singer. This may account for the fact that community size does not affect range in societies where stress is present.

Although the number of cases examined in the present study is small, the hypothesis that there is a relationship between painful stimulation in infancy and a tendency toward bold and exploratory behavior in adults is strongly supported. The finding raises the possibility that other aspects of behavior may be similarly affected. If the effects of infantile stimulation on human behavior are parallel to those observed in the animal experiments, it would seem to suggest that societies which stress their infants may enjoy an overall adaptive advantage which should be reflected in many aspects of culturally patterned behavior. It would seem reasonable, on the basis of the present evidence, to engage in further cross-cultural investigations of this hypothesis.

10

Dance Style and Culture

Alan Lomax, Irmgard Bartenieff, and Forrestine Paulay

A NUMBER of considerations turned the attention of the Cantometrics Project to dance and to film analysis. First, we wished to confirm our impression that the style areas and sets found in the analysis of singing style would be confirmed by a similar analysis of another form of expressive activity. In this way an important working hypothesis of communication studies would be supported: that analogous patterns will be found at the same level in different communication systems (Birdwhistell, 1968a). During the years of systematic listening to tapes and of operations with the descriptive sets thus obtained, it had always been assumed that song style is in part a product of the stance of the singer, of the way he disposes of energy, of the way the singing group operates as a dynamic collective, and of the interflowing of dynamic response between performer and audience. Film offers a way of making such observations and thus of adding the flesh and bones of everyday to our somewhat abstract auditory conclusions.

The most important consideration, however, arose from the operations of the cantometric experiment itself. Of all the clearly significant descriptive parameters on the coding sheet, those having to do with metrical type, with the structural regularity basic to music itself, alone resisted any correlation with social factors or culture history. Birdwhistell suggested the reason for this. He pointed out that both music and song are *derived* and not *primary* communication systems. Unlike the kinesic or the linguistic or the phatic communication systems, music is learned comparatively late and is probably composed of formal, intertwined segments of the three primary systems. Thus it was theoretically possible that certain elements in the song or communication might have no other reference than their *derived* origin. Every known culture has some form of highly redundant physical activity recognizable as dance. It occurred to Lomax that the rhythmic or metrical aspects of song may be derived from dance and that the preferred meters in song are transferred across from the most common metrical patterns of the dance. Song can then be defined as "danced speech." Therefore, if one seeks to

222

evoke the significance of musical meter, one must turn from song to the study of the rhythmic ordering of physical activity in dance.

Our initial hypothesis held that dance itself is an adumbration of or derived communication about life, focused on those favored dynamic patterns which most successfully and frequently animated the everyday activity of most of the people in a culture. Following this suggestion and before beginning the search for metrical pattern in song, we adopted the strategy of searching for the redundant patterns discoverable in the everyday activity of a culture that resembled the stylized forms of its dances. Indeed, this was essentially how Bateson and Mead proceeded in their study of the relationship between child-rearing practices and trance and dance in Bali (Bateson and Mead, 1942).

In what follows, therefore, dance is considered first as a representation and reinforcement of cultural pattern and only secondarily as an expression of individual emotion. Neither the expressive function of dance nor the emotional outlet it gives to each dancer, whether modern choreographer or folk dancer, is denied. What we have seen in scores of films, however, leads inexorably to the conclusion that many aspects of movement, once thought to be idiosyncratic, vary by culture type rather than from person to person.

Each dance type somehow expresses the needs and the nature of a people and one has the impression that the distribution of dance styles on the planet corresponds in some way to the distribution of the families of mankind. Yet, there has been no means of description suitable to comparative study and no body of theory to explain how dance and culture are linked in all societies and in all stages of development. The aim of the present investigation, therefore, becomes one of recording and noting regularities and contrasts in movement pattern sufficiently frequent and gross to produce units universally applicable in cross-cultural studies. In order to distinguish the level of this comparative study of movement from the levels where previous investigators have worked we have given the method a freshly-coined designation, *choreometrics,* meaning the measure of dance, or dance as a measure of culture.

The choreometric approach does not include step-by-step analyses from which dances may be reproduced in detail. The pattern and succession of patterns of step and movements were omitted from our choreometric descriptions, just as in cantometrics details of rhythm and melody were merely summarized because it was felt they referred to cultural but not cross-cultural pattern. Therefore, in what follows there will be no discussion of formations, postures, steps, or successions of these, but instead a rating of dance and movement in extremely general qualitative terms.

This strategy emerged from the experience of the cantometric study. Song was viewed as the most repetitious, redundant, and formally patterned of all oral communications. The operating presumption was that those patterns most prominent and crucial in the everyday interaction of the culture would become even more redundant and frequent in the song style of that culture. This increase of redundancy made song socially louder than speech and thus more effective as a group-organizing and group-orienting form of communication.

Choreometrics tests the proposition that dance is the most repetitious, redundant, and formally organized system of body communication present in a culture (Hanna, 1965). The dance is composed of those gestures, postures, movements, and movement qualities most characteristic and most essential to the activity of everyday, and thus crucial to cultural continuity. By treating these elements redundantly and formally, dance becomes an effective organizer of joint motor activity. Dance supplies the metronome to meter and becomes the regulator of the rhythm of social interaction. Dance captures, regulates, or orders the energy and attention of groups of people, and thereby acquires the weight of general community approval. Thus dance functions to establish and renew consensus at moments when a society, without further discussion or explanation, is ready to act in concert.

As a matter of fact, we know that both dance and song occur most frequently in ritual situations—during religious ceremonials and community festivals of birth, maturation, courtship, marriage, harvest, death, and the like. In song one tends to find cultural features upon which there is maximal community consensus, since these are the utterances which everyone present is willing to voice or heed collectively. In dance those postures and qualities of movement should be discovered which are so familiar, so acceptable, or for some reason so important to a particular human community that all will take pleasure in continually watching or repeating them. These patterns of action ought to be of maximal importance to the actual physical survival of the culture and thus should be esteemed not merely as desirable, but as necessary as breath and food. Here the reader should remember that choreometrics does not describe a series of postures or steps, but the dynamic qualities that animate the activities of a culture. Thus a very outlandish passage of movement in a dance may present, in a stylized way, a movement quality that runs through all the humdrum activity of everyday.

DANCE STYLE AND WORK

Song performance style has been shown to vary cross-culturally and directly in many respects in relationship to subsistence activity. The social structures of the song teams of a society seem to resemble those of its work teams. The evidence of film is more direct. We find many examples of the carryover of posture from work stance into dancing stance, of work-team shape into choreographic shape. Since both work and dance are blueprints for group organization and interaction, one might suppose that this pair of models would vary together cross-culturally. If dance has a social function it should be to reinforce modalities of interpersonal and group organization that are most crucial in the main subsistence activity of a culture.

We looked at more than 200 films for analogies between work style and dance style. It was in the process of this examination and during the attempt to give a consistent description of our findings that the present coding system came into being. We discovered that wherever we had adequate records of work and dance from the same culture, the same or very similar qualities generally animated both members of the pair.

This conclusion cannot be supported by firm statistical evidence because we have completely coded both dance and work from only 21 cultures. Nevertheless, the following table of the paired similarities of these 21 work and dance sets indicates that, for a majority of the cases and in a great variety of cultures, work and dance movement styles are virtually identical (Table 58). The best results are obtained by comparing work to dance, not

Table 58. *Rank order of similarities of work to dance profiles from 21 cultures.*

Ranks of cultural similarity					
1	2	3	4–5–6	11-Quartile	21-Median
Me'udana	Japan	Maring	Afro-	Eskimo	Pomo
Kerala		Pakistan	American		Kraho
Tadjik		Portugal	Binga		Kung
Iroquois		Ellice Is.			
Pitjanta					
Samoa					
Cook Is.					
Dogon					
Guruna					
Massa					

dance to work. Dance, it appears, has a more crystallized, culture-specific pattern than work. In work, the identifying, categorizing function central to the arts is modified somewhat by the practical necessities of tasks.

In comparing the dance profiles from 21 cultures to all other profiles from the same 21 cultures, the following results come from the computer:

1. The work profile from the named culture was first in the ranked listings in almost half of the cases (10 out of 21).

2. The work profile from the named culture was in the first three ranks in two-thirds of the cases (14 out of 21).

3. The work profile from the named culture was within the octile in the ranked listings in about three-quarters of the cases (16 out of 21).

4. The work profile from the named culture was above the median in the ranked listings in all of the 21 cases.

This remarkable finding supports the primary hypothesis of the study: that the movement style in dance is a crystallization of the most frequent and crucial patterns of everyday activity.

Among those cultures studied were the seal-hunting Eskimo and the Tadjik villagers of Persia. In both groups, work and dance tend to be solo performances, but the resemblance ends there. The style differences between the two cultures, whether produced by climate, tradition, or function, provide us with a useful set of contrasts.

The principal dance of the Netsilik Eskimo hunters occurs during the winter months, when a sufficient amount of food is available for a number of families to pass several weeks together in the same camp. Dancing takes place in a large communal igloo and consists of solo performances. One after another, the greatest hunters stand up before the group, a large flat drum covered with sealskin in the left hand, a short, club-like drumstick in the other. Over to the side sit a cluster of women chanting away as the hunter drums, sings, and dances. The performer remains in place holding the wide stance used by these Eskimos when they walk through ice and snow or stand in the icy waters fishing. Each stroke of the short drumstick goes diagonally down and across to hit the lower edge of the drum and turn the drumhead. On the backstroke it strikes the other edge, reversing the motion which is then carried through by a twist of the left forearm. The power and solidity of the action is emphasized by the downward drive of the body into slightly bent knees on the downstroke and the force of the trunk rising as the knees straighten to give full support to the arm on the upstroke. The dance consists largely of these repeated swift and strong diagonal right-arm movements down across the body, backed by the whole force of the solidly held trunk and responded to with steady rotation of the left forearm. A good dancer must stand and drum in this fashion for a long time without failing in the rhythm or losing his drive.

A look at Eskimo seal hunting or salmon fishing shows this same posture and pattern of movement in use—a harpooning, hooking movement. The salmon-fisher stands hip-deep in the clear waters of the weir, thrusting his spear down and across, lifting the speared fish clear of the water, twisting it off the barb and threading it on the cord at his waist in a series of swift, strong, straight, angular movements tied together by powerful rotations of the forearm. At the seal hole on the ice pack, where the hunter may wait in complete stillness during five frozen hours before the nose of the seal appears, there is time for only one thrust of the spear: a miss spoils a day's hunting in subarctic temperature. His harpoon, then, flies in a lightning stroke, diagonally down across the chest with the full force of the compact and solidly held trunk behind it. Again this movement is immediately reversed.

In song and story, the Eskimo hunter is praised for his speed, strength, good aim, and high stamina. The dance dramatizes these very qualities. At leisure the hunter, the food provider of his group, repeats the essentials of his crucial work activity in dance before a seated audience of the women who wait for him in camp every day, receive the game, and process it into edible food and clothing. The presence of women in the dancing scene is significant, for women are frequently absent or inactive in the dances of the primitive world. Eskimo women, who play a part in the productive operation equal to that of the men, portray this role precisely in the scene described, by singing a song in the "chewing" rhythm they use all day as they soften the skins brought by their men.

A contrast of style is found in the analysis of work and dance movement of the Tadjik. In the Near and Middle East, males dominate public activities—in ritual, politics, work, and dance; and in the Tadjik work and dance scenes there were, in fact, no women to be seen in the grain fields or on the dance ground. Each Tadjik male tills the earth, plants his seed, harvests his wheat, and dances alone or accompanied, usually by other males, while his womenfolk remain at home. In the harvest scene, one sees isolated single figures of males, each one busy with threshing and winnowing on his own plot of land, just as in the Eskimo film one sees lone hunters, each at his seal hole, dotted across the icy landscape.

The Tadjik dance takes place in the open, where the males of the village form a circle around a succession of male dancers who move alone or with one partner to the accompaniment of an oboe and a stringed instrument. He walks sinuously with heel placed precisely ahead of toe, like a farmer moving in a narrow furrow. His arms shape light, easy, curving gestures like those his culture employs in winnowing grain or brushing heaps of chaff. Thus, again, in this Tadjik material, the movement of life is taken across into the dance, rhythmized and treated redundantly for an audience which is fascinated by a refined and formalized presentation of a way of action familiar and essential to everyone present. These paired analogies between work and dance are most convincingly presented in a series of training films in preparation. The reader interested in further details will find examples of contrasting dance profiles in the following chapter, where the similarity of the patterns of dance and everyday movement in a single cultural context is found again and again.

The kinesic studies of Birdwhistell (1952, 1959c) have shown that all human beings are constantly immersed, throughout their lives, in a stream

of body communication, whose central shapes and modes are culturally determined and learned. This anecdote illustrates his finding: A young American woman in company must cross her legs in the way prescribed by that particular social context or else her improper posture may bring conversation to
a halt or a woman present may signal a change of position. At one level, then,
all body movement can be regarded as a communication of the mores, customs, and role relationships found in a particular culture. All these vary from
culture to culture and, therefore, must be a part of the training of any young
individual before he joins the culture as an adult. Dance, however, comes
relatively late in the learning process. A child joins his culture by learning
how to move in the style of his culture. Later, when he begins to use the
formal dance patterns, whether he is light footed or a shambler in the dancing throng, he brings to the dance floor those qualities of and potentials for
movement which he has already acquired from his culture. In general, then,
the people of a culture dance as they move in everyday life.

When the American girl moves onto the dance floor, expecting to be en-
joyed and treated as a female, she must comport herself physically in at least
some of the ways that our culture provides for the identification of females
ready to mate. Such a young woman obviously does not want to be treated as
a pre-adolescent, a married woman in purdah, or an old lady, and her way of
carrying herself will make this clear to her potential partners. When, however, she falls into the repeated patterns of the dance itself, she will make a
further condensation of longer stretches of the everyday movement of her
culture, repeated over and over again to compose the formal structure of
the American dance of her period.

Since our intent is not to translate or evoke the entire content of any
movement series, we take these dance phrases, with their strongly punctu-
ated and highly crystallized sequences, as our primary data. When we find
analogous bits occurring with notable frequency in life activity outside the
dance, we assume that the bit in the dance and the bit in life stand for each
other. When we discover similarly structured bits or phrases of movement
redundantly used in dance and in everyday life, we feel confident that we
have found stretches of movement that form a basic part of the movement
style of the culture.

Our description of a dance style does not attempt to evoke the particles of
movement either in the physical, physiological, or kinesic sense, but to characterize the way in which the actors accomplish their goals. An action, a
scene, a dance, a culture is described in terms of the relative presence or
absence of certain movement qualities and certain pervasive body attitudes.
The rating system used is based on the Laban effort-shape scheme (Laban
and Lawrence, 1947), which facilitates systematic observation and descrip-

tion of the quality of human movement: how man disposes of his energy in space and time, and how a certain disposition of energy can shape space.

Our first effort-shape codings from films produced so much detail that the easily observable differences between the body styles of different cultures tended to disappear. We saw the need for a different and grosser set of criteria than those provided by Laban's effort-shape system. Our predecessors in using the Laban system had been working, essentially, with the analysis of individual patterns in estimating the aptitudes of job candidates or treating the physical problems of maladjusted persons who used a Western European cultural or subcultural body style familiar to the observers. To describe the potentials, diagnose the problems, and assist in the adjustment of these individuals, one needed a system for differentiating idiosyncrasies of movement.

The cross-cultural comparison of movement style, however, raised problems of another sort. We were working at a different level—the social and cultural, not the individual. Knowledge of cultural base lines could no longer be assumed; indeed, it was clear that these base lines themselves shifted drastically as the films took us across the borderlines of culture areas and regions. The details that the Laban system picked out actually interfered with our steady perception of cultural differences. We needed coarser scales in order to capture the characteristic stances and modes of using energy that underlie all social interaction, all work, and all activity in a particular culture. These redundant patterns of movement style form part of the heritage of learned behavior belonging to a culture just as much as its language and its customs.

As Birdwhistell put it, "Humans move and belong to movement communities just as they speak and belong to speech communities." (Personal communication) The founder of kinesics here reported on his discovery that there are kinesic "languages" and "dialects" which are learned by culture members just as speech is learned, and which have a matching distribution with speech, languages, and dialects. However, since cantometrics found frameworks of communication which cut across the the barriers of language and culture to bind human beings into continent-sized communication families, the objective of our dance analysis was to develop a system for describing and mapping movement style families of the same dimensions. Further, the aim was to see if the distributions of dance style matched the distributions of song styles. And so, over the course of eighteen months of work with film data, the elements of the Laban effort-shape system were adjusted to the needs of cultural rather than personal style. Parameters emerged that were combinations of two or more of the effort concepts plus elements taken from Laban's earlier movement theories. The resultant choreometric coding system—especially the first part—is thus a specialized outgrowth of Laban's effort theory. Here it was that Bartenieff's years of work in physical therapy, medicine, and psychiatry stood the research in good stead, since she was already prepared to adapt her frame of reference to the scientific task at hand.

The dances of urban America were not studied in this first stage. It was felt that, like urban music, they would be hard to define since their styles so frequently represent the evanescent fads flowing among subcultures. Instead, we worked with movies of folk and primitive societies to find "pure" cases where movement style is more stable. Any observer, no matter how new to the field, is impressed by the extraordinary uniformity of movement style in any non-complex society. A film collection drawn from all the major world culture areas enabled us to compare a series of these more or less pure and stable cases. The extreme contrasts we found presented the full range of the descriptive terms with which we were experimenting. Those qualities and ranges which have turned out to be useful in clustering cultures in normal ethnographic sets or ordering them on complexity scales were retained as primary elements in this descriptive system. In fact, the stylistic patterns they define are among the most redundant behavioral elements in social interaction. Birdwhistell (1957) early recognized the existence of these dynamic qualifiers of movement style. However, since he has not been particularly concerned with cross-cultural comparisons, he has not pursued the matter in other papers.

> ". . . we have recently abstracted and isolated an order of body motion behavior which serves as a cross-reference system for the smaller complexes of activity which form the major components of the kinesic stream. Termed the set-quality complex, this cross-referencing identification behavior seems to be categorizable into the major groupings which are characteristic of mammalian social groups. In order to maintain organized social interaction, the membership of such social groups must internalize special complex signals which cover the varied expectancies of the group concerning age, sex, health, mood, body build, territoriality, rhythm phase, toxic state. . . . These special assemblages of behavior, which I am calling motion qualities, serve to provide a cross-referencing order to any interaction. This behavior is abstractable and manipulable." (Birdwhistell, 1957)

These "motion qualities" run through all the behavior of a culture, controlling the way in which culture members handle energy as they go about their everyday lives. It is at this level that body style can be compared cross-culturally; profiles of such movement qualities can be handled by the similarity wave program in the same way as the song performance profiles to establish areas and regions of dance style (see following Chapter).

The sample will, for some time, be too small for the final establishment of stable areas and regions. Even so, the similarity wave program has found regional clusters that compare in a remarkable way with the distributions picked out for song style. The 43 cultures from which we have extracted dance profiles fall into eight regional sets: (1) Amerindia; (2) Australia; (3) New Guinea; (4) Maritime Pacific; (5) Africa; (6) Europe; (7) and (8) Old High Culture, east and west, whose similarity scores above the quartile (Table 59) form two super-regional sets.

The world of the primitive Pacific splits away from the more complex cultures of Africa and Eurasia, with Australia and New Guinea clustering in a special subgroup. This circum-Pacific tribal area, which includes the Amerindian cultures of North and South America, has turned up again and again in cantometric research. Its pervasive stylistic homogeneity may trace one of the ancient distribution patterns of human culture.

The second cluster is Afro-Eurasian. Within it the super-region, Old High Culture, emerges again with a linked similarity between the dance styles, east and west, of the Indian subcontinent. In this analysis, the Maritime Pacific emerges as a regional isolate with weak affiliations to the Indian subcontinent. Africa's dance style affiliations with the nearby Orient and India correspond to only one aspect of cantometric findings, owing to the nature of the sample in which only two out of the five African cultures are typically agricultural Bantu (Dogon, Afro-American). The European subsample, which

Table 59. *Percent overall similarity of the dance style profiles for eight world culture regions.*

All regions are compared to all other regions and the figures in this table show those similarities that are significant at the quartile or above. Dashed line indicates quartile.

Amerindia	Australia	N. Guinea	Maritime Pacific	Africa	Europe	Old High Culture E.	Old High Culture W.
	N. Guinea 84	Australia 84					
Australia 82	Amerindia 82						
N. Guinea 81		Amerindia 81					
							Old High Culture E. 79
						Old High Culture W. 78	
					Old High Culture W. 74		
Europe 74							
			Old High Culture W. 73		Amerindia 73		

hardly represents the European stylistic variety, falls out of the regional similarity rank altogether. In movement, Europe is closest to Amerindia, as it is in its cantometric scores for melodic style.

The similarity wave comparisons of movement style in 43 cultures produce more interesting results (Table 60). With one or two exceptions, all the single dances from single cultures fall statistically within their own proper regions, and at the same time these sets of similarities link culture regions in a web that makes good sense historically. The percentages in Table 60 score the proportion of times each dance polls an above-quartile similarity with all the dances of one of the seven regions. In effect, it is a statistical mapping technique like that presented in Chapter 3 for song style.

In the next paragraphs the dance style regions so far discernible will be described in a summary fashion. The sample size permits only a preliminary résumé, yet the productive power of the small, early sample of cantometrics indicates that this first geography of the dance may be confirmed by further study. One extremely interesting point is that the primitive cultures of the Pacific again form a cluster with indications of several subgroups of historical interest within this grand dance style region.

Amerindia. The handful of northern Amerindian cultures, tightly linked in song performance style (Blood, Blackfoot, Eskimo, Iroquois), again show high similarities in dance style. The Tarahumara of Mexico have equally strong ties with North and South America, just as they do in cantometric scores. The California gatherers, the Pomo, go along with two of the three South American incipients (Suya, Kraho) in evincing a rooted kinship to New Guinea movement style, the least complex in our sample. The mean cantometric similarity of Kraho to all cultures of New Guinea is 70 percent. Amerindian dance style proclaims an ancient and distant affinity with northwestern Europe, perhaps an echo of the Arctic hunter origin of both regional traditions.

Australia. The four Australian dances coded include each other in the first quartile of similarities, though usually at a low level. All have about an equal level of similarity to the New Guinea set. Their affiliations link them closely to dances from the South American sample. As with the songs, one has the impression in Australia of an extremely specialized, homogeneous and, at the same time, varied style. Thus, although all the "Abo" songs and dances seem to belong to one grand tradition, the dance repertoire presents a dazzling variety of content, design, and texture.

New Guinea. New Guinea is the most homogeneous of the movement style regions we have thus far studied. The dance profiles consistently operate in the same way, showing a 100 percent similarity with each other, a high level of similarity with Australia, distant connections with Amerindia, and none elsewhere. The mass all-male pageants, on which many New Guinea groups

Table 60. *Frequency of above-quartile cultural similarities of dance profiles, organized into seven style regions.*

The percentage figures in this table record the frequency with which the dance of a given culture appears in the upper quartile of similarities for all cultures in a given region. Thus, for example, Iroquois score in the upper quartile of similarity for 88 percent of the cultures in Amerindia.

	Amerindia	Australia	New Guinea	Maritime Pacific	Africa	Old High Culture	Europe
Amerindia							
Iroquois	88	75	60				50
Eskimo	100	50	20	20			25
Blood-Blackfoot	88	50	40				25
Tarahumara	75	50	60				50
Mehinaco	75	75	60				
Pomo	63	25	60			8	50
Suya	63	50	100				
Kraho	63	75	80		20		25
Australia							
Pitjanta	38	100	80			8	
Wik	63	100	60				25
Austra	63	100	100				
Aranda	50	100	100				
New Guinea							
Me'udana	50	100	100				
Dani	50	100	100				
Maring	50	50	100				
New Guinea	50	50	100			8	
Pasum	38	75	100			8	
Maritime Pacific							
Maori	25	25		60	60	23	50
Samoa				60	60	46	
Cook Island	13			80	60	46	
Ellice Island	13			60	60	54	
Africa							
Guruna				60	100	46	
Kung Bushmen	13			40	75	23	50
Dogon				40	100	39	25
Afro-Americans				40	80	46	
Bahima, U	13			40	60	31	50
Old High Culture							
Muria (Gond)				60	60	54	
Pashtu				60	60	54	
Tadjik				60	40	54	
Korea, UR				20	80	54	25
Bhotija	13			40	60	54	
East Tibet				40	20	69	
Pakistan				40	40	62	
Chinese	13				20	69	25
Japan, UR				20	40	62	
Malabar				20	20	77	
Uzbek				20	40	69	
Berber		25		20	20	62	25
Bedouin	38	50	80			8	50
Europe							
Georgia					75	62	
West France	50	25	80			8	75
England	50	80	40				75
Portugal	88		40			8	25

seem fixed, are notable for a tropical brilliance of costume, but the dancers all conform to one basically simple movement structure.

Maritime Pacific. The mean level of similarity drops 10 or 15 points within this cluster. Again, as in the cantometric scores, Pacific cultures show about the same level of similarity to each other and to the African set. Perhaps of even more interest, however, are the strong ties of Samoa, Cook Island, and Ellice Island dancing to some of the simpler dance styles of Old High Culture (Gond, Pashtu, Tadjik). These dances are all marked by a certain set of complexity features, particularly by a preference for subtle peripheral, curvilinear movement, modulated in an undulating and flowing fashion.

Africa. The African sample which includes several of the cultural extremes of the continent, is very different in its composition from the cantometric sample: it consists of one African Hunter culture (Kung); one imperial cattle culture with Cushitic affiliations (Bahima); Fulani cattle culture (Guruna); and two complex West African, or West African-derived, cultures (Dogon and Afro-American). These dances bear a provocative similarity to one another. The Kung and the Bahima are more similar to Africa than to any other region, but have an almost equal attachment to Europe and the Maritime Pacific. Thus, just as in song, these cultures exemplify two distinct peripheries of African style, the first pre-Bantu, the second Cushitic. The style of the Guruna, a pastoral group near Lake Chad (belonging to the cluster), is centrally African with decisive affiliations to Oceania. The wildly energetic, hip-swinging dances of Dogon and Afro-America form a tight subcluster at the level of 82 percent; moreover, the high (100 and 80 percent) attachment of these two profiles to Africa and their relatively weaker ties to other regions put them at the center of the African cluster.

Europe. The Caucasian Georgian dance style has a strong stylistic affinity with African movement style, a weaker one with Old High Culture. Indeed, the tightly coordinated Georgian dances are performed with typically Oriental loops and delicate peripheral development. When the sample includes Russian and Balkan dances, their obvious similarity to Georgian dances will emerge. The four-square leg dances of England and western France strongly resemble each other, but show stylistic similarity, as does Portuguese dance, to the styles of New Guinea and Amerindia. This strange connection may be a product of a very meager sample which does not represent the variety of European dance style; nevertheless, northwestern European dancing, with its attachment to the one-unit system of body attitude and simple reversal, properly shows its strongest ties with the four-square, solid-trunk style of the primitive Pacific.

In spite of many obvious problems, the success of this early sorting of culture by dance style points to the need for the assembly of a properly representative sample of world dance film. The style map is still almost empty. The dances of Siberia, Central Asia, Southeast Asia, Indonesia, Latin America, most of Europe, Africa, and South America remain to be examined. Yet the present study certainly promises good results. Generally, the similarity clustering of dance style profiles produces the same regional sets, clustered in the same way, as the song style regions. This is all the more reassuring since two different systems of description were used in the analysis. Furthermore, the songs and the dances were derived from different ritual and functional settings in the cultures. Thus it appears that we have found two ways—in the separate analyses of song and dance style—of locating and identifying a basic stylistic level in culture. This level seems to shape both song and dance style, and the likelihood is that it controls the form that many other activities take. From the point of view of communication, the function of this level seems to be primarily one of identification. The dance or song style proclaims what culture, age, and sex group those present belong to. Thus it provides continuity and support to all interaction. This is the level of the base lines that control the continuities of all behavior, for example, tempo, energy, flow, length and complexity of statement, level of group contact, voice set, sex role, stance, and the like. The special business of song and dance is to reiterate and reinforce the stylistic grids that identify the members of a culture and supply the functional models for their everyday activity. Here lies the value of song and dance style analysis to the humanistic sciences. All human beings identify themselves and others in terms of relative positions of behavior on these qualitative scales of style. Across thousands of years, artists have worked to crystallize and refine these stylistic spines, upon which, they sensed, the survival of their cultures depended. Cantometrics and choreometrics identify this level of human expressive behavior so that all styles may be compared and evaluated.

As with song style, the first contribution of dance analysis is to point to historically significant families of movement. Now we turn to individual parameters of the choreometric system to see whether they arrange dance styles in an evolutionary sequence.

BODY ATTITUDE

Inspection of more than 200 films from all five continents convinced us that in simple cultures most individuals tend to adopt the same body attitude no matter what the activity and in spite of differences of age and sex. Here we find an aspect of movement that is social, functional, and general, rather than individual.

We were not, of course, the first to notice this. Birdwhistell, for example, assumes that a kinesic observer begins with a description of the base lines of any given movement scene. First, the postural dialect and "ideolect" of the individual must be evaluated. (Ideolect: a coined word meaning an individual pattern of speech.) Only then can the special features of his kinesic conversation be recorded. Underlying the interchange in any scene are the postures normal to a given culture. Maintenance of an erect posture is a universal human problem. Its solution depends on climate, terrain, and many other factors. Thus the particular stance normal to a group of people becomes a cultural statement so that at a distance a person may be identified as a member of a certain tribe merely from his silhouette or his stride.

The fundamental connection of stance and the modes of handling changes in energy had been earlier observed by Laban:

> "Without attempting to offer even a sketch of the history of movement, it can be said that in certain epochs, in definite parts of the world, in particular occupations, in cherished aesthetic creeds or in utilitarian skills, some attitudes of the body are preferred and more frequently used than others. . . . It is easy to understand how the *selection of and preference for certain bodily attitudes create style;* yet, we must remember it is in the *transitions between positions that an appropriate change of expression is made,* thus creating a dynamically coherent movement style. We can connect bodily attitudes with either harmonious or grotesque transitional movements. The fact that any deviation from the main fashion or style of an epoch has been looked upon as abnormal and lacking in style, or that such deviations have even been considered ugly and wrong is due to a peculiarity of the human herd instinct. Communities seem to regard a certain uniformity of movement behavior as indispensable for safeguarding the stability of the community spirit. They also tend to stress a common ideal of beauty, very often connected with a utilitarian value, especially esteemed in the community of a particular epoch. We see here how the attitudes of powerful warriors or hunters, of scholars or priests, artisans and draughtsman, . . . of society at one period or another are considered to be the only beautiful and stylistically right attitudes." (Laban, 1960)

Where Laban discusses stylistically "right" attitudes, we speak of patterns of redundant behavior, and among them, cultural preferences for certain body attitudes. We define body attitude as the limiting postural state from which the individuals in a culture develop their activities and from which their movement unfolds. Put another way, body attitude is the base line from which culture members develop activity and expend energy—their active stance. It is the final postural result in the culture member of interaction with his total natural and human environment. It is an interaction encompassing his biological inheritance, his cultural adaptation, and his life experience.

In scanning many films, we came upon a primary distinction in type of body attitude: (1) movement in which the trunk is treated as *one unit*, and (2) movement in which the trunk is treated as *two units*. In (1) the actor or dancer handles his trunk as a solid, block-like structure. In (2) there are clearcut twists at the waist or undulating movements spreading from the center of the torso into other segments of the body, connected with movements of either upper or lower limbs. The extremes of this contrast are illustrated by a stevedore heaving a hand truck and the sensuous movements of a belly dancer.

Figure 59 shows the trans-regional distribution of the one- and two-unit systems of body attitude. The one-unit body attitude dominates the Amerindian and Eurasian worlds. The two-unit body attitude centers in Negro Africa with extensions through India into Polynesia. This distribution matches the cantometric mapping of a number of song style traits that connect the styles of southern India with the Pacific and with Negro Africa.

A solid trunk provides a powerful support for up-and-down and back-and-forth movements, where speed, strength, and weight are primary considerations. Thrusting, penetrating, shoving, lifting, hurling, and pounding with short-handled tools develop effectively from a single-unit body attitude. Thus the everyday activities of hunters and fishers, which consist of aggressive penetration of the space in front of them, are built around a one-unit system. In the primitive agriculture of the Americas and New Guinea as well, where digging sticks are used and where agriculture is largely limited to clearing land and digging root crops, this powerful, frontally directed, one-unit system seems to prevail.

In the two-unit system, contrastive movement appears in the upper and lower halves of the trunk; the dancer or actor twists at the waist. We first noticed this flexible movement style in films of African herders moving among their cattle without disturbing them, controlling the animals on each side by turning and reaching across them to guide the strays with the touch of their staffs, and threading their way through the herd with a pace very like that of the animals themselves. In films of African millet agriculture the workers twisted at the waist as they planted the seed, hoed the land, and harvested the ears of grain. In their dances, the hips and upper body rotated, pulsed, leapt, almost like two totally independent entities, sometimes moving in different rhythms and giving rise to bodily polyrhythm. Outside of Negro Africa we observed a less crystallized two-unit system, somewhat resembling the African body attitude style, in the belly dances of the Arabs and of the Near East, as well as in the soft and insinuating undulations of the Polynesians and Micronesians.

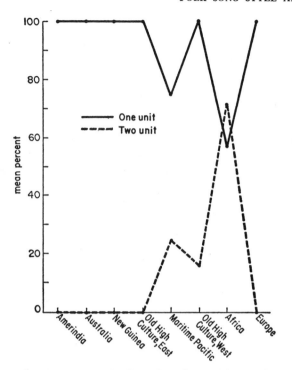

Fig. 59. Body attitude and region. This graph
shows the relative prominence of the two main
types of body attitude in eight world regions.
The one-unit system is most common everywhere
except in Africa, where the two-unit system, with
twist at the waist, is the principal characteristic.

It is suggestive that Negro Africa scores highest for the two-unit system
with the Maritime Pacific culture area next. The erotic orientation of both
African and Oceanic culture is too well known for comment; the independently moving, rotating pelvis, so clear in African behavior and dance, is here
purposefully erotic and sexual. This movement mimes, recalls, and reinforces
the sexual act, especially the woman's part in it. Thus a constant current of
pleasurable, erotic feeling runs openly through much of African life, warm-
ing it like sunlight. Hanna (1965) has found West African dances designed
to instruct young girls in how to please their husbands. In male initiation
rites, boys are taught the sexual skills they will need as heads of polygynous
households.

The expansion of the African agricultural system depended upon the involvement of women in agriculture, on the synchronized activity of large
labor gangs, on the polygynous family, and on the increasing and budding

lineage systems that the fertility of the women supported. Without the high birthrate, without the ardent participation of both women and men in swift-paced communal labor in the blazing heat, the Negro people could never have conquered the African continent. The overtly sexual content of their songs and dances and the constant pelvic play in everyday movement supported the main institutions of the society (polygyny, expanding lineage villages) and gave a pleasant and stimulating tone to the whole of life. More work gets done, a high birthrate is maintained in polygynous families, and the electric current of sexuality touches everyone.

The erotic two-unit body attitude has not so far been observed in the highly masculinized dances of the American Indians. A rapidly increasing population was not a good for these hunters, fishers, and primitive cultivators. The feminine, the pelvic, the fertile was not the favored mode in these aggressively oriented economies. Thus the two-unit system seems to be infrequent among incipient producers (Amerindian agriculturists are classified as incipients) and to appear in the evolutionary series with full-fledged animal husbandry (AH) and cultivation (CA) in the tropics.

In most Amerindian movement so far observed in this study—and this includes one film of sign language—we have found the one-unit system (with straight-line transitions) the predominant pattern. Although in India we found an almost orchestrally varied use of the body in traditional dancing, the tendency toward a two-unit system is absent in Japan. The Japanese usually handle the trunk as one unit, but achieve a complex command of space by loops and a variety of other transitions. A rather similar pattern appears among northwestern Europeans whose most constant body attitude is a held, one-unit system. The apparently homogeneous distributions of different types of body attitudes suggest that this aspect of behavior is highly resistant to change, and that tendencies in movement style may be of very great antiquity. The people of northwestern Europe were fishers, fowlers, and shepherds, and only marginally farmers, until fairly recent times. This way of life still goes on in border areas such as the Hebrides. Until recently, therefore, the one-unit system so prevalent among hunting peoples round the Pacific was a suitable adaptation for the people in this culture area. We may surmise that this survival from an ancient predatory economy—this "hunter's style"—is in a very real sense a suitable contemporary adaptation for northwestern Europe. It must be remembered that for the last ten centuries, like so many Norsemen, the peoples of this area have pursued a path of aggressive exploration and conquest, which established their control over most of the habitable globe.

TYPE OF TRANSITION

Body stance emerges as the stabilizing fin of movement style. A second and equally diagnostic stylistic feature is the characteristic way in which culture members handle transitions in movement. When movement changes direction, the nature of the transition between the old and the new paths defines the design or overall form of the movement, as well as the change in the intensity of effort. Seven categories define the types of transitions observed in our film sample. We range these categories in a scale of increasing complexity from the most simple form of transition to the most complex. The simpler transition types usually occur in only one plane. Curved and looped transitions, however, usually involve three dimensions. By the use of the loop transition the actor seems to wind his way through space, changing direction with ease and then finding a freer access to surrounding space.

Although probably all cultures employ all of the following modes of transition, one type or one cluster of types so dominates the activity of one culture as to give it a distinctive character.

    A. *One- or two-dimensional*
       1. Vague
       2. Simple reversal
       3. Cyclic
       4. Angular
       5. Rotation
       6. Curved
    B. *Three-dimensional*
       7. Looped

In simple reversal, the path of action is simply retraced, as in rubbing, digging, or beating. In cyclic action the movement retraces a circular or curved pathway, as in cranking a car. In other types of transition, the observer can note the changes of direction along an angular, rotating, or curved path. Finally, with looped movement, the action moves through three dimensions. Of course, several kinds of transition occur in every culture. Most cultures, however, may be classified in terms of highs at the two extremes of the scale—simple reversal or loop. Simple reversals (back-and-forth, up-and-down, side-to-side movements) and other straight-line transitions seem to prevail in the primitive world, whereas looping or curved use of space reaches its peak in East Asia (Fig. 60).

Although the relative frequency of one or another type of transition radically affects the character and feeling tone of the dance from region to region, these distributions do not appear to be the product of tradition. The distri-

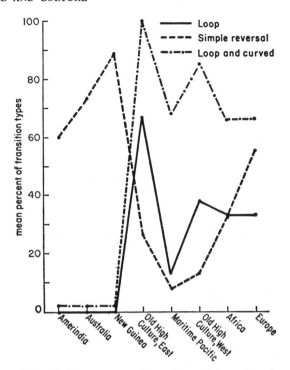

Fig. 60. Dance reversals and transitions found
in various cultures.

butions illustrated in Figure 61 indicate that transition type is strongly related to the level of productive complexity. The reader will note that simple
reversal decreases from a high of 57 percent among extractors to a low of 22
percent among irrigationists. Conversely, the three-dimensional use of space,
indicated by the presence of looped transitions, mounts with subsistence complexity. Looped movements are absent among simple producers. Curved
transitions, although common to all productive levels, again reach a 50 percent level only among irrigationists. All this corresponds to our strong impressions from films where we saw aboriginal Australians, Amerindians, and
New Guinea Highlanders handling every activity, including the dance, with
short, jerky, two-phased movements like rubbing, chopping, and digging.
On the other hand, among the peasants of the Orient, the limbs describe
three-dimensional spirals and large figure-eight movements in both dance
and daily life. It seems both obvious and logical that transition in movement
should grow more elaborate in structure as a more complex productive technology makes further demands on the body for control.

A spiral, looping approach permits complementary and asymmetrically op-

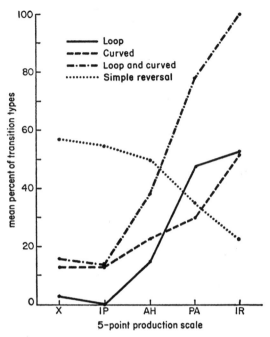

Fig. 61. Transition types: the five-point production scale. Transition types seem to bear a positive relationship to the scale of productive complexity. One-plane, simple reversal falls off
sharply in complex cultures. Both curve and loop
are tied to increased productive range. Three-dimensional loop is strongly associated with Plow
Agriculture (PA) and Irrigation (IR). The increase of the two types of rounded transition
seems to be clear indication of rising complexity
after the introduction of animal husbandry.
   Loop: chi sq/2 df = 22.81; gamma = .8934;
P < .001. Curved: chi sq/3 df = 14.77; gamma
= .6891; P < .01. Simple reversal: chi sq/3 df =
6.83; gamma = .5166; P < .10. Statistical splits:
Loop—X,IP/AH/PA,IR vs. Median; Curved—
X,IP/AH/PA/IR vs. Median; Simple reversal—
X,IP/AH/PA/IR vs. Median.

posed use of the hands and is optimal for crafts such as knitting, crocheting,
and knot-weaving, which depend upon delicate manipulation within narrow
limits. This complex, spiral approach to space is applied to a very wide
range of activities in certain cultures, especially in the Orient. The rice shoots
go into the mud of the paddy field with a complex, spiral, binding move-

ment of the fingers, just as strips of fiber are woven into the broad hat of the paddy field worker with a delicate coiling movement of the wrists and fingers. Both these supple spiraling movements are again mirrored in the savagely woven lightning of Samurai swordplay. An elaborate movement style, with emphasis of hand and finger play, subtly touches most Oriental high-culture dancing. Looping also occurs in African dance, but with a completely different emphasis. Through his spiraling movement the Negro dancer seems to fling himself into the space that surrounds him.

The discovery that transitions in movement grow steadily more complex along the scale of social and productive complexity matches the cantometric finding that the level of ornamentation in song rises with cultural complexity.

NUMBER OF ACTIVE BODY PARTS

On the first line of the choreometrics coding sheet the rater checks which of sixteen body parts are clearly and actively engaged in a given action sequence. The cross-cultural findings in regard to this aspect of movement remind one of the scores for consonantal complexity and wordiness in song. The finding is that, on the whole, primitive people employ a smaller number of body parts at any given moment in dance and everyday life than do people of complex cultures. Furthermore, areas that favor a one-unit system of body attitude and simple non-looping transitions score low in the number of body parts involved in any one activity. The one-unit system, in conjunction with linear transitions, limits the play of the body in space and thus reduces the number of parts that move independently.

Dancers of Australia, New Guinea, and Amerindia generally move the whole leg and arm rather than using these limbs segmentally. The high scores for a large number of active body parts turn up in regions where many body parts, including the fingers, toes, mouth, eyes, and eyebrows are activated. Thus India, with a maximum of types of transition and a discriminating use of many movement elements, is the territory of the most complex movement style thus far observed in our sample. When this complexity score is set up along the production scale, a clear-cut relationship emerges: an increase occurs with plow agriculture and a very sharp rise with irrigation (Fig. 62).

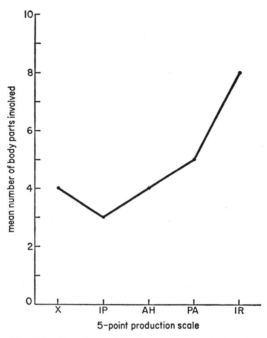

Fig. 62.   Number of body parts: the five-point
production scale. The number of body parts involved in activity seems to increase in complex
cultures, especially in Oriental irrigation societies.   Chi   sq/2   df = 8.19;   gamma = .6172;
P < .02. Statistical split: X,IP/AH,PA/IR vs.
Median.

COMPLEXITY OF EFFORT–SHAPE

The Laban system provides a way of describing each activity or fraction of
an activity in terms of its effort and shape components. *Shape* is the adaptive
form of movement which has to do with the actor's adjustment to the space
around him. When Laban speaks of *effort,* he is talking about the way in
which the energy of the movement is modulated to produce the rhythmic
quality in movement. Sixteen basic components form the constellations of
the Laban effort-shape system.

Shape	*Effort*
Horizontal: narrowing ↔ widening	Space: direct ↔ indirect
Vertical: sinking ↔ rising	Force: strong ↔ light
Sagittal: retreating ↔ advancing	Time: sudden ↔ sustained
Flow: folding ↔ unfolding	Flow: bound ↔ free

Rating the relative presence or absence of these qualities in a large body of film turned out to be an impractical task. Moreover, we discovered that these descriptions were too detailed for the areal cross-cultural differentials with which this research was concerned.

The two expert raters found, however, that they could agree closely on the level of complexity of use of effort and of shape elements. A filmed activity was judged on the number of elements present, how many and how various were their combinations, and how selectively these elements were joined in serial behaviors. A tired woman scrubbing a floor might repeat the same back-and-forth, in-and-out, strong-and-light pattern and would be given a low rating on the effort complexity scale. In contrast, a good boxer, weaving, bobbing, crouching, punching, and jabbing, combined many effort qualities in a complexly textured series.

The effort scale runs from effort fleetingly evident to a full range of effort used with high selectivity. The scale of shaping complexity proceeds from the simple folding and unfolding of the limbs, with no well-defined spatial character, to full use of all forms of shape in various combinations. Examples from our film sample will indicate how various cultures fall along these scales. In the snake ritual of Arnhem Land, where a row of men kneel beneath a long wooden horn, a single effort quality pervades the whole activity. As they bow to their knees, roll on one side, then recover and raise themselves from the dust, these aborigines never deviate from a tempo of movement so slow as to make the whole episode resemble a dream. One effort quality—slowness—dominates the whole of this ritual. In everyday activities as well, Australian movement tends to be characterized by a kind of monochrome of efforts, with little variation within any one sequence. It is interesting, however, that in the dance films so far studied we observe something different—a monotonous, cyclic build-up of two effort elements (strength and speed) emerging from the usual rather neutral base line.

The Eskimos appear close to the Australian Aborigines on the three rating scales discussed previously. On the effort scale, however, they appear considerably more complex. In moments of high drama, such as the killing of a seal on the ice or spearing fish, Eskimos combine speed, directness, and strength, and join these qualities in varied and shifting combinations. This high use of energy is kept up through long phrases when several activities are slung together into one highly efficient chain of action—spearing, hauling out, removing the barb from, and stringing the fish—repeated over and over as a unit, without pause.

In more complex cultures, such as India, one may see the whole panorama of effort-shape combinations and changes of the elements displayed in one activity. In spite of regional differences between Indian areas, high selectivity of effort use appears everywhere, supported by subtle changes in shape.

Indeed, as the sample grew, it became evident that complexity of shaping and use of effort increased together along the scale of productive complexity. If the culture regions sketched in our preliminary survey—Australia, New Guinea, Amerindia, Oceania, Africa, Old High Culture—are ranged along this same scale, both these levels rise steadily from left to right. Apparently, the number of movement components available in a repertoire and constantly in use is a good index of the relative complexity of a culture in an overall sense. More concretely, an Australian will tend to apply the same small repertoire of movement style patterns to every activity, whereas an Indian peasant (at the other end of the scale) will use a larger and more varied repertoire of movement, applying these with high selectivity in each task.

Figure 63 indicates that these two scales are good measures of social com-

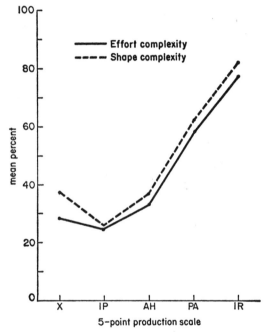

Fig. 63. Effort and shape complexity: the five-point production scale. As indicated by a rise in mean percentage, the level of both effort and shape complexity shows sharp increase among complex producers. Effort complexity: chi sq/3 df = 19.84; gamma = .7782; P < .001. Shape complexity: chi sq/3 df = 29.56; gamma = .8560; P < .001. Statistical split: X,IP/AH/PA/IR vs. Median.

plexity. A sharp rise of both mean curves appears with plow agriculture and steeply increases at the level of irrigation. The correlation with other complexity measurements set forth in this volume can scarcely be disregarded. From left to right, two movement complexity scales rank movement situations in which an increasing number of crystallized and articulated dimensions appear. In other words, in the more complex technologies, a larger vocabulary of movement modalities may be brought to bear upon the dance or on any given task, a shift which is clearly roughly analogous to the results from cantometrics, phonotactics, and from study of concept load. At these levels, too, more definers are engaged in increasing the specificity of a given stretch of communication. This conclusion and others on the foregoing pages provide convincing evidence that, at least at the complexity level, cultures define themselves in similar ways in song and dance.

11

Choreometric Profiles

Irmgard Bartenieff and Forrestine Paulay

A SERIES of typical choreometric profiles follows. Each one is a rating of a separate dance. They cover the same range as the cantometric profiles that appear earlier in this volume. We hope that the ethnologist acquainted with these cultures will find himself at home in the descriptions that accompany these précis of dance movement.

ESKIMO (Fig. 64)

Source: Footage of the Netsilik Eskimo was provided by Educational Services, Inc., Cambridge, Mass., especially the film "Eskimo Life: Fishing at the Stone Weir," filmed by Asen Balikci and Quentin Brown.

In much Eskimo work movement is concentrated in the forearm and hand and executed in front of the body. Relatively few body parts come into play in any one activity—usually trunk, forearm, and hands. Posture is slightly stooped, with legs wide apart and knees somewhat bent. This body attitude, "frontal plane with right and left stress," dominates the life of the Eskimos indoors and out. The square design of Eskimo skin clothing underscores this impression, but other American aboriginals, who appear virtually nude in films, present an equally solid, squared-away posture. It is a body attitude that provides a sturdy base of concentrated and stable power from which strong, direct, thrusting, chopping, and slashing movements may be launched and quick recovery made.

According to Balikci, the supervising ethnologist on this film, the energetic, abrupt, quick movement (G6-10) so typical of Eskimo style, generates body heat and helps to keep these people alive in the subzero Arctic temperatures. Certain Eskimo movements—the single blow of the fist that kills the harpooned seal, the thrust and recovery of the fishing spear in the salmon weir—are the swiftest we have observed in any culture. Eskimo movement style, like their way of singing, is prototypical for Amerindia, but seems to be a specialized adaptation to the demands of an Arctic environment. Like

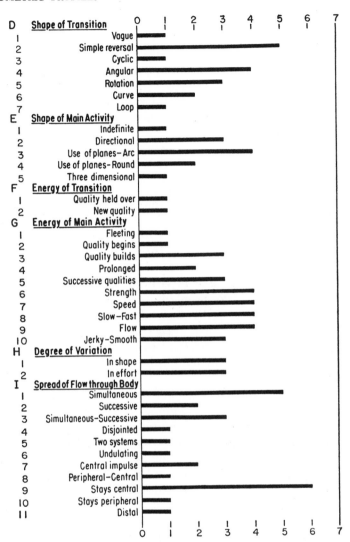

Fig. 64. Eskimo drum dance. The four body parts used are the
trunk, whole arm, forearm, and whole leg. One-unit body attitude: frontal plane with right-left stress.

most simple producers, the Eskimos rather frequently employ the simple
reversal transition (D2). They also employ angular and rotating transitions
(D4, 5) at the wrist and elbow, tieing a series of small actions together like
beads along a string. Eskimos normally sling together long chains of movement—spearing the fish, retrieving it, stringing it—with no intervention of

pauses between phrases or whole acts. Thus, although Eskimo style is, on the whole, low in complexity (H1, 2), its shaping elements of angular, rotating transitions (D4, 5), and linear arrangement (E2) foster a high output of energy in the use of effort; it is fast, strong, and direct. When every component in this combination is strongly emphasized, we have what Laban termed the "fighting attitude," important perhaps in certain survival patterns and not in others. The drummer-dancer reproduces this fighting attitude with somewhat less intensity.

IROQUOIS (Fig. 65)

Source: "The Longhouse People," produced by the Canadian Film Board, deals largely with the ceremonial life of the Handsome Lake Cult, but also depicts work and everyday activities.

A small number of body parts, principally whole arm, whole leg, lower leg, or forearm, is engaged at any one time. A one-unit system prevails throughout the film, with little or no twisting or bending in different segments. Whether one sees these people in their buckskins or in contemporary dress, handling tractors and automobiles, they give the impression of dynamic erectness because of their vertically held body attitude. Many of their dances, however, are characterized by a compact, wide stance with a slight stoop and marked right and left turning of the whole body, i.e., frontal-plane, right and left stress.

Emphasis on simple reversal (D2) and angular transition (D4), plus the verticality of the body stance, contribute to an appearance of measured linearity. An old man stretches out his arms toward his grandchild and encloses her gently between his hands, as if they were two rather stiff pincers. He moves with a straight, long-legged, gliding gait toward his friends. Again, at the harvest, a group of men and women bend straight down and forward from the hips in line-like movement, which persists even in the husking of the corn and the braiding of the corn husks into festoons. The Iroquois rate fairly low on complexity (H1, 2) and this, along with the other characteristics mentioned, puts them into the Amerindian subgroup of the circum-Pacific region.

AUSTRALIA AND NEW GUINEA (Fig. 66)

The movement profiles of the two regions are more similar (84 percent) than any other pair in the sample. Both score low on body attitude, transition, and complexity scales, indicating an even simpler and somehow cruder movement style than that of northern Amerindia. Outside of Amerindia

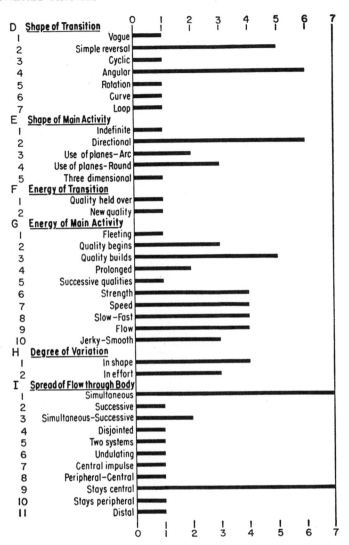

Fig. 65. Iroquois dance. The four body parts used are the trunk, whole leg, whole arm, and head. One-unit body attitude: frontal plane with right-left stress.

only Australia and New Guinea show a complete absence of curved or looped transition (D6, 7) combined with a low level of complexity (H1, 2). Australian movement, however, seems more intense than that of New Guinea because of its tendency to repress generalized bodily activity and localize movement in one limb or even one area of the body. In much New Guinea

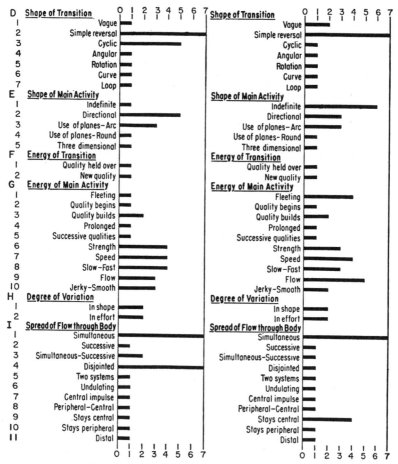

Fig. 66. Similarity of dances in two regions.
Left: Australian dance. Three body parts are used: head, trunk, and whole leg. One-unit body attitude: body axis held.
Right: New Guinea Maring dance. Three body parts are used: trunk, forearm, and whole leg. One-unit body attitude: body axis held.

movement, on the other hand, specifically among the Maring, there is a generally low intensity of energy and a tendency to employ vague transitions. A consistent movement profile with features distinctive for Australia has been noted in films from the central desert, Arnhem Land, the York Peninsula, and in documentaries on the life of the acculturated Aborigines. The New Guinea sample, coming from the Central Highlands, the Sepik River, Baliem Valley, and the D'Entrecasteaux Peninsula, also maintains a high order of homogeneity, in spite of the wide geographical and cultural range represented.

AUSTRALIA

Source: "Arnhem Land," Australian Film Board; "The Story of Stone Age Man," and "Aborigines of Australia," Australian News; "Aboriginal Dances From Cape York," Australian Institute of Aborigines and Australian Information Service.

Like many other hunting and fishing peoples, the Australians treat the trunk as a solid block; the one-unit body attitude prevails in all activities. The restriction in the number of body parts actively engaged in any one task makes their score here the lowest in our sample. In ritual performance this may drop to two or even one. Another peculiarity is that the dancers seem able to segment the body and involve widely separated and not normally connected body parts in a disconnected series of movements. For instance, the pectoral muscle of a dancer may quiver and then a muscle along the inner thigh may tremble in response; meantime stillness is maintained in the rest of the body.

The main Australian transitions are simple reversal and cyclic, with an occasional use of an angular shift of direction (D2, 3, 4). In their daily work, movement consists almost exclusively of two phasic back-and-forth transitions as they use short choppers, digging sticks, or rubbing stones. This pattern persists in the life of the acculturated Aborigines seen in a modern housing development. The children, standing under a shower, wash their heads in a straight, back-and-forth, rubbing motion; the women put clothes on a line with a confined, straight-line reach-up-and-then-down.

Restrictions appear in the use of surrounding space, and in the limitation of effort elements in a typical Australian phrase (H1, 2). One ritual, for instance, emphasizes only the quality of slowness. Again, the Australian ability to move one body segment back and forth in one place with no change of quality is rare elsewhere in the world. When the Australian dancer wears body paint and a strange headgear, he does indeed look like a supernatural. A group of these highly trained Aborigines, coordinating their movement but limiting it decisively to one body segment that moves in one way, gives a remarkable impression of synchrony, but it is a synchrony that arises from restriction and control, in contrast to the flowing style of the Kung, for instance, that animates every part of the body and links a group of Kung dancers in a myriad of mirrored interchanges.

Australian Aboriginal movement style is unique in our sample as being low in complexity and extreme in specialization. On the one hand, the Australian dances resemble those of Old High Culture in the selective control of body. On the other, they are like the styles of New Guinea in emphasizing few body parts, the one-unit system, simple reversal, and little shaping or effort differentiation. One might say that both groups adapt to their environment, but without trying to reshape it.

MARING, NEW GUINEA

Source: Many reels of unedited film shot by Marek and Allison Jablonko, lent by the Film Archive of the National Institute of Neurological Diseases and Blindness, Washington, D.C.

The overall impression of Maring movement profile is of extreme simplicity and, in contrast to the Australians, of generally low intensity. The number of body parts involved is usually limited to only three at any one time—the trunk, arms, and legs. The body is handled as a solid unit without any particular emphasis other than the maintenance of a simple upright posture. In dance, the Maring employ simple reversal (D2) to the virtual exclusion of all other types of transition. Every action has the same spatial layout, either forward and back or straight up and down.

A great deal of Maring activity seems to have no clearly defined direction or intent (E1). Effort is handled in a fleeting way, being neither put forth strongly, nor prolonged, nor handled in successive style (G1, 4, 5). Frequently gestures in communication or in work are but briefly maintained and end with an abrupt drop-off of energy. The Maring do not seem to hurry or to be intentionally deliberate (G6, 7, 8). They introduce little variation in handling either shape or effort (H1, 2). The whole body often moves as if all parts were joined in one solid unit (I1); in other words, a Maring handles his body or one limb as one segment instead of with successive articulations of the parts.

The dance, too, consists of the repetition of simple and often undifferentiated patterns. The women dance on and on, generally staying in one spot, gently bouncing up and down on the balls of their feet. Meanwhile the men jog back and forth in loosely organized groups, occasionally breaking into a trot to meet and sometimes to join another group on the dancing ground. Their step is a simple up-and-down movement, with small shifts in speed, that exactly resembles their drumming technique. Essentially men and women share the same diffuse and somewhat indefinite movement style.

MARITIME PACIFIC—SAMOA AND ELLICE ISLANDS (Fig. 67)

Samoa—Source: "A New Day in Samoa," New Zealand Embassy.
Ellice Islands—Source: Encyclopedia Cine E416, 417 Ellice Is.

Since the dance profiles from these two Maritime Pacific cultures resemble each other at the 80 percent level, we reproduce them together so the reader may see the level of identity for himself. First of all, the shift from earlier circum-Pacific profiles is abrupt. We enter a world where movement is both

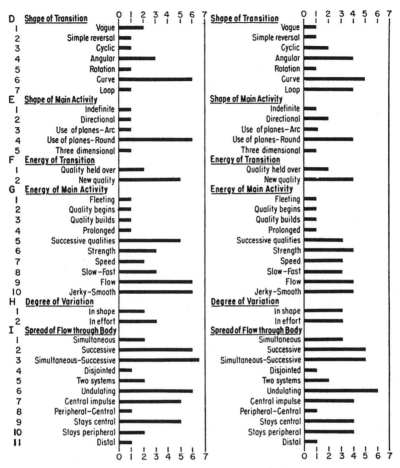

Fig. 67. Samoan and Ellice Island dances.

Left: Samoan: Six body parts are used: trunk, shoulders, whole arm, forearm, hands, and whole leg. Two-unit body attitude, body axis spreading.

Right: Ellice Island: Eight body parts are used: chest, pelvis, whole arm, forearm, hands, whole leg, lower leg, and feet. Two-unit body attitude, body axis spreading.

more complex and more complexly integrated than anything so far encountered in Amerindia, Australia, or New Guinea, yet not so complex as the styles of Asia and Africa.

Regions usually score high (6 and 8) for the number of body parts involved in both movement and dance. The elaborate seated ballets of Polynesia bring into subtle and supple play the hands, forearms, arms, and shoulders. Simple reversal and other straight-line transitions scarcely occur in these styles (D1, 2, 3), while the one-unit system has been replaced by a strong tendency toward two units. In Oceania one does not see the full pelvic twisting so common in Africa but an undulating, wave-like movement spreading from the waist, sometimes causing the pelvis to rotate and breaking up the rigidity of the solid trunk. This feminized feeling is enhanced by a strong tendency to use curved rather than straight-line transition, along with occasional three-dimensional, looped transition (D6, 7). Among Samoans and Ellice Islanders we see the effect of effort used as transition, so that an effort develops at the end of a movement and forms a smooth bridge to the following movement (G2, 3). Polynesians do not seem to punctuate their activity with bursts of strength or speed, but achieve variety by gradually introducing a series of different effort qualities into the undulating and flowing line of their movement. A slowly developing lightness is delicately and quickly interrupted, and then blends into strength, tempered by indirectness. Such combinations of efforts lend the movement of Polynesia a complex and fluid quality without sharp-edged focus, but with an easy and flowing rhythm. Moreover, Polynesian movement is notably more complex than that of the cultures described earlier in this series of profiles. The use of more body parts in phrases linked by curved and looped transitions are both signs of this increased level of complexity and of a possible tie with the body style of East Asia. Indeed, the behavior of Ellice Islanders involves the use of more body parts and more looped transitions than was observed in Samoan films—traits which may point to some relation between Micronesia and East Asia.

AFRICA (Fig. 68)

Source: Footage from the Dogon, shot by Pierre Gaisseau.

The African movement patterns we have analyzed stand somewhat higher on most complexity scales than those of Polynesia and Micronesia, but are not so complex as those of the peoples from Old High Culture.

The most dramatic and outstanding feature of Dogon movement, indeed of much Negro African dance south of the Sahara, is the two-unit system. The torso is divided into two units, and sharp twists at the waist set up an opposition between the pelvis and thorax or between the upper and lower parts of the body. In the Pacific an undulating movement spreads from the center of the torso, but in Africa the upper and lower body halves may be engaged in different activities and move in different directions, not only in the hip-swinging dances of Africa and Afro-America, but in work activity, as well. For instance, a Dogon woman, planting seed in the fields,

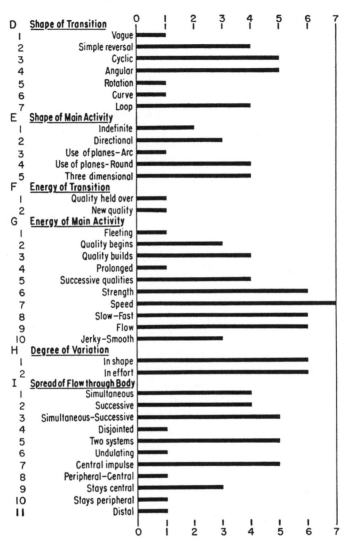

Fig. 68. African Dogon dance. Six body parts are used: head, shoulders, chest, pelvis, whole arm, and whole leg. Two-unit body attitude: upper-lower, with twist.

drops the millet grain into a furrow with her left hand and then, as she steps across the hole, pulls dirt across it with her right foot.

The Dogon profile is notable for the number of types of transition employed in movement. Curving and looping transitions are frequent, but simple reversal, cyclic and angular, are just as frequent (D2, 3, 4, 6, 7). Because of contrastive use of a variety of transition, shaping, and effort qualities, Dogon dancing gives the impression of extreme liveliness and high excitability. Rounded, serpentine, or linear shapes flow out (G9) into space (E4, 5) on either side of the body; phrases begin with bursts of energy (G2), or a succession of efforts may appear, one after another, to build up to a final climactic peak at the end of a phrase (G3). Speed (G7) and power flow through all African movement, but speed especially, enhanced by spurts of acceleration, reaches an unequalled peak in the twisting leaps of the male Dogon dancers. Dogon dancing displays an orchestral use of the body where the upper and lower halves develop different supporting but complementary rhythms. It is with this polyrhythmic handling of the body, combined with dramatic bursts of strength and speed, that the African dancer produces an effect of orgiastic excitement. All is change here, with repeated initiations of streams of energy flowing from the center to the periphery and involving a wide variety of shapes and efforts along the way. In Dogon movement style, as in African song performance style, we have come upon a sexually oriented communication system, highly charged with erotic excitement.

OLD HIGH CULTURE WEST (MALABAR–MYSORE) (Fig. 69)

Source: Malabar, Mysore—"Therayattam," Indian Information Service.

This profile shows more levels and kinds of complexity than any in the series thus far. The score for the number of body parts engaged in both dance and everyday life is the highest in the series—ten. The eyes, eyebrows, and mouth play a formal and necessary role in the dance drama. Although there is no twisting at the waist, a tendency in body attitude appears that gives this dancing somewhat the quality of a two-unit system. We call it "vertical with diagonal stress," an accentuated position of one shoulder against the drive of the opposite hip. This contralateral stress forms the basis of a subtle relationship between sections of the trunk and contributes to a rich and delicately shaded style that resembles both the undulating movement of Samoa and the peaked excitement of African dance. All the straight-lined, angular transitions are absent, and for the first time in this series, three-dimensional spiraling or looping movement dominates a style (D6, 7). As a young Indian beauty arranges her coiffure, for instance, her hands curve in and under the loops of dark hair and around each other like moving tendrils of vines (E5). Again, as in Africa and Polynesia, one quality after another comes into play and the increased selectivity in developing qualities gives rise to a style of subtle variations (G2, 3, 4, 5). This web of shifting qualities flows in a complex interplay between parts of the trunk and the extremities. In the movement style of southern India we reach the peak of variety complexity (HI, 2), and subtlety found in our study thus far.

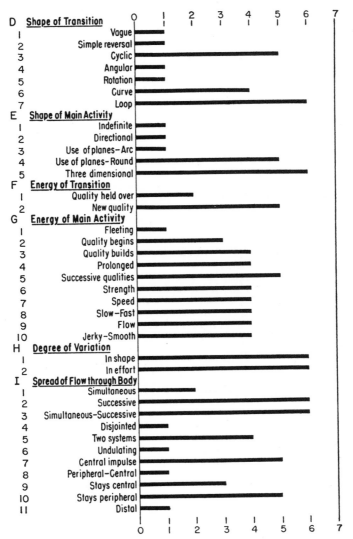

Fig. 69. Old High Culture Malabar-Mysore dance. Ten body parts are used: head, face, eyes, chest, whole arm, forearm, hands, whole leg, lower leg, and feet. One-unit body attitude: vertical with diagonal stress.

ENGLAND (Fig. 70)

Source: "Morris Monday," English Country Dance Society.

This coding describes the famous British Morris dance—a leaping, prancing, all-male ceremonial performance with its roots in the pagan past of West-

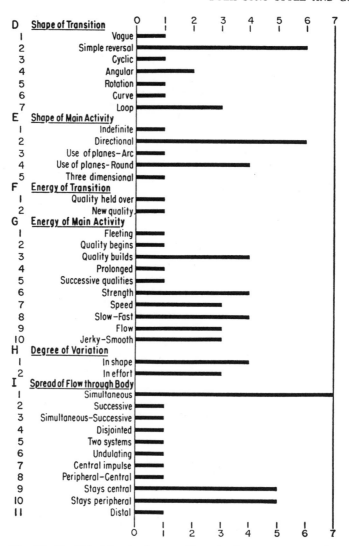

Fig. 70. English Morris dances. Four body parts are used: whole arm, forearm, whole leg, and lower leg. One-unit body attitude: vertical, held.

ern Europe. Its movement style is, in most respects, simpler than anything else encountered beyond the level of incipient agriculture. In many respects the profile resembles that of the Amerindian hunters. Perhaps this points to a very ancient stylistic connection between the old extractive cultures of northwestern Europe and the paleolithic in Siberia and North America. At any rate, the Morris dance scores fairly low on the number of body parts engaged (four). A one-unit system keeps the pelvis rigid in a markedly vertical posture. A break away from primitive simplicity occurs, however, at the level of transition. Although simple reversal and other straight-line transitions are most frequent, the presence of a considerable amount of looping (D7) and of rounded shapes (E4) links this style with that of Old High Culture. The force of the trunk is brought into simultaneously initiated actions, while the energy is characterized by a steady inflow of strength and speed (I1, 9; G6, 8). Complexity in use of shape and effort is only moderate, about the level of the Eskimo whose movement style is similar to that of Western Europeans in so many other respects.

These brief profile summaries show the reader how choreometrics can evoke the quality of a culture by taking a comparative look at its movement style. The system is still in an early stage of development. Whereas cantometrics is a consensus-tested rating scheme that touches upon most of the major features of performance, choreometrics has not yet been thoroughly tested for consensus and does not yet have an established approach to cohesiveness, synchrony, group form, and group dynamics. Results so far, however, indicate that a means for successfully comparing dances and dance styles does exist.

12

The Choreometric Coding Book

Alan Lomax, Irmgard Bartenieff, and Forrestine Paulay

THIS system permits a measured description of dancing or movement by means of agreed-on qualitative rating scales. The viewer may register on these scales his judgments as to the relative presence or absence of qualities such as speed, strength, or linearity in the activity he observes. This set of qualitative measuring rods allows dances to be compared cross-culturally; it produces distributional maps of dance style that make very good historical sense; and it has generated a fruitful study of the functional interrelationship of dance and movement and culture styles. Choreometrics has not been tested for consensus, since this will require the creation of fairly elaborate and expensive rating films, but the two expert coders have found themselves in general agreement as they worked with it day by day.

Choreometrics ignores the problem of the unit; it is not concerned with a step-by-step, phrase-by-phrase result so that dance can be reproduced in its entirety from a written score. It reaches out to another level, to the level of identification where signals, constantly flowing in the kinesic stream, characterize all present in terms of age, sex, occupation, and, most especially, cultural affiliation. Birdwhistell (1957) calls this "cross-referencing identification behavior" and shows that it provides the supportive base line for all interaction. Choreometrics, however, does not seek to describe the particulars or the content of these identifying sets, but to evaluate a sufficient number of their salient qualitative aspects so the movement style of a culture may be delineated. In simpler cultures, one such description distinctively characterizes most activity, whether male or female, dance or everyday. Naturally there are differences between individuals, between behaviors, between persons of different ages and sexes, but these differences are likely to grade away from a base-line movement signature whose imprint may be recognized throughout an area. This movement style model, notable in the stance adopted by the people of the culture and in the tempo of their activity, must be learned early in life and is shared by everyone in simpler cultures.

In every culture a model of movement style serves two main functions for all individuals: (1) *Identifying:* It identifies the individual as a member of his culture who understands and is in tune with its communication systems. (2) *Formative:* It forms and molds together the dynamic qualities which animate the behavior of a culture member in speaking, dancing, working, walking, making love—in fact, in all his activities. These models may be quickly identified in the dances of a culture, for here movement pattern becomes most formalized and repetitious. Once identified, they may be used in the comparison of activity cross-culturally and the discovery of key patterns in all sorts of behavior within one culture. One day, indeed, these models or descriptions very much like them will be needed at the micro-analytical level where the postural units of communication are described, because the chains of units, no matter how small, are tied together by the ebb and flow of energy.

The choreometric rating method grew out of a survey of movement style on film. About 200 films from many cultures and of many levels of excellence were reviewed in the first stages of the work. Subsequently a smaller set of selected films was analyzed with two stages of the present coding system. A first statement of some of these results has been presented in the previous chapters. The coding book found in the following pages is Part 1 of a three-part technique for the evaluation of the gross features of social behavior in cinema. Although designed with the needs of dance analysis in mind, we hope it will be useful in evaluating all social behavior.

The cinema has thus far served the ethnologist largely as a way to supplement and preserve observations already recorded in his notebooks, or relationships already analyzed out of his field work. The movie reminds him of what the field was really like, just as the football film reminds the coach about how his team played a game. Mead, Birdwhistell, and others have pioneered in using film to record and set forth the structural details of particular cultures and communication systems (Birdwhistell, 1966; Mead, 1952; Scheflen, 1965). Choreometrics, however, is an attempt to employ film as a source and a tool in the comparative and historical study of cultures and of human behavior.

We regard the vast, endlessly provocative, prejudice-laden, existing sea of documentary footage as the richest and most unequivocal storehouse of information about humanity. We do not agonize over its limitations or those of the persons who shot or edited it. We come to it with an observational approach like that used by the ordinary person in everyday life, which enables him to differentiate constantly between different classes of visual experiences and to behave appropriately in relation to these varieties of experience.

As in the study of song performance, we do not require an elaborate or exhaustive film record of a culture. Made confident by other similar observational experiences, we trust the redundancy of the behavior and of the cultural setting to evoke patterns that, in a comparative context, indicate stable cultural structure. The most inept travelogue can yield information of importance to the cultural taxonomist and the student of movement style. Everyday documentary footage can be a dependable source of information and theory for the culturologist and the humanist. Of course, a film has more factual value if it contains many long shots of at least thirty seconds duration, not interrupted by change of angle or introduction of close-up or any other editing device that interferes with the simple unfolding of the visual event.

The heading of the coding sheet (Fig. 71) provides space for the identification of the film, the culture, the subsistence level, the activity, and the setting being rated. The coder should specify whether his observations apply to one brief action, a whole episode or dance, or the whole film. A movement style may be so pervasive that in one culture it changes very little, no matter what is being done; or it may be varied enough to require a number of ratings. We have yet to come upon a culture where the several ratings were not clearly and closely related to one another.

A copy of the choreometrics coding instruction book used at the Cantometrics Project is reproduced below.

THE CHOREOMETRIC CODING BOOK

The coder records an impression of an overall or dominant behavioral style of movement that animates a whole scene or activity. He should not attempt to count or to break down actions or scenes into separate parts or small components, but to record his careful judgment as to what strong, clear patterns characterize the whole scene, segment, or film being observed.

(A) Most Active Body Parts

Here the coder checks those body parts which are clearly and constantly engaged in the activity observed, i.e., the body parts in which the most movement changes occur. Check hand only when fingers and palm are used in a manipulative way or for clear-cut wrist actons. Check fingers when relationships between fingers are differentiated.

Directions: Check (O) in the M column if the male group notably uses a particular body part; check (O) in the F column if the female actively uses a particular body part; both will be checked when men and women both employ some part of the body more or less equally.

(B) Number of Body Parts

——1. *The total number of active body parts added up from the field of scores in (A).* The coder thus notes the number of body parts used during the whole film or long sections thereof.

MOVEMENT CODING SHEET

SHELF LIST #:_____ CULTURE:_____GP. #:_____AREA:_____

P.T5:_____ P.T8:_____ NAME OF FILM:_____ SOURCE:_____

ACTIVITY:_____

SCENE:_____

Frames: (Continue on back)

USE OF BODY

(A) Most Active Body Parts (Check as many as needed)

M F		M F		M F		M F	
0 0	1.	0 0	6. Trunk	0 0	11. Whole arm	0 0	16. Whole leg
0 0	2. Head	0 0	7. Shoulders	0 0	12. Upper arm	0 0	17. Upper leg
0 0	3. Face	0 0	8. Chest	0 0	13. Forearm	0 0	18. Lower leg
0 0	4. Mouth	0 0	9. Belly	0 0	14. Hands	0 0	19. Feet
0 0	5. Eyes	0 0	10. Pelvis	0 0	15. Fingers		

(B) Number of Parts Used

_____1. Total number in film   _____2. Number per activity
M | F (Add total from A)   M | F (Enter mean number per scene)

(C) Body Attitude (Score only clear patterns, leave remainder blank.)

(dominant) M F		(secondary) M F	(rare, but important) M F
0 0	1. One unit	0 0	0 0
[0 0	2. Two-plus units	0 0	0 0
[0 0	3. Body axis held	0 0	0 0
0 ¦ 0	4. Vertical	0 0	0 0
0 0	5. Frontal-R-L	0 0	0 0
0 0	6. Frontal	0 0	0 0
0 0	7. Vertical	0 0	0 0
0 0	8. Body axis spreading	0 0	0 0
0 0	9. Up-low, no twist	0 0	0 0
0 0	10. Up-low, twist	0 0	0 0
0 0	11.	0 0	0 0
0 0	12.	0 0	0 0

NATURE OF TRANSITION AND MAIN ACTIVITY (7-pt. scale)

(D) Shape of Transition

M   F
( ) ( ) 1. Vague
( ) ( ) 2. Simple reversal
( ) ( ) 3. Cyclic
( ) ( ) 4. Angular
( ) ( ) 5. Rotation
( ) ( ) 6. Curve
( ) ( ) 7. Loop
( ) ( ) 8.

(E) Shape of Main Activity

( ) ( ) 1. Indefinite
( ) ( ) 2. Directional
( ) ( ) 3. Use of planes—Arc
( ) ( ) 4. Use of planes—Round
( ) ( ) 5. Three dimensional
( ) ( ) 6.

(F) Energy of Transition

( ) ( ) 1. Quality held over
( ) ( ) 2. New quality
( ) ( ) 3.

(G) Energy of Main Activity

M   F
( ) ( ) 1. Fleeting
( ) ( ) 2. Quality begins
( ) ( ) 3. Quality builds
( ) ( ) 4. Prolonged
( ) ( ) 5. Successive qualities
( ) ( ) 6. Strength
( ) ( ) 7. Speed
( ) ( ) 8. Slow—fast
( ) ( ) 9. Flow
( ) ( ) 10. Jerky—smooth
( ) ( ) 11.

(H) Degree of Variation

{ } { } 1. In shape
{ } { } 2. In effort

(I) Spread of Flow Through Body

( ) ( ) 1. Simultaneous—all body parts move as one unit.
( ) ( ) 2. Successive—neighboring body parts successively involved in an action.
( ) ( ) 3. Simultaneous—successive.
( ) ( ) 4. Disjoined—non-neighboring body segments moving in immediate succession.
( ) ( ) 5. Two system—two or more body rhythms occurring at the same time.
( ) ( ) 6. Undulating—in successive movements; joints consistently fold or unfold.
( ) ( ) 7. Central impulse—movement begins in the central portion of body.
( ) ( ) 8. Peripheral-central—movement starts in extremities and spreads to center.
( ) ( ) 9. Stays central—action of torso is engaged in the movement.
( ) ( ) 10. Stays peripheral—torso is held in clear opposition to movement in extremities.
( ) ( ) 11. Distal—movement remains limited to forearm, hands, fingers.

Fig. 71. The movement coding sheet used in the Choreometrics Project.

_____2. *The average number of body parts generally engaged in any one activity, per culture.* Here the coder can note the number of body parts employed per activity in a culture—this figure may be less than B1.

(C) Body Attitude

Body attitude is the basic postural set from which the individual develops his activities and from which all forms of movement unfold. Put another way, body attitude is the base line from which the individual develops activity and expends energy—his active stance. This parameter does not describe posture in an anatomical sense, but the essential dynamic which runs through all or most of the postures of an individual. Our finding is that in any one scene, indeed in any one culture, most actors employ the same or very similar body attitudes.

Under the heading "Dominant," record your impression of the body attitude which most of the actors in the scene employ most of the time. Under "Secondary," record a clearly present but secondary body attitude. Under the column "Rare but Important," note the presence of a body attitude which may occur infrequently but has a clear importance and relevance to the behavior of the group being studied. As above, check (OM) for male, (OF) for female and both for use by both. Check only those items which are clearly present—omit checking others. Either Line 1 or 2 will, however, always be checked, with at least one other dominant body attitude.

_____1. *One unit.* Here the trunk is used like a solid block, with little or no movement at the waist; it functions as a one-unit system. There is an impression of solidity that runs from the shoulders to the hips. No twists appear at the waist between the thorax and the pelvis.

_____2. *Two or more units.* This body attitude is in sharp contrast to the previous one. The trunk is *not* handled as one unit; two or more sections of the trunk move simultaneously or successively in opposition to each other. Twisting may appear at the waistline or undulating movements may flow between belly, shoulder, and hip.

One-Unit Systems

_____3. *Body axis held.* The trunk is held as a solid unit with no clear stress on height or width, and the legs provide a narrow base of support. By "narrow base" we mean that the feet are no more than five or six inches apart.

_____4. *Vertical held.* Trunk used as a solid unit with a clear stress on erectness or height. The legs provide a narrow base of support.

_____5. *Frontal plane, right or left stress.* Trunk used as a solid unit with width emphasized and legs providing a wide base of support, i.e., the

feet are kept more than five or six inches apart. Emphasis here is on unilaterality, i.e., movement seems to divide the body into two halves along
the spine: right arm, right leg, and right side move together; left arm,
left leg, and left side move together.

_____6. *Frontal plane the same as the previous type, except that unilaterality
is not emphasized.* Trunk is a solid unit, width and height are emphasized, legs wide apart. Bilateral use of the limbs is favored.

Transitional Systems
(between one- and two-unit systems)

_____7. *Vertical-diagonal stress.* The limbs are used in a contralateral way,
e.g., the right shoulder area is opposed and supported by the left hip
area. Erectness and height are clearly emphasized. Legs provide a narrow base. Related to one-unit body attitude. Also coded Number 1.

_____8. *Body axis spreading.* Movement spreads through the trunk succes-
sively in an undulating way. Related to a two-unit system. Also coded
Number 2.

Two-Unit Systems

_____9. *Upper-lower; no twist.* The upper torso moves as a separate unit
against the lower torso or vice versa. The two halves of the torso may
also move simultaneously in different patterns, which do not involve
twisting at the waist.

——10. *Upper-lower; twist.* The upper or lower torso move singly or simultaneously in twisting opposition to each other. Twisting at the waist
is accentuated.

(D) Shape of Transition

*Sections D through G deal with the movement quality in main activ-
ities. The relative importance of each quality is rated on a 7-point scale.
The lower part of each scale is applied to qualities and situations which
are of very little importance in the scene or film studied: "4" attributes
moderate but clearcut importance to a trait; "5" and "6" record prominence of a quality in a scene; "7" is the symbol for a dominant, striking,
and frequent occurrence. Leave blank if no judgment applies. Enter
"9" if not sure what to decide about the presence or absence of a quality.*

Human movement of any kind must change direction. In other
words, the actor on reaching the limit of extension of a limb must either
pull back or change direction. One may imagine this moment as a linking point or hinge joining two phases of a movement. This moment of
transition can be characterized as generally curvilinear, angular, loop-

ing, etc. In order to make this judgment, the rater observes what seem to be the most frequent types of transition used by the actors in the scene being studied.

_____1. *Vague.* When most transitions are unclear and impossible to characterize, code "vague."

_____2. *Simple reversal.* Here the limb of the actor returns toward the starting point by exactly retracing its forward or outward path. In other words, movement continues by a simple reversal of direction. This type of transition is most common in forms of simple repetitive activity like digging, stamping, chopping, and pounding, which frequently involve such patterns as in-and-out, back-and-forth, up-and-down.

_____3. *Cyclic.* Here the limb of the mover returns to its starting point by following a circular path. The continuity of movement is established through repetitious cycles of actions. This is another movement form frequently occurring in simple repetitive activities. Continuous repeats of round and round.

_____4. *Angular.* An action proceeds in one direction, then takes a second path at an angle to the first. The linking point is such that the transition resembles the juncture of two intersecting lines. Angular is coded whether the action moves into another plane or simply turns a corner.

_____5. *Rotation.* Continuation of activity is accomplished through a change of direction or plane by rotary action within the active limb. In other words, a twist at the elbow or the shoulder or some other joint is responsible for the change of direction observed.

_____6. *Curve.* The continuity of activity is accomplished through a change of direction or plane along a rounded or curved line. In other words, the link between two phases of activity or the juncture of the two segments of a movement is curved rather than angular. This curved line, however, must be continued within one plane. Otherwise code "Loop."

_____7. *Loop.* Here the continuity of activity occurring in two or more planes of space is linked together by a multi-dimensional curve or "loop." In other words, the actor links three different dimensions together by means of "loop" transition.

(E) Shape of Main Activity

On this scale, the coder records his impression of the various ways in which movement develops and defines patterns in space. Point 1 deals with a vague, indeterminate, and virtually non-directional unfolding. In Points 2–5, movement becomes increasingly directional and space defining. Point 5 defines movements that divide space into clearcut, three-dimensional shapes.

____1. *Indefinite*. Movement in which there is no clear emphasis on direction; a vague unfolding or folding of some part of the body.

____2. *Directional*. Here code one-dimensional or line-like movements that clearly emphasize a specific direction.

____3. *Use of planes—Arc*. Here code movements in which one limb or segment thereof moves in a fan-like fashion, thus describing an arc in space.

____4. *Use of planes—Round*. Code here the style in which the actors create rounded forms in one plane of space by successive folding or unfolding of the segments of a limb.

____5. *Three-dimensional*. Behavior of the type described in 4, except that the limb or limbs carve space into three-dimensional rounded shapes.

(F) The Energy of Transition

Movement not only changes direction but it is notable that, at the moment or point of change, there may be a shift in the kind and intensity of energy that the actor is using. In other words, the moment of transition itself can be handled lightly or emphatically, quickly or slowly, etc. Note the difference between the two main kinds of transition:

____1. *Quality held over*. The quality of the first segment of a movement is simply held over, i.e., the qualitative level of energy that appears within an action is maintained at the same level throughout the changes in direction that occur. For example, an action may continue to be slow throughout the directional changes within one activity.

____2. *New quality*. A new effort quality may appear when there is a change in direction in an activity, i.e., when the direction of movement shifts, a new effort quality also appears.

(G) Energy in Main Activity

We conceive of movement as being divided up into segments linked or defined by changes in direction. The members of a culture tend to conform their movement to some standard way of applying efforts or handling energy. In one movement style most phrases may seem to be very vague or lax, i.e., more or less without strong pulsations of energy. In another, movements may begin with explosive releases of energy. The following list of qualities provides the coder with an opportunity to note the most characteristic ways in which the actors expend energy. He should rate his judgment about the degree of importance of the following qualities along a seven-point scale.

____1. *Fleeting*. Very slight or diminished emphasis in movement.

____2. *Quality begins*. Movement phrases tend to begin explosively.

____3. *Quality builds.* Movement phrases have a build-up of energy and may end explosively.

____4. *Prolonged.* A clear and consistent level of energy is maintained throughout an action or movement phrase.

____5. *Successive.* Different ways of expending energy appear successively through an action or movement phrase.

____6. *Strength.* Most movement seems to be characterized by an emphasis on strength.

____7. *Speed.* Most movement phrases observed seem to be characterized by speed, or by accelerations.

____8. *Slow-fast.* The main tempo to which most of the movement phrases conform is here rated on a seven-point scale. Record the predominant rate at which most activities in a scene seem to proceed.

1. Very slow
2. Slow
3. Moderately slow
4. Normal

5. Moderately fast
6. Fast
7. Very fast

____9. *Flow.* The degree to which a fluid quality is stressed throughout an activity.

____10. *Jerky-smooth.* Here the rater uses a seven-point scale to rate the way that an action proceeds—whether jerkily or smoothly.

1. Very jerky
2. Jerky
3. Somewhat jerky
4. Neutral

5. Somewhat smooth
6. Smooth
7. Very smooth

(H) Degree of Variation

Movement texture is, in a sense, most strongly affected by the movement repertoire that the person or culture employs in shaping and relating to the world around him. Some mentally disturbed or physically handicapped people and some very simple cultures approach their surroundings with only one or two ways of handling effort or space. Other cultures may use a number of patterns which vary their movement repertoire.

In this section, the expert coder may record his conclusions about the variety of ways which the members of a culture or the actors in a scene habitually adopt in transforming energy and shaping space in different forms of movement. Two seven-point scales are provided for this purpose. "1" or "2" on the scale means very little variety, a very limited style. "6" or "7" indicates a very complexly textured or extremely varied approach to action, either in dance or in everyday life. Each of these points on the scale, however, is characterized by a certain level or kind of development and we have attempted to define and describe these levels of variety in relation to effort and space in a preliminary and tentative fashion in order to guide the coder in his choice of a rating.

Variation in Shape refers to the clarity, variety, and complexity of the ways in which space is shaped by the actor.

_____1. *Indefinite*. Code here movement which is difficult to characterize because it is almost random in character or consists of folding or unfolding of limbs with no well-defined direction. The focus of action is vague: *inward* or *outward* from the body may be its only assignable characteristic; there is no such clearcut direction as *backward, sideward,* or *forward,* for instance.

_____2. *Emergent direction*. Code when the path is clear but choice of direction is limited, that is, most movement is *forward-backward* or *up and down* only.

_____3. *Clear dimension*. Here movements have clear direction. They define dimensions or planes. Two-dimensional shaping may be observed in the hand. The areas of space used are still somewhat limited.

_____4. *Directional*. The direction of movement is sharply delineated throughout the action. The action pattern may be characterized as clearly forward or across and down. There is access to all the directions of space that surround the actor. Some two- and three-dimensional shape activity will probably be seen to occur in the hands.

_____5. *Emergent shape*. Here three-dimensional activity of the limbs appears in transitions (loops), while the main activity is essentially directional or confined to one plane.

_____6. *Shape*. The whole body and all the limbs may participate in clearcut three-dimensional activity and transitions.

_____7. *Highly varied*. The whole body and all limbs may be involved in the development of many different combinations of three-dimensional movement activity.

Variability in effort refers to the amount of variation which the actors habitually employ in the disposition of energy in behavior.

_____1. *Indefinite*. The situation coded here is one in which the disposition of energy is so vague and unpatterned as to appear to be randomly ordered. There may be no distinguishable emphasis upon any one movement quality or set of qualities so that no clear impression emerges.

_____2. *Developed*. One or two effort qualities are emphasized at the expense of all those available in the effort repertoire—these are usually strength and/or speed. The strong, powerful movements of hunters, fishers, and incipient producers and the like are generally coded here.

_____3. *Developing range.* A wider variety of effort qualities appear here along with the use of opposites such as fast and slow, light and strong.

_____4. *Clearly developed.* Code here those situations in which most activities observed can be clearly described in terms of their energy components as predominantly forceful, i.e., thrusting, slashing, stabbing; or as predominantly gentle, i.e., gliding or flowing.

_____5. *Emerging balance.* Emphasis on the forceful qualities earlier discerned now includes some of the opposites, i.e., thrusting, slashing, plus gliding or flowing. Qualities are also combined in a variety of ways.

_____6. *Balanced development.* There is a balance between the amount of forceful and gentle uses of energy throughout the activity and a shift between those two extremes. More subtle transitions between these and other qualities appear in a great variety of combinations.

_____7. *High variability.* Here code for high selectivity of energy qualities and many variations in transition from one quality to another. The movement qualities appear in many different combinations. There is much variation in the way that one quality emerges out of another.

(I) Spread of Flow Throughout the Body

Here use 7-point scale to attribute to each scene or culture studied its characteristic manner of handling the flow of energy between regions of the body. Three points are covered: (1) the temporal character of flow, (2) the part of the body in which it originates, and (3) the direction of its spread.

_____1. *Simultaneous.* The degree to which all body parts involved in the activity move at the same time.

_____2. *Successive.* The degree to which the neighboring body parts involved in a movement move in clear succession.

_____3. *Simultaneous-successive.* This was a scale employed in an earlier rating sheet in which simultaneous and successive were treated as opposing qualities. This scale need not be coded, since the points are covered in "1" and "2."

_____4. *Disjoined.* Two clearly isolated body parts, not contiguous to each other, move in immediate succession. In other words, two or more separated parts of the body move one after another. For instance, the head nods and then the foot wags. This disjoined activity may be repeated again and again.

_____5. *Two-system.* Two or more body rhythms that occur at the same time during one action.

_____6. *Undulating.* Successive movement in which the neighboring body parts move in a smooth, rippling way; movement seems to flow through the joints one after another in a constantly folding or unfolding manner.

_____7. *Central impulse.* The energy of movement is initiated in the central portion of the body (between the pelvic girdle and the rib cage) and spreads thence into the extremities.

_____8. *Peripheral central.* Movement starts in the extremities and gradually involves the center.

_____9. *Stays central.* Activity in which the torso stays engaged in the movement at all times.

_____10. *Stays peripheral.* The torso is held in clear opposition to the movement of the extremities.

_____11. *Distal.* The movement is limited to the forearms, hands, and fingers, with no active support or participation of the torso.

13

Folk Song Texts as Culture Indicators

Alan Lomax and Joan Halifax

SCHOLARS and enthusiasts in the field of folk song have long believed that the orally transmitted poetry of a people, passed on by them as part of their noncritically accepted cultural heritage, might yield crucial information about their principal concerns and unique world-view. However, in spite of extensive study and collection of folk song texts, little has been done in a systematic way to test this idea. One of the very few such attempts is Sebeok's analysis of Cheremis lore (Sebeok, 1956, 1959, 1964). The present study develops the hypothesis: that folk song texts, if analyzed in a systematic fashion, give clear expression to the level of cultural complexity, and a set of norms which differentiate and sharply characterize cultures.

Folk tales have been studied with methods similar to those used here. A comparison of the results of these studies to the present analysis of folk song texts suggests that folk song texts yield information about norms more readily than folk tales. The explanation for this lies in the relative position of the two genres on one all-important communication scale—redundancy.

It could probably be demonstrated that the field worker and the culture member recognize a "traditional piece of folk lore" because it and most of its stylistic components occur in ordered juxtaposition more frequently in the discourse of a community than do other sequences. Folk tales consist of standard plots, characters, characterizations, literary devices, "runs," and other bits of discourse joined together in fixed and standardized sequences and in fixed interaction contexts. Given any one culture, the teller of the tale relates to his audience in a patterned way and repeats highly patterned material; the whole tale and most of its elements form part of an enduring stock of discourse used by the culture bearers over generations.

Folk song is far more redundant than folk tale since not only does it recur in steady functional relation to the daily lives of a people and is composed of stock literary devices and favored subject matter, but it is also redundant in its intonation patterns (musical form) and its vocalization patterns (vocal timbre). Folk song may be recognized in the discourse of a cul-

274

ture simply because it is more redundant at more levels than any other form of utterance.

This feature of high redundancy confines folk song in two respects, both augmenting its value as a diagnostic tool. First, the formalities of melody and meter tend to limit the choice of the singer and song maker to a set of stock phrases, devices, and poetic forms. Ballad scholars point to incremental repetition as a main characteristic of the medieval ballad. Parry and Lord (1954), in their studies of the folk epics of Yugoslavia and elsewhere, proved that the touchstone of the traditional epic, as opposed to the literary epic, is the frequency of repeated bits. Lord (1960) showed that the Yugoslav *guslar* can recompose as he sings because he can fall back upon a huge store of learned poetic passages. Thus, 80 or 90 percent of the verse in folk epics, in Lord's view, consists of formal devices, winnowed by generations of communal choice. If the sprawling folk epic is so redundant, the brief song forms that make up the major part of folk and primitive song are far more so. In few cases does a song form require more than 30 seconds to sing; a 10-second phrase is a comparatively long musical segment. These brief bits of discourse, linked tightly together by the inexorable demands of tempo, severely limit the input of text. Further restrictions are imposed by the other redundancy features present, such as melody, rhythm, and phonotactic structure (Chapters 1 and 6).

Given the highly redundant nature of folk song and the fact that song is usually a group communication device serving to focus the attention of groups, to organize them for joint response, and to produce consensus, it seems obvious that the texts of songs will be limited to those matters, attitudes, concerns, and feelings on which the community is in maximal accord. If this is not the case, a song is not likely to hold its audience and it probably will not pass into oral tradition, where acceptance means that consensus has taken place over and over again through time. Thus, in theory, song texts ought to be heavily loaded with normative cultural indicators. Indeed, it would be logical to assume that the textual patterns might be culturally more specific than those coded by cantometrics. The results of this first study seem to confirm this hypothesis.

The analytical tool employed was a simplified form of the General Inquirer System, developed at Harvard by Stone and Hunt (1963), in its third revision by Benjamin Colby. This dictionary was devised for computer analysis of texts. Each tag entry in the lexicon stands for one of a limited number of categories of words. In this way, when a given word appears in a text, the computer assigns it to its predetermined category and adds a score of one to the category count. Large bodies of text, punched out on cards, can be broken down into a set of categories chosen by the researcher and tailored to the questions at hand. Since Colby's analysis of folk tale texts from a number of cultures showed promising results, we determined to begin our experiments in folk song study by taking advantage of the dictionary he had used. An outline of this dictionary may be consulted in various articles by Colby (1966a, b).

Any such rough classification of all the words in any language is bound to suffer from ambiguity. Is "corn," for example, to be classified as a vegetable, a plant, a food, a Kentucky mountain distillate, or old-fashioned music? Perspicacious editing can obviate some of these problems, but in the end, the editor must still decide whether, for instance, to classify corn as a vegetable, a natural object, or a food. For this and other reasons, we decided not to commit our research immediately to an established computer program, since computers can immediately produce file cabinets of error rather than merely a wastebasket or so of mistakes. Therefore, for some months we hand coded a small number of songs, using the Santa Fe dictionary, furnished by Colby, as our starting point (Colby and Spencer, 1967).

In the beginning, only six songs were analyzed, one each from Navaho, Acoma, Uvea, Japanese, U.S. southern white (hereafter called "Kentucky"), and southern Negro. Significant differences and similarities in these first profiles were immediately apparent. The Navaho song text resembled that of Acoma alone; the two American English-language songs seemed very similar to each other, and polar to the Indian songs; Uvea and Japan stood somewhere between. We found that the number of coding categories (74) often exceeded the number of concepts contained in any one song. Furthermore, the placement of a great many words remained doubtful because there were so many bordeline cases of choice between concepts. For this reason, we decided to reduce the number of concepts composing the system. This simplification emerged after considerable experimentation with the song texts themselves and the dictionary was judged adequate largely when it produced clear and interesting distances among the six songs. In its final form, it represents Colby's approach, considerably modified in conference by Arensberg, Halifax (who did the actual coding), and Lomax. The 74 main categories, together with their 184 sub-categories, were boiled down to 22 in the Concept Classifier that emerged from this phase of the work (Fig. 72).

The dictionary was tested on a larger collection of songs: 3 Navaho songs (one of them a cycle of 9 one-line songs), 5 Uvea songs, 3 Japanese songs, 3 traditional Kentucky mountain ballads, and 3 American Negro songs. The size of the sample was, of course, limited by the exigencies of hand coding. Research experience in cantometrics, however, had indicated that only a small number of songs per culture was necessary to define culture differences, provided that the songs were typical and long-popular in the given tradition. Study of the five traditions from which the songs were drawn indicates that all those chosen were both typical and popular.

1) TIME-BEING
04- aspect
07- attitude
09- being
21- doing, done
69- time

2) THE UNIVERSE
33- Greek elements
66- sky, weather

3) ORIENTATION &
      SEQUENCE
55.1,3- position

4) SENSORY
49- observe
62- taste, color
67.1,3- hear, sound

5) ACTION & MOVEMENT
32- go
41.1,3- kinesthetic
43- movement
55.2- action deter-
      mining a position
72- travel

6) WANT, GET, PRO-
      CURE, RETAIN
30- get, want
59- retain
01- ask

7) COGNITIVE
11- cause
14- if, know
29- general
37- identify
38- interrogative

8) OBJECTIVE WORLD
46- natural objects
48- artifacts
[53.1,3- natural place

9) DIMENSIONS
26- form
57- quantity (general)
58- quantity (specific)
65- size

10) FAMILY
12- children
36- home
39- kin
40- kin

11) COMMUNITY
16.1,2- community
51- person, selves
52- person, others
53.2- social place

12) COMMUNICATION
15- communicate
41.2- dance
67.2- music

13) SOCIAL POSITIVE
01- affection
05- assist
08- beautiful
24- efficacy
25.1- positive
      evaluation
31- give
35.1- health
45- right way
54- pleasure

14) SOCIAL NEGATIVE
02- anger
06- attack
18- death
19- destruction
20- difficulty
25.2- negative
      evaluation
35.2- sickness
44- negative
61- sad
70.1- tired
73- withdraw

15) AGE
34.3- comparative age

16) STATUS
68- status reaction

17) ROLE
60- role

18) WORK
74- work

19) BODY
10- body parts
13- clothing
23- eat, drink
27- Freud, anal, oral
70.2,3- asleep, awake

20) SEX
28- Freud, male, female
34.1,2- birth, growth
42- marriage
63- female
64- male

21) EGO
16.3- alone
50- person-self

22) DOMINATION
22- domination

Fig. 72. Categories of word types (revised from Colby, unpublished).

The total number of words in the collection comes to somewhat over 2,000. The coding process and the statistical methods used go back to a null hypothesis basic to the General Inquirer System: that under random conditions, any word, and thus category, can appear with any frequency in any context. If, then, the frequency of any given category in a given culture is notably higher than the frequency of the same category in other cultures, one may conclude that the item points to a special focus of interest in the concept or field represented by it. When the raw scores (word counts) were completed in every category for every song, each word count was expressed as a percentage of the total number of words per song. A mean percentage figure for each category was obtained by adding the percentage scores for all words coded in that category. Thus, six profiles were produced and compared for the sum of their similarities.

CONCEPT PROFILE SIMILARITIES

The summative similarity scoring system, devised by Berkowitz, is based on the notion of conjoint distribution (Chapter 4). Consider the example in which two texts, A and B, are to be compared in terms of a set of 10 categories into which all their words fall. Ten percent of the words in Text A and 15 percent of the words in Text B fall in Category 1. Then, since Category 1 occupies 10 percent of the textual space in both A and B, the two texts are held to be 10 percent similar in respect to this category. A like conjoint score is derived for all 10 categories. The total of these 10 scores gives the total conjoint similarity for the two texts. In like manner, conjoint similarities are calculated for all other pairs of texts (C, D . . . N) in the sample. A table of all these figures will present the relative distances among all members of A—N.

Table 61, compiled in this manner, shows the relative distance of the six sets of songs from each other. This table was calculated by adding and taking

Table 61. *Similarity table for six sets of songs in terms of the concept profile per culture.*

	Navaho	Acoma	Uvea	Japan	U.S. Negro	Kentucky	No. of words
Navaho		.51	.47	.59	.44	.47	379
Acoma	.51		.66	.57	.61	.60	206
Uvea	.47	.66		.69	.68	.66	202
Japan	.59	.57	.69		.64	.68	186
U.S. Negro	.44	.61	.68	.64		.77	507
Kentucky	.47	.60	.66	.68	.77		562
					Total number of words		2,042

the percentage of the raw scores across each category in a cultural sample. In essence, this approach regards each text sample as though it were one long song.

Considered in this way, it appears that, as analyzed by the 22-category dictionary, the concept profiles of all cultures in this set are at least 44 percent alike in the content of their song texts. This figure would not be interesting if we had not arrived at about the same score in comparing the cantometric profiles of the 2,557 song performances from the 233 cultures we have matched with the *Ethnographic Atlas*. The low scores for similarity between cantometric profiles average approximately 40 percent.

Table 62 is composed of the same similarities arranged in order of rank. The midpoint of similarity of this set is about 61 percent. If only those scores lying above the midpoint are regarded as positive indications of similarity, the following statements can be made:

1. Navaho is dissimilar from the other five cultures.
2. Acoma is most similar to Uvea and has a borderline similarity to U.S. Negro.
3. Uvea is most similar to Japan and U.S. Negro and is somewhat similar to Acoma and Kentucky.

Table 62. *Rank order of similarity scores, compiled from Table 61.*

	Navaho (N)	Acoma (A)	Uvea (U)	Japan (J)	U.S. Negro (USN)	Kentucky (K)
					K–77	USN–77
			J–69	U–69		
			USN–68	K–68	U–68	J–68
			A–66			
		U–66	K–66			U–66
				USN–64	J–64	
Midpoint		USN–61			A–61	
		K–60				A–60
	J–59			N–59		
		J–57		A–57		
	A–51	N–51				
	U–47					
	K–47		N–47			N–47
	USN–44				N–44	

4. Japan is most similar to Uvea and Kentucky and somewhat similar to U.S. Negro.

5. U.S. Negro is highly similar to Kentucky, quite similar to Uvea, less similar to Japan, and barely similar to Acoma.

6. Kentucky is highly similar to U.S. Negro, quite similar to Japan, and fairly similar to Uvea.

These relative measures of distance correspond in some respects to one's impressions of overall resemblances and connections of the six cultures. The system does make a pair of Kentucky and U.S. Southern Negro folk cultures, which are in fact a product of the same region, were shaped by the same major cultural heritage (northwestern Europe), and therefore should logically be most similar. This strong similarity emerges in spite of the striking divergence of the two sets of songs: Kentucky—*Hangman's Tree, Farmer's Curst Wife, Streets of Laredo* (all ballads); Negro—*Swing Low, Sweet Chariot* (spiritual), *Po' Laz'us* (prison ballad), *Whoa Buck* (field work song). A folklorist is struck by the contrasts between these songs in theme, in subject, in style, and in mood. Here concept analysis shows its usefulness as a tool in cross-cultural comparison.

Uvea, Japanese, and the two U.S. cultures are all decidedly more complex technologically than Navaho and Acoma and might be expected to be similar to each other, as, in fact, they are. The Amerindian pair seems unrelated to the rest of the sample. Table 62 has one serious flaw, however. Navaho is listed as most similar to Japan, instead of to nearby and culturally similar Acoma. For this reason, we tried another tack, computing another set of scores where the raw percentages for each category were computed song by song rather than over the cultural samples. These scores were

Table 63. *Relative frequency of each concept category per culture.*

The high scores in each category are italicized. The high scores for each culture form a distinctive profile that contrastively, at least, presents a formative world-view. Sex and Domination, as scored here, form two little complexity scales.

	Navaho	Acoma	Uvea	Japan	U.S. Negro	Kentucky
1. Time-being	.20	.13	.13	.16	.07	.06
2. The universe	.04	.14	.04	.01	.003	.003
3. Orientation and sequence	.06	.10	.03	.02	.06	.03
4. Sensory	.03	.03	.01	.02	.01	.04
5. Action and movement	.04	.07	.21	.06	.16	.10
6. Want, get, procure, retain	0	.004	.02	.02	.002	.04
7. Cognitive	.03	.04	.02	.03	.04	.03
8. Objective world	.04	.12	.13	.17	.10	.06
9. Dimensions	.03	.01	.02	.05	.03	.03
10. Family	.05	.04	.02	0	.02	.02
11. Community	.08	.07	.05	.04	.09	.09
12. Communication	.14	.10	.02	.04	.03	.03
13. Social positive	.17	.03	.03	.07	.05	.03
14. Social negative	0	.01	.03	.14	.08	.07
15. Age	0	.004	0	.02	.01	.03
16. Status	0	0	.04	0	.002	0
17. Role	.01	.04	.07	.02	.07	.04
18. Work	0	.03	.006	.007	.01	.002
19. Body	.05	.002	.04	.03	.01	.02
20. Sex	0	.02	.04	.05	.06	.07
21. Ego	.06	.02	.05	.06	.09	.14
22. Domination	.007	.008	0	.02	.02	.09

then averaged by category. In this way, the effect of each song's special contribution to the final score is reflected in each profile. Table 63 gives these six profiles.

The results of similarity comparison scores computed from this table are presented in Table 64. In general the results outlined in this table resemble those that appeared in Table 61: (a) the minimum similarity score is high—50 percent; and (b) the distance between the highest and lowest scores is about 30 percent. There are two important changes: Navaho scores as most similar to Acoma, just at the midpoint; and Acoma shows up as equally similar to the other two simpler cultures, Navaho and Uvea.

Table 64, in which the influence of each song is more clearly felt, appears, then, to be an improvement of Table 62. Two additional reasons influenced our decision to work with this table, rather than with the first: (a) a song is a unit of communication with an overall message of some kind, with an internal unity and order that relates (how, we do not yet understand) its congeries of concepts; (b) it turns out that, at least with texts of clearcut similarity, the General Inquirer technique is extremely efficient at the level of the individual song. Comparing all songs in our sample to each other, the

Table 64. *Similarity table for six sets of songs:*
cultural averages of profiles per song.

	Navaho	Acoma	Uvea	Japan	U.S. Negro	Kentucky
Navaho		.66	.55	.61	.55	.52
Acoma	.66		.66	.61	.63	.55
Uvea	.55	.66		.69	.74	.63
Japan	.61	.61	.69		.70	.67
U.S. Negro	.55	.63	.74	.70		.80
Kentucky	.52	.55	.63	.67	.80	

most similar pair were two versions of the same British-American ballad, *The Farmer's Curst Wife* (score—92 percent). The rank order of similarities between the sets of song texts in the six cultures appears in Table 65.

These measures of textual likeness scale in a way that corresponds to the overall similarities of the cultures themselves, especially if the concept of complexity is considered (Table 66). Navaho and Acoma, both Amerindian and both comparatively simple, form a distinct cluster. The similarity of Uvea and U.S. Negro is reminiscent of the links between Africa and Polynesia on cantometric charts. Japan is tied to the more complex cultures but is not close to any of them. The two U.S. cultures increase in similarity. A field of pertinent data drawn from the *Ethnographic Atlas* shows that this range of distances corresponds to the position of these cultures along a scale of complexity. (Since no coded data were available for Uvea, the ratings for nearby Fiji were used for illustrative purposes.)

If the factors listed in the column headings of Table 66 are considered, the six cultures may be arranged in a complexity scale as follows: (1) Navaho, (2) Acoma, (3) Uvea (Fiji), (4) Japan, (5) U.S. Negro, and (6) Kentucky. This order matches the sets of distances between the concept profiles of these cultures.

Table 65. *Rank order table of similarity scores derived from Table 64.*

Navaho	Acoma	Uvea	Japan	U.S. Negro	Kentucky
				K-.80	USN-.80
		USN-.74		U-.74	
			USN-.70	J-.70	
		J-.69	U-.69		
			K-.67		J-.67
	N-.66				
Midpoint--A-.66---	U-.66------A-.66			--------------------------------Midpoint	

Table 66. *Social complexity ratings for the six cultures.*

	Main production type	Type settlement	Size settlement	Number extra-local hierarchies
Navaho	Incipient producer (IP)	Semi-sedentary	200–399	0
Acoma	Incipient producer (IP)	Village	1,000–3,000	0
Uvea	Horticulture with fishing (HF)	Village	50–90	2
Japan	Irrigation agriculture (IR)	Complex	50,000	4
U.S. Negro	Plow agriculture (PA)	Complex	50,000	4
Kentucky	Plow agriculture (PA)	Complex	50,000	3

Another measure relating to complexity may now be considered. The average number of concept categories per song per culture is a measure of concept density. We do not believe that the size of our collection materially affects the issue. The most complex, the longest, and the most representative songs, were drawn from each collection. Table 67 presents, in order of rank, the density measures derived for the six cultures.

Table 67. *Concept density per culture.*

	Total number categories	Total number songs	Average number of categories per song
Navaho	40	11	3+
Acoma	48	5	9+
Uvea	55	5	11
Japan	39	3	13
U.S. Negro	54	3	18
Kentucky	55	3	18+

It seems unlikely that, even if the sample had been larger, this scale would have been affected, except possibly in the Kentucky-U.S. Negro comparison. Many Navaho and Acoma songs consist largely or entirely of nonsense syllables. Nine of the eleven Navaho examples (McAllester, 1954) are connected elements in a two-line Sway Dance song series. The simplest of these brief songs consists of one word: Hello, hello, hello. . . . In Table 67 each song is considered as a separate unit. The likelihood is that if a large number of Navaho songs had been processed, the average number of concept categories per song score would have remained very low, although we have not tested this hypothesis on any of the long night chants.

Uveans, although they sing long complex songs, have many one- or two-line lyrics. Japanese songs often are like small imagist poems, brief but concept-crammed, and the longer texts tend to be fairly repetitious. Southern Negro folk songs are far more brief and repetitious than the songs of Kentucky mountaineers. If more Negro and Kentucky songs had been coded, the Kentucky score probably would have been higher than the Negro. It appears, in general, that the scale of density scores devised from textual analysis compares favorably with other measures of complexity applied to the same cultural set.

This density measure becomes more interesting when it is related to one of our most basic cantometric complexity indicators—text wordiness, or the relative variety of syllabic material per sung line (Line 10). In Table 68

Table 68. *Concept density and wordiness of text.*

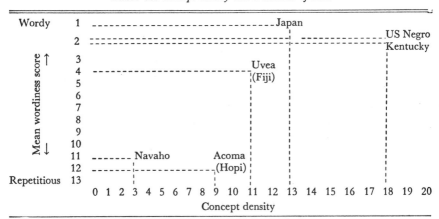

we have cross-tabulated the six cultures, on the ordinate by mean sample score for text wordiness and on the abscissa by concept density. Two substitutions were required: Hopi for Acoma and Fiji for Uvea. These substitutions can be accepted as legitimate because the ratings for wordiness are virtually identical for all Pueblo cultures and for all Western Polynesian cultures in our sample. The correlation between the two measures is obviously strong, offering additional evidence that social complexity is expressed with mutual reinforcement at many levels of the sung communication. In other words, the degree of verbosity and the variety of countable concepts in song texts tend to vary directly and in the same way with the level of productive complexity.

Before proceeding to discuss other complexity indicators, it must be pointed out that some form of musical complexity may occur at every level of social and technological development. Complex vocal polyphony and polyrhythm are, for example, far more common among primitive gatherers than among other groups. The melodic forms common to most Amerindian hunters are larger and more complexly organized than the most common melodic types found in the villages of Western Europe. Such examples could be multiplied indefinitely, but, without going further, it must be stated categorically that the simple-to-complex scale, used throughout this article, cannot be thought of as a measure of increasing musical or aesthetic complexity. It is, however, useful in showing how certain traits of song composition shift in relation to cultural differentials familiar to ethnologists.

CONCEPT FOCUS AND CULTURE PATTERN

Another measure of social complexity, which is also a measure of social difference, may now be derived from the textual material of this study. If the categories in each song sample are rank ordered by relative frequency and profiled, it can be seen that activity is more evenly distributed across the profiles of the more complex cultures—in other words, that profile smoothness increases with complexity (Table 69).

We measured the comparative smoothness of the six profiles by counting the number of categories required to fill approximately 50 and 60 percent of the category space per culture. From this calculation, a table of profile smoothness emerges which conforms to previous complexity measurements (Table 70). It indicates that the simpler the culture, the fewer concepts are found in its principal concept space and, conversely, in more complex cultures, more concepts are required to fill the principal song concept space.

The categories that fill the principal concept space of each song sample serve to differentiate and to define each culture. This idea is illustrated in Table 71, where the reader will find a list of the concepts with which each culture fills up 50 or 60 percent of its concept space.

Each of the categories is listed in the order of its numerical importance within a sample. Where two categories have the same percentile score, as in the Uvea and Kentucky sets, both are given. A reexamination of the texts shows that each of these principal concept sets defines the main statements and the most frequent concerns expressed in the song texts. The Navaho songs particularize very little; they state, for example, that the sound of the ceremonial drum calling people together is a fine thing, and that some experience is beautiful or pleasant. The Acoma singer is also concerned with continuity, but in a far more specific way; he is concerned with bringing rain from the sky to the cornfields through prayers addressed to the rain gods at the four cardinal points. In the complex poems of Uvea, lineage

Table 69. *Rank ordered frequency of concept category by culture.*

Navaho		Acoma		Uvea	
Time	20	Universe	14	Movement	21
Social positive	17	Time	13	Time	13
Communication	14	Objective world	12	Objective world	13
Community	08	Orientation	10	Role	07
Orientation	06	Communication	10	Community	05
Ego	06	Movement	07	Ego	05
Family	05	Community	07	Universe	04
Body	05	Cognition	04	Status	04
Universe	04	Family	04	Body	04
Movement	04	Role	04	Sex	04
Objective world	04	Sensory	03	Orientation	03
Sensory	03	Social positive	03	Social positive	03
Cognition	03	Work	03	Social negative	03
Dimension	03	Sex	02	Want	02
Role	01	Ego	02	Cognition	02
Domination	007	Dimension	01	Dimension	02
		Social negative	01	Family	02
		Domination	.008	Communication	02
		Want	004	Sensory	01
		Age	004	Work	006
		Body	002		

Japan		U.S. Negro		Kentucky	
Objective world	17	Movement	16	Ego	14
Time	16	Objective world	10	Movement	10
Social negative	14	Community	09	Community	09
Social positive	07	Ego	09	Domination	09
Movement	06	Social negative	08	Social negative	07
Ego	06	Time	07	Sex	07
Dimension	05	Role	07	Time	06
Sex	05	Orientation	06	Objective world	06
Community	04	Sex	06	Sensory	04
Communication	04	Social positive	05	Want	04
Cognition	03	Cognition	04	Role	04
Body	03	Dimension	03	Orientation	03
Orientation	02	Communication	03	Cognition	03
Sensory	02	Family	02	Dimension	03
Want	02	Domination	02	Communication	03
Age	02	Sensory	01	Social positive	03
Role	02	Age	01	Age	03
Domination	02	Work	01	Family	02
Universe	01	Body	01	Body	02
Work	007	Universe	003	Universe	003
		Want	002	Work	002
		Status	002		

Table 70. *Number of concepts in principal song concept space.*

	Navaho	Acoma	Uvea	Japan	U.S. Negro	Kentucky
The number of categories required to fill approximately 50% of category space	3	4	4	4	5	5
The number of categories required to fill approximately 60% of category space	4	5	5	5	6	7

chiefs and supernaturals change the face of nature and bring its goods to the human community. The Japanese songs deal with the manipulation of the world of objects, with food, with human products, and with their harmful and beneficial effects on people. The Negro is even more active in the real world, but, because he is in painful conflict with his social environment, he calls upon the supernatural to remove him to a more comfortable and egalitarian afterworld. Finally, in the British ballads that were the center of the Kentucky repertoire, the individual struggles singly against social evils, strives for power, and finds love and death closely entwined.

Table 71. *Rank order of principal concept categories.*

Navaho	Acoma	Uvea
Time	Universe	Movement
Social positive	Time	Time
Communication	Objective world	Objective world
		Role
Approx. 50 percent		
Community	Communication	Community
	or	Ego
	Orientation	
	or	
	Movement	
Approx. 60 percent		

Japan	U.S. Negro	Kentucky
Objective world	Movement	Ego
Time	Objective world	Movement
Social negative	Community	Community
Social positive	Ego	Domination
	Social negative	Social negative
Movement	Time	Sex
Ego		Objective world
		or
		Time

If our small collection of songs is good witness, complexity brings with it an ever-increasing concern with the world of objects, with particularization and individuation, with worldly power, with ownership, and with the problems and needs of the individual. As interest in controlling the natural and human environment emerges, so too does anxiety, a sense of evil, and of alienation.

Four concept categories seem generally to decrease in importance along this row of cultures.

1. *Time*—words of being and condition. There is a corresponding overall rise in the importance of words relating to movement, to action in or upon the environment.
2. *The Universe*—the sky, the earth, and the elements. A high for this category occurs only in Acoma. It represents the concern of these desert gardeners with rain, as they address their ritual chants to the four quarters of the heavens (orientation is high only in the Acoma sample).
3. *Communication*—speech, music, and the dance. For the Navaho, desert farmers and shepherds living in small family settlements, the main occasion for song is the ritual gathering, where the most important value seems to be the pleasure of communication in dance and music with their fellow tribesmen.
4. *Social Positive*—all concepts relating to the good, right, beautiful, healthy, powerful, and supportive. The principal concern of the Navaho seems to be to "accentuate the positive." Social negative does not occur once in their scores. One main object of their songs seems to be to minimize any sort of social conflict.

This relationship is presented in Figure 73.

If these categories are related, it might be surmised that one function of song among simpler, as contrasted to more complex, societies is to depict mankind, rather than individuals, in a somewhat passive but positive relationship to the natural and social environment. Lumped together, these scores form a "simplicity" scale that matches the complexity scale already cited:

Navaho	Acoma	Uvea	Japan	U.S. Negro	Kentucky
55	40	22	28	15	12

The songs of the Navaho and Acoma, the high scorers here, consist almost entirely of nonsense syllables. The function of nonsense syllables in song is, first of all, a means of producing consensus. All the singing group has to agree upon is that a certain series of verbal bits is pleasurable and appropriate. In this way any source of conflict or anxiety is kept out of the texts.

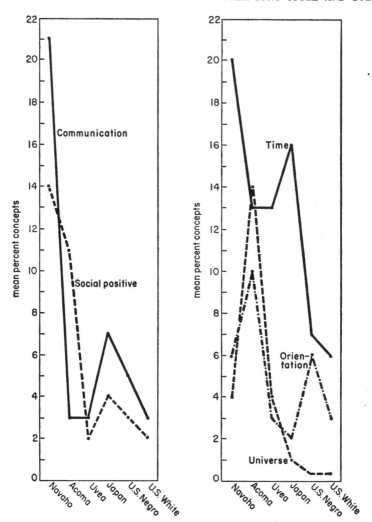

Fig. 73. Five concept categories which are more frequent among
simple than complex cultures.

Left: The categories of "Social Positive" and "Communication"
seem to be more frequent among the simpler members of this
culture sample.

Right: Concept words relating to time, to features of the material universe, and to orientation tend to decrease as cultures grow
more complex.

It looks very much as if these four simple categories occur in conjunction with non-explicitness and that both together may function for conflict reduction.

Nine categories generally tend to increase in importance along the complexity scale. Their various interrelationships appear in Figures 74 and 75.

In Figure 74 the provocative link between Objective World and Social Negative immediately strikes the imagination. It appears to be a correlate of several conjoined cultural features. First of all, it is related to the increasing degree of explicitness or specificity that seems to accompany increasing productive complexity. This relation was fully established in Chapter 6, but here it turns up as an increase of words that define the world of things. In this surprisingly tight correlation of Objective World and Social Negative, there seems to be confirmation of the old truism—that the more you have, the more you want, or in economic terms, that needs always increase more rapidly than the efficiency of the productive system in satisfying them. This factor of unattainable need brings with it a load of frustration, anxiety, and anger, which seems to be part of the tragic freight of all civilized societies. That this correlation may not be a necessary one is suggested by the manner in which the pair, Objective World and Social Negative, relate to two other variables—stratification and ownership.

This relationship suggests the explanatory hypothesis that a concern with the definition of the Objective World assumes a socially negative character in societies where an exclusive control is established over the world of things and human products by an elite, property-owning group or groups.

In Table 72, Murdock's ratings for five factors relating to level of local and

Table 72. *Stratification and ownership in six cultures.*

The material for these tables is excerpted from Murdock (1962–1967) Local Hierarchies (col. 32); Extra-Local Hierarchies (col. 33); Class (col. 67); Caste (col. 69); Inheritance of Land (col. 74); Primogeniture (col. 75).

	Navaho	Acoma	Uvea	Japan	U.S. Negro	Kentucky
1. No. of local hierarchies	3	4	3	3	2	2
2. No. of extra-local hierarchies	0	0	2	4	4	3
3. Class and caste	None	None	Wealth only	Both complex	Both complex	None
4. Inheritance of land	None	Equal between all heirs	Equal between all heirs	Patrilineal	Equal	Equal
5. Primogeniture	None	Equal	Equal	Primogeniture	Equal	Equal
6. Exclusivity of control	None	Little	Some	Total	Great	Considerable

extra-local government, to stratification, and to the exclusivity of the inheritance system are given. In Line 6 each culture is scored for its resultant probable level of *exclusive control over property*. Navaho and Acoma have low scores on the exclusivity scale; Uvea, with wealth distinctions and clan chiefs, has some exclusivity; Kentucky, with its high score for extra-local government, is rated as considerably exclusive; and the United States Negro, who certainly has lived beneath a complex class and caste system, has a high score. In Japan there is a system of totally exclusive control of real property through its inheritance by the first-born male, advantaged by a rigid system of stratification and backed up by strong centralized government.

This summary seems worthy of amplification. Among the Navaho there are no leaders, elite, or owners who control the disposition of property and there is, accordingly, no feeling of conflict over the real world and the products of human labor. The Acoma, with another level of local hierarchies, have clan chiefs, but their principal business is to lead the community observances that bring rain and food to all the people. Thus, a signal difference between Navaho and Acoma texts is a rise in the importance of the Role category. The principal role mentioned in the Navaho texts is Changing Mother, the mythical female creator of the Navaho universe. In the Acoma songs, the main roles cited are clan leaders and the Gods of the Rain and the Clouds, but exclusive control of productive resources is not an issue since land is equally divided among all the heirs of both sexes (Fig. 73).

The score of two for extra-local hierarchies in Western Polynesia (Table 72) signals the presence of hereditary lineage chiefs whose authority, however, is not based upon a stratification system nor upon exclusive control of the land. The system of lineage chiefs is frequently referred to in the song texts themselves, and their role is to distribute goods among the people and to direct them in joint enterprises for the benefit of the community. Uvea, too, has the highest score in the category of movement, an index of the dynamic relationship that Polynesians have to their physical and social environment (Fig. 74).

In Japan the Movement category falls sharply to the same level as in Acoma. Much of Japan's poetry, art, and dance reminds us of stopped motion, of still life, and frozen perfection. At the same time, the Object and Social Negative categories reach their highs in the Japanese songs we studied. Specificity (identification of everything in the outer environment) reaches its peak, along with Social Negative, the category that includes all words pertaining to prohibitions, withdrawal, difficulty, pain, punishment, conflict, illness, withdrawal, anger, and the like. Traditional Japanese society had an upper-class elite, a rigid caste system, four levels of government over the local level, and a system of exclusive inheritance of property by the eldest male in the father's line. Thus, the land, the products of human labor, and most

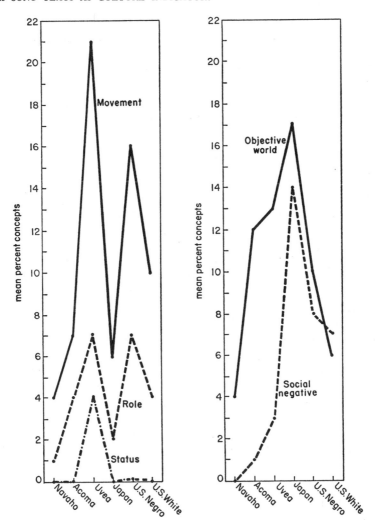

Fig. 74. Movement, role, status, Objective World, and Social
Negative along the six-culture scale.

Left: The songs of Uvea are shown to resemble those of the U.S.
Negro sample in status, social role, and dynamic movement.

Right: The relative frequency of words describing the Objective
World seems to vary with the frequency of concepts having to do
with pain, fear, rejection, and illness. The parallel becomes especially close in Japanese song texts.

of the real world were controlled by an elite or owned by the senior males. Control was denied to women, children, and the majority of males. Moreover, in this highly specific world every object and every feature of the landscape was carefully labeled because it belonged, usually, to someone else who was likely to be very powerful. These labels in effect said, "This is not to be touched; this area is not to be invaded without retribution."

In this world where the authority of elder, elite males limited access to the whole natural and human surround, the individual naturally felt despair as he repressed his anger. Meanwhile an atmosphere of still perfection was the ideal to be achieved. Not only is this true in the descriptive literature about Japanese culture, but it is vividly expressed in the concept load of Japanese peasant songs as the General Inquirer System analyzes them. The collection we consulted has many very bawdy songs, which we would have analyzed if we had found comparable material in the other collections. The theme of one of these, however, should be cited, since it so well illustrates the psychological consequences of the pattern we have discussed. The singer boasts through many verses about the feats, the length, and the size of "my penis," perhaps a compensatory statement for men whose freedom to act aggressively was limited to their own bodies.

In the Negro sample the categories pertaining to motion and to role and status rise together as do these same concept sets in the Uvean sample. This is the main link between these two genres, and here the similarity ends. The Negro scores for Social Negative and the Objective World are still close, though there has been a sharp drop-off from the Japanese pattern. The Negro moves through a society controlled by an elite upper caste of whites and, in the recent past, lived under a system of hereditary slavery. Although property was inherited equally, most of it was actually owned by the white elite. In his religious songs, therefore, he does not praise beneficent leaders, but appeals to a compassionate Lord to come and carry him away from this harsh world. In his secular ballads, his thoughts turn to violence. In his blues, ego rails against the unfaithful loved one and the isolation of a lonely, powerless, and deprived individual.

In the Kentucky songs, a new pattern appears. Although Objective World and Social Negative are still coupled and still important, this pair has been replaced by another set, Ego and Dominance. Stratification only distantly affected the Southern backwoodsman. The main theme of the songs (and tales) is that of Dick Whittington: the individual male (or female) facing life alone. This pattern is unique in our sample and is special to Ireland and the U.S. Southern backwoods. Its essential component, as scored by Murdock, is the smallest of families, living in widely dispersed settlements, where the males completely dominate productive activity and put a premium on virginity in their brides. There is great respect for age and for customs hal-

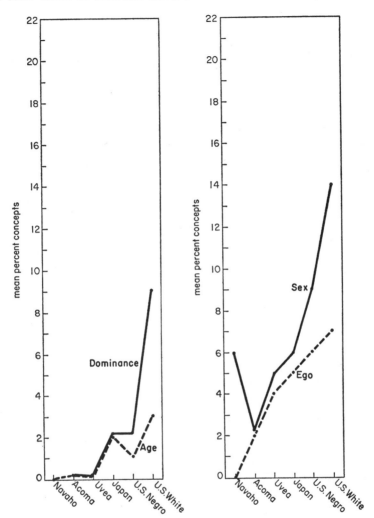

Fig. 75. Four concept categories that are more frequent among complex cultures. As cultures become more complex, they show a greater preoccupation with distinctions having to do with dominance, with age, with sexual differentiation, but especially with the ego. The strong pattern that ties sexual dominance and sexual conflict with alienation is illustrated.

lowed simply for being old; the Age category here reaches its peak in the sample. The main subject matter of songs is sexual conflict; love brings on illness or death. The ballads recount the dangers and difficulties that typically and uniquely beset the adolescent Westerner moving through the *rite de passage*—to find a mate and personal fulfillment in the small nuclear family, the only social institution in the system which provides security and an approved erotic outlet for the mature individual. A great many of the songs in this tradition are principally sung by women and they concern themselves with feminine anxieties surrounding marriage. This pattern is defined in the set of high scores unique to Kentucky: Ego, Dominance, Age, and Sex (Fig. 75).

The folk songs of northwestern Europe frequently deal with the issue of whether the individual will be able to satisfy his personal sexual needs and thus win a place for himself or herself in the adult community. This matter is less in doubt in most simpler non-European societies. Therefore, it may be surmised that the special function of these European songs was first, to prepare the individual for the almost inevitable disappointment consequent to staking his or her whole personal future on one overburdened relationship; and second, to reinforce the importance of the small family so that this institution, crucial to the survival of the culture, would have the unquestioning allegiance of everyone in the society.

The paired rise of Ego and Dominance corresponds to a correlation familiar to workers on the Cantometrics Project: the steady increase of solo-wordy songs with increasing social complexity. The concept here is that, as culture becomes more hierarchical, the singer enacts the role of exclusive dominance (a term of Arensberg's, first discussed by Lomax (1962) and then elsewhere in this volume).

The dominant leaders of complex societies must couch their instruction to their followers in precise terms. Thus we find an increase of text-laden, sharply enunciated songs and a resultant rise in wordy and precise explicitness (Table 73), as a concomitant of an increase in social complexity. It is

Table 73. *Explicitness, as defined by cantometric measures.*

	Wordy	Nonsense	Precise	Slurred	Explicit	Non-explicit
1. Navaho	0	100	60	40	0	100
2. Hopi (Acoma)	0	100	33	67	0	100
3. Fiji (Uvea)	45	55	82	18	45	55
4. U.S. Negro	82	18	36	64	36	64
5. Japan	91	9	80	20	80	20
6. Kentucky	80	20	100	0	80	20

notable that the two highest ranking cultures on the scale of explicitness are Japan and Kentucky, where single individuals emerge as powerful political leaders or military heroes.

Earlier it was demonstrated that specification in the world of objects goes hand in hand with increasing complexity and explicitness. Thus, we were led to develop an even richer index of specificity, bringing under this umbrella those concept categories having to do with the description of the cultural and personal as well as the physical environment. This highly denotative set was compiled from the word counts in the following categories:

8. *The Objective World:* animals, plants, minerals, features of the physical world, tools, cultural products (aside from clothing which was put into the Body set)

9. *Dimensions:* size, weight, form, quantity, both specific and general

17. *Role:* any attribution of age, except for kinship terms and children which were classified under Family

20. *Sex:* attributions on the basis of sex distinctions

21. *Ego:* I, me, mine, alone

The total activity in these categories yields an index of specificity that rises in an expected way along our little scale of simple to complex cultures.

	Navaho	Acoma	Uvea	Japan	Negro	Kentucky
Specificity Index:	2.3	4.5	5	6	6	6

Of the six elements in the specificity index, the category Sex shows the steadiest increase along the culture scale. Actually, the only entries in the Sex category are for occurrences of the words: *he, his, him, she, her, hers*—terms that divide up the world between the two sexes.

	Navaho	Acoma	Uvea	Japan	Negro	Kentucky
Percentage of Sex category:	0	2	4	5	6	7

The sharpened focus of specificity around the category Sex seems to have a connection with another general concomitant of increasing social complexity—the tendency toward a severe and punishing sexual code. In fact, Murdock (1964) has shown that there is a high correlation between the complexity of size of settlement and the severity of sexual sanctions. This correlation (Table 74) applies in a rough way to the present sample.

Table 74. *Size and settlement types in six cultures.*

	Navaho	Acoma	Uvea	Japan	U.S. Negro	Kentucky
Settlement type	Semi-sedentary	Village	Village	Complex	Complex	Neighborhood
Size of largest town	200–399	1,000–3,000	50–90	50,000	50,000	50,000

The stage is now set to offer another striking illustration of the primary hypothesis of this paper—that the function of song texts is to set forth and reinforce the principal interaction norms of a culture. It has already been observed that Kentuckians and, to some extent, all northwestern Europeans, live in a social web that is almost empty compared to the people of other cultures. The only institutional form within which individuals are trained to interact with each other diurnally throughout life is the small nuclear family. In such a family, in which exclusive dominance is split between the feminine or masculine sides, the most important distinction would be his or hers —especially since these cultures have a high index of specificity and have institutionalized private property. Therefore, an increase of Category 20, which deals with this distinction, should appear in complex societies, with small families living in isolation with clearcut male dominance. Table 75 indicates that such is indeed the case.

Table 75. *Song specificity index: Social factors relating to group affiliation.*

Line 2 from Murdock, cols. 30 & 31; Line 3 from Murdock, cols. 14 & 15; Line 4 from Murdock, cols. 19, 20, 21, 22, and from personal communication of C. Arensberg; Line 5, Murdock, cols. 52–62.

	Navaho	Acoma	Uvea	Japan	U.S. Negro	Kentucky
1. Specificity index	2.3	4.5	5	6	6	6
2. Settlement type	Small compact	Small compact	Small compact	Large compact	Large compact	Large scattered
3. Size of family	Small extended	Large extended	Small extended	Small extended nuclear	Small stem nuclear	Small independent nuclear
4. Other important lifelong associations	Clan Sibs Outfits	Clan Lineages Barrio Corvees	Clan Sibs Corvees	Hamlet Associations Guilds	Cults	None
5. Female participation in subsistence	Great	Some	Considerable	Considerable	Considerable	Little

This scaled data seems to match the demands of the model that has been sketched in our hypothesis and in the analysis of texts. In the three complex cultures an increasing preoccupation with interaction of males and females does appear in song texts, with a high in Kentucky. The pairing of love and death in the Kentucky texts would appear to be an outgrowth of extreme isolation and a conflict over dominance which the Kentuckian, of the six cultures discussed, experiences in its most extreme form. Preoccupation with sexual problems is reinforced when adherence to a severe sexual code is believed to be the concern of a masculine deity who intervenes in human affairs. This relationship is exhibited in Table 76, where Murdock's ratings for sexual sanctions are paralleled with his ratings for the relative involvement of

High Gods with human concerns. In Kentucky severe sexual standards are reinforced by supernatural concern.

Table 76. *Severity of sexual sanctions and supernatural reinforcement.*

Sexual codings from Murdock, col. 78, High Gods from Murdock, col. 34, which gives four ratings for High Gods: (0) none, (1) not involved with human affairs, (2) involved but not supportive of human morality, and (3) supportive of human morality (as derived from Swanson, 1960).

	Navaho	Acoma	Uvea	Japan	U.S. Negro	Kentucky
Severity of sexual sanctions	Sanctions	Permissive	Permissive	Severe	Permissive	Severe
High Gods	None	Uninvolved	Absent	Unconcerned with morality	Concerned with morality	Concerned with morality

A recent informal survey of folk song texts from many cultures indicates the essential correctness of the model suggested above. Love songs seem to be the major type in areas such as the Mediterranean and the Near and Far East, where sexual sanctions are severe and reinforced by religious sanctions. The sighing, yearning lover who feels that he is dying from his passion is rarely found among the simpler, less alienated cultures of the world, or at least has left few traces in traditional song. The Navaho singer refers to erotic experiences frequently but usually obliquely and always casually, as in Text No. 67 from McAllester's work (1954) where one song runs:

> Woman of Bare Ridge (Star Lake)
> Woman of Bare Ridge,
> Even though it is very far from your home country,
> Even though it is very hard,
> Let's go to the Place of Wild Onions, we two.

Burrows (1945), in his work on Uvean songs, remarks with wistful surprise that he found no serenades among the amorous Uveans, although he did observe that many texts were laden with erotic double entendre. Apparently in Uvea love songs are not sung, but when love becomes a matter of public concern, it is with bawdy reference, as in:

> Coconut shell stuck up in the pandanus crotch,
> Come daybreak, a rat has eaten it!

Many Japanese peasant songs are extremely erotic in content, with vivid references to sexual organs, but their overall import is frequently aggressive, hostile, or, as in the following instance, melancholy. Here, the parallel with the love songs of Europe, such as *Old Smokey,* is apparent, although the Japanese poem is more pain-filled.

> The ribs of the umbrella
> Have fallen apart;
> The paper is also torn,
> But with bamboo
> Tied together.
> Do not throw it away,
> Dear Rokuro
> Though I
> Also am torn,
> Don't desert me.
>
>   (Embree, 1944)

It appears that, if the General Inquirer technique is tactfully handled, folk song texts can typify the cultures from which they are drawn. The sample on which this idea has been tested is small, but the results are encouraging since the rewards have been great in relation to the time invested. During the next research phase of the Cantometrics Project, texts from a large and representative sample of world cultures will be analyzed, this time using the computer instead of hand counts, and with a somewhat redesigned dictionary of concepts. The aim of this research will now be not merely to demonstrate the special, diagnostic power of song texts among other communication media but to add a dynamic constituent to stylistic analysis.

Style analysis, in this first experimental phase, has shown that:

1. Song performance can characterize a culture in terms of basic structural elements such as complexity and subsistence level, political structure, stratification, complementarity, and sexual mores.
2. Dance performance looks at culture in terms of the dynamic components of its interaction patterns. It locates regions of comparative complexity and synchrony and differentiates these in terms of varying sets of movement qualities.

With textual analysis, however, one turns from these somewhat abstract aspects of culture to concrete, verbally stated themes which can give substance to the description of life style. In the texts one discovers what is valued or disdained, where pain and satisfaction lie; one finds some of the principal dimensions of the psychic constellation that bounds a sector of the human universe. The importance of each of these concepts in a culture is subject to verification, first by analyzing and comparing another sample of texts, and second by checking the independent data of the ethnographer for the behavior the concept profile reveals. In a very real sense such an empirical approach permits a culture to define itself. The coders and the computer operations record the relative frequency of certain classes of words and develop profiles of frequencies which may be compared cross-culturally. Each culture is viewed in terms of its relative position on a series of ranges where other cultures are evaluated. Each aspect of the classification bears the stamp of the intelligence it represents. Such descriptions, despite their built-in limitations, are likely to be genuine and close to the bone of cultural fact. In a sense, then, style analysis turns the task of developing a much-needed dynamic taxonomy of human things over to mankind itself—to the varied families of man, each of which has set forth its pattern of preferences, though sometimes cryptically, in its songs, tales, and traditions.

14

Cantometrics in Retrospect

Conrad M. Arensberg

It is heartening to see here the maturation of five years of intensively creative cooperation. It is rewarding to be able to look back over the discoveries
of Alan Lomax's lifelong search for the meaning of the world's folk songs.
This book is rightly Alan Lomax's, although the particular methods used in
song and dance analysis were co-creations. The meaning discovered lies
rightly in anthropology, in the study of human nature, human culture, and
comparative social life and civilization.

A collector with a wide and varied experience, a classifier, interpreter, and
organizer of folk song archives, Lomax has trained himself and us others to
seek out pattern and style in the many contents of culture, first in music but
soon far beyond it in ritual and ceremony, in communication, and now in
work, social life, and social organization. The search has led us into the many
nonmusical aspects of culture so variously evolved and formed by people
after people. We sought order and interconnections in the numerous and
varied cultural data; in the elements of music, sometimes unique and sometimes shared; and in the roster of human cultures from the simplest to the
most complex. We move in this statement from "him" to "us," for the book
also rightly belongs to the rest of us who worked together. The project led
us, in one way or another, through world ethnography, whose facts cultural
anthropology has at last begun to codify, systematize, order, and explain.

Science is never built single-handed. The path of discovery in this field
leads from musical performance to work and subsistence, from singing roles
to types of family, kinship, and settlement, from political orders to interpersonal and sexual relationships and child-rearing patterns. None of us knew
the whole range of these, but we did know many parts of the range. Furthermore, the cultural data—though not the music, for which the first compilation and classification yet carried out is reported here—had already been organized into compendiums incorporating the results of a hundred or more
years of field observation. These compendiums now make possible an empirical comparison of the ways of life of the peoples of all the continents,
ready to be matched against the musics they make. The most accessible of

300

these is the *Ethnographic Atlas,* a codification of the Human Relations Area File (HRAF), both the fruit of George Peter Murdock's work.

We were fortunate to have crucial guidance and encouragement in using the *Atlas* from Murdock himself, who is still at work, not at Yale but in Pittsburgh, and ever glad to assist other scholars in the use of his library and systematic classification of world culture data, now continuously in expansion at the hands of others. There is, of course, much current dispute in anthropology about the common rubrics (kind of datum, data-class) of culture, but there is also a growing agreement on the definition of many basic traits and institutions. For these there is no better compendium and no better classification of ethnographic materials than the HRAF. We had to rework many rubrics of the data back to the constituent behaviors making them up in the original ethnographer's descriptions. Still the rubrics for cultural materials the world over that HRAF uses and the classes into which they are grouped for cultural comparison seem, in overall terms, substantially correct, and have come to represent a fairly acceptable standardization of the terms of our science. As we have used them—grouped in scales or combined into indexes of behavior—they have emerged as taxonomic tools of a high order.

The book reports many questions, many answers, and many proofs of answers. They are addressed again and again to two great banks of data: the folk songs of the world and the customs of the peoples of the world. The project was a cooperative effort of many persons and many disciplines. It was empirical natural science, even if about human beings, in that both for song and for cultures and cultural behavioral questions were addressed to the whole recorded range of variant, naturally occurring data. Thus it was an empirical musicology, with our questions put not to an *a priori* theory of music, but to the real, reported variety of songs recorded on the spot. It was also empirical anthropolgy with pertinent questions put to the real and reported spectrum of all cultures and institutions, the universe of man's varied social and evolutionary experience. Subjective as musical feeling is, and personal as role and behavior in social life appear, now both the recognition and the identification of artistic performances and the comparison of culturally instituted behaviors are accomplished objectively in modern scientific observation of man and man's psyche and activity, without loss to his humanity or his genius. An understanding of art, of man's nature, and of his culture can be broadened, deepened, and quickened by uncovering the associations, the dependencies, the derivations which unite the various aspects of man's emergence and invention. Thus, our theme of song and culture is both anthropology and musicology, both the study of an art universal in human societies and the exploration of a universal part of human culture. In short it is expressive style, or the one characteristic occurrence of it found in song. It is a search for art's connections with the rest of culture.

The Cantometrics Project of folk songs and culture was cross-disciplinary, even though its primary subject matter was music. To establish the empirical ranges of known sung behavior and to apply these as measures to a world collection of song was to turn from interpretation and empathy to classification and codification; it was to look upon music as behavior, and to seek its distributions in relation to other behaviors: whether communicative, expressive, evocative, or operant. The project was cross-disciplinary in that musicology, ethnohistory, linguistics and ethnolinguistics, psychology, communications theory, sociology, cultural anthropology, and, of course, statistical method and computer mathematics all had a part in it. It was cross-fertilizing too; the ideas arranged against the data of anthropology and musical style came from many sources in these disciplines and from the many diversities of our professional experiences. The book identifies each source of idea and each support for it as it leads onward to new correlations and new insights, tests, and tables of proofs. What the book can only partially reflect, unfortunately, is the endless hours of devotion, discussion, and trial, the excitements of the search, the orchestration which Lomax provided, the sharing that genuine collaboration evoked.

These were full hours for all of us, each in his own way. As co-director, my own part was monitory and contributory, requiring a steady outpouring of knowledge of scientific method and of ethnographic detail of many peoples and places. This knowledge I was often happily surprised to discover I possessed and I was always delighted to find that it was seized upon avidly for further use, reworking, and elaboration. Perhaps I began with too little faith in scientific collaboration, too much experience of arid debate over definitions and proofs. There was nothing arid here, and teamwork had real meaning. What disciplined me, and shepherded us all, was our common object in the immensely rich and varied collection of folk music materials before us, the hard data of the rich and endlessly variegated folk musics, as performed by the tribes of mankind and recorded by scholars on high-fidelity apparatus. Here was a world of human cultural creation and variation that we must somehow explain; it was both intractable as fact and inspiring as art and human expression.

Here also stood the computer and the tapes, with which each idea could be quickly tried and each prediction about song quickly verified. It was for us all an exciting and rigorous research experience. The evocative power of the music of the so richly different peoples of the world was not lost on us, even if we had not collected all of it ourselves at the dance-ground or fireside. It stimulated the least musical among us to some feeling of the aesthetic force that animates both the native singers and the professional musicologists, who, by performing and recording these songs, celebrate the musical experience of mankind. But always the cold water of ethnographic and psychological analysis and the cool logic of the relentless computations held us down, quite properly, to the science we all practiced. The book reflects that animation and that restraint.

The good luck we met in our search for the meaning of musical performance in folk song form, primarily, but also in dance and song text seems a victory for social science. The discovery of so many detailed and significant correlations between musical performance and technical and social organization, spelled out in the book, is encouraging. It was a heartening demonstration of the power of the empirical classification of cultural materials which has grown up in ethnography, has reached codification in the work of Murdock, and gained further usefulness in many studies, not least in the work of Udy and Child. It was a vindication of the flexible and imaginative use of the computer and a reminder of the power and rigor of statistical method, as elaborated by Berkowitz and Erickson, who report it in Appendixes 1 and 2. We were aided here by Columbia's Bureau of Applied Social Research, whose director Alan Barton gave us unstinting support.

The faith that the committees of the National Institute of Mental Health showed in our use of social science with this new kind of cultural data in the collected tapes and dance films seems to us to have won its reward in the demonstration that strong and meaningful connections unite folk song and folk custom, music, and culture. We are confident of our identification of the many links that connect song in its various styles and complexities to the varied ways of winning livelihoods, ordering community and political structures, and structuring relationships among persons and between men and women. To have demonstrated that order exists in the welter of musical and cultural materials and connects the normative and the institutional on a worldwide scale seems to us to have taken a fair step forward. Of course we are subject to replication and corroboration, to refutation on the grounds of error and bias, or to verification and correction.

Nevertheless, we are confident that we have documented the interconnections we have found. Song performance is expressive art and its style springs from, is dependent upon, and takes its shape from the form of society. As societies differ in subsistence, in complexity, in male and female initiative, in ephemerality or stability of personal relationships, etc., so do the peoples of the cultures which organize such societies live different lives.

One of the central problems of social science and of ethnology (cultural and social anthropology), one of the central issues in the theory of the evolution of human culture has long been just this point upon which song and culture touch. That issue is the nature and function of symbols. In the scheme of interconnected behaviors that makes up an integrated human culture, the sentiments of one institution are often expressed, evoked, reaffirmed, and reinforced by the transfer of the associated symbolizations of its own sentiments to the contexts and situations of another institution. This phenomenon is a central mechanism in the theory of ritual and religion and a standard mechanism of politics, where the loftiest patriotism and the fairest justice are often linked, at least oratorically, to home and mother, to sweethearts and loved ones. Examples run, of course, from the sublime to the banal. The point here is that the symbolizing of emotional evocation is both contrived and spontaneous, both personal expression and the capture and quickening of audiences, wherever it occurs. The natural, human use of symbols is, as in language itself, ever varied and creative; every performance is necessarily a new event, but also necessarily an ordered statement within a prescribed and proper form. Transformational grammar, in modern anthropological linguistics, has shown us very clearly in recent years the dynamic emergence of new sentences in the rigidly structured regularities of utterance making up particular languages, where the form is predictable by the analyst but the always fresh creations of the speakers are not. In song and dance, too, as in ritual in general, form and creation alternate, and the connections of song and culture before us in this book may have something new to say about the nature of ritual and symbolic behavior in general.

The invention, elaboration, and use of symbols and symbolic behavior is widely held to be one of the critical, if not the most critical, mark of the emergence of human beings. With man, the brain emerged into new powers unmatched in the animal kingdom; and not least among the functions of the brain was the storing, the comparing, the equating, and the generalizing of experience which is mediated through symbols. Man's special creations of language, tools, arts, and rituals, all involve behavior with symbols and express his unique powers, to communicate, to stimulate and harness his own emotions, and to control his fellows through theirs. It is not usual to think of these last creations, of man's arts and rituals, as a storage, marshalling, and operation of enlarged powers. But a moment's reflection reminds us that in them, as in language and toolmaking, there lies the same cortical control of emotion, the same separation of immediate reaction and further purpose or reference, the same storing up for future use and newer purposes of information and skill as lie in the transmission of meaning or the designs of aid to technique. The difference lies in the subject matter. Arts and rituals do not so much apply the symbols of cognition and of technical application to the things and conditions of the external world as they apply the symbols that refer to man's own nature within, to his emotive processes, and to the evocation and control of these processes in other human beings.

What, then, is art, including song, if not symbolism? The songs, it turned out, were quite clearly related to the conditions and the organization of social life and of personal experience in it. It was wrong to think of the songs as only expressive. They were also very similar in form to the customs and institutions of culture and were not merely mnemonic reference to them. They seemed to evoke, not the actual behaviors of everyday life, but the models in terms of which everyday social activities are structured. We have learned that the significant connection of song with work was not that song directed work or that work fed the singers, but rather that song reflected work in the similarities of the roles of the persons common to their working and their singing. Thus if work, for example with hunters, emphasized the male role over the female role, then song did likewise.

It is in patterns, in style, then, that the connections lie. Song and non-song share such ways of behaving. Even the lustiest self-expresser is following prescribed and ordered patterns, takes part in recognizably ordered relationships, feels right in doing so, and wins his audience in their recognition of his doing as they do. Yet the result is music, however different the forms and tight the patterns, bound as they are to the institutional experience of his people.

We are bold enough, in the book, even to touch on evolutionary speculations. Many of the cantometric scales and the cultural comparisons treat worldwide correlations of levels of technical, social, and political organization. Like the evolution of culture, society, and technology, the evolution of the arts is not yet firmly known, or even adequately conjectured. Establishing a connection between the elaboration of human creativity in art with human accomplishment in the support and ordering of man's ever larger numbers and wider polities, has always been a necessary theme of culture history, prehistory, and anthropology. The evolution of both art and society does not merely involve gross correlations in necessary conditions and preconditions, of which a better understanding is steadily being won in biological and cultural science. It may also present these very coincidences in style and in shifts in the calibrations of the sung communication which we have discovered. The symbols of each stage of mankind seem to exhibit some common form with the things and institutions of each stage. What is art for a hunter is not art for an imperial court or for the atomic age, because the experiences to be symbolized are shaped so differently.

We know that art is born and renewed in ritual and ceremony, in the creation and reiteration of the symbols rousing fellow human beings. Art is not invented in lonely self-realization, as we are prone to think from modern experience. Song likewise was and is mostly public, though we sing to ourselves when we are off and away. In origin, on the male side, one can feel sure from the evidence of archeology and ethnography that when the elders or the shamen find game for the hunters or heal the sick, their evocation of the drama of crisis, their arousal of shared emotion, their heightened feeling and common decision in the first little human bands, must have been very early moments in the development of art, ritual, and politics. If the arts of music, dance, and drama have grown from the sounds and figures of ceremony, so have the masks of dancers and mummers and their symbolic body paints and facial smears grown into sculpture, painting, and the decorative arts, embellishing and transferring meaning and emotion to mundane things. The historian of culture can trace each art's evolution from the drama of religious rite and shared ecstasy to the specialized repetition and re-evocation of such values in feeling and meaning in lonelier, more private or more prosaic contexts. Perhaps all art is like Wordsworth's poetry, the dramatic emotion of ceremony and crisis ritual—the tone and consensus of public assembly and communal decision—formed and shaped and ordered to be "recollected in tranquillity."

Thus it seemed significant to all of us that when the Cantometrics Project put to work fruitful hypotheses from communication theory, it also came close to the secret of the nature of culture patterns, the role of symbols in culture, and the theory of ritual in anthropology. Song, it turned out, is very quickly and rigidly ordered behavior, yet, at the same time, expressive and evocative. Symbols, of course, are shorter and quicker than what they symbolize; they may share form with it, but they are more tightly structured. They are also manipulated at will to express, to evoke, and to direct. Durkheim, the pioneer French sociologist, had held symbols, his *representations collectives,* to be the elementary essential forms, first of religion, then of all human social life. In them he found the essence of what we now call human culture. These collective symbols, he insisted, were creations of man that, once created, existed external to him to stand for his experience, especially for his social experience of his volatile fellows, shaping and directing their experience anew. Leslie White, the American evolutionist or "culturologist," insisted that culture is the prime separator of men and animals in evolution, and insisted that culture was and is nothing more than symbolling. Nadel, the British social anthropologist who most advanced the theory of anthropology in his country, thought, too, that culture was central to man's way and referred it to the crystallization of "the recurrent regularities of the behavior of persons with and upon one another and in respect to one another." That is, it is essential to the ever-denser habits of a human social life more complex than that of any animals and to the symbols referring to such habits. Surely Durkheim, White, and Nadel, to name only three anthropologists, seemingly so different in their theories at first sight, were really all equally correct.

All art, but especially song, symbolizes behavior. Durkheim and Nadel agree that it is special behavior, formed like and performed "in respect to" other behaviors. It is even close to that special behavior Durkheim called "the sacred," which category of activity is known only to human beings; he defined it empirically as any possible object or condition of human activity distinguished only by its being additionally treated with a special emotional regard not accorded the profane. But it has other symbolic characteristics.

Song is quickly ordered. A cantometric style, Lomax and Grauer perceived, is established in the first few bars of any song. The key to symbolism lies in this. The ritual and the sacred are like song and dance in their rigid ordering, but less quickly formed and less quickly done. Both are expressive and evocative. But song is the shortest beat, the quickest establishment of form, the maximum regularization and evocation of the part for the whole. In the book we argue at length this summatory quality of song. The quality is essential in the symbolic statement of experience, and song seems the most summatory art of all.

The identification of pattern, form, short and long beat, behavioral regularity and recurrence, symbol and symbolized, style and culture, in short, most of the insights which paid off as ideas in our ordering of the two kinds of data, would not have been possible without the interactional theory with which we operated. Two things have been necessary for the application of scientific, operational method to ethnology and cultural anthropology. They have been long in coming. They are necessary in every science and are attained separately and uniquely in each historic science. These are capable of yielding such classifiers as the production scale: an empirical universal taxonomy and a method of definition and comparison of phenomena.

The first is a general and standard codification and classification of the real, recorded, variable data in efficient terms covering the cultural behavior of the peoples of the world. With such a standard classification as has marked the growth of the other natural sciences it is possible to work directly with the full range of real behavior rather than through suppositions and assumptions. Anthropology has always been distinguished among the social sciences in its kinship with and origin in natural history and biology. It has rightly insisted on the identification of the universals of human behavior and human culture and on the testing of generalizations across the worldwide and evolutionary variations of the human record. If we have learned anything about music, song, and man, it is because cantometrics has sought to ask not, what is music, but what are the musics of mankind? The cultural data and their distributions have also been equated with questions seeking an exhaustive empirical taxonomy of the culture traits or customs of all mankind, eventually to be compared to the systems that organize behavior and survival through all the biological phyla. The second requisite is less familiar. It is the operational method for the definition of phenomena. Although, as has already been suggested, this operational method is most appropriate to social and cultural data, anthropologists have not been greatly involved in developing it. We made good use of it in the Cantometrics Project, however. Without a strong commitment to operational definition of cultural data in the

universal operations appropriate to the description and comparison of behavior, we could not have hit upon the ideas for search through the compendiums of cultural data available to us for correlations with music, nor could
we have identified the elements of common form uniting song and the non-
expressive parts of culture. This approach was first suggested by Chapple and
Arensberg (Chapple and Arensberg, 1942; Arensberg, 1952) and later further advocated in anthropology by Nadel, and in sociology by Homans
(1950) and by Whyte (1961).

A valid operational definition of culture and culture pattern reduces them,
as Nadel insisted, to verifiable regularities of behavior of interpersonal
events. It specifies who did what was done, in what order, and in what frequencies. It checks asserted social and cultural phenomena with the ethnographer's record of what happened, who did what things, to and with whom,
and how often and in what recurrent or nonrecurrent circumstances. It turns
each rubric of cultural anthropology or sociology back into verifiable histories, personal acts, and utterances. Field work, natural history, and operational definition of our terms keep anthropology a natural science as well as
a human history. As our methods develop so will our understanding, and
with it our ability to place these data alongside those of the other sciences,
where watching and comparing sentient organisms, communicating nervous
systems, and complex ecosystems (of which man's are only the most complex) is slowly being cultivated into true knowledge.

APPENDIX 1

Data Systems and Programming

Norman Berkowitz

THE data bank of the Cantometrics Project contains about three-quarters of a million discrete items, distributed over eleven separate coding systems:

1. Cantometrics
2. Choreometrics
3. Phonotactics
4. Musical instruments, distributions
5. Instrumental ensembles, distributions
6. Length of musical segments
7. *Ethnographic Atlas*
8. *The World Ethnographic Sample*
9. Child-rearing (Barry, Child, and Bacon, 1957, 1959)
10. Work teams (Udy, 1959)
11. Miscellaneous information from Harvard School of Social Relations (Whiting, personal communication)

Operations on these data are manifold; some of the more common research needs include:

1. Comparison of attribute states and scale scores over cultures and other sampling units
2. Geographic mapping of specific attributes
3. Statistical tests of interattribute association and correlation between scaled variables, both within and between coding systems
4. Comparison and classification of multivariable style units (i.e., coding-frequency profiles).

For these and other operations on the data, a variety of output formats have been designed, with easily readable presentations, where possible with English word renderings of attributes, variables, and relationships. The more frequently used formats are described and illustrated in the following pages.

DATA ACCESS AND MANIPULATION: REDODATA

Most of the research operations demand the availability of any given item (or derivative thereof) in the bank, in the form either of a predicate or of a distribution variable. Frequent redefinition and transgeneration is also required. Data units must be grouped or logically combined, rescaled, made conditional for one another, or used arithmetically. To obviate the loss of time and programming effort that would be entailed in such preparation on a problem-by-problem basis, a special language, REDODATA, was developed, during the period November, 1965, to July, 1966, to facilitate the automatic and flexible redefinition and transgeneration of data.

The Interpreter is composed of a supervisor, a translator, and component subroutines, and accommodates about 150 transformations per run. A RE-DODATA program consists of a limited number of specifications controlling input-output options and system logic, followed by a series of Variable Definition Forms (VDF). Each Form produces a desired transgeneration. A VDF, in turn, consists of a sequence of free-form functions, of which there are nine different types. The syntax of a VDF corresponds closely to "Polish" notation—operator, then operands.

The following two VDFs will demonstrate something of both the semantics and the syntax of the language. The first example generates the percent frequency of the co-occurrence of either the literal three in variable six of data bank D or the literal TEXT in variable two of D and anything other than literal A in variable sixteen of bank K.

Card 1. F1 = PERCNT X 2
Card 2. X2 = EXIST (D6 (3) + D2(TEXT)) (− K16 (A))

The second example generates index or discrete states 1 or 3 : 1 if the expression enclosed within the first encountered parentheses is true; 3 if this expression is false and the expression within the third set of outer parentheses is true. Otherwise the literal 0 is returned. The STRING function (see Card 3) returns the percent frequency of the words enclosed by parentheses in the string of characters bounded by M6 and M50. The symbol F (Card 5) denotes the result of a separate VDF, while symbols U, M, and E are data bank names.

Card 1.   F4 = LOGIC (X1 GE 50.5 PL F2 GR 0 OR U16 EQ(DATE))
Card 2.C (   ) (X52 NE 0)
Card 3.   X1 = STRING M6 (HE, HIS, HIM) M50
Card 4.   X52 = (3.7*E6/X 4**3 − 7* (E4 + E9))
Card 5.   X4 = SQRT (F2)

The system allows for three forms of output. Given S subject size and T transgenerated variables, they are:

1. S x T structure in binary for predicate usage
2. S x T structure in BCD for generating table listings
3. T x S structure punched on cards (with identification number in columns 73–80) for vector usage as in SCATS, MAPPS, etc.

Description-Tabulation Programs

The bulk of the computer output can be described as specialized, highly formatted retrieval of portions of the stored information, many cases accompanied by statements of statistical relationship (e.g., gamma and chi-square). This general grouping of output formats includes the following:

1. Cross-tabulated plots, with relevant statistics (SCATS).
2. World geographic maps of trait distributions (MAPPS).
3. Profiles of song style and culture traits (PROFILES).
4. Ranked data state distributions (LINLIN).

SCATS

By far the most frequently used research tool, the cross-plotting program SCATS provides a test for correlation or association between scaled variables, ordered classes, and binary states. Program output consists of:

1. Pearson product-moment coefficient or rank order correlation for pairs of scaled or ordinal variables.
2. Up to nine versions of n-fold summary tables [1] with a maximum of 13 cells in either direction, each with associated chi-square and index of order association (gamma) (see Appendix 2 for definition).
3. A variable-sized scatterplot.
4. A mapping of subject identification in the perspective of the plot.

The scatterplot (Fig. 1) is determined by linear interpolation between computed maxima and minima and plot size. Axis scales follow largely from the specifications for summary tables. Means and variances for each discrete state are printed on the plot face or just below.

[1] Given a variable with a decimal distribution ranging from zero to some constant N, and another composed of, say, six qualitative states denoted by the mnemonics TOP, BOT, SID, MID, C, −O (one to three alpha-numeric characters apiece), then the following summary table cell specifications or "splits" are syntactically valid:
SID, BOT/C, −O/TOP/MID . . . MEDIAN
. . . QUINTILES (Blank fields indicate carryover of above ordering.)
SID/BOT, C/−O, TOP, MID . . . ZERO
. . . 20/50/150

The relationship displayed was given more immediate meaning when accompanied by the visual aid of subject identification in plot orientation (Fig. 2). The mapping results from minimizing the Figure 1 plot area, while coordinate location accuracy is maintained.

Overall specifications for SCATS include a population size of up to six hundred (which can be delimited at object time) and two hundred plots per run. The number of plots actually performed depends upon both the number of variables used once and the number used more often. Current limitations for each are forty.

```
      X-AXIS= PRODUCTION TYPE ' B ' - SCALED - X / IP / AH / PA / IR.        MU07

      Y-AXIS= PERCENT 2-PT. PRECISE.                                    CA37

              X                             PA
                     IP            AH                IR
        ++++++++++++++++++++++++++++++++++++++++++++++++++++++++++
        99.00+                2              1       3+ 100.00
        97.00+                                        + 98.99
        95.00+                                        + 96.99
        93.00+                                        + 94.99
        91.00+               1              1         + 92.99
        89.00+               3              1        2+ 90.99
        87.00+                                        + 88.99
        85.00+                                        + 86.99
        83.00+                                        + 84.99
        81.00+                                        + 82.99
        79.00+             2              1           + 80.99
        77.00+        1                                + 78.99
        75.00+                                        1+ 76.99
        73.00+                                        1+ 74.99
        71.00+                                        1+ 72.99
        69.00+               1              1        1+ 70.99
        67.00+               1                        + 68.99
        65.00+                                       XX+ 66.99
        63.00+                            1           + 64.99
        61.00+                            1           + 62.99
        59.00+                                       1+ 60.99
        57.00+                                        + 58.99
        55.00+                    1                   + 56.99
        53.00+                            1           + 54.99
        51.00+                            1           + 52.99
        49.00+                            2          1+ 50.99
        47.00+                            XX          + 48.99
        45.00+                            1           + 46.99
        43.00+                                        + 44.99
        41.00+                                        + 42.99
        39.00+                                       2+ 40.99
        37.00+ 1                                      + 38.99
        35.00+                                        + 36.99
        33.00+         1                    1         + 34.99
        31.00+                                        + 32.99
        29.00+ 1              4              1         + 30.99
        27.00+                                        + 28.99
        25.00+              2              1           + 26.99
        23.00+              XX                        1+ 24.99
        21.00+                                        + 22.99
        19.00+ 1            4              1           + 20.99
        17.00+ 2                                       + 18.99
        15.00+                                        + 16.99
        13.00+                                        + 14.99
        11.00+          2                              + 12.99
         9.00+ 1              7                        + 10.99
         7.00+ 1       XX     2              2         + 8.99
         5.00+XIX      1      1                        +  6.99
         3.00+ 1                                       + 4.99
         1.00+                                         + 2.99
         0.  +15       12     15             1         + 0.99
        ++++++++++++++++++++++++++++++++++++++++++++++++++++++++++
              X                             PA
                     IP            AH                IR
        MISSING CONTOUR MEANS FOR DISCRETE CATEGORIES ARE   6.33
        VARIANCE FOR DISCRETE ABCISSA CATEGORIES ARE  110.  375. 1099.  801.  895.
```

Figure 1, Appendix 1. Computer produced scatterplot. The label at the top describes the x and y axes, in this case the five-point subsistence scale, derived from Murdock, lines 7–11, and percent precise enunciation, derived from the cantometrics coding sheet, Line 37. The scatterplot field beneath the label is defined by the x axis in five points and by the y axis in percents. The number of cultures per coordinate position is indicated by a digit at that point. The mean percentage, per subsistence type, is indicated by a double x (XX). The variances for each point on the x axis are shown below.

```
        X-AXIS= PRODUCTION TYPE ' B ' - SCALED - X / IP / AH / PA / IR.              HU07

        Y-AXIS= PERCENT 2-PT. PRECISE.                                              CA37

            ++++++++++++++++++++++++++++++++++++++++++++++++
    99.0-101.0+                          401IBA     601FRU 305HAK
    99.0-101.0+                          414SAM            311MAL
    99.0-101.0+                                            311LAQ
    91.0- 93.0+                          413COO     605HIL
    89.0- 91.0+                          309GON 413MAN 627KUR 305JAP
    89.0- 91.0+                          409GIL            403BAL
    79.0- 81.0+                          303KIR 310HNQ 601DSS
    77.0- 79.0+          413MAO
    75.0- 77.0+
    71.0- 73.0+                                            611NME
    69.0- 71.0+                          409PAL     601CHE 613EQY
    67.0- 69.0+                                     632IND
    63.0- 65.0+                                     603HEB
    61.0- 63.0+                                     619AMH
    59.0- 61.0+                                            633KER
    55.0- 57.0+                          401HAN
    53.0- 55.0+                                     603WFR
    51.0- 53.0+                                     601SLO
    49.0- 51.0+                                     601BAS 311VIE
    49.0- 51.0+                                     603NOR
    45.0- 47.0+                                     607SIC
    39.0- 41.0+                                            303TUR
    39.0- 41.0+                                            613SHL
    37.0- 39.0+411MAN
    33.0- 35.0+          119CUN                      629TUR
    29.0- 31.0+405W.A                    105QUE 516BET 609AND
    29.0- 31.0+                          301YAK 615TUA
    25.0- 27.0+                          407MOT 501DOG 601DRA
    23.0- 25.0+                                            311BUR
    19.0- 21.0+301YUK                    402MUR 513BEM 607KIT
    19.0- 21.0+                          411CHO 621BED
    17.0- 19.0+207WAB 219ALA
    11.0- 13.0+          113NCA 203PAP
     9.0- 11.0+211KIO                    117GOA 515BAH
     9.0- 11.0+                          310PWO 516TAN
     9.0- 11.0+                          414TIK 519YOR
     9.0- 11.0+                          501MAL
     7.0-  9.0+211TET                    517BUL      307TIB
     7.0-  9.0+                          521SAL      601GEO
     5.0-  7.0+301AIN    205NAV          407MID
     3.0-  5.0+405N.A
    -1.0-  1.0+101ONA 213PAI 107JIV 206TAO 402VUN 511SOT 521SUS 611QUE
    -1.0-  1.0+107CON 213WAS 107CAM 206LAG 407DAN 515CHA
    -1.0-  1.0+115GUA 215POM 109CAM 207CRE 407ABE 517FUT
    -1.0-  1.0+115GUR 217HAI 113KRA 207YUC 411NAK 519TOM
    -1.0-  1.0+117MOT 217SAL 115YAR        503MAM 521CAR
    -1.0-  1.0+203SER 219CAR 119LAC        503SHI 603LAP
    -1.0-  1.0+211CRE 509BUS 119TZO        503MAY 617HAU
    -1.0-  1.0+213FLA    205MOH            511LOZ
            ++++++++++++++++++++++++++++++++++++++++++++++++
        X       X    IP   IP    AH     AH    PA    IR
        X       X    IP   IP    AH     AH    PA    IR
```

Figure 2, Appendix 1. Subject identification mapping. The position of each culture in relation to the scatterplot is indicated by an abbreviation of its tag name preceded by its regional and areal code number. Thus, the label in the lower left-hand corner of the mapping (213FLA) stands for *North American Indian, Great Basin, Flathead*. When more than one culture falls within a coordinate position, the computer expands that area of the mapping accordingly. See the lower, or zero, field above.

MAPPS

The MAPPS program presents trait distributions across world geography on a specially designed projection. The trait maps which are the output (Fig. 3) provide a quick visual check on hypotheses of historic and functional links between areas, as well as a measure of regional homogeneity on some specific attribute. Of the dozen mapping program options, those most frequently used by the staff are:

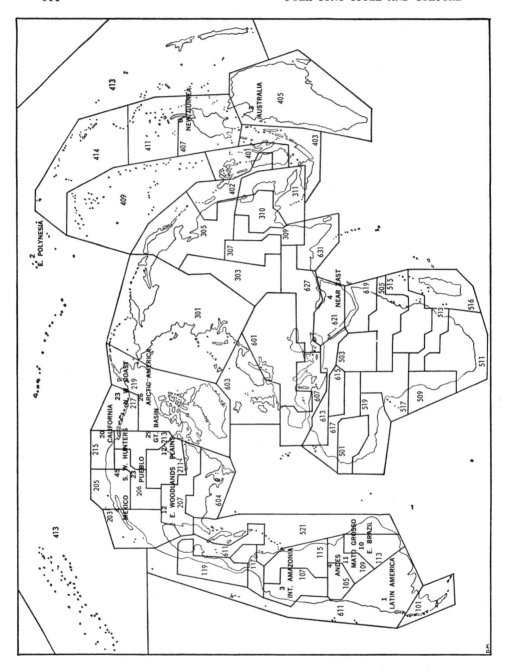

1. Joint mapping of up to three distributions for the purpose of determining associations.
2. Literal or median, quartile, or other lower bound criteria for partial mapping.
3. Substitution of English for ordinal states.
4. Mapping of culture or area names alone in cases of predicate subset definition.
5. Homogeneity maps (see Chapter 4).

An acetate overlay depicting rough geographic borders of masses and culture areas is used in conjunction with the computer-printed maps. The printout displayed in Figure 3 was reproduced with the overlay in place.

PROFILES

The principal researchers spent several thousand man-hours listening to and coding the song material and were anxious to confirm their fundamental hypothesis of homogeneity of song styles for world areas and cultural groups. The earliest developed computer program, CANTO PROFILES (see Appendix 3), provided the staff with two formats in which song data were presented for specified world areas or cultures. One profiling method mapped the percent frequencies of all coding states onto the format of the cantometrics coding sheet, with three to thirteen scale positions for the thirty-seven lines. The second mapped the states of primary, secondary, and tertiary importance per line onto a profile-like grid.

A similarly organized display summarizing grouped ethnographic data was developed next. CULT PROFILES output differs from the above format both in the number of activity states per variable and in the semantics of codes. Years of use gave the research staff immediate recall of the more than two hundred coding points in the cantometric system. This was not so for the ethnographic data. In place of codes, therefore, ten English characters for each state were mapped onto levels of a twenty-fold percent scale. The

---

Figure 3, Appendix 1. Computer mapping application. A special projection of the world was chosen which represented the relative size of the land masses and which centered the world so that lines of migration could be made vivid. The latitude and longitude for each culture and culture area was translated into the most accurate possible coordinates for the computer and the names of the 233 cultures and 56 areas were positioned over those locations. Slots for printing out statistics were left blank by each name. In the present case the computer compiled all the cases of "Simple Group" style and printed out the names of all the areas above the median on this type—an acephalous group, singing in unison, employing wide intervals, much repetition of text and a one-beat accompaniment. The computer map outlines the main Amerindian style area.

cultures in the grouping or population subset are listed in the right-hand margin of the profile.

LINLIN

From the study of song profiles, it became apparent that knowledge of particular cantometrics lines or activity states, cross-culturally, was required for style pattern assessments. Distribution range, modality, skewness, etc., are displayed in LINLIN (line-by-line) output. This system arrays sets of grouped subjects in rank orders according to the extent of an activity state and returns all complementary states for the variable under consideration.

For the first eighteen months the subject groupings referred to above were based entirely on geographic order. Since the middle of 1966, the above four retrieval models have been modified to enable REDODATA output to determine set membership.

CLASSIFICATION AIDS

Since the distributions of cantometric codings per sample unit (area or culture) were presumed to characterize styles, linked to each other in a pattern of historically and functionally determined similarities and contrasts, a system of numerical taxonomy was the next programming development.

A primary requisite in any taxonomic scheme is a standard of comparison —an index of similarity or of "distance" between units of classification. A search of the literature, especially Sokal and Sneath (1963), indicated that although similarity coefficients in one form or another (association, correlation or distance, for example) have been employed extensively, most of these are calculated on a binary data structure. Cantometric variables, in many cases scaled, cannot be reduced to this basis without loss of significant information.

Beginning with crude approximations, a similarity measure (see also Chapter 4) was designed and put in use by June, 1965. With few modifications it has been the basic unit in the cantometrics taxonomic system. For a set of discrete activity states, the measure reduces to the common area under two intersecting histograms (one for each taxon). In the case of scaled lines, where distance between coding states must enter the calculation, a series of positive corrections is made. Each of these is based on the product of an intra-weighting constant and the common area remaining from previous iterations while one function is held constant and the other is translated over a multiple of fixed units. Given, then, $f_{i,j,k}$ (where i runs over taxa, j over variables, and k over states per variable, and furthermore the condition that the sum over k for fixed i and j is constant) the similarity index is derived as:

$$S_{i_1 i_2} = \frac{1}{\left(\sum\limits_{j=1}^{v} w_j\right)} \sum_{j=1}^{v} w_j \sum_{r=0}^{n_j-1} \sum_{k=1}^{n_j-r} \sum_{\substack{a=-1 \\ (a \neq 0)}}^{1} (c_{j,k,k+ra}) \left(\text{minimum} \left({}_r f_{i_1,j,k}, {}_r f_{i_2,j,k+ra}\right)\right)$$

where ${}_0 f_{i,j,k} = f_{i,j,k}$

$\quad\quad {}_r f_{i,j,k} = {}_{r-1} f_{i,j,k} - \text{minimum} \left({}_{r-1} f_{i_1,j,k}, {}_{r-1} f_{i_2,j,k+ra}\right)$

$\quad\quad$ (W): variable weighting vector (for all similarities displayed in this book, a unit vector)

$\quad\quad$ (C): intra-line weighting matrix

TOTAL SIMILARITY

This index is an integral part of a program called TOTAL SIMILAR-ITY, which accommodates up to 233 taxa and a maximum of 100 variables, each with up to ten activity states. Output consists of:

1. Similarity matrix (S), rounded to the nearest integer, with rows and columns identified by subject name.
2. A graphic-ranked distribution of scores, called "similarity waves," with subject identification for each subject unit. The median of the distribution is used for the cutoff criterion unless a literal parameter is supplied.
3. A frequency distribution graph of all scores.
4. Optional preservation of (S) on tape in binary for further manipulations.

The program was recently modified to allow for a prescribed subset of the total subject population to be excerpted for calculation, with a resultant rectangular matrix. Part of a similarity wave can be seen on p. 79.

On a few lines a serious problem of classification is created by an extreme disproportion of world frequencies over attribute states. For example, orchestral rubato is absent in 86 percent of the world's songs. Because this trait is so rare transculturally its relative absence is taxonomically non-specific. In the original calculation of similarities all coding states, including those that are taxonomically inefficient, contributed equally to the total score. Therefore we devised a modification of the program input that would make the contribution of each attribute to the similarity score inversely proportional to its world frequency. This modification is derived as follows:

Given f_x as the frequency per subject of an activity state with, say, four complementary states, the modified frequency

$$f'_x = \frac{2f_x}{P_x + max\,(P_1, P_2, \ldots P_5)}, \text{ where } P_x \text{ is the worldwide frequency}$$

(or probability) of the activity state.

TOTAL SIMILARITY HOMOGENEITY ANALYSIS FOR .....THE 305 JAPAN VI CULTURE

CULTURE AREAS	TOTAL-D RK.NO.SIM	PC CULTURE/ SIMILARITY MEDIAN-D QUARTILE-D RK.NO.SIM RK.NO.SIM	REGIONAL-D 1/2 REG.-D RK.NO.SIM RK.NO.SIM	CULTURES
PATAGONIA...101	34 2	51 2 58	51 26 1 58	
ANDES...25	33 2	51 2 53		
INTERIOR AMAZONIA...107	35 2	53 3 55		
MATO GROSSO...109	27 3	53 20 56		
EASTERN BRAZIL...113	42 4	49 39 57		
GUIANA...115	22 4	44		
CARIBBEAN...117	51 2	52 21 2 56		
CENTRAL AMERICA...119	29 3	55 25 4 56		
MEXICO...203	29 7	55 22 2 58	17 1 59	
SOUTHWEST HUNTERS...205	19 3	50		
PUEBLO...206	36 4	52 40 1 55		
EASTERN WOODLANDS...207	31 4	57 1 57	20 1 62	
PLAINS...211	15 4	50 41 1 55		
GREAT BASIN...213	41 4	53 29 1 55		
CALIFORNIA...215	28 5	54 16 4 56		
NORTHWEST COAST...217	24 5	54 30 2 56		
ARCTIC AMERICA...219	23 5	50 42 2 56		
P-MALAY...402	18 4	50 34 2 57	13 1 67	(PAIWAN,)
NEW GUINEA...407	37 8	50 37 1 58		
MICRONESIA...409	14 4	62 3 75	14 1 74	(TURKMA))
MELANESIA...411	38 5	75 5 75	1 3 75	(HAKKA ,S KORE,AMAMI))
EASTERN POLYNESIA...413	40 5	72 5 72	2 2 72	(ITBET ,SHERPA))
WESTERN POLYNESIA...414 39	1 3	63 4 73	9 2 66	(MNONG ,LUA ,)
CENTRAL ASIA...303	13 4	67 5 73	3 5 73	(VIETNA,THAILA,MALAYA)BURMA ,LAOS ,)
EAST ASIA...305	12 6	67 8 67	4 3 76	(IBAN ,TAGBAN,)
HIMALAYAS...307	8 3	72 9 72	2 5 76	(BALI ,JAVASU,)
TRIBAL S.E.ASIA...310	4 4	64 10 70	5 1 70	(EGYPT))
URBAN S.E.ASIA...311	11 4	70 11 70	10 1 70	(TUAREG)KUNTA ,)
MALAY...401	9 2	66 12 66	11 1 72	(ANCHEB))
URBAN INDONESIA...403	3 7	72 9 72	6 4 72	(KURD ,TADJIK,TURKEY)PASHTU,)
NORTH AFRICA...613	7 3	70 10 70	7 3 70	(GONDOG)INDIA ,KERALA,)
SAHARA...615	50 4	44		
NEAR EAST...621 23	52 9	34 44 1 57		
MIDDLE EAST...627 29	49 7	44 45 1 55		
VILLAGE INDIA...631 32,3	47 6	46	16 1 69	(RUANDA,)
WESTERN SUDAN...501	21 6	55 38 2 54	22 1 66	
EASTERN SUDAN...503	43 6	49		
UPPER NILE...505	48 5	45		
AFRICAN HUNTERS...509	44 5	48 35 2 60	15 1 65	(FON ,)
SOUTH AFRICAN BANTU...511	46 7	46		
CENTRAL BANTU...513	26 6	54 32 3 59	17 1 67	(AMHARA,)
NORTHEAST BANTU...515	52 3	52 36 4 56		
MADAGASCAR...516	25 6	57 24 4 57		
EQUATORIAL BANTU...517	16 6	54 15 6 63		
GUINEA COAST...519	10 6	65 11 6 65	12 3 71 11 1 76	(ANDALU)SICILY,LEON ,)
AFRO-AMERICAN...521	9 7	55 19 5 58	4 60	

TISHA

As a first order of similarity clustering, several formats display score arrays in a manner that will permit the staff to estimate group order and relationship. Typical of these is TISHA (Total Similarity-Homogeneity Analysis) (Fig. 4).

For each of the 56 world areas, the number of member cultures with scores above the median and quartile of the subject's similarity distribution has been calculated; the same for criteria of regional size and half-regional size. Ranks based upon the ratio of these numbers to the total subject size are similarly presented. The names that appear in the right portion of the output represent the members that fall within the last two criteria. At the top of the illustration, mean figures for the subject culture's similarity to world regions for full, median, and quartile cutoffs are presented, along with the rank criterion of the percent frequency.

FORCING FACTORS

Another program, FORCING FACTORS (Fig. 5), indicates which parameters contribute most to the overall similarity between two subjects. When results from clustering are available, the program will serve to define the basic typology responsible for the relative homogeneity of the cluster style. Each variable's contribution to the similarity of pairs is presented in rank order along with the modal activity for one of the paired subjects.

Figure 4, Appendix 1. Total similarity homogeneity analysis (TISHA). The overall similarity of Japan to six regions is presented just below the label: on the left, to the entire distribution; in the middle of the page, to the top half of the distribution; and on the right, to a quarter of the distribution. . . . Under Total-D, the reader can find the position each culture area occupies in the rank order of overall similarity to Japan. Next to this is the number of cultures in each of the areas. Next appears the mean similarity in percentage terms. Thus, Patagonia is 34th in ranked similarity to Japan; it comprises 2 cultures; and its similarity is very low (51 percent). . . . Median-D repeats this same information for the relationship of the top half of the distribution to Japan. Quartile-D covers the same ground for the areas above the quartile in similarity to Japan. Regional-D and one-half Regional-D are means of finding what proportion of the members of Japan's world region fall in its similarity set. The computer runs down the rank order of similarity until it counts the number of cultures in Japan's world region. Then it prints out those names to the right. Regional-D looks at the whole regional number; one-half Regional-D looks at half. Double parentheses indicate cultures that appear in both lists; single parentheses, cultures that fall in only one.

SIMILARITY FORCING FACTOR ANALYSIS OF 521AFRO-AMER WITH 519GUINEA CO.

ONE VARIABLE SIMILARITY	521AFRO-AMER MODAL PERCNT	MODE	CUL.2 PERCNT	VAR. WEIGHT	VARIABLE TITLE
98 *********	88	MAXM'L	89	(1.0000)	S09) RHY. BLEND-O
98 *********	80	NONE	84	(1.0000)	S26) RUBATO-V
98 *********	71	ACCOMP	73	(1.0000)	39) ACCOMP.-UNACC
97 *********	82	UNISON	85	(1.0000)	R12) GROUP RHY.-V
97 *********	78	NONE	69	(1.0000)	S23) EMBELLISHMENT
96 *********	40	NO VAR	39	(1.0000)	R16) MEL. VAR.
96 *********	56	DIATON	52	(1.0000)	S21) INT.WIDTH
95 *********	61	MAXM'L	57	(1.0000)	S08) TONAL BLEND-O
95 *********	58	5-8	58	(1.0000)	20) RANGE
95 *********	48	MEDIUM	41	(1.0000)	S25) VOLUME
94 *********	39	WD-NON	39	(1.0000)	S10) WORDS TO NON.
94 *********	30	CN.POL	35	(1.0000)	R14) GROUP RHY.-O
94 *********	89	NONE	83	(1.0000)	31) GLOTTAL SH.
93 *********	61	GOOD	35	(1.0000)	S05) TONAL BLEND-V
93 *********	59	MAXM'L	45	(1.0000)	S06) RHY.BLEND-V
93 *********	59	POLY.	61	(1.0000)	R07) ORCH. ORG.
93 *********	81	CHORAL	89	(1.0000)	38) SOLO-CHORAL
92 *********	37	V. LOW	36	(1.0000)	S19) PCS.OF FINAL
92 *********	83	NONE	91	(1.0000)	30) TREMULO
91 *********	98	NONE	88	(1.0000)	S27) RUBATO-O
91 *********	48	NONE	19	(1.0000)	S28) GLISS
91 *********	53	NORMAL	36	(1.0000)	S36) ACCENT
90 *********	66	MEDIUM	52	(1.0000)	S24) TEMPO
89 *********	44	POLY.	54	(1.0000)	R04) VOCAL ORG.
87 *********	44	SHORT	50	(1.0000)	S17) PHRASE LENGTH
87 *********	95	ENSEMB	82	(1.0000)	40) SOLO -ENSEMBL
86 *********	68	SYMN.	54	(1.0000)	R18A)PHRASE SYMM.
85 *********	47	OV'LAP	36	(1.0000)	R01) VOCAL GROUP
83 *********	76	WIDE	47	(1.0000)	S33) VO. WIDTH
83 *********	57	INTERM	50	(1.0000)	S35) RASPINESS
82 *********	49	NORMAL	19	(1.0000)	S37) CONSUN.
81 *********	56	MIDDLE	65	(1.0000)	S32) REGISTER
81 *********	59	INTER	36	(1.0000)	S34) NASALITY
79 *********	60	INTL'K	38	(1.0000)	R02) ORCH.RELATION
78 *********	54	SIMPLE	58	(1.0000)	R03) ORCH. GROUP.
77 *********	53	SI.LIT	45	(1.0000)	R15B)MEL. FORM
74 *********	80	SIMPLE	52	(1.0000)	S13) OVERALL RHY-
74 *********	82	NONE	56	(1.0000)	29) MELISMA
72 *********	31	IC.	20	(1.0000)	22) PCL. TYPE
69 *********	52	2/.1/2	69	(1.0000)	R18) NO.OF PHRASES
67 *********	87	SIMPLE	46	(1.0000)	11) OVERALL RHY-V

Figure 5, Appendix 1. Similarity forcing factors output helps one to find which states on which parameters are responsible for the similarity of any two areas—in this case of the Guinea Coast performance profile to that of Afro-America. The first line tells the reader that cantometric Line 9 makes 98 percent of its possible contribution to the closeness of the two areas. This is partly to be explained by the fact that 88 percent of Afro-America and 89 percent of Guinea Coast performances are scored "maximal" for rhythmic blend in the orchestra. All the other statements on this page can be read in the same fashion.

FACTOR ANALYSIS OF Q–MATRICES

Experiments with factor analysis of Q-matrices have provided the basis for a formal taxonomy of styles. The coefficients entered in the cells of the matrix are product-moment correlations between standardized mean profiles. Notwithstanding the loss of information that results from the use of means as sole characterizers, the intercultural correlations present a pattern basically similar to that of the similarity scores, and the clusters defined by the factors seem generally consistent with those derived, though in smaller subsets, from the similarity waves and TISHA.

Author's Note: Programs for factor analysis and rotations (varimax and biquartimin) used in this investigation were taken from the Harvard Multivariate Statistical Analyzer (MSA) library, and were written by William W. Cooley, University of Pittsburgh; Paul R. Lohnes, University of Buffalo; and Kenneth J. Jones, Harvard Graduate School of Education (copyright, 1965, by the authors).

APPENDIX 2

Statistical Notes

Edwin E. Erickson

THE CANTOMETRICS CROSS–CULTURAL SAMPLE

IN THE search for associations between song styles and lifeways, the basic units of sampling were assemblages of generally not fewer than ten songs apiece, each presumed to represent the most frequent modes of public song performance style in a given society. The 233 source societies (listed at the end of Chapter 2) whose songs form the basic sample were chosen to satisfy three conditions:

1. Cultural distinctiveness: each group, whether autonomous (e.g., "tribal") or a subunit of some larger entity, such as a nation, is clearly the bearer of distinctive lifeways and traditions, and possesses a clear identity.
2. Inclusion in the *Ethnographic Atlas* or the existence of sufficient coverage in ethnographic descriptions to permit a full range of cultural codings in the format of the *Atlas* (many of the ratings were made by project staff and consultants).
3. Maximal worldwide coverage of culture types and singing styles.

Complete and balanced coverage of the total corpus of man's music was an impossible goal, given the present state of field collection of folk music and the absence of a world archive or even a central list of collections. A visit by Lomax to the Soviet Union brought in Siberian, Central Asian, Caucasian, and Russian samples. No material, however, became available for the Chinese area, little for Tribal India, and, in spite of considerable effort, South America, Mexico, and Oceania are not as well represented as other regions, such as Africa and Europe, where more recording has been done in recent years.

Thus, even 233 cultural samples, assembled from a total of 3,525 codings, cannot be taken as a completely balanced view of world song, at least in the sense of sampling balance expressed by Murdock (1966) —the even representation of large culture-historic regions. Nevertheless, two subsamples structured to approximate this criterion produced the same outlines of style geography. The boundaries of style regions and the relationships between

322

them were unchanged in both subsamples. Furthermore, nearly all the associations between song style and lifeways discovered in the main sample proved to be statistically significant in the corrected subsamples. This constancy encourages the belief that the Cantometrics archive has captured most of the important dimensions of world style variability.

The subsamples were drawn to control for two kinds of bias. The most obvious sources of statistical bias in any cross-cultural study are the inclusion of large clusters of historically related peoples and the overweighting of any specific regional set. In the first case, it could be argued that intertrait correlations were merely the artifacts of joint origins and diffusions, rather than the outcome of similar functions in culture; in the second case, not only is there the possibility of historical bias, but the averages and other parameters of comparison can be skewed to such an extent that the sample cultures are not being tested generally against each other so much as specifically against those in an over-sampled region. Given both the demonstrably broad geographic distributions of similarity and the apparent durability of song styles, complete control for historic biasing is obviously impossible. Nevertheless, such effects can be minimized by eliminating close historic congeners from the sample and making sure that the maximal range on all test variables is represented.

Two subsamples, constructed on distinct but related criteria, were chosen for the purpose of testing the correlations discovered in the full sample. The first of these, designated in the culture list as the *select sample* (S), was designed both to minimize the effects of close historic interdependence and to ensure maximal and balanced representation of culture types and song styles. Given the aims of coverage and balance, the criteria of inclusion were necessarily judgmental, rather than probabilistic. The second subsample, called the *random test sample* (T), was selected by random drawings from a list of cultures presumed not to be in close historic relationship with one another, and was designed to impose a more rigorous test of independence of cases.

The first step in the construction of the 120-member select sample was a search of style similarities and cultural codings to establish the ranges of variability in the whole sample. Next, a provisional list was prepared, including one culture from each of the fifty-six areas in the geographic roster. Additional cultures were added to this list from areas in which there were marked variabilities of cultural or song-style codings. The list was then scrutinized for probable culture-historic duplication. For Africa and the circum-Mediterranean, decisions on the degree of historic relatedness were based on Murdock's (1966) classification of culture clusters (i.e., groups of culturally similar, historically related societies).

When the select sample was being assembled, the same author's (Murdock,

1967) worldwide classification of culture clusters was not available. For the rest of the world, therefore, the degree of historic interdependence was gauged in terms of linguistic relationship (reckoned from a classification of languages in the cantometric sample prepared by Roger Wescott), geographic propinquity, and overall ethnographic similarity. The outlines of the roster, after the exclusions were made, turned out to be largely congruent with the cluster borders established in Murdock's world classification. Finally, the sample was stratified, following Murdock's recommendation (1966) that about equal representation be given to each of three macro-regional units: North and South America, East Eurasia and the Insular Pacific, and Africa and the circum-Mediterranean. This was done by rejecting, at random, a certain number of cultures from Africa and the circum-Mediterranean. The resulting, more or less even, distribution compares with one of about 25 percent each for the first two units and 50 percent for the third, in the large sample.

In a few cases, cultures with fairly recent historic connections were permitted to remain together in the select sample, when this was necessary to meet the criterion of inclusiveness. For example, in the Pacific region, close linguistic congeners were admitted in order to afford a balanced coverage of the widely dispersed but very under-recorded Polynesian stylistic world. In this case, however, care was taken to choose cultures with the most contrastive song codings. The same criterion required the inclusion of the New Mexican Spanish and the Quechua-Mestizo samples, along with Andalucia and Quechua (Q'eros). For several reasons, these latter inclusions are not likely to have introduced serious bias. All four are mutually quite different in key song codings. They are distributed over different production scale categories: Quechua-Indian (IP), Quechua-Mestizo (IR), Andalucia (PA), and New Mexico (IR). All show a considerable degree of mutual contrast in their cultural codings. Thus, there is little probability that an historically determined distribution will give rise to a spuriously high correlation. Indeed, on the production scale correlations, any trace of retained feature between, say, Quechua-Indian and Quechua-Mestizo will actually lower the measure of association.

All associations between song style and lifeways discovered on the large sample were tested on the select sample, and only those that stood at approximately the same level on the latter as on the former are presented in this book. The select sample appears to be quite sensitive to the biases of gross regional imbalance. Several of the correlations that failed to stand the test of the small sample turned out to involve features of song style strongly present in Africa, suggesting that the pattern of association had been generated by a disproportionate pileup of positive cases.

The 85-member random test sample was constructed from a list of cultures, each one of which clearly belongs in a separate cultural cluster in the Murdock world classification. Only one level of choice was imposed on the sample; as in the preceding case it was stratified to ensure a balanced representation of regions. After the list of cultures representing all the clusters in the large sample had been prepared, the names were grouped in macro-regional blocks. Then, a drawing of names was made within each block, using a table of random numbers. The cultures thus chosen were checked against the list of geographic coordinates given in the cluster classification to ensure that no two of them were very close neighbors. The criterion of separation was that suggested by Murdock—a minimum of three degrees of latitude or longitude in the tropics, four or five degrees in the temperate zones (the latter for societies more than 35 degrees from the Equator), and six degrees in the Arctic. One culture of each neighbor pair was rejected at random, and, where possible, another from the same cluster was substituted.

Every one of the relationships between song style, on the one hand, and the production scales and *Atlas* codings, on the other, presented in the graphs of Chapters 6 and 7, was tested on the random sample. All but four of them retained statistical significance. Those that failed to pass the test involved vocal counterpoint, orchestral counterpoint, and orchestral polyrhythm; these features are so rare in the world sample that they could not be represented adequately in the smaller one. Table 1 presents the results of the random sample test.

MEASURES OF ASSOCIATION AND SIGNIFICANCE

MEAN FREQUENCY GRAPHS

The graphs presented throughout this book are designed to provide a quick visual impression of trends in relationship, usually between a discrete but ordered variable (for example, a production scale) and a continuous variable (typically the percent frequency of some style attribute). In most cases, the plotting points represent the means of all cultural frequencies for each discrete scale category.

GAMMA

Association between variables is measured by *gamma*, the Index of Order Association (Hays, 1963), which expresses the degree of monotonic co-variation between two ordinal scales. The index ranges from $+1.0$ to -1.0. For simplicity the gammas presented on the graphs are given as absolute values (the direction of co-variation is easily perceived in the slope of the mean curve).

Table 1, Appendix 2. *Random test sample, cross-cultural associations.*

	N	Gamma	Significance level (chi square)
1. *Five-Point Production Scale*			
Mean size of local communities	57	0.7891	.001
Settlement pattern	76	0.5470	.001
Class stratification	82	0.8315	.001
Political development (extra-local hierarchies)	75	0.8038	.001
Wordiness of song text	85	0.8562	.001
Precision of enunciation	85	0.7612	.001
Moderate delivery	85	0.5361	.005
Solo and explicit	85	0.7053	.001
Solo, explicit, and moderate	85	0.8771	.001
Repetitiousness of song text	85	0.8654	.001
Slurred enunciation	85	0.7703	.001
Non-explicit song text	85	0.7622	.001
Wide melodic intervals	85	0.8009	.001
Narrow melodic intervals	85	0.5553	.02
One-beat orchestral rhythm	76	0.7827	.001
Unison orchestral rhythm	62	0.8049	.001
Tonal cohesiveness	83	0.5382	.005
Embellishment	85	0.7267	.001
Free rhythm	85	0.4926	.005
2. *Eight-Point Production Scale*			
Tonal cohesiveness	83	0.6897	.001
Rhythmic cohesiveness	83	0.5718	.005
Polyphony	83	0.5013	.05
Elaborateness (embellishment and rubato)	85	0.7687	.001
Interlocking vocal group	83	0.8310	.005
Overlapping vocal group	83	0.5105	.05
Simple alternation	83	0.6566	.005
Exclusive dominance	85	0.7038	.001
3. *Layering Index*			
Mean number of instruments	85	0.5457	.02
Elaborateness	85	0.7041	.001
4. *Productive Complementarity*			
Polyphony	62	0.5850	.02
Polyphony for female choruses	49	0.5691	.05
5. *Pre-Marital Sex Sanctions*			
Narrow voices	56	0.8148	.001
Wide voices	56	0.7637	.001
Nasality	56	0.6484	.01
Tonal cohesiveness	54	0.8000	.02
6. *Number of Extra-Local Hierarchies*			
Unison orchestral rhythm	54	0.8700	.001
Accompanying orchestral rhythm	54	0.5261	.01
7. *Vocal Width*			
Tonal cohesiveness	83	0.8998	.001

STATISTICAL SPLITS

Since gamma is calculated over a matrix of joint frequencies in discrete classes, any continuous variable in the test must be divided into categories. Thus, the percentage scale on which the relative importance of style traits per culture is measured is usually split at the median (occasionally, at the quartiles) of the ranked cultural frequencies. The treatment of the ordinal (production) scale varies with the hypothesis of association being tested. In some cases, it is predicted that the relative importance of a style trait will increase steadily with each step in the scale; in others, it is predicted that significant differences lie only between larger segments of the scale. Accordingly, ordinal categories are held separate or lumped in the calculation of the index. Table 2 of this Appendix illustrates the extreme varieties of statistical splitting on the abscissa.

Table 2, Appendix 2. *Statistical splits illustrated.*

a. X-Axis: Five-point production scale
   Y-Axis: Percent one-beat orchestral rhythm

	X	IP	AH	PA	IR	
Above median	13	9	13	2	0	
Below median	3	5	13	7	11	N = 76 cultures

Statistical split: X/IP/AH/PA/IR vs. Median

b. X-Axis: Five-point production scale
   Y-Axis: Percent narrow melodic intervals

	X, IP, AH	PA, IR	
Above median	30	23	
Below median	56	11	N = 120 cultures

Statistical split: X, IP, AH/PA, IR vs. Median

STATISTICAL SIGNIFICANCE

In most cases, the statistical significance of differences (taken as the probability that the observed differences could have occurred by chance) over the categories created by the gamma splits is reckoned from the chi-square distribution. In a few instances, where the sample was too small, or an expected frequency was too low to permit the calculation of a chi square, either the Mann-Whitney U-Test (Siegel, 1956) or Fisher's Exact Test was employed.

APPENDIX 3

Summodal Profiles for Nine World Song Style Regions

THE nine pages of statistics that follow are the "summodal profiles" for the nine world song style regions described in Chapter 4. Each summodal profile summarizes all traits of all songs, whether solo or choral, accompanied or unaccompanied, in each region. The numbers 1–13 lying above the heavy black line divide each parameter into the maximum number of thirteen coding points. Not all the phenomena in song could be rated in an equally fine-grained way, and for this reason the parameters have varying numbers of points. They are, however, distributed symmetrically and uniformly so that the seventh, or mid-point, of each parameter falls under the "7" on the scale and the end points lie at "1" and "13."

The one- or two-digit numbers give the percent frequencies with which each trait on a rating line appears in the total corpus of songs for the region. The caption title of each line is given to the left, and after this caption appears the name of the most prominent and sometimes the second most prominent point per line on that particular profile. For the purposes of this first comparative survey, sets of points forming clusters of traits or "sides" of lines are frequently clumped for comparative purposes. For instance, the main or modal coding on Line 1 in the South American summodal profile is 2, or "solo," with a frequency of 27 percent. The second main occurrence is "unison group" and here points 5 and 6 are considered as one, giving a total of 24 percent for this state. In some cases traits are cited to draw the reader's attention to an unusual or important bias in a line.

Point 1 on this Line 1 is "non-occurrence," or no singing group, a condition which, of course, does not occur in this song style study. Point 1 in parameters 2–9, 11–14, and 21–22 stand for null conditions on these parameters. ∅ on Line 4 is recorded only as a coding error. Others, such as ∅ on Lines 7, 8, and 9, simply mean no orchestra. For further clarification of the points on the lines, consult the coding book, Chapter 3. Occasionally, the total percents for the points in a line add up to more than 100 percent. This is a result of "double-coding" where an ambiguous situation has been described as partaking of two traits.

Table 1, Appendix 3. *Summodal profile for South America—230 songs.*

Name of coding line	Main traits	Points on coding line with percents of occurrence for each												
		1	2	3	4	5	6	7	8	9	10	11	12	13
1. Vocal group	Solo, Unison		27		5	7	17	17	9	1	4	1	1	10
2. Orch. relationship	None, Heterogeneous	65	9	5			3		15	3				
3. Instrumental group	None, 1 Instrument	66	19			3	8	2	3					
4. Vocal organization	Monophony, Polyphony, or Unison	1			33			26			11			28
5. Tonal blend-vocal	Non-cohesive	34			18			35			11			
6. Rhythmic blend-vocal	Very diffuse	40			24			16			15			4
7. Orch. organization	None	67			19			9						5
8. Tonal blend-orch.	None	85			2			7			1			5
9. Rhythmic blend-orch.	None	86			3			4			5			2
10. Words to nonsense	Repetitious	1				4		37			51			7
11. Overall rhythm-vocal	Irregular		2				15			9		66		8
12. Group rhythm-vocal	None, Unison	40	33			14		3				2		7
13. Overall rhythm-orch.	None, Solo	65	16				3			2		7		7
14. Group rhythm-orch.	None	85	7			2		5						
15. Melodic shape	Undulating, Descending	10				4				70				15
16. Melodic form	Simple litany, Complex strophe	5	8	11	1	4	12	3	2	5	13	18	11	7
17. Phrase length	Short, Medium	4				11			30			42		12
18. Number of phrases	1 or 2, 8+	21		3		4	6		6	2		12		46
19. Position final tone	Lowest	55			19						15		5	6
20. Range	5-8, 3-5	6			35			38			14			6
21. Interval width	Wide, Diatonic	1			11			24			49			15
22. Polyphonic type	None, Counterpoint	69	2				3		8		3			15
23. Embellishment	None, Some								5			37		57
24. Tempo	Slow, Medium	2			15		36			37		9		1
25. Volume	Soft, Mid	9			36			35			12			7
26. Rubato-vocal	None, Some	9				12			32					47
27. Rubato-instruments	None	6				2			9					83
28. Glissando	Some	10				29			35					26
29. Melisma	None, Some	6						28						65
30. Tremolo	None, Some	10						29						61
31. Glottal shake	None, Some	11						36						53
32. Register	Mid, Low	9				13			45			24		10
33. Vocal width	Speaking, Wide	1		17			46		27			7		1
34. Nasalization	Marked, Extreme	22			51			17			8			2
35. Raspiness	Great, Intermittent	10			42			28			15			4
36. Accent	Relaxed or Normal	9			20			33			33			5
37. Consonants	Slurred, Normal					6			43			33		18

Table 2, Appendix 3. *Summodal profile for North America—374 songs.*

Name of coding line	Main traits	Points on coding line with percents of occurrence for each												
		1	2	3	4	5	6	7	8	9	10	11	12	13
1. Vocal group	Unison, Solo		29		2	16	31	2	14	1	2	2		1
2. Orch. relationship	Accompanying, None	26	47	13					10	3				
3. Instrumental group	1 Instrument, Unison	26	37			15	20	1	1					
4. Vocal organization	Unison, Monophony				32			57			2			8
5. Tonal blend-vocal	Diffuse	31			10			41			16			1
6. Rhythmic blend-vocal	Diffuse, Cohesive	32			7			29			27			6
7. Orch. organization	Monophony, Unison	26			37			31						6
8. Tonal blend-orch.	None	63			4			10			8			16
9. Rhythmic blend-orch.	None	63			1			10			18			8
10. Words to nonsense	Repetitious	2			4			25			59			10
11. Overall rhythm-vocal	Irregular			1			26			1		69		3
12. Group rhythm-vocal	Unison, None	32	59		3		5							
13. Overall rhythm-orch.	1-beat	25	46				17			1		10		1
14. Group rhythm-orch.	None, Unison	61	29		2			7		1		1		
15. Melodic shape	Undulating, Terraced	7				20				62				11
16. Melodic form	Simple, Complex strophe	6	5	21	3	5	32	2	4	3	3	8	9	
17. Phrase length	Medium, Short	3			15			41			32			9
18. Number of phrases	8+, 1 or 2	29		11		11	6		13	3		8		18
19. Position final tone	Lowest	50			27					16		4		3
20. Range	5–8, 10+				18			46			34			2
21. Interval width	Wide				2			18			70			9
22. Polyphonic type	None	91		2			2		3		1			2
23. Embellishment	None, Some				2			16			39			43
24. Tempo	Medium, Slow			7		31				51		11		
25. Volume	Mid	5			25			36			27			7
26. Rubato-vocal	None	3					6			19				72
27. Rubato-instruments	None	1								9				91
28. Glissando	Some	2					21			62				16
29. Melisma	Syllabic	2						36						62
30. Tremolo	Some or None	10						45						45
31. Glottal shake	Some or None	17						44						39
32. Register	Mid, Low	7			17			41			31			4
33. Vocal width	Speaking, Wide	3	14				49		31		4			
34. Nasalization	Marked	15			52			24			8			1
35. Raspiness	Great, Intermittent	9			47			32			11			1
36. Accent	Forceful	15			32			32			20			2
37. Consonants	Slurred, Normal	1			4			45			41			9

Table 3, Appendix 3. *Summodal profile for the Insular Pacific—309 songs.*

Name of coding line	Main traits	Points on coding line with percents of occurrence for each												
		1	2	3	4	5	6	7	8	9	10	11	12	13
1. Vocal group	Unison, Alternation		14		6	13	32	2	18	2	1	4	7	1
2. Orch. relationship	None, Accompanying	61	14	13				1		3	7		1	
3. Instrumental group	None, Unison	61	10				4	22		3				
4. Vocal organization	Polyphony, Unison	1			18			37			4			41
5. Tonal blend-vocal	Cohesive	17			5			31			23			24
6. Rhythmic blend-vocal	Cohesive	18			8			18			17			38
7. Orch. organization	None, Unison	61			8			26						4
8. Tonal blend-orch.	None, Cohesive	71						3			5			22
9. Rhythmic blend-orch.	None	72			2			10			8			8
10. Words to nonsense	Wordy, About half repeated	18			26			29			19			8
11. Overall rhythm-vocal	Irregular, Free			2			23			1		47		28
12. Group rhythm-vocal	Unison	19		64		5		5						5
13. Overall rhythm-orch.	None, 1-beat	61			19			14			1	4		1
14. Group rhythm-orch.	None, Unison	72			15			5	8					
15. Melodic shape	Undulating, Arched	13					1			77				10
16. Melodic form	Simple litany	14	5	6	1	3	15	2	2	2	12	21	15	2
17. Phrase length	Long, Medium	16			21			37			18			7
18. Number of phrases	1 or 2, 8+	19		5		7	4		7	2		14		44
19. Position final tone	Lowest	44			21			18			9			8
20. Range	3-5, 5-8	6			41			27			20			6
21. Interval width	Diatonic, Wide	2			13			53			30			2
22. Polyphonic type	None, Drone	54		14			2		12		11			6
23. Embellishment	None, Some				2			9			23			66
24. Tempo	Slow, Medium	7		16	29					36		11		
25. Volume	Loud, Soft	9			26			28			26			11
26. Rubato-vocal	Much, None	31						8			24			37
27. Rubato-instruments	None	1						3			5			92
28. Glissando	Some, Prominent	8						28			40			24
29. Melisma	Syllabic, Some	10						38						52
30. Tremolo	None	6						15						79
31. Glottal shake	None	4						14						83
32. Register	Mid, Low	4			12			49			29			7
33. Vocal width	Wide, Speaking	1		9		33		37			19			2
34. Nasalization	Little or Marked	8			31			30			20			11
35. Raspiness	Little or Intermittent	7			26			32			24			11
36. Accent	Relaxed or Moderate	6			19			32			31			12
37. Consonants	Precise or Normal	6			27			31			18			18

Table 4, Appendix 3. *Summodal profile for Africa—666 songs.*

Name of coding line	Main traits	Points on coding line with percents of occurrence for each												
		1	2	3	4	5	6	7	8	9	10	11	12	13
1. Vocal group	Overlap, Alternation		16		8	2	7	1	18	4	24	7	6	6
2. Orch. relationship	Accompanying, Complementary or None	25	21	20		3	1		6	2			9	13
3. Instrumental group	Unison, Some overlap	25	17			21	22	1	1			2	6	4
4. Vocal organization	Polyphony, Unison				20			27			4			49
5. Tonal blend-vocal	Cohesive	19			1			19			31			30
6. Rhythmic blend-vocal	Cohesive	20			3			9			23			46
7. Orch. organization	Polyphony, Unison	25			9			28						38
8. Tonal blend-orch.	Cohesive, None	43						9			16			32
9. Rhythmic blend-orch.	Cohesive, None	42						2			11			44
10. Words to nonsense	About half repeated	4			21			41			27			7
11. Overall rhythm-vocal	Simple						63			3		23		10
12. Group rhythm-vocal	Unison	19	60			2		8		1		1		11
13. Overall rhythm-orch.	Regular	25	13				50			3		7		3
14. Group rhythm-orch.	None, Polyrhythm	43	14					17		14		12		
15. Melodic shape	Undulating, Descending	6								65				29
16. Melodic form	Litany	9	9	5	1	4	9	11	5	3	20	10	9	5
17. Phrase length	Short	2			6			28			42			22
18. Number of phrases	1 or 2	23		3		3	4		2	2		15		48
19. Position final tone	Lowest	45			31					15		6		4
20. Range	5–8, 10+	1			16			45			32			6
21. Interval width	Diatonic, Wide				6			46			41			7
22. Polyphonic type	Parallel, Counterpoint	47			1		9		18		11			13
23. Embellishment	None	2			3			12			20			63
24. Tempo	Medium, Fast		5			16			52		24			2
25. Volume	Mid, Loud	1				14		45			35			5
26. Rubato-vocal	None	10					4			8				78
27. Rubato-instruments	None	3								3				94
28. Glissando	Some, Prominent	7					24			46				23
29. Melisma	Syllabic, Some	12						34						55
30. Tremolo	None	2						10						88
31. Glottal shake	None	5						23						72
32. Register	Mid	4			25			44			24			3
33. Vocal width	Wide·	1		13			17		42		22			5
34. Nasalization	Marked, Intermittent	10				36		33			15			6
35. Raspiness	Intermittent, Marked	5				37		40			15			2
36. Accent	Moderate, Forceful	4				28		47			17			3
37. Consonants	Slurred	1				7		26			56			10

Table 5, Appendix 3. *Summodal profile for Old High Culture—422 songs.*

Name of coding line	Main traits	Points on coding line with percents of occurrence for each												
		1	2	3	4	5	6	7	8	9	10	11	12	13
1. Vocal group	Solo, Alternation		45		9	1	10	9	12	3	5	1	4	1
2. Orch. relationship	Accompanying or none, Heterophony	34	22	13			1	2		16	7		2	2
3. Instrumental group	None, Unison	34	17				24	14	4	3		1		1
4. Vocal organization	Monophony, Unison	2			55			24			13			6
5. Tonal blend-vocal	None, Diffuse	56			12			28			5			
6. Rhythmic blend-vocal	None, Diffuse	58			14			15			10			4
7. Orch. organization	None, Polyphony or Unison	36			11			21			9			24
8. Tonal blend-orch.	None, Diffuse	54			3			22			10			10
9. Rhythmic blend-orch.	None, Cohesive	54			4			8			13			22
10. Words to nonsense	Wordy	51			25			16			5			2
11. Overall rhythm-vocal	Free, Simple or Irregular						31			2		30		37
12. Group rhythm-vocal	None, Unison	57	26			13		1						2
13. Overall rhythm-orch.	None, Simple meter	33	7				28			4		17		11
14. Group rhythm-orch.	None, Accompanying	53	7			6		22		7				4
15. Melodic shape	Undulating, Arched	14				2				75				9
16. Melodic form	Through composed, Simple litany	27	10	7	2	8	10	3	1	1	10	12	8	1
17. Phrase length	Medium, Long	12			24			39			21			4
18. Number of phrases	8+, 1 or 2	43	4			5	3		7	3		14		22
19. Position final tone	Lowest	48			24					19		7		2
20. Range	5–8, 10+ or 3–5	2			28			36			30			3
21. Interval width	Narrow	1			48			27			20			4
22. Polyphonic type	None	92		3				1						3
23. Embellishment	Considerable, Extreme	25			21			33			14			8
24. Tempo	Slow, Quite slow	5	22			32				25		14		2
25. Volume	Mid	3			21			47			23			6
26. Rubato-vocal	Extreme, None	40					8			17				34
27. Rubato-instruments	None, Some	11					4			11				74
28. Glissando	Prominent, Some	17					45			28				10
29. Melisma	Some, Much	22						55						23
30. Tremolo	None, Some	14						28						58
31. Glottal shake	Much	35						31						34
32. Register	Mid, High	8			22			46		12	21			3
33. Vocal width	Narrow	20	46				17		12		3			2
34. Nasalization	Extreme	52	36					7			3			2
35. Raspiness	Great, Intermittent	7	38					31			18			6
36. Accent	Moderate	3			21			51			22			3
37. Consonants	Precise, Normal	17			40			24			14			4

Table 6, Appendix 3. *Summodal profile for Europe—383 songs.*

Name of coding line	Main traits	Points on coding line with percents of occurrence for each												
		1	2	3	4	5	6	7	8	9	10	11	12	13
1. Vocal group	Solo, Unison		45		8	6	21		14	1	2		1	1
2. Orch. relationship	Solo, Accompanying	59	22	7		3	1		2	1			1	5
3. Instrumental group	Solo, Unison	60	16			11	9							3
4. Vocal organization	Monophony, Polyphony				52			19			1			28
5. Tonal blend-vocal	None, Cohesive	51				5		16			17			11
6. Rhythmic blend-vocal	None, Cohesive	52				5		7			13			23
7. Orch. organization	None, Polyphony	59				5		4			1			30
8. Tonal blend-orch.	None	76				1		6			10			7
9. Rhythmic blend-orch.	None	76				1		2			8			14
10. Words to nonsense	Wordy	47			29			17			6			1
11. Overall rhythm-vocal	Simple, Irregular						51			2		35		13
12. Group rhythm-vocal	None, Unison	52	39			1		5						3
13. Overall rhythm-orch.	None, Simple	59		4			28			1		8		1
14. Group rhythm-orch.	None, Accompanying	74		2		1		19		1				2
15. Melodic shape	Undulating	11					2			77				10
16. Melodic form	Simple strophe	6	4	14	1	13	42	1	1	1	4	8	6	
17. Phrase length	Medium, Short	2			9			47			37			5
18. Number of phrases	4 or 8, 3 or 6	18		8		9	26		11	9		6		13
19. Position final tone	Lowest, Mid	37			24			49		25		10		4
20. Range	5–8, 10+				12			49			33			6
21. Interval width	Diatonic, Wide				7			72			17			4
22. Polyphonic type	None	70		5					11		11			3
23. Embellishment	None, Some	2			7			16			30			45
24. Tempo	Slow, Medium	2		17		35			33		13			
25. Volume	Mid, Loud	1			21			46			27			6
26. Rubato-vocal	None, Some or Much	15				14			33					38
27. Rubato-instruments	None	2				3			7					88
28. Glissando	Some, Prominent	2				24			47					27
29. Melisma	Syllabic, Some	8						39						53
30. Tremolo	None, Some	5						37						58
31. Glottal shake	None	7						18						76
32. Register	Mid, High	7			22			49			21			1
33. Vocal width	Wide, Speaking	1		13			35		32		17			2
34. Nasalization	Marked, Intermittent	5			39			34			16			5
35. Raspiness	Intermittent, Little	4			23			39			27			7
36. Accent	Moderate	3			23			61			12			
37. Consonants	Precise, Normal	7			43			41			9			1

Table 7, Appendix 3. *Summodal profile for Australia—32 songs.*

Name of coding line	Main traits	Points on coding line with percents of occurrence for each												
		1	2	3	4	5	6	7	8	9	10	11	12	13
1. Vocal group	Unison, Solo		39			3	36	21						
2. Orch. relationship	Accompanying, Heterophony	12	33	12					33	9				
3. Instrumental group	Unison	13	19				22	47						
4. Vocal organization	Unison, Monophony				44			50						6
5. Tonal blend-vocal	Poor, None	44						53			3			
6. Rhythmic blend-vocal	None, Good	44						25			31			
7. Orch. organization	Unison	16			19			63						3
8. Tonal blend-orch.	Diffuse, None	34						47			6			13
9. Rhythmic blend-orch.	Cohesive	34						9			38			19
10. Words to nonsense	About half repeated	13			9			56			22			
11. Overall rhythm-vocal	Simple, Irregular		3				42				3	36		15
12. Group rhythm-vocal	Unison, None	42	55					3						
13. Overall rhythm-orch.	1-beat, Simple	9	56			30						5		
14. Group rhythm-orch.	Accompanying, None	31	16					47			6			
15. Melodic shape	Descending, Undulating or Terraced	8				24				29				39
16. Melodic form	Litany, Simple strophe	3	6	17		3	22		6		8	22	14	
17. Phrase length	Long, Medium	16			29			36			16			4
18. Number of phrases	1 or 2	15		12		9	6		15			15		29
19. Position final tone	Lowest	76				18				6				
20. Range	5–8, 10+	3				16		47			34			
21. Interval width	Narrow, Diatonic					63		34			3			
22. Polyphonic type	None	94	3						3					
23. Embellishment	Considerable, Some				3			66			28			3
24. Tempo	Medium, Slow			18		21			33	27				
25. Volume	Mid, Loud					26		38			35			
26. Rubato-vocal	None, Some	15					9				24			52
27. Rubato-instruments	None										6			94
28. Glissando	Prominent, Some	3					53				34			9
29. Melisma	Syllabic, Some							38						63
30. Tremolo	None, Some	15						24						61
31. Glottal shake	None	3						3						94
32. Register	Mid, Low				7			53			31			9
33. Vocal width	Narrow, Speaking	13	40				38		10					
34. Nasalization	Marked, Extreme	44				56								
35. Raspiness	Great, Extreme	19				63		19						
36. Accent	Forceful					47		25			28			
37. Consonants	Slurred					13		22			56			9

Table 8, Appendix 3. *Summodal profile for Arctic Asia—92 songs.*

Name of coding line	Main traits	Points on coding line with percents of occurrence for each												
		1	2	3	4	5	6	7	8	9	10	11	12	13
1. Vocal group	Solo		70				1	5	4	8	3	1		7
2. Orch. relationship	None	85	5	9					1					
3. Instrumental group	None	85	2				13							
4. Vocal organization	Monophony	1			71			12			3			13
5. Tonal blend-vocal	None	73			7			21						
6. Rhythmic blend-vocal	None	74			3			9			4			10
7. Orch. organization	None	84			2			14						
8. Tonal blend-orch.	None	86									2			12
9. Rhythmic blend-orch.	None	86			1			5			5			2
10. Words to nonsense	About half repeated	7			14			27			35			17
11. Overall rhythm-vocal	Irregular			1			35			4		53		6
12. Group rhythm-vocal	None	72		14		3		4						6
13. Overall rhythm-orch.	None	84		12							1		3	
14. Group rhythm-orch.	None	86		14										
15. Melodic shape	Undulating	6				2				86				5
16. Melodic form	Litany	2	2	11	2	1	12	1	6	4	5	23	25	6
17. Phrase length	Short	2			4			25			49			21
18. Number of phrases	1 or 2	13		5			1	4		5	1		15	57
19. Position final tone	Lowest, Mid	38			19					24		11		7
20. Range	3-5, 5-8				48			39			12			1
21. Interval width	Wide, Diatonic	1			2			34			42			22
22. Polyphonic type	None	87		1			3		2		1			5
23. Embellishment	None, Some or Considerable	8			13			24			26			30
24. Tempo	Medium	2		3	34					47		12		1
25. Volume	Mid, Soft			28				60			12			1
26. Rubato-vocal	Some, None	8				15				46				31
27. Rubato-instruments	None									7				93
28. Glissando	Some	5				22				46				27
29. Melisma	Some, Syllabic	13						52						35
30. Tremolo	None, Much	23						22						55
31. Glottal shake	Much, Some	67						20						13
32. Register	Mid, Low	3			9			41			40			6
33. Vocal width	Speaking, Wide			11			39		31		10			9
34. Nasalization	Marked	8			60			18			7			8
35. Raspiness	Great, Intermittent	8			34			29			26			2
36. Accent	Moderate	5			21			46			25			3
37. Consonants	Normal, Slurred	1			13			46			30			9

Table 9, Appendix 3. *Summodal profile for Tribal India—19 songs.*

Name of coding line	Main traits	Points on coding line with percents of occurrence for each												
		1	2	3	4	5	6	7	8	9	10	11	12	13
1. Vocal group	Alternation						10		35	40	15			
2. Orch. relationship	Accompanying	11	26	47					16					
3. Instrumental group	Unison	11	11			16	58			5				
4. Vocal organization	Unison							74						26
5. Tonal blend-vocal	Cohesive, Medium					8		40			52			
6. Rhythmic blend-vocal	Cohesive							5		89				5
7. Orch. organization	Unison, Polyphony	11				11		53						26
8. Tonal blend-orch.	Medium	21						42		11				26
9. Rhythmic blend-orch.	Cohesive	21						11		26				42
10. Words to nonsense	About half repeated, Wordy	11			21			47		21				
11. Overall rhythm-vocal	Regular						50			5		35		10
12. Group rhythm-vocal	Unison			95				5						
13. Overall rhythm-orch.	1-beat, Simple	8		56			36							
14. Group rhythm-orch.	Unison, Polyrhythm	21		32				21				26		
15. Melodic shape	Undulating	15							80					5
16. Melodic form	Litany	4	4	9		4	13	4		4	22	13	22	
17. Phrase length	Medium, Short				17			48			22			13
18. Number of phrases	1 or 2	14				5	5		14	5		23		36
19. Position final tone	Lowest	70		25						5				
20. Range	5–8, 3–5				42			58			5			
21. Interval width	Wide, Diatonic							42			53			5
22. Polyphonic type	None	74		11			11		5					
23. Embellishment	Some, Considerable				25			25			30			20
24. Tempo	Medium			5		18				59		18		
25. Volume	Loud, Mid							47			47			5
26. Rubato-vocal	None	10								10				80
27. Rubato-instruments	None						5			11				84
28. Glissando	None						16			11				74
29. Melisma	Syllabic, Some							42						58
30. Tremolo	None							16						84
31. Glottal shake	None							16						84
32. Register	Mid					9		64			27			
33. Vocal width	Speaking, Narrow			42			47		8					3
34. Nasalization	Marked, Intermittent	4		58				35			4			
35. Raspiness	Intermittent			28				64			8			
36. Accent	Moderate	5						79			16			
37. Consonants	Precise, Normal				53			47						

BIBLIOGRAPHY

This compilation is based on references contributed by the authors of this volume and on selected publications which have been helpful in preparing the manuscript and in conducting the Cantometrics Project.

ALLPORT, G. E.
1961 Pattern and growth in personality. Holt, Rinehart and Winston. New York.

ALTENFELDER SILVA, FERNANDO, AND BETTY J. MEGGERS
1963 Cultural development in Brazil. *In* Aboriginal cultural development in Latin America: An Interpretive Overview. B. J. Meggers and C. Evans, editors. Smithsonian Institution Miscellaneous Collections, Vol. 146, No. 1, Washington, D.C.

AMES, DAVID
1967 Music and the musician in Igbo and Hausa societies: a comparative examination. Prepared for UCLA African Studies Center Colloquium on "Critical Standards for the African Arts." To be published with other papers written for the Colloquium by the University of California Press, J. Povey and K. Wachsmann, editors. Berkeley, California.

ARENSBERG, CONRAD M.
1952 Behavior and organization. *In* Social psychology at the cross roads. John Rohrer and Muzafer Sherif, editors. Harpers, New York.

ARENSBERG, CONRAD M., AND SOLON T. KIMBALL
1965 Culture and community. Harcourt, Brace & World, New York.

ARIETI, S.
1955 Interpretation of schizophrenia. Robert Brunn, New York.

AX, A. F.
1953 Physiological differentiation between fear and anger in humans. Psychosomatic Medicine 15:433–442.

BANKS, ARTHUR S., AND ROBERT B. TEXTOR
1963 A cross-polity survey. The M.I.T. Press, Cambridge, Mass.

BARRY, HERBERT, III, IRVIN L. CHILD, AND MARGARET K. BACON
1957 A cross-cultural survey of some sex differences in socialization. Journal of Abnormal and Social Psychology, 55 (3):332–337, 447.
1959 Relation of child training to subsistence economy. American Anthropologist 61 (1):51–63.

BATESON, GREGORY, AND MARGARET MEAD
1942 (reissued in 1962) Balinese character: a photographic analysis. "Special Publications of the New York Academy of Science," New York Academy of Sciences, New York.

BATESON, GREGORY, RAY L. BIRDWHISTELL, HENRY W. BROSIN, CHARLES F. HOCKETT, AND NORMAN A. McQUOWN
(In press, expected publication date, 1969) The natural history of an interview. Grune and Stratton, New York.

BEAGLEHOLE, ERNEST
1947 Some modern Maoris. Oxford University Press, New York.

BERNDT, R. M., AND C. H. BERNDT
1964 The world of the first Australians. University of Chicago Press, Chicago, Ill.

BIRDWHISTELL, RAY L.
1951 Border County: A study in socialization and mobility potential. Doctoral dissertation, University of Chicago, Chicago, Ill.
1952 Introduction to kinesics. University of Louisville Press, Louisville, Ky.
1957 Kinesics in the context of motor habits. Read at December 28, 1957 meeting of the American Anthropological Association. Unpublished. (Available from Eastern Pennsylvania Psychiatric Institute, Philadelphia, Pa.)
1959a Contributions of linguistic and kinesic studies to the understanding of schizophrenia. *In* Schizophrenia: an integrated approach. Alfred Auer-

back, editor; pp. 99–123. Ronald Press, New York.

1959b The frames in the communication process. Read at October, 1959 meeting of the American Society of Clinical Hypnosis. Unpublished. (Available from Eastern Pennsylvania Psychiatric Institute, Philadelphia, Pa.)

1959c Paralanguage: 25 years after Sapir. In Lectures on experimental psychiatry. Henry W. Brosin, editor. University of Pittsburgh Press, Pittsburgh, Pa.

1962 An approach to communication. Family Process 1 (2) :194–201.

1963 Body signals: normal and pathological. Unpublished. (Available from Eastern Pennsylvania Psychiatric Institute, Philadelphia, Pa.)

1966 Some relationships between American kinesics and spoken American English. In Communication and culture. Alfred J. Smith, editor; pp. 182–189. Holt, Rinehart and Winston, New York.

1967 Some body motion elements accompanying spoken American English. In Communication: concept and perspective, Lee Thayer, editor. Spartan Books, New York.

1968a In press. Body behavior and communication. International Encyclopedia of the Social Sciences. Macmillan, New York.

1968b In press. Communication as a multi-channel system. International Encyclopedia of the Social Sciences. Macmillan, New York.

1968c In press. Communication without words. In L'aventure humaine. Paul Alexander, editor. Société d'Études Littéraires et Artistiques. Paris.

BLACK, J. W.
1949 Loudness of speaking: The effect of heard stimuli on spoken responses. Journal of Experimental Psychology 39:311–315.

BOWLER, N. W.
1957 A fundamental frequency analysis of harsh vocal qualities. Dissertation Abstracts 17:2706.

BRODY, M. W.
1943 Neurotic manifestations of the voice. Psychoanalytic Quarterly 12: 371–380.

CAILLOIS, ROGER
1961 Man, play and games. English translation by Meyer Barash. Free Press of Glencoe (Crowell-Collier), New York.

CARNEIRO, ROBERT L.
1962 Scale analysis as an instrument for the study of cultural evolution. Southwestern Journal of Anthropology 18 (2) :149–169.

CARNEIRO, ROBERT L., AND STEPHEN F. TOBIAS
1963 The application of scale analysis to the study of cultural evolution. Transactions of the New York Academy of Sciences, Series 2, Vol. 26, No. 2:196–207.

CARNEIRO, ROBERT L., STEPHEN F. TOBIAS, DAISY F. HILSE, AND BARBARA D. REYNOLDS
1965 Trait list to be used for the study of cultural evolution. Sixth edition. Unpublished. (Available from American Museum of Natural History, New York.)

CARPENTER, EDMUND, AND MARSHALL MC-LUHAN (editors)
1960 Explorations in communications: an anthology. Beacon Press, Boston, Mass.

CHAPPLE, ELIOT DISMORE, AND CONRAD M. ARENSBERG
1940 Measuring human relations: an introduction to the study of the interaction of individuals. The Journal Press, Provincetown, Mass. Part of Series: Genetics Psychology Monographs, Vol. 22, No. 1.

1942 Measuring human relations. Genetic Psychology Monographs. Genetic Psychology Press, Provincetown, Mass.

CHILD, IRVIN L., AND LEON SIROTO
1965 BaKwele and American esthetic evaluations compared. Ethnology 4 (4) :349–360.

COLBY, BENJAMIN N.
1966a The analysis of culture content and the pattern of narrative concern in texts. American Anthropologist 68 (2):374–388.

1966b Cultural pattern in narrative. Science 155 (3712) :793–798.

COLBY, BENJAMIN N., AND ROBERT S. SPENCER
1967 A quantitative analysis of pattern and content in Eskimo folk tales. Museum of New Mexico Press, Santa Fe, N.M. (Includes description of the Sante Fe Dictionary.)

CONDON, W. S., AND W. D. OGSTON
1966 Sound film analysis of normal and pathological behavior patterns. The Journal of Nervous and Mental Disease 143 (4):338–347.

COULT, ALLAN D., AND ROBERT W. HABENSTEIN
1965 Cross tabulations of Murdock's World Ethnographic Sample. University of Missouri, Columbia, Mo.

DARWIN, CHARLES
1955 Expression of the emotions in man and animals. Philosophical Library, New York.

DAVIS, DOROTHY M.
1940 The relation of repetitions in the speech of young children to certain measures of language maturity and situational factors. Journal of Speech Disorders 5:235–246.

DAVITZ, J. R., AND LOIS J. DAVITZ
1959 The communication of feelings by content-free speech. Journal of Communication 9:6–13.

DENENBERG, VICTOR, PAUL V. CARLSON, AND MARK W. STEPHENS
1962 Effects of infantile shock upon emotionality at weaning. Journal of Comparative and Physiological Psychology, 55:819–820.

DENENBERG, VICTOR, AND S. A. SMITH
1963 Effects of infantile stimulation and age upon behavior. Journal of Comparative and Physiological Psychology 56:307–312.

DIAMOND, STANLEY
1960 The search for the primitive. In The image of man in medicine and anthropology. Iago Galdston, editor. International Universities Press, New York.
1963 The uses of the primitive. In Primitive views of the world. Stanley Diamond, editor. Columbia University Press, New York.

DIEHL, C. F., R. WHITE, AND K. W. BURK
1959 Voice quality and anxiety. Journal of Speech and Hearing Research 2:282–285.

DUNDES, ALAN
1962 From etic to emic units in the structural study of the folktale. Journal of American Folklore 75:95–105.
1964 The morphology of North American Indian folktales. FF Communications No. 195. Suomalainen Tiedeakatemia, Academia Scientiarum Fennica, Helsinki.

DUNPHY, D., P. STONE, AND M. SMITH
1965 The general inquirer: further developments in a computer system for content analysis of verbal data in the social sciences. Behavioral Science 10:468–480.

DURKHEIM, EMILE
1915 The elementary forms of the religious life. Translated from the French by Joseph Ward Swain. George Allen and Unwin, Ltd., London.

DYEN, ISIDORE
1964 A lexicostatistical classification of the Austronesian languages, Memoir 19. International Journal of American Linguistics.

EBEL, R. L.
1951 Estimation of the reliability of ratings. Psychometrika 16:407–424.

EISENBERG, P., AND E. ZALOWITZ
1938 Judging expressive movement: III, Judgments of dominance feeling from phonograph records of voice. Journal of Applied Psychology 22:620–631.

ELKIN, A. P., AND TREVOR A. JONES
1953 Arnhem Land music (North Australia). *Reprinted from* Oceania, Vol. 24, No. 2. The Oceania Monographs No. 9. The University of Sydney, Australia.

FAIRBANKS, G., AND W. PRONOVOST
1939 Pitch of voice and expression of emotion. Speech Monographs 6:87–104.

FILMS FOR ANTHROPOLOGY AND SOCIOLOGY, THIRD EDITION. Audio-Visual Services. The Pennsylvania State University. University Park, Pa.

FORD, CLELLAN S., AND FRANK A. BEACH
1951 Patterns of sexual behavior. Ace Books, Inc., New York.

FORD, CLELLAN S., E. TERRY PROTHRO, AND IRVIN L. CHILD

1966   Some transcultural comparisons of esthetic judgment. The Journal of Social Psychology 68:19–26.

FREEMAN, LINTON C., AND ALAN P. MERRIAM
1956   Statistical classification in anthropology: an application to ethnomusicology. American Anthropologist 58 (3):464–472.

GILLIS, FRANK J. (editor)
1953–1967   Ethnomusicology, Vols. I–XI. Wesleyan University Press, Middletown, Conn.

GILLIS, FRANK, AND ALAN P. MERRIAM (editors)
1966   Ethnomusicology and folk music: an international bibiliography of dissertations and theses. Special Series in Ethnomusicology, No. 1. Wesleyan University Press, Middletown, Conn.

GOLDMAN-EISLER, FRIEDA
1955   Speech-breathing activity—a measure of tension and affect during interviews. British Journal of Psychology 46:53–63.
1956   The determinants of the rate of speech output and their mutual relations. Journal of Psychosomatic Research 1:137–143.

GOLDSCHMIDT, WALTER
1960   Exploring the ways of mankind. Holt, Rinehart and Winston, New York.

GRAUER, VICTOR
1965   Some song style clusters: a preliminary study. Ethnomusicology 10 (3):265–271.

GREENSON, RALPH R.
1950   The mother tongue and the mother. International Journal of Psychoanalysis 31:18–23.

GRIFFIN, JAMES B.
1967   Eastern North American archeology: a summary. Science 156 (3772): 175–191.

GUILFORD, J. P.
1957   Psychometric methods. McGraw-Hill, New York.

HALL, EDWARD TWITCHELL
1959   The silent language. Doubleday, Garden City, N.Y.
1963   A system for the notation of proxemic behavior. American Anthropologist 65 (5):1003–1026.

HAMBURG, DAVID A.
1963   Emotions in perspective of human evolution. In Expressions of the emotions of man. P. Knapp, editor; pp. 300–317. International Universities Press, New York.

HANNA, JUDITH
1965   African dance as education. In Dance and education now, 48–52. Impulse Publications, San Francisco, Calif.

HANNETT, FRANCES
1964   The haunting lyric, the personal and social significance of American popular songs. Psychoanalytic Quarterly 33:226–269.

HARMAN, H. H.
1960   Modern factor analysis. The University of Chicago Press, Chicago, Ill.

HARVARD DICTIONARY OF MUSIC
1960   Willi Apel, editor. Harvard University Press, Cambridge, Mass.

HAYS, WILLIAM L.
1963   Statistics for psychologists. Holt, Rinehart and Winston, New York.

HERZOG, GEORGE
1938   A comparison of Pueblo and Pima musical styles. Journal of American Folklore 49:283–417.
1939   African influence on North American Indian music. Christian Science Monitor, Sept. 15, 1939.

HEWES, GORDON W.
1957   The anthropology of posture. Scientific American 196 (32):123–128, 178.

HOCKETT, CHARLES F.
1955   A manual of phonology. Waverly Press, Baltimore, Md.

HOMANS, GEORGE C.
1950   The human group. Harcourt Brace, New York.

HYMES, DELL (editor)
1964   Language in culture and society: a reader in linguistics and anthropology. Harper and Row, New York.

IWAO, SUMIKO, AND IRVIN L. CHILD
1966   Comparison of esthetic judgments by American experts and by Japanese potters. The Journal of Social Psychology 68:27–33.

JOURNAL OF THE INTERNATIONAL FOLK MUSIC COUNCIL

1949–1967 Volumes I–XIX. W. Heffer and Sons, Cambridge, England.

KOHUT, HEINZ
1951 The psychological significance of musical activity. Music Therapy 1:151–157.

KONGAS, ELLI-KAIJA, AND PIERRE MARANDA
1962 Structural models in folklore. Midwest Folklore 12 (3): entire issue. Indiana University, Bloomington, Ind.

KRAMER, ERNEST
1962 The judgment of personal characteristics and emotions from nonverbal properties of speech. Progress report submitted to College of Literature, Science, and the Arts, Department of Psychology, The University of Michigan, Ann Arbor, Mich.

LABAN, RUDOLF
1956 Principles of dance and movement notation. MacDonald and Evans, London.
1960 The mastery of movement, second edition (revised by Lisa Ullman). MacDonald and Evans, London.
1966 Choreutics. Lisa Ullman, editor. MacDonald and Evans, London.

LABAN, RUDOLF, AND F. C. LAWRENCE
1947 Effort. MacDonald and Evans, London.

LABARRE, WESTON
1947 The cultural basis of emotions and gestures. Journal of Personality 16:49–68.
1954 The human animal. The University of Chicago Press, Chicago, Ill.

LABOV, WILLIAM, AND JOSHUA WALETZKY
1967 Narrative analysis: Oral versions of personal experience. In AES essays on the verbal and visual arts. June Helm, editor. Proceedings of the 1966 Annual Spring Meeting, American Ethnological Society. The University of Washington Press, Seattle, Wash.

LANDAUER, THOMAS, AND JOHN W. M. WHITING
1964 Infantile stimulation and adult stature of human males. American Anthropologist 66:1007–1028.

LEVINE, SEYMORE
1956 A further study of infantile handling and adult avoidance learning. Journal of Personality 25:70–80.
1959 Emotionality and aggressive behavior in the mouse as a function of infantile experience. Journal of Genetic Psychology 94:77–83.
1960 Stimulation in infancy. Scientific American 205 (5):2–8.
1962 Effects of infantile stimulation. In Roots of behavior. Eugene L. Bliss, editor. Harper and Row, New York.

LEVINE, SEYMORE, AND RICHARD F. MULLINS
1966 Hormonal influences on brain organization in infant rats. Science 152:1585–1592.

LINDHOLM, BRYAN W.
1962 Critical periods and the effects of early shock on later emotional behavior in the white rat. Journal of Comparative and Physiological Psychology 55:597–599.

LOMAX, ALAN
1955–1956 Nuovi ipotesi sul canto folcloristico italiano nel quadro della musica popolare mondiale. Nuovi Argomenti. Alberto Moravia and Alberto Carocci, editors. Rome. No. 17–18, Nov. 1955–Feb. 1956:109–136.
1959 Folk song style. American Anthropologist 61 (6):927–954.
1960 The folk songs of North America. Doubleday, Garden City, N.Y.
1962 Song structure and social structure. Ethnology 1 (4):425–451.
1967 Special features of the sung communication. In Essays on the verbal and visual arts. June Helm, editor. Proceedings of the 1966 Annual Spring Meeting of the American Ethnological Society. The University of Washington Press, Seattle, Wash.

LOMAX, ALAN, AND VICTOR GRAUER
1968 In press. World folk song styles. Wesleyan University Press, Middletown, Conn.

LOMAX, ALAN, AND EDITH TRAGER
1964 Phonotactique du chant populaire. L'Homme, Revue Francaise d'Anthropologie, Janvier–Avril, 1–55.

LORD, ALBERT B.
1960 The singer of tales. Harvard University Press, Cambridge, Mass.

MAHL, GEORGE F.
1959 Exploring emotional states by content analysis. In Trends in content

analysis. I. Pool, editor; pp. 89–130. University of Illinois Press, Urbana, Ill.

1962 The expression of emotions on the lexical and linguistic levels. *In* Expression of the emotions in man. P. Knapp, editor. International University Press, New York.

MAHL, GEORGE F., AND GENE SCHULZE
1962 Psychological research in the extralinguistic area. Prepared for Interdisciplinary Work Conference on Paralanguage and Kinesics, May 17–19, 1962. Indiana University, Bloomington, Ind.

MARANDA, ELLI
1965 Myth and art as teaching materials. Occasional Paper No. 5, Social Studies Curriculum Program, Educational Services Incorporated, Cambridge, Mass.

MARKEL, NORMAN N.
1961 Connotative meaning of several initial consonant clusters in English. *In* Monograph series on languages and linguistics 14:81–87, Georgetown University, Washington, D.C.

1965 The reliability of coding paralanguage: pitch, loudness, and tempo. Journal of Verbal Learning and Verbal Behavior 4 (4):306–308.

MARKEL, NORMAN N., AND ERIC P. HAMP
1960–1961 Connotative meanings of certain phoneme sequences. Studies in Linguistics 15 (3–4):47–61. University of Buffalo, Buffalo, N.Y.

MARKEL, NORMAN N., RICHARD M. EISLER, AND HAYNE W. REESE
1967 Judging personality from dialect. Journal of Verbal Learning and Verbal Behavior 6 (1):33–35.

McALLESTER, DAVID P.
1954 Enemy way music. Reports of the Rimrock Project—Values Series No. 3. Papers of the Peabody Museum of American Archeology and Ethnology, Cambridge, Mass.

McLUHAN, MARSHALL
1964 Understanding media: the extension of man. McGraw-Hill, New York.

McQUOWN, NORMAN A.
1957 Linguistic transcription and specification of psychiatric interview material. Psychiatry 20:79–86.

MEAD, MARGARET
1949 (first published 1928) Coming of age in Samoa. Mentor Books, New York.

1951 Night after night. Review of movies: a psychological study, by Martha Wolfenstein and Nathan Leites. Transformation: Arts, Communication, Environment 1 (2):94–96.

1954 The swaddling hypothesis: its reception. American Anthropologist 56:395–409.

1961 National character and the science of anthropology. *In* Culture and social character: the work of David Riesman reviewed. S. M. Lipsit and L. Lowenthal, editors; pp. 15–26. Free Press, Glencoe, Ill.

1963 Anthropology and the camera. *In* The encyclopedia of photography. Willard D. Morgan, editor; vol. 1, pp. 166–184. Greystone, New York.

1964 Continuities in cultural evolution. Yale University Press, New Haven, Conn.

MEAD, MARGARET, AND FRANCIS COOKE MACGREGOR
1951 Growth and culture: a photographic study of Balinese childhood. (With photographs by Gregory Bateson). Putnam, New York.

MEGGERS, BETTY J.
1964 North and South American cultural connections. *In* Prehistoric man in the New World. Jesse D. Jennings, and Edward Norbeck, editors; pp. 511–523. The University of Chicago Press, Chicago, Ill.

MERRIAM, ALAN P.
1957 Yovu songs from Ruanda. Zaire, Nrs. 9–10, Nov.–Dec., 933–966.

1964 The anthropology of music. Northwestern University Press, Evanston, Ill.

1967 Ethnomusicology of the Flathead Indians. Viking Fund Publications in Anthropology, Sol Tax, editor, No. 44. Aldine, Chicago, Ill.

MERRIAM, ALAN P., AND WARREN L. D'AZEVEDO
1957 Washo Peyote Songs. American Anthropologist 59 (4):615–641.

MOSES, PAUL J.
1954 The voice of neurosis. Grune and Stratton, New York.

MURDOCK, GEORGE P.
1959 Africa, its peoples and their culture history. McGraw-Hill, New York.
1962–1967 Ethnographic Atlas. Ethnology, Volumes 1–5.
1964 Cultural correlates of the regulation of premarital sex behavior. *In* Process and pattern in culture. R. Manners, editor; pp. 399–410. Aldine, Chicago, Ill.
1967 Ethnographic atlas: a summary. Ethnology 6 (2) :107–236.

NADEL, SIEGFRIED FREDERICK.
1951 The foundations of social anthropology. Free Press, Glencoe, Ill.

NAROLL, RAOUL
1956 A preliminary index of social development. American Anthropologist 58:687–715.

NETTL, BRUNO
1954 North American Indian musical styles. Vol. 45. Memoirs of the American Folklore Society, Philadelphia, Pa.
1956 Music in primitive culture. Harvard University Press, Cambridge, Mass.

OSTWALD, PETER F.
1960a Sound, music and human behavior. Music Therapy 10:107–125.
1960b Visual denotation of human sounds. Archives of General Psychiatry 3:117–121.
1961 Humming, sound and symbol. The Journal of Auditory Research 3:224–232.

PARRY, MILMAN, AND ALBERT B. LORD
1954 Serbocroatian heroic songs. Harvard University Press, Cambridge, Mass.

PEACOCK, JAMES L.
1967 Javanese clown and transvestite songs: Some relations between "primitive classification" and "communicative events." *In* AES essays on the verbal and visual arts. June Helm, editor. Proceedings of the 1966 Annual Spring Meeting of the American Ethnological Society. The University of Washington Press, Seattle, Wash.

PIKE, KENNETH L.
1954 Language in relation to a unified theory of human behavior. Summer Institute of Linguistics, Glendale, Calif.

PITTENGER, R. E., C. F. HOCKETT, AND J. J. DANEHY
1960 The first five minutes. Martineau, Ithaca, N.Y.

PROPP, VLADIMIR
1958 Morphology of the folktale. Publication 10. Indiana University Research Center in Anthropology, Folklore and Linguistics, Bloomington, Ind.

REESE, GUSTAV
1954 Music in the Renaissance. W. W. Norton, New York.

ROBERTS, HELEN H.
1936 Musical areas in aboriginal North America. Yale University Publications in Anthropology No. 12, New Haven, Conn.

ROBERTS, JOHN M., AND BRIAN SUTTON-SMITH
1962 Child training and game involvement. Ethnology 1 (2): 166–185.

ROBERTS, JOHN M., BRIAN SUTTON-SMITH, AND ADAM KENDON
1963 Strategy in games and folk tales. Journal of Social Psychology 61, 185–199.

ROUGET, GILBERT
1954–1955 A propos de la forme dans les musiques de tradition orale. Les Colloques de Wegimont, 1, Paris-Bruxelles.

SACHS, CURT
1962 The wellsprings of music. Martinus Nijhoff, The Hague.

SACHS, CURT, AND ERICH VON HORNBOSTEL
1961 Classification of musical instruments. (Translated from the original German by Anthony Baines and Klaus P. Wachsmann.) Galpin Society Journal, XIV, March 1961:3–29.

SAPIR, EDWARD
1949 Selected writings of Edward Sapir. David G. Mandelbaum, editor; pp. 533–543. University of California Press, Berkeley, Calif.

SEBEOK, T. A.
1956 Sound and meaning in a Cheremis folksong text. *In* Essays on the occasion of his sixtieth birthday. For Roman Jakobson. Compiled by Mor-

ris Halle, Horace G. Lunt, Hugh Mc-Lean, and Cornelius H. Van Schooneveld; pp. 430–439. Mouton and Co., The Hague.

1959 Approaches to the analysis of folksong texts. Ural-Altaische Jahrbuche 31:392–399.

1964 Structure and content of Cheremis charms. In Language in culture and society. Dell Hymes, editor; pp. 356–365. Harper and Row, New York.

SEBEOK, T. A. (EDITOR)
1960 Style in language. Wiley, New York.

SEBEOK, T.A., AND LOUIS ORZACK
1953 The structure and content of Cheremis charms, Part 2. Anthropos 48:760–772.

SCHEFLEN, ALBERT E.
1965 Stream and structure of communicational behavior: context analysis of a psychotherapy session. Behavioral Studies Monograph No. 1, Eastern Pennsylvania Psychiatric Institute, Philadelphia, Pa.

SHULTER, RICHARD, JR.
1961 Peopling of the Pacific in the light of radio-carbon dating. Asian Perspectives 5 (2):207–212.

SIEGEL, SIDNEY
1956 Nonparametric statistics for the behavioral sciences. McGraw-Hill, New York.

SOKAL, ROBERT H., AND PETER H. A. SNEATH
1963 Principles of numerical taxonomy. W. H. Freeman, San Francisco and London.

SPENCE, J. T., AND B. A. MAHER
1962 Handling and noxious stimulation of the albino rat: effects on subsequent emotionality. Journal of Comparative and Physiological Psychology 55:247–251.

STEPHENS, WILLIAM N.
1963 The family in cross-cultural perspective. Holt, Rinehart and Winston, New York.

STEWARD, JULIAN H., AND LOUIS C. FARON
1959 Native peoples of South America. McGraw-Hill, New York.

STONE, P. J., AND E. B. HUNT
1963 A computer approach to content analysis: studies using the General Inquirer System. Proceedings of the Spring Joint Computer Conference from American Federation of Information Processing Societies Conference; vol. 23, pp. 241–256. Spartan Books, New York.

SUTTON-SMITH, BRIAN, AND JOHN M. ROBERTS
1964 Rubrics of competitive behavior. The Journal of Genetic Psychology 105:13–37.

SUTTON-SMITH, BRIAN, JOHN M. ROBERTS, AND ROBERT M. KOZELKA
1963 Game involvement in adults. The Journal of Social Psychology, 60:15–30.

SWANSON, G. E.
1960 The birth of gods. University of Michigan Press, Ann Arbor, Mich.

THOMAS, ELIZABETH MARSHALL
1959 The harmless people. Knopf, New York.

THOMPSON, S.
1958 Motif-index of folk literature, 6 volumes. Indiana University Press, Bloomington, Ind.

TRAGER, G. L.
1958 Paralanguage: a first approximation. Studies in Linguistics 13:1–12.

TSCHOPIK, HARRY S., AND WILLARD RHODES
1951 Music of the American Indians: Southwest. Folkways Records and Service Corp., New York.

TURNBULL, COLIN M.
1959 Legends of the BaMbuti. The Journal of the Royal Anthropological Institute 89, Part 1:45–60.

1960a The Elima: a premarital festival among the Bambuti Pygmies. Zaire 14:175–192.

1960b Field work among the Bambuti Pygmies, Belgian Congo: a preliminary report. Man 60:36–40.

1960c Some recent developments in the sociology of the BaMbuti Pygmies. Transactions of the New York Academy of Sciences, Series II, 22 (4):275–283.

1961 The forest people. Simon and Schuster, New York.

1963 The lesson of the Pygmies. Scientific American 208 (1):28–37.

UDY, STANLEY H., JR.
1959 Organization of work: a comparative analysis of production among non-

industrial peoples. Hraf Press, New Haven, Conn.

WEININGER, O.
1956 The effects of early experience on behavior and growth characteristics. Journal of Comparative and Physiological Psychology 49:1–9.

WEININGER, O., W. J. McCLELLAND, AND R. K. ARIMA
1954 Gentling and weight gain in the albino rat. Canadian Journal of Psychology 8:147–151.

WELLESZ, EGON (EDITOR)
1957 The new Oxford history of music. Vol 1, ancient and Oriental music. Oxford University Press, London.

WESCOTT, ROGER W.
1967 Strepital communication: A study of non-vocal sound-production among men and animals. The Bulletin, New Jersey Academy of Science 12 (1):30–34.

WHITE, DOUGLAS R.
1966 Index of societal samples used in cross-cultural studies. Societal Research Archives System, Department of Anthropology, University of Minnesota. Unpublished MS. (Available in mimeographed form from Department of Anthropology, University of Minnesota, Minneapolis, Minn.)

WHITE, LESLIE A.
1949 The science of culture. Farrar, Straus and Young, New York.

WHITING, JOHN W. M.
1961 Socialization process and personality. In Psychological anthropology: approaches to culture and personality. F. Hsu, editor. Dorsey Press, Homewood, Ill.

1965 Menarcheal age and infant stress in humans. In Sex and behavior. Frank Beach, editor. Wiley and Sons, New York.

WHYTE, WILLIAM FOOTE
1961 Men at work. Richard D. Irwin, Homewood, Ill.

FOLK SONG TEXT SOURCES

BELDEN, H. M.
1940 Ballads and songs. Collected by the Missouri Folklore Society. University of Missouri Studies, Columbia, Mo.

BURROWS, E. G.
1945 Songs of Uvea and Futuna. Bernice P. Bishop Museum Bulletin 183. Published by the Museum, Honolulu.

DENSMORE, FRANCES
1957 Music of Acoma, Isleta, Cochiti and Zuni Pueblos. Smithonian Institution Bureau of American Ethnology Bulletin 165, U.S. Government Printing Office, Washington, D.C.

EMBREE, J. F.
1944 Japanese peasant songs. Memoirs of the American Folklore Society, Vol. 38, Philadelphia, Pa.

GOLDSTEIN, K. S.
1965 The unfortunate rake. Folkways Records FA2305, New York.

LOMAX, JOHN A., AND ALAN LOMAX
1934 American ballads and folk songs. Macmillan, New York.

1957 Cowboy songs and other frontier ballads. Macmillan, New York.
1959 Leadbelly. Folkways Publishers, New York.
1966 Folk song USA. Signet, New American Library, New York.

McALLESTER, DAVID P.
1954 Enemy way music. Reports of the Rimrock Project—Values Series No. 3. Papers of the Peabody Museum of American Archeology and Ethnology, Cambridge, Mass.

SEEGER, CHARLES
N.d. Folk music of the United States, versions and variants of Barbara Allen. From the Archive of Folk Song, Library of Congress, AAFS L54, Washington, D.C.

SHARP, C. J., AND M. KARPELES
1932 English folk songs from the Southern Appalachians. Oxford University Press, London.

SMITH, REED
1928 South Carolina ballads. Harvard University Press, Cambridge, Mass.

FILM SOURCES

Some of the major sources for ethnographic and documentary films appear in the list that follows. It is with the help of these agencies that we have obtained much of the material rated on the Choreometrics Project. Some of these publish excellent catalogs, others are able only to furnish lists, but all will be useful to the person beginning to use ethnographic film. No attempt has been made to be exhaustive or complete. In a future publication, full acknowledgment will be made to many individuals and institutions that have loaned us films for the dance study.

A Brief List of 16mm Sound Motion Picture Films on Folk Music and Folk Dance with Rental Distributors. Compiled by the Archive of Folk Song, Library of Congress. Ethnomusicology 11 (3) :375–385.

Audio-Visual Services
Pennsylvania State University
University Park, Pennsylvania 16802
(Distribute Encyclopaedia Cinematographica films; excellent catalog of "Films for Anthropology and Sociology")

Australian News and Information Bureau
636 Fifth Avenue
New York, New York 10020
(Films on Australian Aborigines)

Brandon Films, Inc.
221 West 57 Street
New York, New York 10019
(Selection of films on music and dance)

Carpenter Center for the Visual Arts
Harvard University
19 Prescott Street
Cambridge, Massachusetts 02138
(Varied)

Comité du film ethnographique
Musée de l'Homme
Palais de Chaillot
Paris, France
(Varied; see "Catalogue des films ethnographiques francais," Cahiers du Centre de documentation, Départment de l'information, UNESCO, May 1955, No. 15)

Contemporary Films, Inc.
267 West 25 Street
New York, New York 10001
(Distributors for British Information Services, National Film Board of Canada, United Nations, and National Association

for Mental Health, all of which publish separate catalogs)

Educational Services Incorporated Film Studio
55 Chapel Street
Newton, Massachusetts 02158
(Series of films suitable for schools, but excellent in ethnographic content, of the complete life cycle of the Netsilik Eskimos —9 films)

Encyclopaedia Cinematographica
Institut für den Wissenschaftlichen Film
34 Göttingen, den Nonnenstieg 72
East Germany
(Index, in German, of films on Europe, Africa, Asia, the Americas, and Oceania. Most of these films can be obtained from Audio-Visual Services, Pennsylvania State University. Perhaps the most useful source at present. Their index makes it possible to choose among a series of authentic and simply photographed brief films which present a wide range of activities in primitive societies, including work, ritual, dance, etc. G. Wolf, editor.)

Films Made by Americans in the Pacific Which Have any Anthropological or Ethnographic Significance. Prepared by Colin Young, Chairman, Department of Theater Arts, University of California at Los Angeles, Los Angeles, California 90024

Ideal Pictures, Inc.
321 West 44 Street
New York, New York 10036
(Agency for distribution of Japan Information Services films)

Indiana University
Audio-Visual Center

Bloomington, Indiana 47401
(Varied)

Media Center—Film Distribution
University of California Extension
Berkeley, California 94720
(Varied)

Museum of Modern Art Film Library
11 West 53 Street
New York, New York 10019
(Varied)

National Film Board of Canada
680 Fifth Avenue
New York, New York 10019
(Films on the Eskimo and Canadian Indians)

National Institute of Neurological Diseases
and Blindness
National Institutes of Health
Bethesda, Maryland 20014
("A Catalogue of Research Films in Ethno-

pediatrics" includes good selection from
Oceania, but for restricted use only)

New York Public Library
Donnell Library Center Film Collection
20 West 53 Street
New York, New York 10019
(Varied)

New York University Film Library
26 Washington Place
New York, New York 10003
(Varied)

Premier Catalogue sélectif des Films ethnographiques sur l'Afrique noire.
Catalog of films on Black Africa, published by UNESCO, 1967. Gives distributors. Jean Rouche, editor.

Program in Ethnographic Film
19 Prescott Street
Cambridge, Massachusetts 02138
(Excellent list, "Films for Anthropological Teaching," prepared by Karl G. Heider)

Index